W9-CAX-513

DATE DUE

FEB 1 ^

After *The Grapes of Wrath*

Essays on John Steinbeck

In Honor of Tetsumaro Hayashi

After *The Grapes of Wrath*
Essays on John Steinbeck
In Honor of Tetsumaro Hayashi

Edited by

Donald V. Coers

Paul D. Ruffin

Robert J. DeMott

 Ohio University Press/Athens

This project was initiated by *Texas Review* Press and represents a collective effort involving both *Texas Review* Press and Ohio University Press.

Ohio University Press, Athens, Ohio 45701
© 1995 by Ohio University Press
Printed in the United States of America

99 98 97 96 95   5 4 3 2 1

Library of Congress Cataloging-in-Publication Data

After the Grapes of Wrath: essays on John Steinbeck in honor of Tetsumaro
   Hayashi / edited by Donald V. Coers, Paul D. Ruffin, and Robert J.
   DeMott.
        p.   cm.
   Includes bibliographical references (p.).
   ISBN 0-8214-1102-0
   1. Steinbeck, John, 1902-1968--Criticism and interpretation.
I. Hayashi, Tetsumaro. II. Coers, Donald V., 1941-
III. Ruffin, Paul D., 1941- IV. DeMott, Robert J., 1943-
PS3537.T3234Z565 1994
813'.52--dc20   94-18228
                                                        CIP

Table of Contents

Part III: Interview

Part IV: Bibliography

Tetsumaro Hayashi

I am very proud to be a small part of this book dedicated to Tetsumaro Hayashi. I think fondly of the time when John Steinbeck and Ted Hayashi finally meet in Japanese-American Heaven. They will fly along in perfect companionship through the azure sky and fleecy clouds, and they'll stop off at the Big Dipper Bar and Grill for a cup of tea or a good drink. They are sure to have a fine time together!

—Elaine Steinbeck

Acknowledgments

In mid-August of 1992 at Steinbeck Festival XIII in Salinas, Ted Hayashi delivered a speech entitled "Steinbeck's America and My America." Virtually everyone in the auditorium that afternoon knew that Ted was leaving Ball State University to assume new teaching duties at Kwassui Women's College in Nagasaki, Japan, so his speech was both a retrospective of his remarkable forty-year academic career in the United States and a touching farewell. That evening Bob DeMott, Kevin Hearle, bookdealer Florian Shasky, Don Coers and his son John had a leisurely supper together at a local family-style Mexican restaurant. During the course of that meal, Bob observed that someone really should do something special to honor Ted's contribution to Steinbeck studies. Someone else raised the possibility of a collection of commemorative essays, and the present volume had been conceived. The collection was originally planned as a special issue of *The Texas Review*, but Ohio University Press, upon hearing of the project, recognized its international importance and asked to assume production.

In the two years following that warm and informal genesis in Salinas, the editors have incurred many debts in bringing the project to fruition. Expressions of gratitude are due the following: Julie Fallowfield of McIntosh and Otis and Florence Eichen of Viking/Penguin for numerous felicities; John Timmerman, Calvin College, Yasuo Hashiguchi, Yasuda Women's University, and Kiyoshi Nakayama, Kansai University, for their generous contributions; Jason Puskar, Honors Tutorial College research assistant at Ohio University, and Cheryl Joy Allman, administrative assistant for *The Texas Review*, Sam Houston State University, for their invaluable assistance in preparing the manuscript; doctoral student John Marsden, Ohio University, for his meticulous indexing; Jim Johnson of Carmel, California, for providing photographs for the dust jacket; Barbara Whitehead of Smithville, Texas, for the dust jacket design.

We thank for their research assistance Michael T. Dumas, Curatorial Assistant at the Harvard Theatre Collection; Grace Shackney, Assistant to the Artistic and Managing Directors, the McCarter Theatre of Princeton, New Jersey; Jim Miller, Chair, and Maureen McIntyre, Professor, Division of Theatre and Dance, Sam Houston State University; Robert E. Parks, the Robert H. Taylor Curator of Autograph Manuscripts at the Pierpont Morgan Library, New York City; the Director and staff of the Harry Ransom Humanities Research

Center at the University of Texas at Austin; Susan Shillinglaw, Director, Steinbeck Research Center, San Jose State University; Margaret J. Kimball, Head, Special Collections and University Archivist, Stanford University; Zola Molitor, Rights and Permissions Manager, University of Texas Press; Jean Ashton, Director, Rare Books and Manuscript Collection, Columbia University; Elisabeth Dyssegaard and Linda Ostashevsky of Farrar, Straus and Giroux, Mary Jean Gamble, Steinbeck Librarian, John Steinbeck Library, Salinas, California; and Raymond Teichman, Supervisory Archivist, Franklin D. Roosevelt Library, Hyde Park, New York.

We acknowledge our gratitude to Ball State University for its twenty-five-year financial support of the *Steinbeck Quarterly*, the Steinbeck Monograph Series, the Steinbeck Essay Series, the Steinbeck Research Institute, and the Elizabeth Otis/Steinbeck Collection at the Bracken Library—all of which Professor Hayashi had a fruitful relationship with over the years, as evidenced in DeMott's chronological checklist which concludes this collection.

Special acknowledgment is also due Duane Schneider, Director of the Ohio University Press, and his staff, especially Helen Gawthrop, Production Manager, for their patience and encouragement; the staff of Ohio University's Computer Center for technical assistance; Margaret Cohn, Director, Ohio University Honors Tutorial College, for a 1993-1994 Research Internship Award to DeMott; the late John Hollow and Betty Pytlik, past and present Chairs of the Ohio University Department of English, and Eugene Young, Chair of the Division of English and Foreign Languages, Sam Houston State University, for express mail and Xerox privileges; Warren French of the University of Swansea, John Ditsky of the University of Windsor, and Eleanor Mitchell of Sam Houston State University for their careful reading of various portions of the manuscript; Trina Atkinson, Business Manager of *The Texas Review*, for her invaluable assistance in transcribing the interview with Elaine Steinbeck; and Jeannine Jacoby, Office of Graduate Studies, Sam Houston State University, for her multifarious contributions.

Heartfelt thanks to Mary Jeanne Coers for her help with the interview with Elaine Steinbeck, and to Andrea Berger DeMott for her support and advice during the production of this volume.

The editors offer their deepest appreciation to Elaine Steinbeck for her many gracious contributions to this book.

The editors are grateful to the following for permission to quote from works by John Steinbeck:

The editors also cite the following for their permission to use material in this book:

Elaine Steinbeck, for permission to publish the interview conducted by Donald Coers, April 23 and 24, 1993, in New York, and from various unpublished letters and memoranda of John Steinbeck. Unpublished Steinbeck material is copyrighted in the name of Elaine A. Steinbeck © 1994 and used by permission of McIntosh and Otis, Inc.

The John Steinbeck Collection (M263), Department of Special Collections, Stanford University, for permission to quote from three unpublished Steinbeck letters.

The University of Texas Press, for permission to quote a passage from "Discourse in the Novel" from *The Dialogic Imagination* by Mikhail Bakhtin, translated by Caryl Emerson and Michael Holquist, the University of Texas Press, 1981.

The Annie Laurie Williams Papers, Rare Book and Manuscript Library, Columbia University, for use of quotations from the Steinbeck/Williams letter in Roy Simmonds's essay "The Metamorphosis of *The Moon Is Down*."

After *The Grapes of Wrath*

Essays on John Steinbeck

In Honor of Tetsumaro Hayashi

Introduction

Warren French

Although I had been in correspondence with Ted Hayashi about the founding of the John Steinbeck Society since 1966, I did not become closely associated with him until 1970, when I visited Indiana after accepting a position as first chair of the English Department of the newly created Indiana University-Purdue University at Indianapolis. Ted had asked me to serve as President of the ambitious organization during its early years, and I was eager to be close to him in Muncie so that we could collaborate on development plans.

Ironically, we had almost met more than a decade earlier at the University of Florida. He had received his bachelor's degree in British literature at Okayama University in his native Japan in 1953. Intending to specialize in Renaissance studies, he had come to Gainesville in 1954 to study American literature under the sponsorship of Didier and Lotte Graeffe, a remarkable and outgoing pair of international scholars who had served as Ted's sponsors. He remained there until 1957 but left just before I moved there, after which the Graeffes became two of my closest friends and associates. Another mutual friend and influence there was Harry Warfel, whom Ted credits with firing his interest in American fiction, especially *The Grapes of Wrath*.

Harry was a dynamic and demanding scholar who insisted that his graduate students should begin early to develop professionally. One of his noteworthy practices in his American fiction seminar was to require beginning graduate students, instead of laboring over term papers that drearily rehashed past scholarship, to write a short paper on each novel they read and to submit the ones he found promising to academic journals. A number of those whom I worked with at Florida began what have become distinguished careers—J. Paul Hunter, Robert Detweiler, William Friedman, among others—with such fresh, spontaneous efforts; and I suspect that some of Ted's first publications in Japanese journals, like his articles on *Huckleberry Finn* and *The Grapes of Wrath* appearing in the checklist that Robert DeMott has compiled for this tribute, originated from these early efforts, as they reflect the positive and humanistic values that Harry urged through his teachings.

Before I had the opportunity to join this creative group hopeful about promoting humanistic values, Ted had moved on to take a master's degree in library science, specializing in American literature, modestly supposing such behind-the-scenes work might provide the most de-

1

pendable outlet for his talents; and in 1959 he moved to his first full-time position as an Instructor in Japanese and English at Culver-Stockton College, Canton, Missouri, where in 1961 he also became the Associate Director of the College Library.

Although he has always remained a vocal advocate of library building—the Elizabeth Otis/Steinbeck Collection at Ball State is one of his outstanding successes—he could not resist the opportunity that classroom teaching offered to win new readers and fellow workers for the writing he admired passionately. He returned to work for a Ph.D. in Shakespeare and Elizabethan Drama at Kent State University in 1963. He could not forget, however, the impact that Steinbeck's writing had had upon him during his earliest years in the United States, an interest that was reinforced by Steinbeck's publication in 1962 of *Travels with Charley in Search of America*, in which the aging author set out to reacquaint himself with his country in a fashion that inspired the young scholar from another culture to become acquainted with his adopted country.

As early as 1966, he was promoting his plan to establish a society to honor John Steinbeck. At first it was to have been essentially a bibliographical society that would accumulate a record of all materials related to Steinbeck, since there was not even a comprehensive bibliography of his international publications available. Soon, however, Ted realized that his best service to this distinguished author would be to encourage young potential scholars as Harry Warfel had encouraged him by providing them with a forum where promising work might be reviewed and published.

Unfortunately, John Steinbeck was not to see the fruits of this sincere tribute to a monumental talent that has been greatly honored internationally by devoted supporters of humanistic values, but also grotesquely denigrated by the self-seeking anti-humanist forces of depersonalization and socio-political reductivism. Steinbeck died in the same year that the Society was formally organized and set about its multi-faceted work, focused on its principal outlet, the *Steinbeck Quarterly*.

What is most difficult to convey in words is the way in which this enormous effort has been conceived and carried out by Ted Hayashi himself. As far as getting the work done, the word out, the effort promoted for twenty-five years, this enterprise has been a one-man show. I was greatly honored to be asked to serve as President of the Society, until Ted properly took over this role as an acknowledgement of what he had been doing all the time, and then as Chairman of the Board of the now International Society; but my role through all these years has been that of aiding and abetting, hoping that I might have the persuasive powers to help Ted achieve his goals.

I do not wish here, by any means, to suggest that Ted had sought to dominate the action, to shape the work of the society rather than give it needed enthusiastic direction. He has always been most generous in encouraging others, especially young scholars, and in listening to the advice of the responsible support boards he has organized to scrutinize the activities of the society. If Ted has been in anything disappointed, it is that he has had to carry so much of the burden himself that he has not been able to generate broader independent activities that the society might help coordinate and promote. Americans should have ambiguous feelings about the largest auxiliary activity being the Steinbeck Society of Japan, which has produced an enviable record of conferences and publications and a roster of specialized scholars that rivals that of the United States.

Ted Hayashi devoted himself for twenty-five years to seeking support for the society at the same time he had the principal responsibility for carrying out its projects, often supporting them himself. In recent years he has been apprehensive about declining support for these activities, which was *not*, however, attributable to the work of the Society or its purposes, but to an almost universal crisis in the support of the humanities in the American university system. Many other worthy efforts have disappeared, and nearly every effort to intensify humanistic studies, whether by the schools themselves or by scholarly groups or public sponsors, has encountered severe cutbacks in efforts to spread intellectual enlightenment to powerful forces threatened by it.

Ted, like Steinbeck himself, has never been able to quite understand the forces at work here; but while still enthusiastic about the mission he undertook, tired from a quarter century of unremitting effort, he has decided to suspend his activities and return to Japan for a period of contemplation and perhaps fresh inspiration from a new generation. I suspect, however, that he will be back after a period of readjustment. He plans annual seasonal returns to the United States to keep in touch with scholarly developments in this country and the two younger generations of his American family. In the meantime, however, it is appropriate that the effort he has conducted unceasingly for so long a time should be honored by those who respect it as a model one hopes others might follow. Perhaps it is ironic that the spearhead of this effort to keep alive the significance of a distinguished American author should have been attracted from another culture; but it is very likely that it is only someone like Tetsumaro Hayashi, embodying a rare combination of Asian respect for the masters, which often misguides or devitalizes the disciples, with the American "go-getter" spirit, which often turns into a self-glorifying rejection of the values of tradition, who could have undertaken a task that required a certain amount of self-sacrifice along with a seemingly antithetically powerful drive for self-expression.

This book has been assembled by those who cherish their association with Ted Hayashi to carry out the same principles that dominated the *Steinbeck Quarterly*—to provide new insights into Steinbeck's work from new voices, to show that the legacy left by an author now dead for a quarter century is not now relegated to a fixed place in our tradition, but is, like the very tradition itself, subject to constant reexamination and reevaluation. Professor Hayashi himself has recently added to his outstanding list of publications by editing *John Steinbeck: The Years of Greatness, 1936-1939*, papers presented at the Third International John Steinbeck Congress in Honolulu in May 1990. The work of that period has generally been accepted as of permanent value, although new readings and new critical approaches constantly shed light on new sources of value in them. The stature of Steinbeck's subsequent work during and after World War II, however, remains controversial. Most critics have argued that there was a decline in the quality of his writings and have sought to give reasons for it; but others have challenged this judgment.

To follow up the collection that Professor Hayashi has recently edited, the organizers of this collection decided that the most appropriate undertaking to honor him would be a companion volume on the post-*Grapes of Wrath* publications, exploring, as they put it, "new ways of assessing Steinbeck's later work."

The plan is to begin with a discussion of some general issues that became increasingly significant during Steinbeck's later years and even more recently; then to present essays on important individual works, generally in the order of their publication, not looking at them all from a particular critical perspective, but through a variety of approaches that these trail-blazing and highly individualistic scholars feel best suited to bringing out particular merits that each sees in the work under scrutiny. These essays challenge readers to reexamine their own positions. There is much here that can be neither quickly grasped nor hurriedly dismissed.

The collection begins with Cliff Lewis's "Art for Politics: John Steinbeck and FDR." The reason for the importance of this seemingly non-literary subject is that the most conspicuous difference between Steinbeck's career up to 1939, when *The Grapes of Wrath* was published and World War II broke out (two events not just casually linked, since both were what Steinbeck called "outcroppings" that indicated similar underlying conditions), and his career thereafter is that before 1939 he was a determined but obscure and defeatist writer, struggling for

4

recognition that he did not expect; after that he was a celebrity. As Jackson Benson, his biographer, has said in speculating on possible causes of a "decline," "One answer is that what happened was the writing of the novel itself." People no longer asked, "John who?" Millions knew who he was. Many of them loved him; many hated him. The President listened to him.

Such recognition led to another drastic change in his lifestyle. Before 1939, he had carefully avoided any public political commitments; then he became an avid supporter and advisor of President Roosevelt and subsequent Democratic candidates for the office. After his first success with *Tortilla Flat* in 1935, he wrote to his agents that popularity "has ruined everyone I know" and to bookseller Ben Abramson at Chicago, who was one of his principal promoters, "I guess there is no worse thing for a writer than to get an idea his work is important." Could he avoid this fate himself? Would these extraordinary changes have no effect upon the quality of his writing?

Steinbeck did refuse during his lifetime to publicize the extent of his involvement in wartime politics, though he acknowledged his later close involvement in Adlai Stevenson's campaigns and his and his wife Elaine's close relationship with Lyndon B. and Lady Bird Johnson. In the first of his "Letters to Alicia," columns written for *Newsday* from 1965 to 1967 that were his last published works, he jokingly commented on his relationship to four presidents and candidate Stevenson, but added that none of them had ever taken his advice. Cliff Lewis's essay and earlier writings indicate that this is not literally true. They certainly did not take all of his advice, but he made important contributions, especially during periods of national crisis. President Roosevelt was not in condition to undertake the fourth campaign that he thought essential to the national welfare, and Steinbeck provided both the rationale for limited campaigning and important parts of the platform on which it was based. Lewis does not think that such collaboration of artists and politicians can occur again; but I am not sure this is true. Writers as respected as André Malraux and as popular as Jeffrey Archer have occupied high government posts in Europe in recent years, and Václav Havel has even served as President of liberated Czechoslovakia.

Steinbeck comments on the relationship of writers to politics in another of the earliest "Letters to Alicia" and wonders whether hobnobbing with the power elite might not corrupt them; but, citing without naming Robert Lowell and Norman Mailer, he discusses incidents which suggest that artists might be able to exercise greater influence over the government than the government could over them. It would depend upon the writers' access to the halls of power. The reason artists have had little influence on the American government for years is that our recent choices for the highest office are not likely to have known any writers of distinction or to have valued them much. If artists with great communal visions do not play a role in shaping the nation's future, it is because the community rejects them, to its loss.

Certainly, in concluding the discussion of this significant issue, we must observe that serving the government did not always serve Steinbeck's artistic development well. For the first time he had to write under orders, and *The Moon Is Down* and *Bombs Away* both had to be written hurriedly and within government guidelines with the result that, despite the impressive role that *The Moon Is Down* played in heartening the European resistance movement during the Second World War, the two works lack the stylistic power and the almost mystical sense of the author's personal driving involvement with his characters and their plight—qualities one finds in the great books from *The Red Pony* to *The Grapes of Wrath*. What Steinbeck unintentionally learned from his political involvements was that he could, if necessary, write superficial accounts about matters with which he was not intimately involved, an unfortunate lesson that probably contributed to bouts of despair and depression in his later years.

With these thoughts in mind about the pitfalls in an author's life that are surely likely to influence the quality of his performance, we turn with Susan Shillinglaw in the second essay to another matter that has mushroomed in importance in the quarter century since Steinbeck's death, when he could make no contribution to a complicated and often violent debate over "political correctness" and about the treatment of minority groups in everyday affairs and creative works, particularly in determining the canon that should be the focus of American literary study.

Shillinglaw's account of "Steinbeck and Ethnicity" begins with the revisionist critic Louis Owens's summary judgment in 1992 that Steinbeck "doesn't offer a great deal to multiculturalism. His treatment of women and what today would be called people of color leaves a lot to be desired. He was a white, middle class male from Salinas. He was a product of his times." Shillinglaw demonstrates that this conclusion is a considerable oversimplification. What must be borne in mind as she presents a different view of Steinbeck is that Owens is certainly right that he was "a product of his times," but that in his best works he transcended those times and created visions of universal significance.

He was certainly always a deeply concerned sympathizer with underdogs, from the pathetic old Mexican coming home to die in "The Great Mountains" to his retelling of the profoundly moving story of the Jewish defenders of Masada in Biblical times in his "Letters to Alicia"; but it is also true that until his creation of the determined Ma Joad in *The Grapes of Wrath*, the women characters in his novels had been subordi-

6

nate, often ineffectual, and sometimes targets of some personal resentment. He never had any use for the "do gooders" that Thoreau also viciously scorned, waging a personal campaign that comes to a climax in the contrast between the officious middle-class matrons who want to manage everything but their homes and the kindly and generous "girls" outside the law at the Bear Flag Restaurant in *Cannery Row*.

There is only one memorable black character in his fiction, the stablehand Crooks in *Of Mice and Men*, who appears briefly to sound the keynote for that sombre work: "Nobody ever gets to heaven, and nobody gets no land." No Asian figures importantly in his work until the incredible Lee in *East of Eden* organizes the conclave of Chinese savants who provide the keynote for that muddled history by translating the Biblical *timshel* as "Thou mayest," though scholars have questioned the accuracy of this interpretation. There are lots of Mexicans in his works, but as Shillinglaw points out, students today protest his early portrayal of the paisanos in *Tortilla Flat* while recently his portrayal of Mexican revolutionary Emiliano Zapata, one of the most heroic figures in Steinbeck's work, is deconstructed as racist. Certainly Steinbeck did not understand Mexicans as well as he thought he did. His problem becomes apparent in the highly moral but dramatically improbable *The Pearl*, when he rejects the philosophy behind the folktale he is using as a source as "contrary to human direction" and really provides justification for Louis Owens's intimation that Steinbeck's deepest feeling was that everyone, despite cultural differences, aspired toward the highest ideals of middle-class America—small town sons and daughters of the frontier.

The point of these comments is that one should not turn to Steinbeck's writing in anticipation of developing and understanding multicultural differences; he was indeed "a product of his times," and what Edward Margolies said of Steinbeck's great contemporary Richard Wright is equally true of Steinbeck: "He is at his best when he is relating something he had just seen or recording one of his own conversations." Steinbeck's publishers and agents tried to get him to write about the Puerto Ricans in New York City's Spanish Harlem, but he wisely declined on the grounds that even though he had come to think of himself as a New Yorker, he did not understand the situation well enough. As he wrote his agents when he refused to publish the completed "L'Affaire Lettuceburg" and decided to replace it with *The Grapes of Wrath*, "my whole work drive has been aimed at making people understand each other," but he could not be expected to foster an understanding of those he did not understand himself. As a belated adoption of multicultural approaches to literary study demonstrates, one learns most about a culture from those deeply but critically immersed in it. We should not expect Steinbeck to tell us about Mexicans, though he was often tempted to. (We should know Manuel Azuela's work better.) Steinbeck made a significant contribution to the perception of the problems of his culture, and, as always, he must be judged in terms of what he accomplished rather than what he failed to do.

One may be surprised to find this general section of a book on Steinbeck's work after *The Grapes of Wrath* concluding with Robert E. Morsberger's exhaustive study of the scores for the films made from Steinbeck's works; but we must recall that although some of these movies have been based on works from his early period, all of the movies were released after the publication of the major novels, so that all of them and their scores are part of the story not of the obscure "years of greatness" before the publication of the pivotal novel, but part of the celebrity period when a Steinbeck film was an important commission for a composer. The scores are also ironically interesting because they, too, reflect a decline that is in some ways related to a falling off in the author's work. None of the later movies were as enthusiastically received as the first two: director Lewis Milestone's *Of Mice and Men* and John Ford's *The Grapes of Wrath*. The best of the scores are also two of the earliest, both written by the distinguished American composer Aaron Copland for films directed by Milestone, *Of Mice and Men* and *The Red Pony*. Morsberger understandably devotes much of his account to examining the history of these two scores that have had, like the works the films are based upon, a far grander history than most similar efforts.

This new examination of specific works begins appropriately with two studies of Steinbeck's long and eagerly awaited first novel since *The Grapes of Wrath*. *The Moon Is Down* came as a startling shock to reviewers, particularly those whose expectations were based entirely on *The Grapes of Wrath*. The new novel seemed to have nothing in common with its monumental predecessor. It was a short, austere, uncomplicated tract about unfamiliar people in an unparticularized setting far from the United States that appeared to take a detached and ambiguous view of the horrifying international conflict then in progress. It had no epic quality; it was a closet drama in the classic mode of tragedy, occurring in a small place within a short time, and designed to be transferred to the theatre as *Of Mice and Men* had been.

Before looking at the particular problems generated by *The Moon Is Down*, however, we need to recall that though for many authors three years is not a long time between books, Steinbeck had been publishing fiction almost annually during the 1930s; and the readers were impatient for what they hoped would be the sequel to a book that had moved so many so deeply to both love and hatred for its author. We also need to recall that he had published two unprecedented works during the interval that were scarcely noticed because they were not what the public had anticipated or expected from the author. Neither was a novel. One was *Sea of Cortez*, an elaborate, expansive volume full of color plates of specimens of marine life from the Gulf of California, of practically no interest to the general public, along with an account of the expedition during which they were collected, full of heavy philosophical speculations. The second, which the author had not wished published, was a collection of stills from *The Forgotten Village*, a short film he had made in Mexico with voice-over narration that told the story of a dedicated young man's effort to bring modern medicine to his superstition-ridden community.

Despite Steinbeck's venturing into these new forms, neither work marks essentially a break with the past. Although he had decided that he would write no more novels about the condition of California's dispossessed, he still associated with the same companions as during the 30s and was interested in the same questions; and Ed Ricketts was involved in both projects. Steinbeck viewed the two works as escapes from the pressures engendered by the writing and reception of *The Grapes of Wrath*, but he found in Mexico the same problems he thought he had left behind. *Sea of Cortez*, therefore, is here examined in conjunction with a nostalgic return to the 1930s in *Cannery Row*. Even though *The Forgotten Village* is one of Steinbeck's most interesting works—ostensibly a documentary film, but actually a fable in a manner that he would begin to cultivate in fiction, using real people and settings to tell a romantic story—it is omitted here because it is essentially a film of which the printed book provides only a record.

The Moon Is Down, to return to the arguments set forth concerning Cliff Lewis's opening essay on Steinbeck's political involvements, is the first product of a now celebrated author working among new associates on a novel far removed from his accustomed settings. The timing of its appearance was singularly unfortunate. As Roy Simmonds points out in "The Metamorphosis of *The Moon Is Down*," when Steinbeck had become involved with the Roosevelt administration, the novelist had wanted to write about an enemy invasion of an American city—in the manner of Sinclair Lewis's *It Can't Happen Here* (1935). This idea was viewed by the authorities, however, as potentially too destructive to national morale, so that the action was set in an unidentified European country under enemy occupation as a warning to Americans about the need for eternal vigilance. By the time the novel and play appeared, however, the United States was already involved in the war, and clamorous voices demanded that a more belligerent tone should have been taken, though how this transformation could have been achieved

9

in the three months after Pearl Harbor when the works were already in production was not considered.

The result of this disastrous turn of events was that the novel was much more highly valued abroad than in the United States, where, despite the encouragement of President Roosevelt, Steinbeck was already suspected as a subversive by highly placed national security officials and many fellow native Californians. This distressing situation was intensified by the breakup of his first marriage and what can be called the devolution of *The Moon Is Down*. Roy Simmonds relates with great accuracy and thoroughness how the novel became a play and then a movie, showing that attempts to make the action of the successive versions clearer and more acceptable to the public only produced results that were increasingly less successful. Indeed an especially insightful remark that Simmonds makes is his conjecture in a note that "it is perhaps unfortunate" that John Ford, who had directed *The Grapes of Wrath*, did not also direct *The Moon Is Down*. Ford, in a now-too-little-remembered film version of Liam O'Flaherty's *The Informer* (1935), had already displayed a unique talent for turning the relatively static action of a depressing work that focuses on psychological rather than physical warfare into a prize-winning production much honored by the critics by using the medium to create dramatic tension that less gifted auteurs could not achieve. By the time the film was made, however, Ford was busy with other wartime activities regarded as higher priority.

Against the background of Simmonds's sweeping panoramic view of a work that came at the wrong time for Americans but just the right one for the European resistance movement, Eiko Shiraga's essay, which returns us to the original novel, suggests that because it has often been too easily dismissed, much still may remain to be discovered about Steinbeck's artistic strategies in it. The women who play important roles in the narrative have rarely been discussed, because they have been seen as symbolic figures whose actions are determined by the necessities of the plot. Looking at the work from the viewpoint of another culture, however, Shiraga presents an argument pointing out the deft touches by which the writer has suggested the importance of women in a patriarchal situation in which they might ordinarily be seen only as victims in the power struggle between the dominant males.

Since it would be a long time before Steinbeck learned how wrong critics had been about the European response to his emboldening allegory in *The Moon Is Down*, he was again distressed about his future as a fiction writer and anxious to become more directly involved in the war effort. His concern led to several works that are, for different reasons, among his least remembered. *Bombs Away: The Story of a Bomber Team*, was written at the behest of President Roosevelt. Like *The For-*

gotten Village, ostensibly a documentary, it is a fictional allegory about the transformation of frustrated youths into fighting men. It is pedestrian propaganda, ground out by a writer who, though sympathetic with his subject, has no enthusiasm for the genre. *Once There Was a War* is the title under which were published many years later a series of dispatches that Steinbeck was finally permitted to send from the European Theater to the New York *Herald Tribune* in 1943. It contains some excellent writing; but by the time it was available for study, interest in such reporting had evaporated. *Lifeboat*, intended as a film tribute to the dangerous wartime work of the U. S. Merchant Marine, was so transformed by Alfred Hitchcock and Twentieth Century-Fox that Steinbeck wished his name removed from the credits (though it wasn't), and neither he nor his estate has allowed the publication of his original story treatment.

Our review of his career moves thus to almost the end of the war and *Cannery Row* and gives Kevin Hearle a chance to take us back to *Sea of Cortez*. Hearle shows the links between this work and the novel as the final productions of Steinbeck's great involvement with the pre-war world of his native California valleys, isolating his frustrating efforts to find new media and new scenes to advance his career as his personal version of the kind of nightmare that the whole world was experiencing during the devastating years of World War II.

In "The Boat-Shaped Mind," Hearle sums up the relationship between *Cannery Row* and Steinbeck's feeling at the beginning of the period after *The Grapes of Wrath* with the conclusion that his novel is his "funny, bittersweet reply to *Sea of Cortez*'s adventurous optimism about the continual challenge posed by the relationship between language and the world." Drawing upon the speculation of Mikhail Bakhtin to discuss Steinbeck's handling of the problems that have so long engaged semanticists about the complex and shifting relationships between words and things, Hearle's compact, lucid account of an elusive process suggests much about the effect of five years of difficult, often harrowing and tragic experiences on Steinbeck.

I would add only to Hearle's conclusion that the novel is "not a comedy in the classical sense, because Doc doesn't get the girl in the end," that it was not a classical comedy of reconciliation that Steinbeck sought in this work, but rather a "cosmic comedy" suggested by what he identifies and differentiates in his speculations on "The Word" in chapter 2 of the novel. Most of the characters that "The Word sucks up" remain, like the lonely gopher in chapter 31, in the quotidian flux where ignorant armies shatter pastoral dreams; but Doc has transcended this troubled realm to achieve through art the stasis that the speaker seeks in W. B. Yeats's "Sailing to Byzantium." Steinbeck here places Doc in the same position that Salinger places Buddy Glass at the end of "Seymour: An Introduction." The trouble with achieving entropy, however, is, as Salinger discovered, that there is no place to go but to the kind of mortal sleep achieved by Buddy or the immortal sleep of Seymour. Having brought "words" and "things" to rest by infinitely merging them, one is left with no alternative but to repeat indefinitely the account of the road to enlightenment or to lapse into silence (as Salinger has). Some mystics achieve such states, but neither would have satisfied the restless Steinbeck, even if his fleeting vision had not been derailed by the wasteful death of Doc's original, Ed Ricketts, and the degeneration of the bower of bliss Steinbeck anticipated finding in his second marriage. These were accompanied by a growing perception that there were still things wrong with the rest of the world and an obsession that he had to try to do something about them. He had to find a hero who could bring his tales to a more classically comic ending and provide an example for a wayward world. Out of this effort emerged Juan Chicoy guiding his wayward bus from Rebels Corners to San Juan de la Cruz and a regenerated Doc. For the moment, however, Steinbeck was not abandoning *Cannery Row* for Dogpatch but for Byzantium.

Cannery Row was to prove not a new spring, but an Indian Summer before the autumn and winter of Steinbeck's career as a novelist. The disillusionment that underlies *The Moon Is Down* and *Lifeboat* proved not just a product of the wartime madness but the force that Steinbeck struggled to overcome in his later fiction. Debra Barker's essay on Juana's role in *The Pearl* serves unintentionally in conjunction with Eiko Shiraga's on *The Moon Is Down* by stressing also a new importance of the women in Steinbeck's work to establish a continuity in Steinbeck's post-California period. Far apart as the two works seem in setting and in the nature of the situation confronting the characters, both works are basically pictures of naive innocents at the mercy of greedy, ruthless, dehumanized killers who are most successfully thwarted by brave, determined women when their men lose control of the situation. The would-be thieves and killers in *The Pearl* and the invaders in *The Moon Is Down* differ from each other only in the magnitude of their operations and the numbers of their victims; given equal opportunities they would pursue the same course. Though both novels end with morally admirable sacrifices, the future prospects of the admirable characters remain ambiguous, for in *The Pearl* the surviving women still face problems as grievous as those in *The Moon Is Down*.

Indeed, the note that both Shiraga and Barker stress about the new dignity of the women characters is not sustained in subsequent novels. Both works are products of the brief happy period of Steinbeck's second marriage to Gwyn, before he was disillusioned in his expectations about family life; but both have also tested the credulity of many readers, though they have inspired others.

Steinbeck's next effort was his first attempt since *The Grapes of Wrath* and his wartime involvements to produce a long, complex fiction in the *Grand Hotel* manner of bringing together a group of widely assorted strangers who would usually not mingle and letting them impinge on each other as they face crises that can change their lives during a symbolic journey. It proved not even inspiring to many readers, though Steinbeck had had high hopes for it.

Great is the change in the treatment of the women characters from *The Pearl*, which was actually written quite a long while before *The Wayward Bus*, to that novel which has been called misogynistic by respected critics. Brian Railsback, however, proposes the possibility of the influence of Darwin's theories of sexual selectivity, in order to argue that the novel was not intended as a one-sided attack on American Momism, like Philip Wylie's once best-selling *Generation of Vipers*, but rather as an attack on "the inherent weakness of a society that has gone Hollywood, that has tried to cover up biological reality with make-up, booze, or a handsome business suit," in the manner of the palimpsest on the bumper of the bus itself where the tacky word "sweetheart" has been painted over "the grand power of Jesus."

Before leaving this essay to examine another approach to this pivotal novel, one may notice that at this point in the collection, if one is reading it straight through, there is a change that may not be obvious at first in the viewpoint from which critics are approaching the individual works. The essays about earlier works have focused primarily on the qualities of the narrative, judging the effect of these later works on the reputation that Steinbeck established in the 1930s. With this essay, however, as in the subsequent ones about the novels, the emphasis shifts from a concentration on the work to a speculation about the writer. Heretofore, the concern has been with the kind of reading experience that the work offers; it is considered as a possible candidate for attention—one that just happens to be by John Steinbeck—in competition with a multitude of others; but henceforth the focus is on John Steinbeck. The work is assumed to merit attention because he did write it rather than because of its standing with its competition in its own time or from earlier times. The commentators appear moved to bring heavy artillery to his rescue principally by a troubling knowledge that Steinbeck's reputation was being widely questioned.

John Ditsky and Robert DeMott are the two most active, articulate and persistent of what may be called the second generation of Steinbeck critics, appearing on the scene at the time of the foundation of the John Steinbeck Society and the author's death in the late 1960s to reexamine and expand upon the background established five to ten years earlier in the general studies by Peter Lisca, Joseph Fontenrose, F.W. Watt and myself that, despite differences in their aims and approaches, served largely to reinforce each other in the judgments of the individual works. It should be noted that three of these books were parts of series that were just being launched at that time in which the writers had to consider their subject in relation to the aims of the publisher of the series to strive for a consistency in the books that would make them not special pleadings for an individual writer but efforts to show why indeed these particular writers had been selected for the series in comparison with other Americans, past and present.

Ditsky and DeMott have distinguished themselves among the growing number of younger critics attracted to Steinbeck by developing experimental approaches toward the writing of criticism. Both are also poets and strong promoters of poetry with somewhat romantic sensibilities attuned to the power and influence of words more strongly than to the narrative structures that principally engage many fiction scholars.

The essays that we have examined so far are thoughtful and commendable examples of conventional criticism. There is a curious, but I think entirely accidental, similarity between the five essays by men and the three by women that differentiate the two groups. The men's essays, though not avoiding qualitative judgments, are what can be called informational essays, providing new factual material about Steinbeck, his works and his own readings, while the three by women are argumentative essays that focus primarily on new ways of looking at the works. But I don't think any further generalizations can be drawn from such a small sample. Ditsky's, and DeMott's on *Sweet Thursday*, on the other hand, are invitations to readers to join them in an exploration of the work that may not lead to any firm conclusions about the author's intentions or achievements. These are reports of quests by those still engaged in the hunt, whereas the other essays (including those that follow) are reports from the quiet of the study about completed hunts, though not necessarily final ones, since other forays may follow.

Under the circumstances, it would be presumptuous to attempt to summarize the Ditsky and DeMott essays like the others. What is perhaps appropriate, however, is to suggest to readers that they should try to change gears in order to enjoy these papers most fully. One is not in the classroom now, where indeed most papers like those collected here are written to be read, but traveling along with the writers in pursuit of an elusive catch.

One should note that, although both essays are experimental in form and tentative in findings, they do not follow the same kind of course, so that one must adjust one's pace of pursuit to different demands. Ditsky describes *The Wayward Bus* as an "open-ended" novel, and the same adjective might certainly be applied to his speculation that concludes with the admission that perhaps he ends with "only the tip of the iceberg" explored in what may be "a major statement on the vital relationship between writer and work." The essay is like a rambling walk on a crooked and sometimes obscured path, or perhaps it would be more suitable to say in connection with this novel, like a jolting bus ride with frequent stops and starts and little sidetrips to explore the terrain. One thing leads to another, but formalists would find it very difficult to produce an outline imposing a conventional structure upon it. Not everyone can bring off an essay like this one, but Ditsky is always an interesting companion who leads us enticingly on a rambling journey.

DeMott, on the other hand, is not out for a stroll but on the track of elusive game. The goal of his mission is revealed, almost offhandedly, when he finally gets to the heart of his circuitous staking out of Steinbeck's artistic relationship to Al Capp and his famous comic strip by quoting from Steinbeck's Introduction to Capp's *The World of Li'l Abner*: "Who knows what literature is?" Steinbeck's further observation in this same essay, "Our present argument that literature is the written and printed word . . . has no very eternal basis in fact," needs to be applied at greater length to DeMott's argument that Steinbeck was a prophetic postmodernist.

Perhaps *Sweet Thursday* should have been presented as a comic strip or an animated cartoon? Its exaggerations and putdowns and slapstick violence give it much in common not only with Al Capp's themes and satire but also with the style and technique of the Tom and Jerry cartoon films. Would the work have reached the far larger audience that would have appreciated it much more than finicky book reviewers if it had found the form that best suited it?

We are also indebted to Bob DeMott for the splendid guide to the reassessment of *East of Eden*, which I think is likely to become one of the most frequently consulted contributions in this volume, behind only the marvelous long interview with which Elaine Steinbeck has permitted us to conclude. Not only is DeMott's bibliography of great value in itself, but it is an outstanding example of the energy and enthusiasm with which he pursues what other scholars might look upon as drudgery, like his first great contribution to Steinbeck studies, *Steinbeck's Reading* (1984).

After having the long controversy over the novel that Steinbeck regarded as his big one recalled to mind by DeMott's introduction to the checklist, I would also comment that I feel much of the controversy over *East of Eden* has simply been beside the point, since the participants have failed to recognize the true genre of this fictional fantasy/autobiogra-

15

phy. I see it as another attempt, like all of Steinbeck's last six novels, beginning with *The Wayward Bus*, to do what he had steadfastly refused to do in the 1930s: write in popular genres that would appeal to a broad audience. Since DeMott has carried his checklist up to so nearly this present reading, I do not feel that on this occasion I am abusing a captive audience if I carry the discussion one step further by quoting briefly from what is likely to be my final appraisal of the "patchwork leviathan" in *John Steinbeck's Fiction Revisited* (1994), the third and almost entirely new version (the first having been published in 1961) of my Twayne series introduction to Steinbeck's writing:

> Besides essentially talking down to his audience, as the overt moral-izer must, in his enthusiasm he apparently failed to realize that the two narratives he was attempting to juxtapose did not complement each other for another reason . . . one was pastoral history and the other Gothic fantasy.
>
> The two seemingly antipathetic forms can on rare occasions be juxtaposed when the author envisions precisely the reason for the contrast, as William Faulkner does in *Light in August*. But Steinbeck had not found the recipe. (118)

One of the great ironies of Steinbeck's career is that the novels he thought he was writing for a small audience like *In Dubious Battle* and *The Grapes of Wrath* found huge audiences for decades and stirred up great conten-tion, while the novels that he thought might appeal to larger audiences were less successful than he hoped.

One work that was surprisingly popular in its time but that has failed to attract substantial new audiences is not examined in this collection, *The Short Reign of Pippin IV*. If I may quote once more from my new book, I would like to suggest a reason it has been neglected even though it is the most entertaining novel that Steinbeck had written since *Cannery Row*: "The principal shortcoming of this attractive fable is that—like editorial cartoons—it has dated quickly. After only a few years annota-tions would have been needed to make [it] fully comprehensible" (125). My brief reference here to its cartoonlike features was suggested long before I read Bob DeMott's essay on *Sweet Thursday* by Steinbeck's writing during his residence in Paris in 1954 for *Le Figaro*, the daily newspaper famous for its front page "Marianne" cartoons lampooning the foibles of French politicians as Steinbeck's novel does.

With Michael Meyer's "Citizen Cain: Ethan Hawley's Double Iden-tity in *The Winter of Our Discontent*," we reach the end of his career as a fiction writer with another project for which he had high hopes that disappointed both his closest associates and the general public, although

it provided the occasion for belatedly awarding him a well-deserved Nobel Prize for literature. Wisely, Meyer avoids directly attacking the lukewarm response to the novel and its continued neglect, though I think that the very form and thoroughness of his essay implicitly suggest the problem that made this well-intentioned work uninspiring reading.

Meyer's essay returns us to the established forms of literary criticism with a study of the symbols and allusions with which he quite effectively demonstrates the novel abounds. "Symbol hunting," as this type of criticism is sometimes condescendingly called, has fallen under some suspicion because of the excessive claims some practitioners have made for questionable conjectures; but Meyer's extensive findings strike me as well supported and entirely consistent with Steinbeck's known interests and intentions. It is presented with great skill; but what strikes me most after finishing this demanding argument is that if the novel had to carry such a heavy burden of allusions, parallels, and mythical and religious traditions, it is no surprise if it collapses under its own weight. That the novel "forms a subtle warning to America" cannot be denied, but one perhaps must add "too subtle for America." After failing to impress a popular audience with comic-strip techniques, Steinbeck had gone to the other end of the scale and failed to impress a highly literate audience with an overwrought work.

The conclusion that still has to be reached, I feel, after examining this collection of carefully considered and well constructed essays is that after *The Grapes of Wrath* and certainly after *Cannery Row*, Steinbeck's intentions in his fiction were not achieved but his whole career remains especially significant, particularly in terms of changing literary, social and political theories, as an American success story that has cautionary implications for anyone who has risen or thinks of rising from obscurity to celebrity. Steinbeck, as I have often observed, greatly resembles not only the boy Jody in *The Red Pony*, but also Jody's grandfather in the final story of "The Leader of the People." Steinbeck shared the spirit of "westering" and lamented its passing. Unlike Jody's grandfather, however, Steinbeck shook off the sense of defeat that permeated his early fiction by expressing in *The Grapes of Wrath* a hope for the survival of the human community. Even this novel and its immediate successors until *Cannery Row* ended ambiguously and left the shaping of the future in the hands of readers. When he turned, however, to overt moralizing and preaching, beginning with *The Pearl*, his fiction began to lose its hold on his most responsive readers, as appears inevitable when he began to allow the lesson to shape the narrative instead of letting the design emerge from the material as he had advocated in *The Log from the* Sea of Cortez and opening the page "to let the stories crawl in by themselves," as he proposed in *Cannery Row*.

The contributions to this volume finally venture beyond the large-enough-in-itself subject of Steinbeck's fiction to consider two of his most substantial works from his last years that crowned what may be called his other writing. His first professional engagement was actually as a reporter for a New York City newspaper. He soon found that he was not suited for the life of a newshound in the 1920s when reporters battled each other for "scoops," and nothing he wrote in this period has been identified. Beginning in 1936, however, with such reports as "The Harvest Gypsies" on conditions in the migrant camps in California—reports written for the San Francisco *News* and subsequently published with additions as *Their Blood Is Strong*—he began an off and on career as what can best be called an autobiographical reporter-at-large of a volume of work that contains finally more words than his fiction.

From this formidable pile, we have already observed the links between his first personal narrative to be published, *The Log from the Sea of Cortez*, and his fiction, and at last we turn to the one that would be the greatest success and one of the most popular of all his books, *Travels with Charley in Search of America*, and his final major contribution, *America and Americans*, in which he looked back over his country's history and his own life to share with readers his personal feelings about the American past, the present, and possible future.

Geralyn Strecker examines and compares the two books in her essay, and indeed there is a close relation between them, as Steinbeck himself acknowledged that he became interested in writing the second book because it offered him opportunities to discuss things he had thought about while writing *Travels with Charley* but that were not suitable for that book. As Strecker points out, the travel book was a narrative of a journey of rediscovery for an aging observer-critic who felt he was getting out of touch with his country, while *America and Americans* is a philosophical analysis of contemporary America against a background of a grand but often wasteful past and an uncertain future.

Mimi Gladstein, one of the strongest voices devoted extensively to criticism of Steinbeck's work and its reception, concentrates in "*America and Americans*: The Arthurian Consummation" on the importance of this last publication to Steinbeck himself "as a capstone and culmination of his career." She points out how he turned what had started out to be a series of brief comments to accompany a book his publishers planned as a montage of memorable pictures of the United States by prominent photographers into what Jackson Benson has described as a work which says in different form what he had hoped to be able to say through his unfinished transformation of Sir Thomas Malory's *Morte Darthur*. Certainly one cannot begin to understand Steinbeck without pondering his conception of the importance of the Arthurian myths and the many sides of his complex and widely neglected meditation on America's land and its people.

The last words here should go to Tetsumaro Hayashi, reminding us that despite his devotion to John Steinbeck—which resulted in a dozen books, including bibliographies, and twenty more that he edited, mostly for the John Steinbeck Society monograph series, and at least thirty articles—he produced much other scholarship. He continued to write about the English Renaissance figures who had been the subject of his doctoral dissertation, especially Shakespeare, Robert Greene and Thomas Lodge. While he was editing the *Steinbeck Quarterly* for twenty-five years, he also prepared books about William Faulkner, Ernest Hemingway, Henry James, James Joyce, Arthur Miller, Herman Melville and Eugene O'Neill, books which often suggested research opportunities for young scholars in the United States and Japan. The scope and variety of his contributions are indicated by the bibliographical checklist that Robert DeMott has compiled to round off this volume of tributes. Tetsumaro Hayashi's energy and thirst for knowledge have inspired his colleagues and friends and have been of great and continuing value to several generations of students.

I reach the end of this account of our efforts to honor Tetsumaro Hayashi by calling fresh attention to the works to which he devoted so much of his professional career with the uncomfortable feeling that I have talked too much when readers should be moving on for their direct encounter with the critics. I add only that even beyond these engaging and often provocative papers, there is an even greater enticement for readers in Donald Coers's long and far-ranging interview with Steinbeck's widow; but no comment is needed here. Elaine can speak for herself—and she certainly has much to tell us that complements the rest of this collection and that the always shy Steinbeck might have been reluctant to share even in his personal narratives.

Part I

General Essays

Art for Politics: John Steinbeck and FDR

Cliff Lewis

The Nazi attack in Europe led to many American artists' participation in government war projects. Writer John Steinbeck was among those whom the Roosevelt administration called upon for assistance. Steinbeck's war contributions to the Roosevelt Administration included suggestions for an espionage program, recommendations to trust Japanese-Americans, and propositions for post-war domestic and foreign policy. And after the war Steinbeck was asked to write a farewell address to a New Deal leader. In Steinbeck's Washington eulogy (1946) for Roosevelt assistant Harry Hopkins, Steinbeck artfully defines a new myth in America's public consciousness—government exists to improve citizens' lives—for which Roosevelt and Hopkins are the symbols. Steinbeck, who kept his political efforts secret, became for FDR loyalists a hidden spokesman for New Deal principles. Drawing largely from unexamined manuscripts,[1] this essay will argue that in the period under discussion, 1939-1946, Steinbeck evolved as an astute yet visionary political writer and, for the innermost circle of the FDR election team, a respected advisor.

The journey that brought Steinbeck to Washington from Salinas, California, began indirectly with his 1936 newspaper articles "The Harvest Gypsies," whose research introduced him to the wretched conditions of migrant workers and to the relief efforts of federal workers. Steinbeck revised the articles in spring 1938 as a pamphlet titled *Their Blood Is Strong*; the pamphlet was one of several projects that evolved into *The Grapes of Wrath* (DeMott xxxiv-xli), the novel that brought Steinbeck in 1939 to the attention of Eleanor Roosevelt and the nation.

Steinbeck's realization that the federal government could alter the appalling migrant conditions, along with the influence of politicially active artists Pare Lorentz and Paul de Kruif among others,[2] induced Steinbeck to appeal to Washington to intervene in reactionary California politics. The Roosevelts had been concerned about the serious labor problems in California. When a Democratic governor replaced a conservative Republican, FDR initiated further federal support to the state. Eleanor Roosevelt, moreover, welcomed personal letters drawing her attention to poverty and corruption, and she directed federal authorities to investigate the reports. With FDR's commitment to correct injustices and Eleanor Roosevelt's proclivity to answer personal appeals, reformers felt the White House welcomed their ideas.

Steinbeck first contacted the President in a cryptic telegram from "The

Steinbeck Committee to Aid Agriculture Organization" February 9, 1939, protesting the threatened "curtailment of the FSA [Farm Security Administration] Camps and relief program"[3] (RL). The Steinbeck Committee also in February telegraphed a one-sentence request to the President asking "for the continuation and extension of the LaFollette Civil Liberties Committee" (RL). The LaFollette Hearings, which opened in San Francisco in 1939, exposed the abuse of American migrant workers and as well the tactics of the Communist Party to organize them.[4] But Steinbeck also used his name to seek help for a friend. On June 14, 1939, Steinbeck telegraphed a request to Eleanor Roosevelt asking the government to continue funding the U.S. Film Service, the organization Pare Lorentz had created in 1938 to fund his documentaries. Perhaps Steinbeck's trip to Washington around June (Benson 402) was for a meeting with Mrs. Roosevelt. Mrs. Roosevelt brought Steinbeck's request to the President's attention. FDR instructed the Director of the Budget to reply to Mrs. Roosevelt; despite Mrs. Roosevelt's support the funding ended (RL). Nevertheless, Steinbeck had committed himself to a project for someone in Washington. On October 16, 1939, he wrote, "I have one little job to do for the government, " and, two days later, "Sorry I committed myself to the Washington thing" (*Working Days* 106, 107). The nature of "the Washington thing" is unknown. A subsequent appeal for another favor resulted in an intriguing relationship between Steinbeck and Washington.

Steinbeck's next request from Washington was self-serving. To acquire quickly Mexican permission for a "marine ecology" trip into its coastal waters, Steinbeck in the fall of 1939 persuaded Paul de Kruif to contact the State Department (RL). For some reason FDR himself reviewed the request and on December 13 sent a memorandum to an aide to determine whether the Navy could employ the John Steinbeck expedition "in connection with information for ONI [Office of Naval Intelligence]." The note specifically directs ONI chief Admiral Andersen to see if he can use Ricketts and Steinbeck "for this [intelligence gathering] purpose" (RL). The Mexican permits arrived without aid from the State Department. No existing correspondence indicates that Steinbeck and Ricketts collected naval intelligence in Mexico. But a few months later, while on a movie project in Mexico, Steinbeck, as we shall see, sent political intelligence to Washington. And since Steinbeck and Ricketts corresponded with Naval Intelligence after Pearl Harbor, it seems safe to assume that the subject of spying must have come up previously.[5] Thus within a year after Steinbeck began asking the Roosevelts for favors, a year in which war started in Europe, Steinbeck began collecting foreign intelligence.

II

Forwarding intelligence about Mexico and recommending a propaganda bureau to influence American public opinion constituted one phase of Steinbeck's war effort. In Mexico to film his documentary *The Forgotten Village*, assisted by Herbert Kline (who directed *Lights Out in Europe* (1940), a film about the Nazi attack on Poland), Steinbeck worried that the lights were dimming in Mexico. There Steinbeck observed the growing influence of Germany. He responded with a typed three-page letter to his uncle Joe Hamilton, Information Officer of the Works Project Administration, warning that deteriorating political conditions required an American response.

Steinbeck's letter of May 1940 described the many levels of fascist threat in Mexico's forthcoming election: "The other candidate is General Almazan. He is a fascist, is being backed by Hearst, by Harry Chandler, and by the [American] oil companies, and by the business interests of Mexico . . . . Unfortunately, he also has the backing of the German element and the German propaganda office . . . . He has promised to raise a rebellion if he isn't elected. . . "(RL).

Steinbeck offered explanations as to why American economic interests supported a fascist system. Steinbeck wrote, "Hearst . . . still has a lot of land down there which he hopes won't be taken from him . . . [and] there is a strong interventionist group in the United States who would like to take over Mexico for . . . Hearst and the Standard Oil Company."

Harry Chandler had huge land investments in the San Fernando Valley, along the Colorado River in Mexico, and exerted influence through his *Los Angeles Times*. According to Daniel Yergin, when the Mexican Government nationalized American oil production in that country, American companies would not purchase Mexican oil. Mexico was forced to trade with Japan, Germany, and Italy. In this dispute, FDR aligned the U.S. with Mexico against the oil companies (276-77).

American public opinion was the second issue Steinbeck believed Washington should consider. Steinbeck warned that the American public received false information from its media about Mexican political events. According to Steinbeck, columnist Walter Winchell wrote that Mexican communists and fascists were cooperating when, Steinbeck said, they battled in the streets. Further, Steinbeck commented, *Life* magazine published pictures of labor marches with captions claiming that the laborers wore storm trooper uniforms, but which Steinbeck identified as their "work uniforms."

Inept American government bureaucracies were the third problem Steinbeck outlined to his uncle. "Ten FBI men arrived lately in Mexico [City]. They are all known . . . [and] they are regarded as spies. They are so obviously FBI men that it is funny. They pose as tourists ... a hammer [hammier] bunch of flat feet never existed." By contrast, "The Germans have absolutely outclassed the Allies in propaganda." To these problems Steinbeck added a fourth, one of attitude: "Our businessmen" are arrogant and "Our young diplomats get drunk and express their contempt ..." for Mexicans (RL). In Steinbeck's view the United States faced a political crisis on its southern border partly of its own making.

Steinbeck recommended that "a propaganda office be set up which, through radio and motion pictures, attempts to get this side of the world together. Its method would be to make for understanding rather than friction." Steinbeck then offered the use of his film crew and volunteered to recruit Hollywood experts who would share the work (RL). Although the letter to Joe Hamilton proposed a propaganda agency, he did not directly advocate an intelligence-gathering organization to replace the incompetent FBI, but the implication exists. Nor does he explain how to deal with the fascist-leaning American businesses.

The letter alerted Washington. Steinbeck traveled to the capital. There on June 24, 1940, he sent Roosevelt a one-paragraph summary reporting that "a crisis in the western hemisphere is imminent, and is to be met only by an immediate, controlled, considered, and directed method and policy" (RL). Roosevelt instructed an aide to bring Steinbeck to the White House "for twenty minutes" the next day. Persuaded by Steinbeck's argument for an American response, FDR offered Steinbeck some form of job. Steinbeck declined. Several weeks after returning to California, Steinbeck wrote of the June meeting: "I hope I made some of it stick" (*Working Days* 114). It did. This meeting confirmed Roosevelt's fears about Nazi penetration, and he "made hemispheric defense a priority." Consequently, in "August 1940 he created by executive order the Office of the Coordinator of Inter-American Affairs (CIAA)" with Nelson Rockefeller its head, with John Hay Whitney chief of the Motion Picture Division (Koppes and Black 51). Neither position was salaried.

A year went by before Roosevelt formed his international intelligence and propaganda units. Steinbeck was one among many to suggest a failure in our gathering of foreign intelligence. For instance, in August 1940 William Donovan, whom the British were training to administer an American spy network that did not yet exist, discussed with FDR speechwriter Robert Sherwood the need for a spy organization.[6] Finally, a year later, FDR accepted Donovan's argument for a "central enemy intelligence organization" and then appointed Donovan the unsalaried Coordinator of Information of what was later designated the OSS and then renamed the CIA (Brown 164-65). When Donovan formed the Foreign Information Service as a propaganda branch of the CIO, Sherwood was in charge of "radio propaganda" and had "800 journalists, broadcasters, and writers" helping him the first year (Brown 170). According to Jackson Benson, Steinbeck's work for that organization in its first year was immense (487). As a result of the June meeting, moreover, Steinbeck had FDR's confidence.

An economic proposal Steinbeck sent FDR two months later also received a hearing. On August 13, 1940, Steinbeck forwarded a scheme to destroy Germany's economy. Noting to Roosevelt that "I find I have a job whether or not I want one," (referring to the June meeting) Steinbeck suggested that FDR meet a friend "with imagination . . . a remarkable scientist" who will "put forth an analysis and a psychological weapon . . . " (RL). In September FDR and the U.S. Treasurer met with Dr. Melvyn Knisley but decided not to act upon his scheme of dropping counterfeit money into the European war zone (Benson 465). Nearly a year passed before Steinbeck returned to Washington.

After working for a year in California on various film and book projects, Steinbeck traveled to Washington in the fall of 1941 to meet with newly appointed CIO Director Donovan to discuss organizing a propaganda unit (Benson 487). A subsequent report from Steinbeck to Donovan leads me to believe that they discussed organizing a Foreign Nationalities Branch within the CIO to collect information from European refugees about their homelands for propaganda or for spying purposes. These refugees, Steinbeck's biographer informs us, were Steinbeck's inspiration for his novel about the Norwegian Resistance, *The Moon Is Down* (Benson 487-88). The function of this branch as a spy network might explain the contents of an extraordinary Steinbeck-Donovan correspondence in December 1941.

Donovan sent FDR on December 15, 1941—eight days after Pearl Harbor—a typed summary of Steinbeck's recommended treatment of Nisei or Japanese-Americans. The arguments of Steinbeck's report suggest that he was aware of California and Washington officials' mistrust of the Nisei. The Hyde Park document demonstrates Steinbeck's confidence in Nisei loyalty; his scheme to assure their continued wartime loyalty is shrewd and wise. As the internment decision remains topical, I quote the entire document.

Memorandum for the President:

The following suggestions have been made to us by John Steinbeck:

1. The Nisei or native born Japanese have condemned the action of Japan and have reiterated their loyalty.
2. In every community the Nisei have very close organizations.

3. Every Japanese foreign born or native born is known to these organizations.
4. There is no reason so far to suspect the loyalty of Japanese-American citizens.

IT IS SUGGESTED:

1. That local civilian defense authorities make contact with these Japanese.
2. That they be given auxiliary status in controlling sabotage.
   (1) They know the language.
   (2) They would be more likely to know of illegal gathering places than whites.
   (3) They have very close check on unknown or strange Japanese.
   (4) Such evidence of trust would be likely to cement the loyalty of inherently loyal citizens.
3. No information need be given them. It can all come from them.
4. Any valuable information coming from them would do much to overturn a distrust of themselves.
5. This can all be done by local authorities.
6. A failure to cooperate would be indicative of disloyalty.

CONCLUSION:

A. By instituting this cooperation, some actual information may be gained and since the Japanese community is settled, such a plan would in effect make the loyal Japanese responsible for the disloyal.
B. In case valuable work were done by the Nisei, it should be published, thus cementing loyalties and driving a wedge between loyal and disloyal Japanese.
C. Organization of this cooperation by the local Civil Defense organizations should be very easy to accomplish.
D. It would constitute a test of loyalty (RL).

In strategic positions throughout this document emphasis is upon the loyalty of these Americans. But Steinbeck acknowledges that "unknown or strange Japanese"—not Americans—should be watched. And before condemning a priori "our inherently loyal citizens," we could administer a loyalty test. However unfair to ask for such a test, it was a shrewd request—given the current distrust and the subsequent judgment—that the Nisei no doubt would have welcomed. The audience was not the Nisei but one suspicious of and unfamiliar with these West Coast citizens. In a few words Steinbeck had tried to educate the President about their community and to persuade him to follow a benign policy.

Consequently Steinbeck's report is organized into three parts: Part one affirms Nisei loyalty and indicates that Steinbeck well understood their insular community. Part two suggests the ways the government officials can use the Nisei community to spy upon "unknown or strange Japanese." His third section reaffirms that the spy system will both succeed in uprooting possible enemies and offer further proof of patrotism.

Today it seems like an extreme proposal even to set before paranoid officials. Over the last forty years we have come to distrust domestic surveillance. We recall the results of McCarthyism and the House Un-American Activities Committee: innocent lives ruined, the loss of our Chinese diplomatic corps. Neither the government's spying upon Vietnam war protesters nor the Church Committee's revelations about the C.I.A.'s abuse of power prepares us for Steinbeck's proposal. We must, instead, recall that fifty-two years ago, when Steinbeck offered his proposal, just a week had passed since the Japanese had destroyed our Pacific fleet and its supporting air power in Hawaii and the Philippines. However unsavory Steinbeck's recommendation that Americans spy on one another, under the circumstances Steinbeck's views show that while he does not doubt the loyalty of Japanese-Americans, he must go to extremes to protect them from those who do. Better to acknowledge that a few traitors might exist and should be caught, and try to protect the rest, Steinbeck may have reasoned.

Steinbeck's "loyalty test" was not offered. In February, 1942, at the insistence of California and Washington political leaders and such prominent Americans as Walter Lippmann, the Nisei lost their freedom. They also lost businesses, homes, and reputations under the Internment Program. Disregarding Steinbeck's knowledge of his employees and neighbors brought national disgrace. A play that he coauthored, *A Medal for Benny*, begun in December, 1942, protested the discrimination against an Hispanic war hero, but it could easily be read in retrospect as a response to the abuse of the Nisei.[7]

Steinbeck's war efforts consisted of more than recommending policies. As Jackson Benson has described Steinbeck's wartime writing thoroughly, I limit my remarks to an outline of Steinbeck's activities. Commencing in the fall of 1941 and into 1943 Steinbeck worked without pay for the CIO, "the Office of War Information, the Writers' War Board, and the [Army] Air Force" (487). In that period he wrote two books for the government: *The Moon Is Down*, which promoted guerrilla warfare, and *Bombs Away*, the result of an exhaustive national tour of air bases, which encouraged the enlistment of citizens into the air force.[8] It is ironic and sad that despite Steinbeck's work on the behalf of the intelligence and military services, other government bureaucracies blocked his application for an officer's rank in Army Air Force Intelligence, and for a while interfered with his freedom to travel abroad because his loyalty was suspect (Benson 508-09).

The F.B.I. questioned Steinbeck's loyalty. From 1936 until his death in 1968 it collected a file on his political life (Robins 96). Because he denounced economic injustice, many Californians thought Steinbeck sympathetic to communism. Communist Party member Howard Fast made this shocking statement: "[Steinbeck] was a CP member when he wrote *In Dubious Battle* . . . we all knew he was a Party member" (Robins 97). (The Communist Party in Poland, as I observed while I was there in 1976, interpreted that novel as hostile, and had banned it.) Fast and J. Edgar Hoover little understood Steinbeck's politics. Nor did Steinbeck at first understand Hoover. In 1939 Steinbeck had forwarded a particularly threatening letter on his life to the F.B.I. with a request for help. But Steinbeck's view changed. As we saw in his 1940 letter, Steinbeck did not respect the professional work of the F.B.I. Nor did he send Hoover his report on the Nisei. It went instead to Donovan to be forwarded to FDR. By 1943, around the time of his application for military service, Steinbeck knew Hoover was investigating him. Steinbeck asked Attorney General Biddle, Hoover's superior, to demand that Hoover discontinue the spying. Hoover lied and said Steinbeck was mistaken to believe he was under investigation (Robins 96). How could Steinbeck have known? Very likely during the army's review of Steinbeck's application, Hoover's agency sent its confidential file on Steinbeck to military authorities. And someone of authority in a military or civilian agency who read it probably reported the file's existence to Steinbeck. Pare Lorentz, an Army Air Force Officer, recalls a meeting with Air Force Intelligence at the Pentagon in 1943 where Lorentz learned that Naval Intelligence recommended Steinbeck be turned down for a military commission. And Lorentz adds that shortly thereafter he warned Steinbeck of the Navy's letter (106). Nonetheless, Steinbeck's letter to Biddle addressed Hoover and not Naval Intelligence. If Steinbeck had an enemy in Hoover, he had friends in Army Intelligence, in the spy chief Donovan, and in the White House. Finally his passport was approved, and he covered the European war for four months as a journalist in 1943. Although his war work for the government had ended, still ahead were two White House campaign projects to write.

Had Steinbeck been unusually patriotic during this two-year period? No. A few names will serve to represent the thousands of notable Americans who served for patriotic reasons as did Steinbeck. We noted that Rockefeller and Whitney and Donovan (who could not afford it) served without pay. Dollar-a-year men left business to serve in capacities such as organizing military production of war supplies. The authors of *Hollywood Goes to War* inform us that John Houseman, Thornton Wilder, and Stephen Vincent Benet worked for the Foreign Information Service for little money (55-56). Film producers Frank Capra and John

Ford enlisted in the service (122); actor Douglas Fairbanks, Jr., whom Steinbeck fictionalized in his war reports, led commando missions against Germans. Steinbeck's reputation of a public spirited citizen is more visible than others because of the written records he left behind. The history of millions of Americans who served longer in or out of uniform is still being written.

III

In 1944, Steinbeck escaped from war and politics by working on his novel *Cannery Row*. In June he agreed to help reelect FDR. We learn of Steinbeck's campaign role in a memorandum from Oscar R. Ewing, Assistant Chairman of the Democratic Committee, who on June 29 sent a note and a Steinbeck "Letter" to Steve Early, FDR Press Secretary. Ewing wrote, "Appropos of the possibility of the President in advance of the Convention, indicating that he will accept the nomination, the Chairman [Robert E. Hannegan] asked me to send to you the enclosed suggestion for a statement that he might make. This was prepared by *John Steinbeck*."[9] The intent of a "Letter" to the Democratic Party—really to the American public—is to explain why FDR sought a fourth term. Roosevelt slightly revised Steinbeck's "Letter" and sent it to Party Chairman Hannegan on July 10, 1944. The next day the revised "Letter" appeared in the newspapers.[10] The "Letter" intended to blunt the Republican criticism of Roosevelt's presumed dictatorial ambition. Steinbeck opened his "Letter" by saying that during wartime the President's "superior officer—the people of the United States" is ordering him through the Democratic Party and the electorate to "serve" again in office. Steinbeck compared the thought of Roosevelt's refusal to serve a fourth term to that of a soldier who wanted "to leave his post in line." As soldiers each must serve his country in wartime (HRC).

The "Letter" noted, however, that FDR "will not run, in the usual partisan, political sense" out of respect for those suffering in combat. Then Steinbeck added a further argument for not campaigning because "I have not the time nor the inclination." Perhaps Roosevelt's health was not up to a strenuous campaign, but the question of whether the President would be nonpartisan was answered in this attack upon Republicans: "And I shall hesitate to abandon the country and the war to a group whose last experience in public power reduced the nation to panic, economic hysteria and leaderless anarchy . . . ." The concluding paragraph reiterates in military language that FDR would serve as the public "ordered" (HRC).

Roosevelt included most of Steinbeck's prose in the newspaper

31

"Letter" or in his Democratic Convention "Address" a month later. Omitted from both was Steinbeck's graphic description of the battlefield: "the young men of America . . . dying in the hell of the beaches and the islands" became in FDR's acceptance speech "days of tragic sorrow."

The success of Steinbeck's June "Letter" brought another request. This time Steinbeck corresponded with Harry Hopkins's aide Howard O. Hunter, who requested platform ideas in 250 words or less for FDR's July 20, 1944, "Convention Address."[11] The exact number of words was not accidental. Roosevelt in a July 15 memo to Hannegan asked for a "Gettsyburg Address type of platform" because "People are tired of the old type—don't read them—don't remember them if they do" (RL). Steinbeck wrote a poetic yet visionary Lincolnesque platform. He sent Hunter the typed page with eleven items titled "Manefesto" [sic]. An accompanying note apologized for his having written 300 words but warned that the ideas were arranged and written for dramatic impact and therefore should not be altered (RL). FDR, who had little feel for language, rewrote it and so erased from history an eloquent political document.

The rhythmic flow of ideas is indeed memorable. Using declarative and parallel sentences, Steinbeck opened each of the eleven statements with the pronoun "We" followed by the verbs "intend," "propose," "believe," and in one instance "will not." The first ten items fall roughly into the categories of either foreign or domestic policies; point eleven asserts that technology and science will make an "abundance" of food and goods available and therein lies "the greatest promise of comfort and security the world has ever seen." Steinbeck's eleven points effectively define what was to become the Truman Presidency, although Truman's policies, as David McCullough's *Truman* shows, had other sources:

Manefesto

1. We intend to win the war quickly and decisively.
2. We propose to create and to help direct a militantly peaceful world organization with the strength to prevent wars.
3. We believe that no people can long prosper in isolation, that all must rise together or sink separately.
4. We propose to cooperate with other nations through trade, association and understanding in order that all people may climb to the new peak of security and comfort which technical developments have made possible.
5. We will not permit methods of production or destruction to be used or controlled by men or nations for the exploitation or enslavement or [sic] peoples.
6. We believe that a free flow of goods and of ideas are [sic] the

foundations of world peace and world development.

7. We believe that a thoughtful and controlled economy can support the farmer on his land, the workman in his job and the merchant behind his counter and we know from brutal experience that uncontrolled economy can and will bring us to the edge of destruction.
8. We propose that our returning fighting men shall be secure in their futures—that they shall have jobs in private industry if possible, but we insist that they shall have jobs.
9. We propose to lower taxes when possible but not at the expense of the welfare, security or strength of the nation.
10. We intend to protect our racial, religious and political minorities from those who would deny them their right to live and develop in our democracy.
11. We believe that in the techniques of abundance lie the greatest promise of comfort and security the world has ever seen. We propose to encourage, develop and control those techniques to the end that the greatest good may indeed come to the greatest number and that peace and plenty may live not only in our nation but in the whole world (HRC).

Roosevelt and his speechwriters absorbed only parts of the poetry into their dreary prose and so lost the moment. Let me cite one example of how the revision muddled items 7 and 10 by hiding them in the middle of the FDR "Address":

Improvement through planning is the order of the day. Even in military affairs, things do not stand still. An army or a navy trained and equipped and fighting according to a 1932 model would not have been a safe reliance in 1944. And if we are to progress in our civilization, improvement is necessary in other fields in the physical things that are a part of our daily lives, and also in concepts of social justice at home and abroad (Rosenman 204).

Although many of the policies, especially the controlled economy and the plans for a U.N., were those of the New Deal, nowhere else are they stated so eloquently. Other goals, such as civil, political, and human rights at home and abroad, and a sharing of our wealth and technology internationally became the hallmarks of Truman's Presidency. FDR's "Address" pointedly omitted references to the civil rights (#10) Steinbeck advocated, other than blandly asserting the need for "social justice." Although Steinbeck's proposal to battle international economic and political totalitarianism anticipated Cold War diplomacy, the proposal today has become an honored one. Altogether, Steinbeck's vision for America is, a half century later, inspiring.

Steinbeck's spelling variation of the word "Manifesto" intended perhaps to offer the modern world a vision equal to one Marx expressed in his *Communist Manifesto*. Yet in style and tone it combines the language of Lincoln that FDR requested, certain policies of FDR, and the civil and human rights view of John Steinbeck. The "Manefesto" represents, I believe, the height of Steinbeck's political expression. More important than his Stevenson correspondence because it was written for a sitting president, the Manefesto's domestic ideas are possibly the base for policies Steinbeck worked into President Johnson's Great Society Program address (Hayashi). It was Steinbeck's last work for FDR.

IV

To most people the death of FDR in spring 1945 followed months later by that of his confidant Harry Hopkins, signaled the end of the New Deal. Steinbeck's praise for the achievements of the New Deal and a statement about its place in the nation's psyche occurred in a memorial service in Washington for Harry Hopkins on May 22, 1946.[12] Three speeches totaling two and a half typewritten pages were delivered at the ceremony. Dorothy Thompson's talk came to one page; Steinbeck's eulogy, delivered by Burgess Meredith, covered less than half a page; and Sam Rayburn's speech about public service consumed the final pages (HRC). It is Steinbeck's original three typwritten pages only, however, that I wish to discuss.

Steinbeck never mentioned Hopkins's name until the middle of the eulogy and then twice after that; he mentioned Roosevelt's name once. The omission of the names shifts the focus from the mundane to the thought that "the man was also an idea." It is the immortal concept of the New Deal that Steinbeck wished the audience to recognize, not the man-symbols for it. Paragraph two resembles in rhythm and tone the *Gettysburg Address* he had studied two years before: "Fourteen years ago the nation lay tortured with fear . . . its industry in ruins . . . [with] a growing cynicism toward government. . . . The nation slowly fought its way out of the wreckage . . . this nation was attacked . . . . leadership continued . . . ." It is evident that Steinbeck perceived his subject as a form of political-economic civil war that the New Deal, represented by Roosevelt and Hopkins, had won over their laissez-faire enemies. The battle over, the burial commences: "Then, within a year of one another, the great leader and his friend and advisor died. And no enemy has forgiven these two men. They cannot be allowed to rest because—only the smallest part of them is dead" (HRC). The ideas that prevailed, we understand, transcend the grave.

34

Steinbeck described the governmental principles that won: in Washington "welfare took precedence over profit . . . . it became rooted in the minds of the people. . . . People should come nefore [sic] profit. . . . The idea is a flame in the eyes of the people." Then Steinbeck denounced the recent weakening of New Deal policies: "Even the legislation designed to protect the nation from plunder was cut off at its source by a powerful, greedy and rich fifth column." In defense of Truman he added, "It is true that the new leadership has endorsed the great idea but it is being mawled [sic] and shouldered and attacked" (HRC).

Next, Steinbeck's purpose became clearer—his address, modeled upon Lincoln's, was a call for rededication:

> We should be here today not to celebrate the memory of Harry Hopkins but to try to determine within ourselves how much of him is dead and how much lives . . . . Have we become weak and cowardly because two brave free men are dead? . . . Must the nation come to know that without a fight compromise will be permitted with the public welfare . . . ? They are not questions Franklin Roosevelt or Harry Hopkins would have considered since to them there was only one answer.

Steinbeck then listed New Deal economic weapons that brought victory in this political Civil War: "dams . . . new forests . . . highways . . . public buildings . . . saved people by the process of building" (HRC).

Steinbeck argued that future Americans would expect a public-spirited government because the New Deal's political-economic emancipation had been planted within Americans' consciousness: "The administration which will ever again permit one third of its citizens to be ill housed, ill clothed and ill fed cannot survive." The memorial to Harry Hopkins and to his "great friend," Steinbeck concluded,

> is carved in the generations. It is chizeled [sic] in the hardest most enduring material we know—the Idea. It flows in the veins and shines in the eyes of the people and it will be there just as enduring in their children. HUMAN WELFARE IS THE FIRST AND FINAL TASK OF GOVERNMENT. IT HAS NO OTHER.
>
> The graves cannot be closed. The men are not dead. (HRC)

Steinbeck's final words as literary executor of the New Deal defined the new federalism for which this civil war had been fought. Unlike Lincoln's Gettysburg dedication, Steinbeck's graveside dedication did not get a hearing. Ceremonial managers failed to appreciate Steinbeck's unspoken comparison between the Roosevelt-Hopkins era and that of

Lincoln. The latter assigned the federal government to protect civil rights; the former assigned the federal government economic responsibility for its citizens. If Steinbeck were bitter about the mismanagement of his eulogy, he had the right to be, for the Steinbeck Washington Address was a fitting response to the burial of the New Deal warriors.

In the writing period discussed, Steinbeck's political transformation is startling. From writing about local poverty in 1936, Steinbeck in 1946 defined for a Washington audience the mythic presence of the New Deal. As an unpaid government employee, Steinbeck composed perhaps some of the best and least-known political prose in our century. Persuaded to spy, to write propaganda, to draft Roosevelt speeches, Steinbeck's political writing nevertheless demanded respect for Mexican citizens, liberty for Japanese Americans, civil rights at home, human rights abroad, and a government that served humanity.

The Steinbeck-Roosevelt connection, however slight, is a commentary upon the access artists had to Washington before the war. As a consequence of war, government grew so large that "experts" replaced amateur consultants such as Steinbeck. Afterwards, writers had presidential access for different purposes: John Hersey attended Truman cabinet meetings for historical documentation; Norman Mailer interviewed candidate Kennedy and wrote a glowing account; but for a writer to submit, as Steinbeck did, domestic and foreign programs is unlikely to occur again. Washington, as David Brinkley has shown, used to be a small town. The Roosevelts reached out to controversial people. And John Steinbeck had the intelligence to blend the practical and the ideal in concise prose. A willingness to listen to people such as Steinbeck may in part explain the ideals for which the Roosevelt Presidency stands.

Notes

[1]Steinbeck's correspondence is on file in the Franklin D. Roosevelt Library in Hyde Park. References to that correspondence are abbreviated *RL* in the text. I wish to thank Robert Parks for his generous help at the Library. Steinbeck's political writing is to be found at the Harry Ransom Humanities Research Center (abbreviated *HRC*) in Austin, Texas. An earlier version of this essay on speech writing appeared previously in Lewis.

[2] Steinbeck apprenticed in the film business with Pare Lorentz, creator for the New Deal of the classics *The Plough That Broke the Plains* and *The River* in the late thirties. He met Paul de Kruif, biologist and coauthor with Sinclair Lewis of *Arrowsmith*, about the same time he met Lorentz, and he retained lifelong friendships with both.

[3] Charlie Chaplin and Helen Douglas asked Steinbeck for the use of his name

in their relief organization. As a Congresswoman Douglas lost an election to Richard Nixon, who implied that she supported communism. Weedpatch, where the Joads go for aid and are introduced to ideas about economic democracy, is modeled after a federal camp.

[4] For material Steinbeck might have used for his novel *In Dubious Battle*, see U.S. Senate Committee Report on the Violations of Free Speech and Rights of Labor, 1939, in Part I of *Report* no. 1150 titled "Employees Association and Collective Bargaining" (11). Exhibit 8307, p.18183, containing the March 28, 1934, "Monthly Handbook for Functionaries," describes the process of recruiting for the Party; its diction is altered slightly in the novel. Handbook: "The unit membership committee . . . passes on him." Mac to Jim: "The committee passes on the report and the membership votes on you." Mac's recruitment of Jim and Mac's organization of the strike follow the directions from the Handbook.

[5] In Steinbeck's *The Log from the* Sea of Cortez he acknowledges that with Ed Ricketts's help, the two of them offered priceless information to Naval Intelligence about the coastal waters around Japanese occupied Pacific Islands (lix-lxi). Such an offer suggests that discussion about collecting marine information along Mexican shores for Naval Intelligence occurred.

[6] Anthony Cave Brown states that the FBI Director "had established a Special Intelligence Service for work in South America . . ." (159) that Donovan and others recognized as ineffective. Steinbeck's name is not mentioned by Brown or by an earlier Donovan biographer, Corey Ford.

[7] A scene dramatized in the play has some similarities to an actual clash between civilians and an army general in California in 1945. The play's climax features an army general threatening to use tanks against an Anglo community who refused to bury an Hispanic Congressional Medal of Honor winner in the town cemetery. The actual clash Bill Hosokawa described involved Anglos and a Japanese-American. On December 8, 1945, General Stilwell presented Mary Masuda a Distinguished Service Cross awarded posthumously to her brother Staff Sgt. Masuda at her California home, where despite threats, she had returned from an Internment Camp. General Stilwell intended the ceremony to be a strong rebuke to the "barfly commandos" who discriminated against Nisei heroes (414).

[8] See Coers for the influence of Steinbeck's novel on citizens of German occupied countries. Benson relates the story that Steinbeck stalled writing *Bombs Away* because of the guilt he felt in sending soldiers to their deaths. Summoned to Roosevelt's office, Steinbeck was convinced by the President's command performance that he had no choice but to write the book. Steinbeck to himself: "I am not going to do this. They will have to get somebody else." After FDR talked about Steinbeck's writing: "Now John, you are going to do what I want you to do—what I want you to do, John." And then Steinbeck: "Yes, Mr. President, I am . . ." (508).

[9] I discovered two political documents, the handwritten "Letter" and the typed "Manefesto," in the Steinbeck Collection at the HRC, and with help from Robert Parks at RL. I discovered a typed version of the "Letter" (minus a page)

and also located the "Manefesto," confirming that Steinbeck indeed worked on the campaign.

[10] Rosenman contains the final version of Roosevelt's July 10 "Letter" (197-98).

[11] Documents at Hyde Park show that Rosenman had written a long acceptance speech for FDR to deliver July 20; FDR rejected it and asked for an "Address." So the call went out through Hunter to Steinbeck for a short speech. An aide and FDR hastily stitched together the Rosenman essay and Steinbeck's "Manefesto" on a train from Chicago to San Diego for the broadcast.

[12] Harry Hopkins had died in the winter, but the memorial service occurred in Washington on May 22, 1946, at the Sylvan Theatre. Of the three eulogies Steinbeck's alone deserves recognition. Someone decided wrongfully that his first two and a half pages were too historical, too descriptive, and used only the last two paragraphs.

Works Cited

Benson, Jackson J. *The True Adventures of John Steinbeck, Writer*. New York: Viking, 1984.

Brown, Anthony Cave. *The Last Hero: Wild Bill Donovan*. New York: Times, 1982.

Coers, Donald V. *John Steinbeck as Propagandist:* The Moon Is Down *Goes to War*. Tuscaloosa: U of Alabama P, 1991.

DeMott, Robert. Introduction. *Working Days*. By John Steinbeck. New York: Viking, 1989. xxi-lvii.

Hayashi, Tetsumaro. *John Steinbeck and the Vietnam War (Part I)*. Steinbeck Monograph Series, No. 12. Muncie: Steinbeck Society, 1986.

Hosokawa, Bill. *Nisei: the Quiet Americans*. New York: Morrow, 1969.

Koppes, Clayton R., and Gregory D. Black. *Hollywood Goes to War*. New York: Free Press, 1987.

Lewis, Cliff. "Steinbeck: The Artist as FDR Speechwriter." *Rediscovering Steinbeck—Revisionist Views of His Art, Politics and Intellect*. Ed. Cliff Lewis and Carroll Britch. Lewiston: Mellen, 1989. 194-217.

Lorentz, Pare. *FDR's Moviemaker Memoirs and Scripts*. Las Vegas: U of Nevada P, 1992.

McCullough, David. *Truman*. New York: Simon, 1992.

Robins, Natalie. *Alien Ink: The FBI's War on Freedom of Expression*. New York: Morrow, 1992.

Rosenman, Samuel I. *The Public Papers and Addresses of Franklin D. Roosevelt, XIII*. New York: Russell, 1969.

Steinbeck, John. *The Log From the* Sea of Cortez. 1951. New York: Compass, 1964.

_____. *Working Days: The Journal of* The Grapes of Wrath, *1938-1941*. Ed. Robert DeMott. New York: Viking, 1989.

U. S. Senate Committee Report on the Violations of Free Speech and Rights of Labor. *Report* 1150, 1939.

Yergin, Daniel. *The Prize: the Epic Quest for Oil, Money, and Power.* New York: Simon, 1990.

Steinbeck and Ethnicity

Susan Shillinglaw

In the spring of 1992, *Nude Zapata* was performed by El Teatro de la Esperanza in San Francisco. The play featured an impassioned Latina conceptual artist, Connie, whose work deconstructs what she sees as the racist 1952 film *Viva Zapata!* Her goal in *Nude Zapata* is to "redeem Zapata from his celluloid prison," where he was bound by the white male establishment—read Steinbeck and Kazan. In the play, writes a lukewarm reviewer, "Steinbeck and his cronies slurp margaritas and conclude they couldn't possibly make 'Viva Zapata' in Mexico, where they'd be surrounded by Mexicans" (Winn).

In February, 1992 I sat on a panel called "Expanding the Canon" at a California Studies conference in Sacramento. My role was to argue that Steinbeck should be reconsidered, not excised, from a multicultural perspective. After all, I began, *In Dubious Battle* (1936) earned Steinbeck a place on a much-touted "Multicultural Reading list for America" compiled a few months earlier by the *San Jose Mercury News* (notably absent was Faulkner). In response to this presentation, an ethnic studies professor from Southern California reported that he had stopped teaching *Tortilla Flat*—a book he liked—because he grew tired of defending Steinbeck. Chicano students, he said, objected to images of lazy, lustful, and drunken paisanos.

That same spring, my students were discussing *To a God Unknown*, and one Chicana, heretofore silent, read the following passage describing a festival hosted by the hero, Joseph Wayne:

> At the pits the Indians moved up and thanklessly took the bread and meat that was offered. They moved closer to the dancers, then, and gnawed the meat and tore at the hard bread with their teeth. As the rhythm grew heavy and insistent, the Indians shuffled their feet in time and their faces remained blank. (130)

They sound like animals, she noted softly.

During the 1992 Steinbeck Festival, *The Californian* ran articles on "Reading Steinbeck," where Louis Owens notes that the author "doesn't offer a great deal to multiculturalism. His treatment of women and what today would be called people of color leaves a lot to be desired. He was a white, middle class male from Salinas. He was a product of his times" (Neary).

These examples summarize the criticism leveled against Steinbeck's treatment of ethnics, particularly Mexicans. But a reconsideration is surely in order for an author who wrote so frequently and searingly about race and ethnicity. One third of his work either is set in Mexico or treats Mexican subjects. And it is of no small significance that his first published story—"Fingers of Cloud," which ran in *The Stanford Spectator* in 1924—treats an ethnic confrontation and his last published book—*America and Americans*—begins with a chapter on race in America. In that late text he writes: "From the first we have treated our minorities abominably, the way the old boys do the new kids in school. All that was required to release this mechanism of oppression and sadism was that the newcomers be meek, poor, weak in numbers, and unprotected . . . " (15). That statement holds one key to Steinbeck's concern with this country's attitude toward ethnics, for since childhood he had abhorred bullies and developed a quick sympathy for outcasts: a handicapped neighbor, foreign laborers. He visited often and spoke Spanish at the Wagners, a Salinas family that had lived in Mexico for three years. Throughout high school and college he worked with Mexicans at the Spreckles sugar plant and on the company's vast farms, hearing stories, sharing jokes. When he finally had a substantial advance from his publisher, his first trip with Carol Steinbeck in 1935 was a three-month stay in Mexico, a country he had long wished to visit and one to which he repeatedly returned.

In short, he wrote about Mexican-Americans, in particular, because they, like his weary dreamers and gritty laborers, lived outside the dominant culture. He wrote about them because the energy and joy of their culture cut against the rigid middle-class morality that he long scorned, and because their lives and values critiqued the prevailing cultural mythos. As California writer and critic Gerald Haslam has noted, Steinbeck must be recognized for *seeing* the diversity of the state's population, for writing about the paisanos of Monterey, for example, at a time when the majority of Californians did not acknowledge the importance or even the existence of mixed-blood Mexicans. Not only did Steinbeck create a voice for these paisanos, but he also invoked prevailing patterns of the American mythos in giving them form.

Another statement made in the introductory essay in *America and Americans* suggests a second reason for Steinbeck's abiding interest in ethnicity. He tells a story about a native American he met when working at Lake Tahoe in the late 1920s:

> Many white people, after association with the tribesmen, have been struck with the dual life—the reality and super-reality—that the Indians seem to be able to penetrate at will. The stories of travelers in the early days are filled with these incidents of another life

separated from this one by a penetrable veil; and such is the power of the Indians' belief in this other life that the traveler usually comes out believing in it too and only fearing that *he* won't be believed. (18)

Compare this vision with one of Steinbeck's own, outlined in a 1930 letter to his Stanford classmate Carl Wilhelmson:

Modern sanity and religion are a curious delusion. Yesterday I went out in a fishing boat—out in the ocean. By looking over the side into the blue water, I could quite easily see the shell of the turtle who supports the world. I am getting more prone to madness. What a ridiculous letter this is; full of vaguenesses and unrealities. I for one and you to some extent have a great many of the basic impulses of an African witch doctor. (*Life* 31)

The playful tone masks the letter's real significance. Steinbeck was no mere realist, either in art or life. Metaphysics intrigued him. Although many of his works have a realistic texture, a journalistic precision, they also contain layers of meaning beneath the surface, a point he often noted in correspondence when he referred to the various "levels" of his books. (*Cannery Row*, for instance, was "written on several levels of understanding and people can take out of it what they can bring to it.")[1] One way that he suggests alternative meaning is through marginal characters, ethnics with radically different perspectives: the Indian Tularecito in *The Pastures of Heaven* (1932), whose face holds "ancient wisdom"; Gitano in "The Great Mountains" (1933), behind whose eyes was "some unknown thing"; Pepe in "Flight" (1938), who acknowledges the dark watchers of Big Sur; the "old Chinaman," who "flap-flapped" mysteriously to the beach at dusk in *Cannery Row*; and the Chinese Lee, who, as one of Steinbeck's self- reliant and wise "self" characters, speaks for the author and plays complex roles in *East of Eden* (1952). These ethnics fascinated Steinbeck in part because they represented a vision that he longed to grasp, that he often suggested in his fiction through their ritualistic significance. Steinbeck was in large part attracted to "others" because of their exoticism and mysticism.[2] A key question, of course, is whether or not he diminishes them by his treatment or if, as symbol or prophet or seer, these ethnics help blend ritual and realism, and thus help reconstruct a vision of wholeness.

Far from exhaustive, this essay will examine representative and sometimes problematic texts about the ethnic presence in America. It will focus on two strains plucked from *America and Americans*: first, Steinbeck's treatment of ethnicity as cultural saga; second, his fascination with the primitive as intriguing and often unfathomable other.

That first published story, "Fingers of Cloud," sets up a significant paradigm for much of Steinbeck's work. As the story opens, Gertie, the restless heroine, flees her home to nearby mountains because she feels a visceral craving for mountaintops, clouds, and beauty. A rainstorm, however, sends her down into a migrant camp, where bleak reality banishes her visionary aspirations. Subsequently the white Gertie marries the "black" Filipino worker, Pedro. He is a violent, sexually charged man, who demands that both Gertie and the reader confront the grim underside of the American experience, the insistent violence that shatters visionary quests. Like so many of Steinbeck's central characters, Gertie is an idealist, and her quest, like Joseph Wayne's or the Joads's or Adam Trask's, is also America's—the hope for a new beginning. Her disillusionment and dark knowledge is also theirs.

For embedded both in the American experience and in Steinbeck's retelling of the nation's Edenic impulse are other stories, ones of racial conflict, sexual excesses, tainted deeds. "Fingers of Cloud" articulates boldly—and with no little artistic uncertainty as to exactly what the 22-year-old author wanted to say—that America's story includes, but often suppresses, ethnic confrontations. For Steinbeck, the saga of continental conquest in broad sweep is a tale of Edenic expectation and consequent disillusionment; and that inevitable fall means, in part, that character and (more insistently) reader glimpse what so often taints the dream: racial and ethnic suppression and violence. The brief first chapter of *The Pastures of Heaven*, for example, ironically deflates the notion of paradisiacal America announced by the title: the archetypal American here is a white corporal chasing renegade Indians, a man who, upon locating them, beats the lot and then ultimately dies of the pox after somewhat more intimate contact with an Indian woman. What Steinbeck acknowledges is that racial and sexual violence is as much a part of the American saga as is the Edenic mythos that the visionaries in the book blithely seek.

That parable of America's dark destiny represents a defining moment in much of Steinbeck's fiction. Repeatedly he undercuts sagas of idealism, dynastic control, or social harmony with less insistent voices and stories of racial and ethnic turmoil. Examples are numerous. In his first epic treatment of Westward epansion, *To a God Unknown*, the hero Joseph Wayne's Mexican friend Juanito discovers brother Benjy's sexual infidelity and kills him, thus enduring as punishment a self-imposed exile. The loss of Juanito, Joseph's most trusted confidant, signals the beginning of his spiral downward. Alone, Joseph falters. Alone, he ignores Juanito's warning to avoid the mysterious rock. The rollicking tale of contractual social harmony, *Tortilla Flat*, is punctured by one tale of sexual infidelity and death—the corporal's—and one of desperation and suicide—Grandfather Ravanno's. And at the conclusion Danny spins into a maelstrom of unbridled destruction and sexual conquest that dismantles the fragile fraternal order. In the short story "Johnny Bear," what must be suppressed in the Buffalo Bar are not Johnny's fragmented words telling of Amy's pregnancy and suicide, but that one phrase that reveals her liaison with a Chinese man. To silence Johnny Bear, Alex smashes his face. A black man is lynched in "The Vigilante," and the violence of that moment is compared, at the conclusion, to a sexual liaison. Curley's wife in *Of Mice and Men* (1937), her own dream of Hollywood stardom snuffed by her marriage, threatens the black man Crook's thin security by giving voice to the lynching threat. By far the darkest vision in the multilayered *Cannery Row* is early glimpsed in the Chinaman's eyes, "the desolate cold aloneness of the landscape . . . [where] there wasn't anybody at all in the world and he was left" (24). In *East of Eden* Adam Trask's vision of fecund California acres is shattered as fully by his wife Cathy's betrayal as it is qualified by the Chinese Lee's interpolated tale of his parents' arrival in California, their own story of migration and hope cut short by Lee's mother's rape and subsequent death.

In short, throughout Steinbeck's work, fragmentary voices of ethnic Americans suggest, like an insistent discordant note, America's violent and oppressive past. Sexuality and violence are implosive in these texts. The stories and episodes convey, I think, not Steinbeck's racism—far from that—but rather his sensitivity to the contradictions at the heart of the American character and experience. Idealism, superficial structures of belief, confidence in American pragmatism, Edenic quests—all are altered or destroyed when touched by subversive violence, repressed knowledge, sexual energy.

More can be said, however, about Steinbeck's sensitivity to the ethnic presence in the West. Tales of California's settlement repeatedly show how intertwined are dominant and marginal voices. In each of his western epics—*To a God Unknown*, *The Grapes of Wrath*, and *East of Eden*—the patriarch is dethroned, his ties to the land severed, and family bonds strained. With the loss of certainty in cultural and familial coherence, voices other than those of the dominant culture emerge and carry the burden of meaning in each text. In the first novel it is the Indians' wisdom and acceptance. In *The Grapes of Wrath* it is Ma Joad's iron will. And in *East of Eden* it is the Chinese Lee's intuitive grasp of *timshel*, the doctrine that he so fluidly accepts and Adam so trenchantly resists. In terms that Werner Sollors uses in *Beyond Ethnicity*, the tension between lines of descent, or inherited privilege and culture, and "a forward-looking culture of consent" (4) is an essential national drama and one that

Steinbeck draws upon in his most ambitious accounts of California settlement.

In his first novel set in California, *To a God Unknown*, for example, Joseph Wayne is the archetypal patriarch, tracing lines of descent. He's also a magnificently wrongheaded visionary, and as such a kind of American fictional icon. He would rule the land, his three brothers, and his wife absolutely; even the self-possession of his sister-in-law falters before Joseph's physical presence. This ungodly god-like man—to apply Ahab's tag to the hero modeled after him—countermands the cycles of nature, first believing that a drought will not return, a foolhardy notion, and then defying the drought when it comes, a wickedly defiant stance. But as hereditary ties and inherited willfulness fail him, other voices are tentatively acknowledged and fragile bonds are forged.

Steinbeck complicates the story of Joseph's dynastic ambitions through rough contrasts between white and Indian characters. Each of Joseph's three brothers is, in his way, as monomaniacal as he: Benjy lusts for women, Thomas craves animal contact, Burton is a religious fanatic. Each brother fixes on a teleological purpose, and if Joseph's vision is the most grandiose, his is nonetheless as confining as their "gods"—women, animals, religious fundamentalism. But Joseph is also engaged with three Indians whose words and actions have symbolic bearing on his life. Each Indian in the book represents knowledge that the hero would suppress. Joseph is linked to Indian alter-egos. Romas gives him practical advice, most pointedly, not to build his dynastic seat under an oak tree; Romas also tells him about drought years. His son, Willie, embodies a vision Joseph ignores: Willie's nightmares of defeat and death become, at last, Joseph's own. Finally, Juanito, his friend and worker, tells him of the mysterious rocks that are both his sanctuary and his tomb. "My mother brought me here, señor," Juanito tells Joseph. "My mother was Indian . . . the Indian in me made me come, señor" (45). The symbolic place intrigues Joseph, and his need to know it—in a word to conquer the ineffable—proves futile. The intangible resists his domination, and he perishes because he does not heed the Indian voice signifying an alternate truth. The Indians in *To a God Unknown* form a kind of chorus that imparts significant and telling information that Joseph does not and, in his myopia, cannot absorb.

The structure of the text also qualifies Joseph's story. Not unlike *The Pastures of Heaven*, this novel is framed by passages that undercut Joseph's dynastic impulses. This is Joseph's first sight of the town of Our Lady, as he enters into the valley he will call his own:

The huts of Indians clustered about the mud walls of the church, and although the church was often vacant now and its saints were worn and part of its tile roof lay in a shattered heap on the ground, and although the bells were broken, the Mexican Indians still lived near about and held their festivals, danced La Jota on the packed earth and slept in the sun. (4-5)

This sentence suggests a long history of Spanish conquest, and yet what survives here—as in the book's conclusion—are the Indians and their pagan ways. In the final chapter, the Indians celebrate the end of the drought with orgies of pleasure, as their throbbing music blends with the sounds of rain and their naked bodies roll in the mud. Indians and nature seem as one. If their resilience as well as their acceptance of cycles of drought and rain offer one foil to Joseph's monomaniacal quest, the Catholic Church—surprisingly—offers another. Father Angelo, who can be as doctrinaire as Joseph is single-minded, nonetheless compromises his faith. It is surely significant that this text ends not with Joseph's solitary death in a parched land but with Father Angelo's gesture of acceptance in the midst of a drenched community. As he listens to the rain in the final chapter, he belatedly remembers that he had, indeed, prayed for rain. No fanatic, he. And in the closing paragraphs, as the sound of the people's pagan rites blend with the life-giving rain, he checks his doctrinaire need to stop their blasphemy. Penance can be administered later, he tells himself. Because the priest accommodates himself to the Indians' paganism, he assures his survival and that of his church. In contrast, although Joseph consults the priest and notes Juanito's warning about the drought, he cannot meaningfully contemplate change or heed warnings. His teleological purpose defines and dooms him.

The wisdom of the Indians' holistic vision thus undercuts Joseph's monomaniacal quest, and their world view ultimately defines meaning in this text, acceptance of what is. Mexicans are as thematically important in *To a God Unknown* as is the exotic Lee in *East of Eden* and as are marginalized women's voices that emerge at the conclusion of important books: *In Dubious Battle*, *Of Mice and Men*, *The Grapes of Wrath*, and *The Winter of Our Discontent* (1961). In each, the female character—like the ethnic—is largely discounted throughout the book, seen only through the eyes of males, silenced. But Curley's wife, the whining Rose of Sharon, the meek Lisa, and the winsome Ellen Hawley find voices or assume a symbolic role at the end of each novel and articulate values that the author endorses. In a "passion of communication," the lonely wife of furious Curley pours out her life's "story" of missed chances to the only audience she's ever had, Lennie, an innocent who cannot hear her (but the reader can). As Rose of Sharon evolves from self-centered girl to empathetic woman, she stops whining and smiles, becoming the text's symbolic center. Lisa's vision of domestic pleasure is what organizer Jim so pointedly and fatally resists. And only Ellen fully recognizes Ethan's desperation: "Take me with you," she pleads. "You're not coming back" (278), words that will save Ethan in the final chapter because he "had to return the talisman to its new owner" (281). Male characters may resist or dismiss the fragmented female voice, but the reader should not. Steinbeck has been accused of creating one-dimensional female characters as often as he has been said to create ethnic stereotypes. Both charges, I would argue, must be qualified by the thematic and cultural significance given alternative perspectives, both female and ethnic. That vision is, in many texts, only haltingly and belatedly acknowledged by central male characters who cannot abandon inherited notions of patriarchal control of family, fate and nature. But the very fragmentation of women and ethnics is precisely the point. Steinbeck's patriarchs cannot heed the words appealing to contractual bonds and readers often discount their import.

II

"How can we conceive of difference without fetishizing it by a separatist and ultimately hedonistic, self-canceling politics of identity?" (E. San Juan Jr. 4)

If, in part, Steinbeck's ethnic characters play key roles in his settlement dramas, they also enact significant parts in a personal and writerly drama. He cast himself early on as an outsider, and for much of his life he identified with marginal groups. His most sympathetic characters don't belong. "For American intellectuals," writes Fred Matthews,

[F]olk romanticism tended to lead not to hatred of "outsiders" and a lust to purge them from the nation, but rather to a sense of guilt about their own society's exploitation of the strangers, and to the desire to protect them from the aggressive majority. In the American context, alienated romanticism created not xenophobia but xenophilia. (qtd. in Sollors 29)

With other modernists, Steinbeck found in the untutored a vital source of artistic expression. Throughout his career Mexican subjects in particular intrigued him because he identified with their otherness—a zest for life, scorn for a dominant culture, and an inherent exoticism and often mysticism. When he was writing *Tortilla Flat*, he wrote to critic and book reviewer Joseph Henry Jackson: "The work has been the means of making me feel that I am living richly, diversely, and, in a few cases and for a few moments, even heroically" (*Life* 119). In 1948, depressed and lonely, he wrote to friends that he needed to go to Mexico, for, he said, there's an "illogic there that I need" (Letter to Lovejoys). Steinbeck discovered a transforming power in ethnicity. He kept returning to Mexico and Mexican subjects as a way to live and he translated that personal need into a cultural need.

In contemporary discussions of ethnicity, however, Steinbeck's impulse is problematic. To attach even compelling qualities to the primitive encodes ethnic stereotypes: the Mexican is perpetually the "other," essentially exotic and strange. This argument is, from one point of view, unassailable, since Steinbeck, a writer of the dominant culture, drew portraits of mystical, untutored, and spontaneous primitives. Louis Owens, for one, recently has argued that Steinbeck's Indians are "purely symbols, walking shadows illustrating the kind of intuitive, nonrational state he and Ricketts celebrate in the *Log*." Passages like this are, in this view, representative:

> [Indians] seemed to live on remembered things, to be so related to the seashore and the rocky hills and the loneliness that they are these things. To ask about the country is like asking about themselves. "How many toes have you?" "What, toes? Let's see—of course, ten. I have known them all my life, I never thought to count them. Of course it will rain tonight, I don't know why. Something in me tells me I will rain tonight. Of course, I am the whole thing, now that I think about it. I ought to know when I will rain." (*Log* 78)

Here, as in *To a God Unknown*, the Indians are one with the land, bound to a vision that has perished in the modern world. But when assessing Steinbeck's acknowledged and frank impulse toward primitivism, I believe that several points must be kept in mind—points that do not, finally, counter the argument that this sympathetic white male, more than any other, avoids encoding identities or that he, more than others, writes fully and deeply in any one book about the Mexican culture. A few observations may, however, qualify the resistance to Steinbeck's ethnic portraits.

First, a holistic vision of character and environment is as essential to Steinbeck's ecological vision in *Sea of Cortez* as it is in *To a God Unknown* or in *Cannery Row*. His biological holism, a conviction that humans must be seen in the context of their environment, often finds an objective correlative in the primitive. For Steinbeck, marginal groups, not the dominant culture, lived non-teleologically and thus accepted "what is." Second, an assessment of Steinbeck's primitivism must acknowledge his range. In his works simplicity and spontaneity cut across racial and ethnic lines: Mack and the boys are as untrammeled as the lusty paisanos in *Tortilla Flat*. Casy in *The Grapes of Wrath* and Doc in *Cannery Row*, both of whom live non-teleologically and holistically, can be as mystical as the Indians in *Sea of Cortez*. Values associated with the Mexican are applied to other characters who live non-teleologically and thus seem "simple" (Dr. Winter), "childlike" (Lennie), or "sentimental" (Doc Burton). Naivete is not, in short, ethnically determined. Finally, Steinbeck is, in fact, as sensitive to the Indians' economic and social plight as he is fascinated by their spiritualism, holism, and zest. It must not be forgotten that as he was working out ideas for *Sea of Cortez* in 1940, he was simultaneously writing a controversial script for *The Forgotten Village*, a documentary set in an isolated Mexican village which contrasts traditional mores— particularly an unquestioned faith in a healer or curandera—with the village's need for modern medicine to combat cholera: the script poses knotty questions about modernity and progress.[3] Nor must the many foils to Steinbeck's intuitive Indians be discounted when measuring his ethnic sensitivity: wily Zapata, artful Pilon, and hardheaded Juan Chicoy are, in the main, vividly realized and incisive portraits. And critics of Steinbeck's primitivism must also acknowledge his firm insights about social reality:

> It is said so often and in such ignorance that Mexicans are contented, happy people. "They don't want anything." This, of course, is not a description of the happiness of Mexicans, but of the unhappiness of the person who says it. (*Log* 99-100)

> To us, a little weary of the complication and senselessness of a familiar picture, the Indian seems a rested, simple man. If we should permit ourselves to remain in ignorance of his complications, then we might long for his condition, thinking it superior to ours. The Indian on the other hand, subject to constant hunger and cold, mourning a grandfather and set of uncles in Purgatory, pained by the aching teeth and sore eyes of malnutrition, may well envy us our luxury. (*Log* 248)

In short, Steinbeck would have readers as fully sympathetic to ethnics as to Okies, working stiffs, bums, and villagers locked in resistance with Nazi oppressors. "In every bit of honest writing in the world," he wrote in a 1938 journal entry,

> there is a base theme. Try to understand men, if you understand each other you will be kind to each other. Knowing a man well never leads to hate and nearly always leads to love. There are shorter means,

many of them. There is writing promoting social change, writing punishing injustice, writing in celebration of heroism, but always that base theme. Try to understand each other. ("*Long Valley* Ledger")

That could well serve as an epigraph to his writing on ethnicity.

All of the author's types and anti-types are sketched fully in *Tortilla Flat*, an engaging account of the adrift in Monterey. *Tortilla Flat*, notes Charles R. Metzger in a sympathetic discussion of the author's diverse portraits of Mexican-Americans, "does not purport to do more than present one kind of Mexican-American, the *paisano* errant, in one place, Monterey, and at one time, just after World War I" (149). To respond further to charges of essentialism in Steinbeck, I wish to examine this most problematic text where, I will posit, Steinbeck deliberately avoids characterizations that depend on an ethnic component.

Chicano critic Philip Ortega, among others, finds Steinbeck's paisanos objectionably flat. "The romanticized stereotype and caricature of the Chicano," he notes,

> is nowhere more evident in *Tortilla Flat* than when Steinbeck wrote that the Chicanos are "clean of commercialism, free of the compli-cated systems of American business, and, having nothing that can be stolen, exploited, or mortgaged, that system has not attacked them very vigorously. (41)

The passage Ortega cites is, I would agree, a crucial one in a text so centrally concerned with identity—but crucial not because it caricatures the paisano. It appears on the second page of the novel, where Steinbeck pointedly defines a paisano by what he is not; he is not a part of the dominant culture and so avoids the most objectionable qualities of that culture. When, in the following paragraph, Steinbeck poses the obvious next question, "What is a paisano?" the response avoids reference to character, to any essentialist premises. The paisano, a name Steinbeck may have used because it lacks a racist context and because its meaning is indeterminate,

> ... is a mixture of Spanish, Indian, Mexican, and assorted Caucasian bloods. His ancestors have lived in California for a hundred or two years. He speaks English with a paisano accent and Spanish with a paisano accent.... His color, like that of a well-browned meerschaum pipe, he ascribes to sunburn. He is a paisano, and he lives in that uphill district .... (2)

Although Ortega objects to ethnic distortion in this passage as well, in essence Steinbeck describes externals, not innate qualities of a Mexican. Throughout these tales, in fact, it is the characters, not the author, who paint with broad strokes. The paisanos show little reluctance to make essentialist distinctions. "Race antipathy" toward Italians "overcame Danny's good sense" (5). Torelli had, Pilon knew, "The Italian's exaggerated and wholly quixotic ideal of marital relations" (42). Portagees "always want to marry, and they love money" (28). To heartily insult a stingy friend is to call him a Jew. Women are best, as Danny and his friends know well, when "lively." Often women are grasping. "That Rosa will want new dresses. All women do. I know them," asserts Pilon (28). He weeps with Danny "over the perfidy of women" (19). It is precisely this rigidity—however comic in context—that Steinbeck avoids in his depictions. Only the paisanos' personalities, not their ethnic identities, are tagged: "Their campaign [against Sweets] had called into play and taxed to the limit the pitiless logic of Pilon, the artistic ingenuousness of Pablo, and the gentleness and humanity of Jesus Maria Corcoran. Big Joe had contributed nothing" (105). Logic, ingenuousness, humanity and Big Joe's uncouthness are the essentialist characteristics of Steinbeck's paisanos.

Steinbeck avoids reductionist attitudes toward ethnics in part because, as is clear from the two paragraphs quoted above, he focuses the reader's attention not on fixed norms but on *questions* of identity. What Danny's house *is* becomes the central concern in a book that takes as its model *Morte Darthur*, tales of knightly prowess where heroes earn for the round table its identity. *Tortilla Flat*, like Malory's epic, is about process. Indeed, although Danny, Pilon, Pablo, and Pirate have distinct and rather complex personalities, they enter the book with indeterminate identities, each in a kind of liminal state. As first introduced, Danny and Pilon are no longer soldiers, nor was Danny a "mule skinner" before the war, as he had confidently labeled himself. Heretofore Danny has not been a homeowner, and when he acknowledges ownership "one cry of pain escaped him before he left for all time his old and simple existence" (13). Pablo is on parole, the months ahead a test of his resolve. Pirate is initially a shadowy presence, for "no one knew him very well, and no one interfered with him" (57), but his character deepens as his pile of quarters mounts. As individuals, each paisano is adrift. In the early chapters, they are occasionally lonely and dissatisfied because obligations—being a tenant or a homeowner—cramp their freedom. Only when all move in with Danny, only as a "unit of which the parts were men" (1) does their identity jell. They become Danny's men. The first sentence of the novel, in fact, articulates Steinbeck's central concern in the text, group identity. "This is the story of Danny and of Danny's friends and of Danny's house. It is a story of how these three became one thing..." (1). The book is not about drunken sots, but as many critics have noted, it is about Steinbeck's theoretical concerns with group man: how a unit functions as a whole and how the identity of that whole is distinct from that of individuals composing the group.

In fact, Steinbeck's paisanos are defined most precisely by the codes they develop as comrades, codes of survival. Together the paisanos exhibit endurance, pluck, and skill; together they are generous to Pirate; together they listen solemnly to the corporal's story; together they are loyal and respect the rhythms of nature and the privacy of friends. The qualities that he identifies with the paisano clan are far from objectionable or, in fact, ethnically determined. Demands of communal living and the paisanos' economic isolation establish identity with far more conviction than "paisano" norms—whatever they may be. As a mutually dependent unit, the paisanos share traits with Steinbeck's Okies and the *Cannery Row* bums who are similarly marginalized by their economic status. The paisanos' virtues are theirs—endurance, pluck, communal spirit. Their plights are similar—the need of a home and space for shared experience. And central to all three books is ecological holism in a community, human interdependence. In each novel Steinbeck works with the part of reality he knew and translates that known truth into the contours of art.

There is also a mimetic defense to be made for the text: these were real figures around Monterey in the 1930s. Steinbeck heard many of the stories first from Sue Gregory, a popular Monterey High School Spanish teacher, president of the Spanish club, and mentor, friend, and counselor to Monterey's paisanos. A couple he heard when he worked with Mexicans in the Spreckles sugar plant during summers in high school and college. And, as demonstrated by countless newspaper accounts in the *Monterey Peninsula Herald*, their exploits were famous around town. This is Edward Martin's story of himself, told to a reporter, Dudley Towe, when he was 97:

"Absolutely, Pilon and me, we was just like brothers. . . . We were always together. When you see one, you wait a few seconds, and then you see the other one. . . . We had a whole lot of fun." Doing what? "We pretty well drinking wine. In Iris Canyon, across the highway from the cemetery. We lived in a box in Iris Canyon behind the willows. A big box. Like a coffin. Made out of tin. We used to get in there to drink wine. Especially when raining. . . . Just drinking, that's all we did. . . . We used to sell bottles, beer bottles, sody bottles. Enough to get more wine. We would get in underneath the box and sleep there. Next morning we would figure what we are going to do to get another bottle of wine. We had a little dog. 'Borracha.' You know what that means in Spanish? 'Drunkard.' Everybody know him here in town. He used to pick him up bottle of wine. We put the bottle of wine on the floor, and he would pick him up and bring it over to us." (14)

In short, Steinbeck's interest in these paisanos is in part psychological—the study of group man—and in part realistic—the "history" of a subculture—and finally in part aesthetic—wrestling with the contours of artistic expression. As a writer who declared with some frequency throughout the 1930s and 1940s that the novel was dead, he restlessly sought alternate forms for expression and self-consciously, in most of his books, wrote about the process of creation. *Tortilla Flat* is as much about the tradition of the oral story telling as it is about a culture that recounts the stories. Cast in a consciously artistic language that captures the rhythms of Spanish (a device that to some ears sounds artificial, to others charming), Steinbeck records the tales he heard as an "outsider." In the first paragraph of the novel, the word "story" appears five times. And the book's "plot" is concerned always with stories: making them (hatching schemes), listening to them, or allowing the reader to watch the paisanos tell them. The *caporal*'s sad tale of lost love, for example, is a "drama that made the experiments of Cornelia Ruiz seem uninteresting and vain. Here was a situation which demanded the action of the friends" (118). A good story engages the paisanos in "action," just as the "story" told by the artist engages the reader in understanding. And engagement in the narrative is, in fact, the book's method, as Pilon reveals when he listens to Jesus Maria's account of the soldiers and Arabella: "The story was gradually taking shape. Pilon liked it this way. It ruined a story to have it all come out quickly. The good story lay in half-told things which must be filled in out of the hearer's own experience" (45). That may well be Steinbeck's artistic credo; certainly it is Pilon's. As the book's most vivid character, Pilon is the consummate artist, creating romantic visions and artful constructs with equal facility. Pilon is the Artful Dodger, the confidence man. He is as fully a study of the possibilities of art as are Steinbeck's other artist figures of the same period: Johnny Bear, whose stories record life with absolute fidelity, stripped of empathy; Elisa Allen or Mary Teller, whose gardens reflect their artistic compulsions; the boy Jody, whose youthful romanticism must be tempered with life's hardest lesson, the reality of death. Steinbeck repeatedly wrote self-consciously about art: the roles artists play, the forms they seek, the plots they create. So, Arthur Pettit's objection to the texture of *Tortilla Flat* may, in fact, be Steinbeck's very point: that the art of story telling is a mixed bag. "Alternately tender and tasteless, subtle and simple, comical and crude, the novel is handicapped by a baffling mixture of moods and motifs which collide rather than meet. The mock-heroic elements conflict with the theme of paradise lost, and we are left uncertain as to which is more important" (195). The uncertainty of art, of many stories told by many personalities, mirrors the instability of the paisanos' culture. And life on the edge—charmingly told, raucous and doomed—is far preferable, in Steinbeck's vision, to entrenched ease—teleologically focused, predictable, and no doubt the subject for an intricately plotted novel that he couldn't write.

III

The Latina artist in *Nude Zapata* is "so mad about a 40-year-old film she's going on strike as a gesture of her rage." For Connie, Steinbeck's *Viva Zapata!* "represents white male domination" (Winn). Indeed, a root cause of Steinbeck's perceived insensitivity to ethnics may be traced to films of Steinbeck's works. There is seepage from popular translations of the novels back to the texts themselves. As a result, an uncritical regard of both may be synonymous. I close with two examples.

On January 10, 1944, bitterly disappointed with *Lifeboat*, the Hitchcock film he had scripted, Steinbeck wrote a letter of complaint to Twentieth Century-Fox Film Corporation:

> While it is certainly true that I wrote a script for Lifeboat [*sic*], it is not true that in that script as in the film there were any slurs against organized labor nor was there a stock comedy Negro. On the contrary there was an intelligent and thoughtful seaman who knew realistically what he was about. And instead of the usual colored travesty of the half comic and half pathetic Negro there was a Negro of dignity, purpose and personality. (*Life* 266)

Steinbeck wanted his name withdrawn from the film.

When Jack Kirkland began writing a script of *Tortilla Flat* for Broadway, Steinbeck was enthusiastic. In September, 1937, he told a reporter for the *Los Gatos Mail-News*, "We are going to have something new in an all-Mexican company. Then we won't have to bother about accent, and all that. The actors won't be able to talk in any other way. We expect to pick up our cast in and around LA." But his concern for authenticity evaporated when he read Kirkland's final script. "[W]e read the thing out loud and it sounded so bad that I got to feeling low. . . ," he wrote his agent.

There are so many little undertones that he has got wrong. I don't want to maintain my book but I would like to maintain the people as I know them. Let me give you an example. Jack makes them want wine and need wine and suffer for wine whereas they want the thing wine does. They are not drunkards at all. They like the love and fights that come with wine, rather than the wine itself. (*Life* 150)

"'I think it will flop,' Steinbeck predicted calmly" to reporter Louis Walther a few days before the New York opening (Walther 11).

In his best work Steinbeck achieved what Hitchcock and Kirkland did not—a balance between fidelity to fact and fidelity to art, between empathy for marginalized Americans and the inescapability of his perspective as an outsider. But artistic balance is a fragile construction. From *Tortilla Flat* on, Steinbeck was engaged in a lifelong debate with critics over the fidelity of his ethnic portraits, over his use of dialect, folklore, and historical sources. Contemporary reviews of *Sea of Cortez* and *The Forgotten Village* throw the debate into focus. Writing for the Springfield, Massachusetts, *Republican*, Eileen Carlson notes that in *Sea of Cortez* one sees "the value of meeting each new experience unfettered by prejudices from previous experiences, to the value of different ideals of civilization—ours and that of the Mexican Indian. . . . Best of all it is splendidly tolerant." Reviewing *The Forgotten Village*, the author's good friend, fellow traveler to Mexico in 1935, novelist and book reviewer, Joseph Henry Jackson, found troubling Steinbeck's implied superiority to the peasants:

Some day a critic will take time to analyze the curious, fatherly-godlike love that Steinbeck manifests for his characters, to examine the chastiseth-whom-he-loveth attitude implicit in so much of Steinbeck's work, the insistent diminishment of his human characters (no not his turtles) by which the author-creator unconsciously magnifies himself in relation to them. (17)

Jackson, with Connie the Latina conceptual artist, faults the outsider's vision. Outsider Steinbeck most definitely was. And "splendidly tolerant" as well. The truth about his art probably lies between the two, but tipping the balance, to my mind, is his intention, his "base theme. . . . Try to understand each other" (Steinbeck, "*Long Valley* Ledger").

Notes

[1]Letter to Joseph Henry Jackson.

[2]See Lewis and Britch, who argue that Steinbeck "characterizes his Indian figures as members of a particular race, who act as they do because of some subconscious predisposition, and who, in like manner, are so identified as Indians by members of Western culture" (128). While I agree that Steinbeck's Indians are associated with a powerful but vanishing culture, I also think that, first, he associates the mystery of the "other" with several ethnic groups, not only Indians; second, that although the figure of the Indian is doomed (most perish) his voice, in its very insistence, survives in the consciousness of the central character and the reader. The fragmentation of the ethnic voice is, I believe, the author's critique of the dominant culture. Therefore, I disagree with Lewis and Britch's conclusion that "Steinbeck has managed to reveal Indian suffering without indicting the white majority as in any willful way the cause of it" (152). Steinbeck's critique of white imperialism is clear enough in the opening pages of *The Pastures of Heaven.*

[3]Steinbeck's closest friend, Edward Ricketts, visited Steinbeck during filming in Mexico, and he strongly opposed Steinbeck's tacit support of progress in the film: medicine is seen as the cure for the cholera epidemic. Education is endorsed as corrective to a bad water supply. Ricketts, in contrast, thought that any outside influence undermined traditional beliefs, and that Steinbeck should simply study and accept what *is*. Ricketts wrote an anti-script to Steinbeck's own.

Works Cited

Carlson, Eileen. "Steinbeck in a Boat: 'Sea of Cortez' Is Marine Biology, Philosophy and Sea Narrative Mixed in Splendid Prose." Springfield *Republican* 21 Dec. 1941: 12.

Haslam, Gerald. "Travels With John," Keynote Address. Steinbeck Festival XII. Salinas, 1 Aug. 1991.

Hearle, Kevin. "Regions of Discourse: Steinbeck, Cather, Jewett, and the Pastoral Tradition of American Regionalism." Diss. UC Santa Cruz, 1991: 136-41.

Jackson, Joseph Henry. "The Bookman's Daily Notebook: Steinbeck Goes All Simple and Just Overdoes It." *San Francisco Chronicle* 1 June 1941: 17.

Lewis, Cliff, and Carroll Britch. "Shadow of the Indian in the Fiction of John Steinbeck." *Rediscovering Steinbeck—Revisionist Views of His Art, Politics and Intellect.* Ed. Cliff Lewis and Carroll Britch. Lewiston: Mellen, 1989. 125-54.

Metzger, Charles R. "Steinbeck's Mexican-Americans." *Steinbeck: The Man and His Work.* Ed. Richard Astro and Tetsumaro Hayashi. Corvallis: Oregon State UP, 1971: 141-55.

Neary, Walter. "Students Drawn to Human Themes of Hope, Equality," *The Californian* 10 Aug. 1992: 1.

Ortega, Philip D. "Fables of Identity: Stereotype and Caricature of Chicanos in Steinbeck's *Tortilla Flat.*" *The Journal of Ethnic Studies* 1 (1973): 39-43.

Owens, Louis. "Grandpa Killed Indians, Pa Killed Snakes: Steinbeck and the American Indian." *Melus* 15 (1988): 85-92.

Peck, Llewellyn B. "Noted Author Returns from European Trip." *Los Gatos Mail News and Saratoga Star* 16 Sept. 1937:1, 4.

Pettit, Arthur G. *Images of the Mexican-American in Fiction and Film.* College Station: Texas A&M UP, 1980.

San Juan, E. Jr. *Racial Formations/Critical Transformations.* Atlantic Highlands: Humanities, 1992.

Sollors, Werner. *Beyond Ethnicity: Consent and Descent in American Culture.* New York: Oxford UP, 1986.

Steinbeck, John. *America and Americans.* New York: Viking, 1966.

_____. *Cannery Row.* New York: Viking, 1945.

_____. "Fingers of Cloud: A Satire on College Protervity." *The Stanford Spectator* 2 (February 1924): [149], 161-64.

_____. Letter to Joseph Henry Jackson. Aug. 1944. The Bancroft Library. University of California, Berkeley.

_____. Letter to Ritch and Tal Lovejoy. 27 May 1948. John Steinbeck Library. Salinas, CA.

_____. *The Log from the* Sea of Cortez. New York: Penguin, 1951.

_____. "*Long Valley* Ledger." Steinbeck Research Center. San Jose State University, San Jose, CA.

_____. *Steinbeck: A Life in Letters.* Ed. Elaine Steinbeck and Robert Wallsten. New York: Viking, 1975.

_____. *To a God Unknown.* 1933. New York: Penguin, 1976.

_____. *Tortilla Flat.* 1935. New York: Penguin, 1986.

_____. *The Winter of Our Discontent.* New York: Viking, 1961.

Towe, Dudley. "Pilon and Me." *Game and Gossip* 20 Jan. 1957: 14-15.

Walther, Louis. "Oklahomans Steinbeck's Theme: Author Says Migrants Altering California." *San Jose Mercury Herald* 8 Jan. 1938: 11, 13.

Winn, Steven. "Curtain Calls." *San Francisco Chronicle* 14 Feb. 1992: D 11.

Of Mice and Music: Scoring Steinbeck Movies

Robert E. Morsberger

Studies of the interaction of the arts, the way in which works of literature, painting, sculpture, and music may inspire each other, have been particularly rewarding for Steinbeck scholars. John Steinbeck's fiction has led to paintings by Thomas Hart Benton and drawings by Orozco, to two operas, a Rodgers and Hammerstein musical, and some memorable film scores, two of which, by Aaron Copland, have been turned into concert music. This paper attempts to show how Steinbeck impacted on Aaron Copland, Woody Guthrie, Alex North, and Leonard Rosenman, how they composed for him, and how in a rippling effect, they influenced subsequent composers.

All too often, concert composers consider film music *kitsch* and think that those who write it are selling out, but it need no more be *kitsch* than scores written to order for opera or ballets. Paul Hindemith, Darius Milhaud, Arthur Honegger, Ernst Toch, Werner Janssen, Heitor Villa-Lobos, Sergei Prokofiev, Dmitri Shostakovich, Sir William Walton, Ralph Vaughan Williams, George Antheil, Aaron Copland, Erich Wolfgang Korngold, and Miklos Rozsa have all composed outstanding music for the movies. Bernard Herrmann distinguished between Hollywood's "film music composers" and composers in Hollywood who occasionally wrote for films (Palmer 236).

Most scores for Steinbeck movies are serviceable but unmemorable— Alfred Newman's for *The Moon Is Down*, Franz Waxman's for *Tortilla Flat*, Hugo Friedhofer's for *Lifeboat*, Victor Young's for *A Medal for Benny*, Antonio Diaz Conde's for *The Pearl*, Leigh Harline's for *The Wayward Bus*. (Harline also composed the songs for *Snow White* and *Pinocchio*.) One Steinbeck film almost had no score at all. A Hollywood anecdote tells how David Raksin, a composer for Twentieth Century-Fox, was informed that Alfred Hitchcock decided not to use any musical score for *Lifeboat*, the film he was making in 1944 from Steinbeck's screen treatment of a film about the Merchant Marine. When Raksin asked why Hitchcock made such a decision, he was told, "Well, Hitchcock feels that since the entire action of the film takes place in a lifeboat on the open ocean, where would the music come from?" Raksin responded, "Ask Mr. Hitchcock to explain where the cameras come from, and I'll tell him where the music comes from" (Thomas, *Music* 15). Eventually, Hitchcock had second thoughts, and Hugo Friedhofer provided a score for the film.

The first Steinbeck movie to be made was *Of Mice and Men*, released late in 1939. Director Lewis Milestone, a cousin of violinist Nathan

Milstein, wanted a distinguished score and persuaded Aaron Copland to write his first music for a Hollywood film. The only film music Copland had previously composed was the score for a documentary called *The City*, which was screened at the New York World's Fair. Copland had read *Of Mice and Men* but insisted on rereading it before accepting the assignment, to make sure it would suit his creative powers. Convinced that it did, he cabled his acceptance and within twenty-four hours was on his way west. "Here," he said, "was an American Theme, by a great American writer, demanding appropriate music" (Copland and Perlis, *Copland: 1900 Through 1942* 297). Running the unscored film back and forth, Copland said, "... I was genuinely moved by *Of Mice and Men* and by the inspired performances, and I found that the scenes induced the music if I turned to them while composing" (Copland and Perlis, *Copland: 1900 Through 1942* 298).

Ordinarily, composers were given only two weeks to produce a film score, but Copland insisted upon six for *Of Mice and Men* and, unlike many film composers who use arrangers (for example, Hugo Friedhofer orchestrated most of Erich Wolfgang Korngold's scores) he did his own orchestration (Dobrin 146). Instead of calling attention to itself Copland's restrained music underscores and intensifies the action in such episodes as the threshing machine and the fight between Curley and Lennie, climaxed, when Lennie crushes Curley's hand, by a grinding dissonant chord that David Diamond called "extraordinary." Diamond added, "This is what film music's all about" (Copland and Perlis, *Copland: 1900 Through 1942* 242).

"After all," Copland wrote, "film music makes sense only if it helps the film; no matter how good, distinguished or successful, the music must be secondary in importance to the story being told on the screen" (Dobrin 152). For *Of Mice and Men*, Copland wanted to avoid the full-blown symphonic orchestration that Erich Wolfgang Korngold and Miklos Rozsa provided, and tried to write instead minimally scored themes reminiscent of folksongs such as the farm workers might have sung or whistled (Thomas, *Music* 175). Thus he used "more natural-sounding instrumentation—solo flute, flutes together, and a guitar for a campfire scene" (Copland and Perlis, *Copland: 1900 Through 1942* 298). "The temper of the music varied with every scene," Copland recalled, "but always I tried to keep away from the overlush harmonies that are so common on the screen and usually defeat their own purpose by overemphasis" (Smith 202). The score for *Of Mice and Men* was nominated for an Academy Award but lost to Richard Hageman's for *Stagecoach*.

In 1942, Copland composed *Music for Movies*, a suite for small orchestra that was derived but not transcribed literally from his scores for *Of Mice and Men, Our Town,* and the documentary *The City.* Two of its five movements, "Barley Wagons" and "Threshing Machines," come from *Of Mice and Men.*

It might be instructive to compare the success of Copland's score for *Of Mice and Men* with other musical treatments of Steinbeck's novel/play. In 1958, Ira J. Bilowit and Wilson Lehr adapted *Of Mice and Men* into a musical play, with lyrics by Bilowit and music by Alfred Brooks. It ran briefly off Broadway but fared poorly. Louis Calta judged that while "Mr. Steinbeck's drama still remains a work of substance and power," the score and lyrics "never quite became an integral part of the drama"; they lack "the necessary passion, grandeur and breadth," and "at no time . . . heighten the intensity of Mr. Steinbeck's prize-winning play . . . " (*The New York Times*). An operatic version by Carlisle Floyd fared no better in 1970; when it was revived in San Francisco in 1974, music critic Martin Bernheimer judged that the simple eloquence of Steinbeck's language sounds "stilted, silly and artificial when blown up for grand operatic treatment."

The main weakness of an otherwise well-done 1981 production of *Of Mice and Men* is the score by George Romanis, which is too often loud, obtrusive, and unsubtle, providing literal transcriptions of folk songs such as "Skip to My Lou," "Turkey in the Straw," the inevitable "Red River Valley," and others. A plaintive rendition of "Shenandoah" accompanies Candy's expression of loneliness and his desire to join George and Lennie. After the murder, we hear "Red River Valley" again, rendered in a funereal manner; and at the end, as George walks alone down a road, carrying his bindle, we hear "Going Home" from the Largo movement of Dvořák's *New World Symphony.* This is not the last shot, however, for during the end credits, we see George and Lennie, timelessly together, walking through a waist-high field of waving wheat. The score is too obvious. Instead of writing original music in a folk idiom, like Aaron Copland, Romanis simply gives us traditional folk songs, nudging us with cornball cues that distract from the dialogue and asking us to accept their use as profound.

For a large screen remake of *Of Mice and Men,* director Gary Sinise avoided the 1980 TV version's flaw of having an obtrusive musical background. He observed, "There are a lot of moments in the story that just cry out for scoring; more *sad* music here, more *crisis* music there. Somebody else would have scored this thing to the hilt" (Winn). Mark Isham's unobtrusive music is effective and Coplandesque but unmemorable.

The second Steinbeck film, released only a few weeks after *Of Mice and Men,* was *The Grapes of Wrath,* which Bernard Herrmann called a film without music (Bazelon 232). Actually, it has a score, consisting largely of "Red River Valley" played variously on the harmonica and concertina, but Alfred Newman (who scored nine additional pictures in 1940) also contributed a jaunty, cheerful theme for the migrants traveling down Route 66.

For less cheerful traveling, Woody Guthrie contributed "I'm Goin' Down That Road Feeling Bad." Guthrie recalled being "packed off" to the studio while *The Grapes of Wrath* was shooting,

> and they set me down on a carpet in a directors harum there, and said, "Now what we want you to do is to sing a song, just don't even think, and without thinking, just haul off and sing the very first song that hits your mind—one that if a crowd of 100 pure blood Okies was to hear it, 90 of 'em would know it."

> This was the first song that popped to my mind, so without thinking, I sung it. They used the song in the picture, "Grapes of Wrath," which had more thinkin' in it than 99% of the celluloid that we're tangled up in the moving pictures today. (Lomax, Guthrie, and Seeger 215)

Telling of his presumed travels and how he supposedly wrote a collection of "dust bowl" songs about "Migratious Oakies," Guthrie commented,

> There was a feller that knew us Oakies, and he knew what it was like in Oklahoma, and he knew about the dust and the debts that covered us up, and he knew why we blowed out to California, because early in the deal, he throwed a pack on his back and traipsed around amongst us, and lived with us, and talked to us, and et with us, and slept with us, and he felt in his heart and knew in his head that us Oakies was lookin' for "A Living WITH Labor"—that man was John Steinbeck. (Guthrie 41)

In a "Foreword" to the collection *Hard Hitting Songs for Hard-Hit People*, compiled by Alan Lomax, with notes on the songs by Woody Guthrie and music transcribed and edited by Pete Seeger, Steinbeck returned the compliment, writing,

> Woody is just Woody. Thousands of people do not know he has any other name. He is just a voice and a guitar. He sings the songs of a people and I suspect that he is, in a way, that people. Harsh voiced and nasal, his guitar hanging like a tire iron on a rusty rim, there is nothing sweet about Woody, and there is nothing sweet about the songs he sings. But there is something more important for those who

will listen. There is the will of a people to endure and fight against oppression. I think we call this the American Spirit. (9)

The compilation of songs was completed by 1940, but for twenty-seven years it was banned as being too radical and was not published until 1967, a year before Steinbeck died, so that his "Foreword" is one of his last pieces published during his lifetime. Folk singer, musicologist, and literary scholar H. R. Stoneback points out that it is unclear just when Steinbeck wrote his "Foreword," but it did appear before the book, making its first appearance in 1945 as liner notes to a recording, *The Woody Guthrie Album* (Stoneback 164).

In it, Steinbeck wrote of the songs of working people in general, that they had "the rhythms of work, and over them, the words of anger and survival" (Lomax, Guthrie, and Seeger 9). During the era of the dust bowl, when Steinbeck sat in the migrant camps, he "heard the singing and I knew that this was a great race, for, while there was loneliness and trouble in their singing, there was also fierceness and the will to fight," and he noted that the opening line of Guthrie's " I'm Goin' Down That Road Feeling Bad" is followed by the determined "Cause I aint gonna be treated that-a-way" (Lomax, Guthrie, and Seeger 8-9). Consequently, Steinbeck believed that the sharpest statement of working people can be found in their songs, for while the written word can be banned, singing cannot be prevented (Lomax, Guthrie, and Seeger 8).

Working people sing of their hopes and of their troubles, but the rhythms have the beat of work—the long and short bawls of the sea shantys with tempos of capstan or sheets, the lifting rhythms, the swinging rhythms and the slow, rolling songs of the southwest built on the hoof beats of a walking horse. (Lomax, Guthrie, and Seeger 8)

As H. R. Stoneback has pointed out in detail, *The Grapes of Wrath* not only also has these rhythms but makes extensive use of folk songs, and after seeing the movie version of it, Woody Guthrie was so moved that he wrote the song "Tom Joad," which condenses the novel into seventeen stanzas that Woody was proud of (Lomax, Guthrie, and Seeger 236-38). Later, in his commentary on it for *Hard Hitting Songs for Hard-Hit People*, Woody noted that the book "ain't got no songs in it that was wrote by deputy sheriffs. It ain't got none wrote by company guards, nor cops, nor snitches, nor guys that set fire to the little shacks of the poor folks along the river bottoms" (Lomax, Guthrie, and Seeger 236). Rather, it contains the songs of those Ma Joad calls "the people that live." Yet another song in the collection, the lesser-known "Vigilante Man," has a quatrain about the murder of Preacher Casy.

Stoneback makes a convincing case that the popular image of Woody Guthrie was largely a fiction, shaped by Guthrie by modeling himself as a Steinbeck character: ". . . the mythic Woody who seems to stand at the center of the American 'folk experience,' is an unacknowledged Steinbeck creation, is in some very real sense a by-product of *The Grapes of Wrath*" (Stoneback 160). In fact, a Texas farmer once told Stoneback that "that Steinbeck writer-feller stole that story from ol' Woody" (Stoneback 166). Though from Oklahoma, Guthrie had never been a farmer nor a dust bowl migrant, but he continually referred to himself as a migrant Okie, writing of the dust bowl migrants as "we" and saying he had tramped all the same roads and been in every town in Steinbeck's novel. He first came to public prominence on March 3, 1940, electrifying Alan Lomax, at a "*Grapes of Wrath* Evening" organized by actor Will Geer to benefit the "John Steinbeck Committee for Agricultural Workers," for which he was promoted as "'Woody'—that's the name, straight out of Steinbeck's 'The Grapes of Wrath' . . ." (Klein 142-43). Stoneback demonstrates that Guthrie wrote almost all of his dust bowl, "Okie," and political songs after *The Grapes of Wrath* and that his public persona, even his prose style, derive from that novel (Stoneback 162). He even named one of his sons Joady. In turn, Stoneback argues, Guthrie's disciples, such as Bob Dylan and other creators and performers of music in a folk idiom are ultimately "heirs to *The Grapes of Wrath*, children of the road, of the tribe of Joad . . ." (Stoneback 169).

Following *Of Mice and Men*, Copland wrote a distinguished score for *Our Town* (1940), also nominated for an Oscar, and a less memorable one for *The North Star*, a wartime melodrama in 1943. Copland probably agreed to work on *The North Star* because it was directed by Lewis Milestone, who had directed *Of Mice and Men*. After the film flopped, Copland did not score another Hollywood film for six years, though in 1945 he scored a documentary for the United States Office of War Information, *The Cunningham Story*.

In 1949 Lewis Milestone once again asked Copland to score one of his films, this time Steinbeck's *The Red Pony*. Though the picture was only fair, Copland's music is his finest for the movies. Virgil Thomson called it "the most elegant . . . yet composed and executed" of Hollywood scores (Berger 87). Bernard Herrmann, himself a distinguished composer of film music, said, "I don't . . . feel that Copland's music for *The Red Pony* is any the less than the music of his symphonies" (Bazelon 235).

Copland refused to write scores on dozens of different subjects, in the manner of many leading Hollywood composers, such as Alfred Newman, who scored over 200 films. Instead, Copland said that he preferred to write only for the sort of material that he found compatible, that composers should be "cast" for a film in the same way that actors and directors are. Clearly, he had an affinity for the work of John Steinbeck. Both of them wrote fanfares for the common man, and though Copland was a New Yorker, both he and Steinbeck did most of their best work when dealing with folk and pastoral themes. In Copland's words, "I admired Steinbeck, and after reading the book [*The Red Pony*], I knew this was a film for me" (Copland and Perlis, *Copland Since 1943* 88).

Roger Manvell and John Huntley write that *The Red Pony* "portrays very closely and sympathetically the sentiment of simple family life on a California ranch" (Manvell and Huntley 113). Copland has called it

> a series of vignettes concerning a ten-year-old boy called Jody [whose name is changed to Tom in the film, probably because *The Yearling*, filmed in 1946, already featured a boy named Jody with an animal], and his life in a Californian ranch setting. There is a minimum of action of a dramatic or startling kind. The story gets its warmth and sensitive quality from the character studies of the boy, Jody, Jody's grandfather, the cowhand Billy Buck, and Jody's parents, the Tiflins. The kind of emotions that Steinbeck evokes in his story are basically musical ones, since they deal so much with the unexpected feelings of daily living. (Copland, *The Red* 2)

Copland composed his film score between February and April 1948; the movie was not shown in theatres until 1949. In the meantime, Efrem Kurtz, newly appointed director of the Houston Symphony, asked Copland to write a work for his first concert, and Copland complied by adapting his score for *The Red Pony* into a suite that has become one of his best-loved works and has been judged "the most popular concert presentation of any American film score . . . " (Thomas, *Film Score* 16). It was first performed on October 30, 1948, prior to the release of the film. The *Houston Post*'s music critic, Herbert Roussel, called the suite "clear, joyous, ingenious, and irresistibly spirited music . . . by turns tender, and bombastic in a light whimsical manner, well studded with humorous dissonance, it made everybody feel good" (Dobrin 154). Copland recalled: "In shaping the suite I recast much of the material so that, although all the music may be heard in the film, it has been reorganised as to continuity for concert purposes" (Thomas, *Music* 177). The suite runs for approximately 21 minutes; the published score is 117 pages long.

Years later, when *The Red Pony Suite* was about to be recorded, Copland wrote to Steinbeck requesting a commentary to accompany the music. At first, Steinbeck replied, on July 17, 1964:

> The music for the Red Pony is very beautiful. I wish the picture could have been as good. Except for the music, I am not unpleased

that this film, to the best of my knowledge, is still held as hostage in a bank vault. [It is now rentable on videotape.] I am glad that the suite is not a captive—your suggestion that I write some sort of commentary for the music also pleases me very much and I would like very much to do it. I would also be happy to narrate it on tape, at least for you to decide whether I can do it well enough. However, you are holding the baton on this.

But when Copland explained that the version with commentary would be for children, Steinbeck had second thoughts. On September 22, he wrote:

This is an old theme with me. The reason I have never written books for children is not because of the children but because of the so-called adults who choose what books may be printed for children. Children have nearly always understood my work—and yours. It is only critics and sophisticates who do not . . . . Children have always understood the little book *The Red Pony*. They have been saddened by it, as I was when it happened to me, but they have not been destroyed by it . . . . When you wrote this suite, being an artist and therefore automatically truthful, you let the sombre come into your music to balance the gaiety and to give it proportion and significance. And children surely understand that as they understand form, being instructed by heartbeat and morning and night. In your original music, I remember that you had a passage which covered an owl's sweep down on a rabbit and you had a fantastic passage during the fight of Jody with the buzzard, which was of course man's defiance of death. Children think a great deal about death, much more than adults do, for to the idcentric child his own death is the death of the world . . . . What I am trying to say, I guess, is that if you want a children's version, you must get someone else to write it for you. Surely you may use my notes as you wish, but sometime I would hope that you will let a group of children hear a "children's version" and soon after hear mine, and judge for yourself, their reaction . . . . Sorry to be so vehement, but this is one of my strong feelings. (Copland and Perlis, *Copland Since 1943* 90-91)

Steinbeck apparently reversed himself again, as he did write an unpublished "Narration," about three hundred words long, which turned up in the Annie Laurie Williams Collection at the Rare Book and Manuscript Library, Butler Library, Columbia University. In it, he tells how the boy grows into a man by experiencing the events suggested by the Suite (French 298). Copland thought this lost the child's perspective;

he called *The Red Pony* a "children's suite because much of the music is intended to reflect a child's world" (Dobrin 154). Julia Smith writes that as an American counterpart to Robert Schumann's *Scenes from Childhood* and Claude Debussy's *Children's Corner*, Copland's suite "has elevated to a high degree the yearnings and aspirations of American children" and has become an American classic (211).

Sometimes a film score is more potent in a concert performance than in a screening of the film. Irwin Bazelon writes that on tape, the score by Leonard Rosenman (who composed the music for Steinbeck's *East of Eden*) for *Fantastic Voyage* "has power, imagination, and a marvelous, contemporary sound texture. With the film, the composer's sound language is so watered down that it bears little resemblance to the recorded version. Other composers and films can be cited for similar transformations" (39). This is certainly true of Copland's music for *The Ped Pony*. The concert suite from *The Red Pony* resembles Copland's three great ballet scores. But in the film, the music is often accompanied by dialogue, the cries of owls, roosters, buzzards, and other birds, doors banging, the wheezing of a sick pony barely able to breathe, the various sounds of the ranch. These are not ordinarily part of a composer's orchestration; Respighi did include the record of a nightingale in *The Pines of Rome*, but ordinarily one does not score music for orchestra and owl. The film music is often interrupted by dialogue and action. If it sometimes helps punctuate dialogue and action, it is in turn punctuated by them, not necessarily to the advantage of the music. Sometimes the film music goes on at length with little or no interruption, as in the main-title theme, the imaginary scenes of knights on horseback and a circle of chickens turning into white circus horses galloping around a ringmaster, the scene when Tom lets the pony run free. Sometimes, the film music goes on for only a few bars. In the concert suite, there are no such distractions or interruptions; everything is pulled together, sometimes rearranged, so that we hear the music for its own sake. If it is still program music that suggests ranch life, so are the scores for *Rodeo* and *Billy the Kid*.

The Red Pony Film Suite has six movements, best described in the composer's own words:

1. Morning on the Ranch
   Sounds of daybreak. The daily chores begin. A folk-like melody suggests the atmosphere of simple country living.

2. The Gift
   Jody's father surprises him with the gift of a red pony. Jody shows

off his new acquisition to his school chums, who cause quite a commotion about it. 'Jody was glad when they had gone.'

3. Dream March and Circus Music
Jody has a way of going off into day-dreams. Two of them are pictured here. In the first, Jody imagines himself with Billy Buck at the head of an army of knights in silvery armour; in the second, he is whip-cracking ringmaster at the circus.

4. Walk to the Bunkhouse
Billy Buck 'was a fine hand with horses,' and Jody's admiration knew no bounds. This is a scene of the two pals on their walk to the bunkhouse.

5. Grandfather's Story
Jody's grandfather retells the story of how he led a wagon train 'clear across the plains to the coast.' But he can't hide his bitterness from the boy. In his opinion 'Westering has died out of the people. Westering isn't a hunger any more.'

6. Happy Ending
Some of the title music is incorporated into the final movement. There is a return to the folk-like melody of the beginning, this time played with boldness and conviction. (Copland, *The Red* 2)

Though all of the concert suite music is in the film, not all of the film music is in the concert suite. The film includes foreboding music to accompany a torrential rain storm that causes the pony to catch a fatal lung infection, music to accompany the tortured breathing of a dying horse, windpipe-slitting music, and a graphic six-minute sequence when the boy fights with buzzards who are devouring the body of the dead pony, Copland's "dissonant music with complicated rhythms" effectively reinforcing the violence (Copland and Perlis, *Copland Since 1943* 88). Tony Thomas judges that "Copland's score for *The Red Pony* is that ultimate in writing for films—music that perfectly does its job yet lives and breathes and thrives even when divorced from the picture" (Thomas, *Music* 177).

The score deserved an Academy Award, but in 1949 the Oscar went to Copland for his next picture, *The Heiress*, based upon Henry James' novel *Washington Square*. Curiously, Copland was not asked to score another picture until twelve years later, when he wrote the music for a United Artists bomb called *Something Wild*. Copland salvaged the music from this disaster by turning it into *Music for a Great City*.

The next Steinbeck movie after *The Red Pony* is *Viva Zapata!* (1952), from an original screenplay by Steinbeck about the Mexican revolutionary leader. It boasts a distinguished score by Alex North. In the 1930s Aaron Copland had helped North get assignments writing music for ballet companies, including Martha Graham's. Next, North joined the Federal Theatre project, wrote incidental music for their plays, and then scored about eighty short documentary films for various government departments. In 1948, he had written incidental music to accompany Elia Kazan's stage production of *Death of a Salesman*, and Kazan liked it so well that when he undertook to direct the film version of *A Streetcar Named Desire*, he used his influence to have North assigned to score the movie. North's innovative music was a landmark, being the first jazz-oriented score written for a feature film, and it earned him an Academy Award nomination (Thomas 181; Palmer 295). Kazan's next picture was *Viva Zapata!*, and once again, he selected North to compose the score, only his second for a feature film. The subject was a compatible one for North, who in 1939 had spent two years in Mexico with Anna Zokolow and her ballet company. North recalls,

> . . . I was able to sop up their music. I met and studied with Silvestre Revueltas, to my mind the top Mexican composer, more interesting than Carlos Chavez because his roots were more indigenous to Mexico . . . . I would go to his classes and he might take his four or five students and go to a bistro and hold the class there. What I learnt from him was invaluable when it came to score *Viva Zapata!* because it's important when you write music based on the elements of another country's music to be able to feel it. I was also very fortunate with this film because Kazan hired me from the start of the production—he and I often wandered around our Mexican locations together, going from village to village. I would jot down little tunes I heard peasants humming or singing. (Thomas, *Music* 182)

At one time Steinbeck considered having "corridos," a running commentary of traditional Mexican songs, "to be written by a wandering poet named John Steinbeck to music by Alex North" and performed by one of Zapata's men, or else "to be accompanied by either guitar music solo or music from our conception of a typical five-piece Mexican Country band" (Steinbeck, "Note"). But this device would interrupt the narrative and was accordingly dropped. Apparently, Steinbeck actually wrote corridos, for Zanuck wrote to Kazan,

> In carefully looking through the script I cannot find one spot where we are compelled to use the corridos. It seems to me that almost

everything we want to know is told clearly in the action and the dialogue. Personally, this makes me very happy, although I doubt whether you will share my elation . . . . (Zanuck 176)

Instead, for background music, Kazan got together a group of Mexican musicians with antiquated instruments and had them play classic Mexican songs and songs of the revolution, which he taped and which became a source for Alex North's score. Instead of creating the customary symphonic background music of the 1950s, like Miklos Rozsa's, North had most of his music function as a natural part of the action—as mariachi bands, military parades, serenades, religious chants, songs and celebrations—all indigenous Mexican modes, to accentuate the ballad-like quality of the film. For the opening main title, "full of Mexican rhythms and dissonant brass chords," North used xylophones and other percussion instruments. During a scene between Zapata and his wife on their wedding night, an oboe d'amore plays a Mexican folk-type melody over marimbas and strumming guitars and mandolins. One death scene is scored with a flute solo in the Aeolian mode (Evans 148).

An often praised highlight of the film and its score is a wordless sequence in which Zapata is captured and hauled off by mounted rurales with a rope around his neck. Seeing his brother taken prisoner, Euphemio Zapata begins pounding a message with two stones, and the message is relayed telegraphically by others pounding stones, until a vast number of peasants congregate from all directions upon the procession of rurales and force them to release their prisoner. North begins his music for this episode by picking up the rhythm of the stones with a bolero-type theme with timbals and bongos, to which he adds a marimba and then flutes, guitars, and plucked strings (Evans 148; Bazelon 95). Tony Thomas notes, "The music grows in scale and intensity as the numbers of men increase, and it reflects their purpose and their pride" (*Music* 183). As Irwin Bazelon observes, "The music acts as a rallying cry, an instrument of rebellious defiance." North called this one of his favorite scenes from all his film scores (Bazelon 222).

North recalls that the climactic musical highlight of the film was a result of Kazan's decision. "In the scene near the end where Brando is to be assassinated, the sound effects men prepared their track, the sounds of horses and soldiers, but when Kazan heard the music for the scene he told them to hold back, that he didn't want to hear horses or footsteps, that he wanted the music to carry the scene up to the point where the massive fusillade of shots cuts Brando to pieces. This was unusual because the emphasis is almost always placed on realism in terms of sound in films. Music and sound effects are too often in conflict, with the music losing" (Thomas, *Music* 183).

For the second year in a row, North was nominated for an Academy Award for his score for *Viva Zapata!* but lost to Dimitri Tiomkin's for *High Noon*. Later North scores include *The Rose Tattoo, Spartacus, Cleopatra*, and *Who's Afraid of Virginia Woolf?*

Claiming that "directors who have engaged a composer with limited or no film experience to score their pictures deserve a great deal of credit," Irwin Bazelon cites Elia Kazan for using Alex North for *Streetcar*, which was followed immediately by *Zapata!*, and Leonard Rosenman for *East of Eden* (Bazelon 45). North has expressed admiration for Rosenman's work, "specifically, parts of *East of Eden*" (Bazelon 222). David Raksin in turn admires both Rosenman and North, "who has almost no peer in the profession . . . " (Bazelon 245).

Leonard Rosenman got his first assignment to score a movie because he had to supplement his meager income from composing by teaching piano. One of his students was James Dean. When Dean was picked for the lead in *East of Eden*, he recommended his teacher and friend to score the film. Christopher Palmer argues that Dean is unlikely to have understood much about Rosenman's "advanced" music, but "he must have intuitively recognized that it was the right kind of music for *him*" (Palmer 302). Rosenman, who had studied under Arnold Schoenberg and was devoted to the twelve-tone serial school of composition, considered himself a composer of serious concert music and balked at Kazan's invitation, suggesting that he try Aaron Copland instead (Evans 171). But Kazan persisted and succeeded in luring Rosenman to Hollywood. However, Kazan objected to Rosenman's use of atonality, and so they agreed on a compromise whereby Rosenman wrote tonal music for scenes involving children and dissonant themes for the adults. Rosenman notes: "Kazan and I worked together to fit the music to the film" (Thomas, *Music* 203). Following a few opening bars of atonal music, the soundtrack launches into the main title music, which is also the motif for Abra, a lushly romantic theme, tonal, triadic, and entirely accessible, which became quite popular. But, as Tony Thomas points out, " . . . the tone of the scoring is sparse and close in style to Alban Berg" (*Music* 203). After the opening credits, the score turns instantly atonal to accompany the evil Kate as she walks through Monterey, followed by her unacknowledged son Cal, to deposit in the bank the latest earnings from her whorehouse. There are two motifs for James Dean's Cal, one "a dissonant pile-up of fourths and thirds, declamatory in nature and suggestive of Cal's latent hysterical violence," the other scored for only two bassoons and two clarinets to convey his loneliness and sense of alienation (Palmer 303). The latter is the most pervasive theme in the film, and to heighten its impact, Rosenman inverts it and provides endless variations on it.

For the scene where Cal enters his mother's brothel, Rosenman wrote music echoing Berg's opera *Wozzeck*, played on an out-of-tune upright barroom piano. ". . . [T]he low-down music that assaults our ears tells us exactly what kind of a house he has entered. In this instance, it is not merely tone color that acts as an emotional signpost, but also the rhythmic style of the music" (Bazelon 103). Following it is Cal's loneliness theme on an oboe, which "swells on a dissonant chord" just before his mother screams upon seeing the intruder as she awakens from a half-drunken stupor (Palmer 305).

For the father, Adam Trask, an austere patriarch whose harshness is modulated by moments of gentleness, Rosenman provided modal music that Christopher Palmer finds reminiscent of Copland's *Appalachian Spring* and *The Tender Land* (Palmer 303). Adam introduces his own theme by humming it as he gloats over the expected success of his experiment with shipping refrigerated lettuce, and the theme is orchestrated in following scenes where the lettuce is picked and packed. Later, when Cal discovers that he can earn enough to replace the fortune his father lost on the lettuce project, he dances joyfully to Adam's theme turned into a "rollicking scherzo" played on the piccolo (Palmer 305).

Likewise, Abra introduces her theme by humming it during a love scene in the ice-house with Aaron; later, ironically, it becomes the love theme for Abra and Cal. Meanwhile, when Cal, spying on Abra and Aaron, reacts with frustrated rage by hurling great blocks of ice down the chute, we hear his violence theme in all its atonal dissonance. The love theme reappears when Cal asks why he hit his brother so hard during a fight, suggesting that he did so because of their rival love for Abra. The following scene has a nocturne for high strings when Cal climbs into Abra's bedroom window to plan a surprise birthday party for his father, the themes of violence, love, and loneliness all combined contrapuntally (Palmer 306; Evans 171).

The movie's final scene, in which Adam Trask, rendered an invalid by a stroke, lies in his sick room, is underscored by ten minutes of austere music, one of the longest passages in films. Cal, Abra, and Adam are all present, and Rosenman counterpoints their main themes to comment on their conflicting characters (Thomas, *Music* 203). In the sickroom, the dialogue is quiet and subdued, as is the music, neither dominating but each reinforcing the other.

At times, Rosenman scored voices almost as if the performers were singers in an opera. He noted that

. . . Julie Harris was a soprano, James Dean a tenor and Raymond

Massey a bass-baritone. The design of the instrumentation and of the thematic material itself was influenced by these vocal ranges and qualities. Often 'holes' were left in the scoring for the voice to be utilized as a sort of speaking instrument. Sometimes in moments of high tension or concentrated dialogue music was not used at all, and entered later for punctuation in quiet reactive moments. (Rosenman, qtd. by Palmer 308)

Though deserving, Rosenman's score was not nominated for an Oscar, which went to Alfred Newman's more conventional romantic score for *Love Is a Many-Splendored Thing*. Another Steinbeck connection of sorts for Rosenman is his winning, twenty-one years later, an Academy Award for arranging and adapting Woody Guthrie's songs for the film *Bound for Glory* (1976).

Though Rosenman continues to write serious concert music, much of it in serial and avant-garde idioms, *East of Eden* launched him on a second career of writing film music. He scored James Dean's second film, *Rebel Without a Cause*, and in it and *East of Eden* contrived, according to Christopher Palmer,

to create what may be described as a James Dean sound. This 'sound' was of major significance in respect of Hollywood film history, for it advanced a process which had been gathering momentum since the early fifties: the gradual loosening of the 19th century romantic stranglehold. (Palmer 294)

The other two composers Palmer chiefly credits for this change are Alex North and Elmer Bernstein. Tony Thomas credits North and Rosenman with having "more to do with bringing the sound of serious mid-twentieth-century music to Hollywood than any other composers . . . (*Music* 205).

Since their careers in film music got off the ground with Elia Kazan's Steinbeck films, Steinbeck indirectly deserves some credit for this development. Steinbeck also influenced Aaron Copland, whose opera *The Tender Land* has been compared to his scores for Steinbeck films. And since Copland has influenced innumerable younger composers, including many who wrote film scores, part of the credit goes to Steinbeck, for whom Copland wrote both his first score, *Of Mice and Men*, and his finest, *The Red Pony*.

Works Consulted

Bazelon, Irwin. *Knowing the Score. Notes on Film Music*. New York: VanNostrand, 1975.

Berger, Arthur. *Aaron Copland*. New York: Oxford UP, 1953.

Bernheimer, Martin. "Opera Review," *Los Angeles Times*, 18 Mar. 1974: IV, 1.

Copland, Aaron. *The Red Pony: Film Suite for Orchestra*. London: Boosey, 1951.

Copland, Aaron, and Vivian Perlis. *Copland: 1900 Through 1942*. New York: St. Martin's, 1984.

Copland, Aaron, and Vivian Perlis. *Copland Since 1943*. New York: St. Martin's, 1989.

Dobrin, Arnold. *Aaron Copland: His Life and Times*. New York: Crowell, 1967.

Evans, Mark. *Soundtrack: The Music of the Movies*. New York: Hopkinson, 1975.

French, Warren. "*The Red Pony* as Story Cycle and Film." *The Short Novels of John Steinbeck: Critical Essays with a Checklist to Steinbeck Criticism*. Ed. Jackson J. Benson. Durham: Duke UP, 1990. 71-84, 297-99.

Guthrie, Woody. *Pastures of Plenty: A Self Portrait*. Ed. Dave Marsh and Harold Leventhal. New York: Harper, 1990.

Klein, Joe. *Woody Guthrie, A Life*. New York: Knopf, 1980.

Lomax, Alan, Woody Guthrie, and Pete Seeger. *Hard Hitting Songs for Hard-Hit People*. New York: Oak, 1967.

Manvell, Roger, and John Huntley. *The Technique of Film Music*. London: Focal, 1975.

The New York Times, 5 Dec. 1958, 38:1.

Palmer, Christopher. *The Composer in Hollywood*. New York: Boyars, 1990.

Smith, Julia. *Aaron Copland*. New York: Dutton, 1955.

Steinbeck, John. "Note to the Reader," Twentieth Century-Fox, July 31, 1950.

_____. *Zapata*. Ed. Robert E. Morsberger. New York: Penguin, 1993.

Stoneback, H. R. "Rough People . . . Are the Best Singers. Woody Guthrie, John Steinbeck, and Folksong." *The Steinbeck Question: New Essays in Criticism*. Ed. Donald R. Noble. Troy: Whitston, 1993.

Thomas, Tony, ed. *Film Score: The View from the Podium*. South Brunswick: Barnes; London: Yoseloff, 1979.

_____. *Music for the Movies*. South Brunswick: Barnes; London: Tantivy, 1973.

Winn, Steven. "'Of Mice and Men' Brings Sinise Full Circle." *San Francisco Chronicle*. 10 Oct. 1992: C. 5.

Zanuck, Darryl F. *Memo from Darryl F. Zanuck: The Golden Years at Twentieth Century-Fox*. Ed. Rudy Behlmer. New York: Grove, 1993.

Part II

Essays on Specific Works

The Metamorphosis of The Moon Is Down: March 1942-March 1943

Roy Simmonds

The second of Steinbeck's play-novels, *The Moon Is Down*, occupies a unique place in his canon, for it is the only full-length work of fiction he published which is entirely devoted to the subject of war in his time. There are, of course, mentions of modern war in other Steinbeck novels—*Tortilla Flat* and *Sweet Thursday*, for example—and there are extended passages in *East of Eden* which examine the impact of World War I on the sheltered community of his hometown, Salinas, California. Although he did write about World War II in non-fictive terms in *Bombs Away* (1942) and in the 1943 New York *Herald Tribune* dispatches he sent from England, North Africa, and Italy, the major war novel anticipated by critics and readers alike never materialized. Despite its popularity with the American reading public, there is no denying the widespread underlying sense of disappointment that *The Moon Is Down* generated on its publication. What everyone had been waiting for was another book on the same epic scale as his previous novel, *The Grapes of Wrath*, published in 1939. This sense of disappointment, certainly among many critics of the day, heralded the beginning of what became known as Steinbeck's "decline," a concept that snowballed in almost self-perpetuating fashion during the postwar years, with some critics declaring (and still declaring) that nothing Steinbeck wrote after *The Grapes of Wrath* bears rereading.

The disappointment that was felt in 1942 can be understood. With critics and readers eagerly awaiting Steinbeck's follow-up to his story of the Joads and their fellow Okie migrants, a prepublication sale had amounted to 285,000 copies, benefitting by being a Book of the Month Club selection, and had far outshone the prepublication sale of 90,000 copies achieved by *The Grapes of Wrath* (Benson 388, 497). Steinbeck could hardly believe that figure of over a quarter-million. "It is kind of crazy," he commented (*Life* 242).

The "craziness" did not end there. It was announced in the month following publication that the movie rights to the book had been sold to Twentieth Century-Fox for the then record sum of $300,000. Three years earlier, the same studio had been able to acquire the movie rights to *The Grapes of Wrath* for a mere $75,000, then considered a very substantial sum. Although both books were bestsellers in their respective years of publication, *The Moon Is Down* has never reached the same sort of long-term sales figure, nor has it gone through so many editions internationally, as *The Grapes of Wrath*. The scripts of both movies were written by Nunnally Johnson; but whereas the 1940 screen version of *The Grapes of Wrath*, directed by John Ford, has become a recognized classic of the cinema and is frequently included in lists of the twenty best films of all time, the screen version of *The Moon Is Down*, directed by Irving Pichel, has been all but forgotten.

Both books had been born from Steinbeck's driving need to express his anger and compassion over contemporary issues, and the unifying themes of the books are powerful and timeless in their depiction of man's inhumanity to man, and in man's ability to confront physically and to overcome morally that inhumanity. But, it has to be said, whereas one book is a masterpiece, the other is not.

The detailed history of the genesis and composition of *The Moon Is Down* is too well known now to be repeated here (see Benson 486-88, 491-92; Coers 6-12). What is perhaps not so much appreciated is the manner in which the presentation of the story and of some of the main characters evolved from novel to play and ultimately to movie as America became more deeply embroiled in the war and the propagandist campaign against the Nazis became more strident and more freely expressible. In this respect, it is pertinent to bear in mind that the novel was published on 8 March 1942, the play first produced on Broadway on 7 April 1942, and the world premiere of the movie presented on 14 March 1943.

I: THE BOOK

While Steinbeck was writing the first draft of his novel, America had not yet been drawn into the war against Germany. By then, Hitler's Third Reich had swallowed up, under the banner of the New Order, Norway and Denmark in the north, France, Belgium, Holland and Luxembourg in the west, and vast tracts of Soviet Russia in the east. Steinbeck's aim in writing the book was primarily propagandist. He deplored the complacent attitude adopted by many of his fellow-countrymen ("It can't happen here"), and he wanted to draw their attention to the plight of the people in the occupied territories and warn them that complacency would not prevent the same disaster from befalling America.[1] Steinbeck's theme certainly was, in Jackson J. Benson's words, "compelling in its currency, yet timeless—foreign occupation and resistance" (488). Two decades later, in his article "Reflections on a Lunar Eclipse," Steinbeck explained that, in order to ensure that the work possessed universal implications, he had "placed the story in an unnamed country, cold and stern like Norway, cunning and implacable like Denmark, reasonable like France," made the names of his characters "as international as I could," and "did not even call the Germans Germans but simply invaders." He did not mention, however, that even the title of the work had also been neutralized (the original title he had given it was *The New Order*), and that the original name given to the fifth columnist character, "Curseling" (echoing the name of the Norwegian traitor, "Quisling") had been changed shortly before publication to the more innocuous "Corell."

Steinbeck planned in the novel to show both sides of the coin. While he was angered and appalled by the reports he read in the office of the Foreign Information Service in Washington of the misery and brutality being suffered by the oppressed multitudes in Europe and Russia, he was also cognizant of the problems and the fears of the soldiers in the occupying forces. The propagandist thrust of the work was therefore intended to be two-edged: to raise the spirits of the oppressed, and to eat into the morale of the invaders. Steinbeck possessed the perception, unusual for those days, that the invaders were equally vulnerable, if not in certain circumstances more vulnerable, than the populations they had overrun. It could not be ignored that the majority of the German soldiery were neither sadistic monsters nor the gullible fools of contemporary popular belief, but themselves human beings projected into a situation not specifically of their making and with the same sort of needs, fears, and longings as the people they had conquered. The recognition of this vulnerability and the exploiting of it could, in Steinbeck's view, sow many of the seeds of final victory.

When the book was published, many critics and readers were, perhaps understandably, somewhat irritated by Steinbeck's literary device of setting his story in an unnamed country invaded by troops of an unspecified nationality. The setting, after all, was recognizably a Norwegian coastal mining community, and who else could the "invaders" be—with their talk of "the Leader" and their memories of the occupation of Belgium during the last war—but Germans? Indeed, several reviewers had no compunction in writing about Norwegian patriots and Nazi invaders. It is possible, however, that Steinbeck had a further reason, over and above his desire to present the work as a timeless and universal metaphor of all oppressed peoples and their oppressors, for being coy about the national identities of his characters. The work had been planned as a second exploration into the play-novel genre, following the success of *Of Mice and Men* (1937). That earlier work had not only been eminently successful as a novel and a Broadway play, but had also been acclaimed in a movie version, directed by Lewis Milestone and released in 1940. So, with the new play-novel, Steinbeck was, even as he was writing it, looking beyond the novel and play versions to a possible movie version. It could have been this factor that had persuaded him to retain the anonymity of setting and nationalities to conform with what was, in 1941, still the establishment's soft-pedalling attitude toward the German government, and thus ensure that *The Moon Is Down* was granted a wide distribution in the nation's movie houses.[2]

Although, in general, the book received good reviews, there was an extremely vocal pocket of influential critics who were incensed by Steinbeck's treatment of the Nazis. These critics not only denounced him for being far too soft in his portrayal of the invaders, but also, as Clifton Fadiman expressed it in *The New Yorker*, for "melodramatic simplification of the issues involved" (59). He accused Steinbeck of basing the work on the comforting fallacy that good will always overcome evil simply because it is, by definition, good. Other critics and readers charged that Steinbeck could have no concept of how desperate life was under Nazi rule, and claimed to foresee the dire consequences that would flow from his advocacy of resistance and of answering force with sabotage and assassination. Such a course, these critics and readers argued, could only result in an inevitable increase in the incidence and severity of the reprisals taken against defenseless civilian populations. The concern felt by these critics and readers was understandable, if possibly unfocussed, in a nation detached by many thousands of miles from the occupied countries, for they had not been given access, as Steinbeck had, to the secret reports emanating from the resistance groups in Europe. If he was unable to confront his critics, Steinbeck could at least privately complain that it was they, not he, who did not appreciate the true desperate nature and depth of the plight of the millions then suffering under the New Order. It had never been his purpose to people his novel with the sort of stock Nazis most readers regarded as the norm. His approach was both more subtle and wiser than that, something on the lines of: "Know your enemy. Do not underestimate him. But never forget his weaknesses." If his critics could reject his portrait of Colonel Lanser as being too reasonable and cultured a man—a man of "certain memories" (88) who was anxious to avoid the bloodshed that would inevitably result from the repetition of active resistance, hostage-taking and execution he had experienced in the last war, a man whose eyes "lacked the blank look of the ordinary soldier" (30), a man who could correct Mayor Orden when he misquoted Socrates—then, as Steinbeck maintained, they could have no concept themselves of what *he* was attempting to achieve.

Ultimate vindication of the book and the thesis Steinbeck propounded in it was not, in fact, fully recognized until after the Liberation, when the whole story of how clandestine copies of *The Moon Is Down* had been printed, duplicated, distributed, and circulated under the noses of the Nazis came to be told.[3]

During the war, the book had become not only a call to arms, but, as Steinbeck had hoped, a definitive statement, relayed across the seas and backed with the authority of one of America's greatest writers, that all was not lost, that there was no possibility of the Nazis winning the war. That was the message, the assurance, the people of Norway, Denmark, Holland, Belgium, Luxembourg, France, and Russia wanted to hear.

II: THE PLAY

In 1949 or 1950, at the time he was working on his third play-novel, *Burning Bright*, Steinbeck told Pascal Covici, his editor and friend at the Viking Press: "There is one disadvantage to the play-novel form. The novel has to go to press and stay that way but little changes take place in the play right up to opening night" (Fensch 134). And so it was with *The Moon Is Down*. While there is no evidence to confirm or refute, Steinbeck may have retrospectively regretted that he had released his fiction text so readily to his agents and publishers before tackling the task of preparing the text for stage presentation. On the other hand, had there not been a stage version to prepare, it is questionable if Steinbeck would in any case have taken time out to revise the novel to any appreciable degree. At the time, he found, for the most part, the process of rewriting for the stage something of a chore, imposed upon him by unavoidable circumstance and influenced by the requirements of the play's director and actors.

What is certain is that during the period between handing over the manuscript of the novel to his agents and publishers and the first night of the play on Broadway he was engaged, almost to the last minute, in making those "little changes" to improve his text: revising dialogue, adding lines, cutting others, and changing emphases. He even transferred dialogue from one character to another for greater dramatic effect, as in the final exchange between Doctor Winter and Mayor Orden, when the mayor is being led out to his execution. The novel text reads:

> . . . In the doorway he turned back to Doctor Winter. "Crito, I owe a cock to Asclepius [*sic*]," he said tenderly. "Will you remember to pay the debt?"
>
> Winter closed his eyes for a moment before he answered, "The debt shall be paid."
>
> Orden chuckled then. "I remembered that one. I didn't forget that one." He put his hand on Prackle's arm, and the lieutenant flinched away from him.

And Winter nodded slowly. "Yes, you remembered. The debt shall be paid." (187-88)

The play version ends on a similar note, but with the final, and significant, exchange of dialogue:

MAYOR. "Crito, I owe a cock to Ascalaepius [*sic*]. Will you remember to pay the debt?"
WINTER. [*Crosses C. to table.*] "The debt shall be paid."
MAYOR. [*Chuckling.*] "I remembered that one."
WINTER. [*Very softly.*] Yes. You remembered it.
MAYOR. The debt will be paid! [*He turns and walks slowly to the door as another explosion is heard, this time closer.*]
[PRACKLE *goes ahead of him. The* SOLDIERS *follow him out as the*]
CURTAIN
COMES DOWN SLOWLY (101)

In the play, Colonel Lanser, the mayor's wife, and Annie, the maid, are not witnesses to the final exchange between Orden and Winter, as they are in the novel. Only Prackle and the two soldiers who are to escort Orden out to the firing squad remain in the room. Winter is next in line for execution if the sabotage continues (as the explosion indicates it already has), so his solemn—and perhaps, on his part, ineffective—personal promise to the mayor in the novel becomes instead not only Orden's declaration to the doctor of his unquestionable belief that they both will be avenged, but also his dire warning to Prackle and the two soldiers of the retribution to come.

An examination of the texts of the novel and play make it clear just how extensive were the revisions Steinbeck carried out on the work after the book had been rushed into print. In the course of this revision, or series of revisions, during the course of the play's rehearsals, Colonel Lanser evolved into a marginally harsher character than he is in the novel. For example, in the book, following Orden's observation that, while herd men might win battles, it is free men who win wars, Lanser replies: "My orders are clear. Eleven o'clock was the deadline. I have taken hostages. If there is violence, the hostages will be executed." Winter then asks him: "Will you carry out the orders, knowing they will fail?" Lanser tells him: "I will carry out my orders no matter what they are" (186). In the play version, the tone of the exchange has been subtly altered. "My orders are clear," Lanser says. "Eleven o'clock is the deadline. I have taken *my* hostages. If there is violence *I will execute them*" [my italics]. Winter's reply also has a different emphasis. No longer is it a question, however rhetorical by implication, that seeks response from a man possibly still open to reason, but a statement recognizing that reason has already been jettisoned in the cause of so-called military expediency. Winter says: "And you will carry out the orders, knowing they will fail." Lanser answers: "I will carry out my orders" (99).

In the first chapter of the book, when the traitor Corell makes his initial appearance, Winter explains to the disbelieving Orden the role Corell has played in paving the way for the successful invasion and occupation of the little town. In the novel, Corell defends himself angrily: "I work for what I believe in! That is an honorable thing" (31). In the play, he justifies his actions more specifically and at greater length: "Doctor, you don't understand. This thing was bound to come. It's a good thing. You don't understand it yet, but when you do, you will thank me. The democracy was rotten and inefficient. Things will be better now. Believe me. When you understand the new order you will know I am right" (12-13).

Lanser's dislike of and contempt for Corell is made explicit in the book, both in that scene and during their two subsequent confrontations in chapter two and, more particularly, chapter seven. In this latter chapter, Corell reveals that he has gone over Lanser's head in making a report direct to the capital on the situation in the town. Corell insists that both Orden and Winter be arrested as hostages and, if necessary, shot. The mayor and the doctor represent, one by virtue of his office, the other by virtue of his profession and wisdom, the authority in the town. Once they have been disposed of, Corell argues, rebellion will be broken. "Do you really think so?" Lanser asks him. "It must be so," Corell replies. Lanser immediately calls in a sergeant and tells him: "I have placed Mayor Orden under arrest, and I have placed Doctor Winter under arrest. You will see to it that Orden is guarded and you will bring Winter here immediately." When the sergeant has left, Lanser warns Corell: "You know, I hope you know what you're doing. I do hope you know what you're doing"(171). In the play, the debate between the military mind and the mind of the political theorist is greatly extended; and Lanser's reluctance in the novel to comply with Corell's new-found authority is replaced in the play by a reluctance based less on humanitarian considerations than on hard-headed appreciation of the logistics pertaining to an army of occupation:

LANSER. [*Shakes his head a little sadly.*] Have you ever thought that one execution makes a hundred active enemies where we have passive enemies? Even patriotism is not as sharp as personal hurt, personal loss. A dead brother, a dead father—that really arms an enemy.

CORELL. [*Almost as though he had grounds for blackmail now.*] Your attitude, sir, may lead you to trouble. It is fortunate that I am— your friend.

LANSER. [*Crosses R. to arm chair; with a little contempt in his voice.*] I can see your report almost as though it were in front of me—

CORELL. [*Quickly*] Oh! But you're mistaken, sir. I haven't—

LANSER. [*Turns to him.*] This war should be for the very young. They would have the proper spirit, but unfortunately they are not able to move guns and men about. I suffer from civilization. That means I can know one thing and do another. I know we have failed— I knew we would before we started. The thing the leader wanted to do cannot be done.

CORELL. [*Excitedly, leaning toward him across table.*] What is this? What do you say?

LANSER. [*Quietly, crosses to R. end of table.*] Oh! Don't worry. I will go about it as though it could be done and do a better job than the zealots could. And when the tide turns, I may save a few lives, from knowing how to retreat.

CORELL. They shouldn't have sent a man like you here!

LANSER. Don't worry—so long as we can hold, we will hold. [*Crossing to CORELL, sadly.*] I can act quite apart from my knowledge. I will shoot the Mayor. [*His voice grows hard.*] I will not break the rules. I will shoot the doctor, I will help tear and burn the world. I don't like you, Corell. I am licking my wounds surely. And—I am giving you wounds to lick. [*Crosses around to front of table R. end.*] Sergeant!

SERGEANT. [*Enters U. L., crosses D.L.C.*] Sir?

LANSER. [*Slowly.*] Place Mayor Orden and Dr. Winter under arrest! (92-93)

The revisions Steinbeck introduced during the gestation of the play cannot be said, however, to have made the work more dramatically viable to any appreciable degree. *The Moon Is Down* does indeed fail artistically as a novel because of an insistence on observing the requirements of drama, and as a play it fails because it is too literary. Steinbeck himself realized this in the aftermath of the play's Broadway presentation and the rather indifferent reviews that had appeared in the New York newspapers. He admitted that the play was "dull," that "probably because of my writing, it didn't come over the footlights," and that it was not "a dramatically interesting play" (*Life* 244). The anonymous *Time* reviewer put his finger precisely on the problem: "The dialogue, more like subdued rhetoric than human talk, often seems stilted and formal when spoken aloud. The play lacks sustained action and commits the dramatic crime of having almost everything exciting take place offstage" ("New Play" 36).

Book and play are peopled for the most part with artificial characters. No matter how one may deplore the viciousness of James Thurber's strictures in his *New Republic* book review, one has a certain sympathy for his declared difficulty in believing the characters in the novel came from the streets and houses of a little town. "They come from their dressing rooms," Thurber averred. "The characters and the language they speak are in keeping with the theatrical atmosphere, from Annie, the irate cook, to Colonel Lanser, the leader of the invaders and his staff. If these are German officers, if they are anything else but American actors, I will eat the manuscript of your next play" (370). Thurber, of course, was overreacting, but his criticism nevertheless had an inner core of truth. It is one of the basic flaws of the work that one cannot unconditionally accept these characters as Norwegian patriots and their German oppressors, as Steinbeck (for all the inconsequential anonymity he imposed upon their nationalities) intended them to be.[4]

The townspeople, in so many ways, seem more akin to Steinbeck's simple paisanos from Monterey translated arbitrarily to an alien setting. This lack of versimilitude may not destroy *The Moon Is Down* as a piece of timeless propaganda—indeed, it may even strengthen it as such—but it seriously damages it as a sustainable work of art created by a writer who had been hailed only three years previously as a master-realist.

The artificiality of the work is patent in some of its simplistic and sentimental dialogue. Simplicity and sentimentality of style, content, and characterization are failings for which Steinbeck has frequently been accused—on many occasions, let it be said, unfairly. Here, however, the criticism is valid. Take, for instance, this conversation in the book between Annie and Joseph, the mayor's servingman, as they prepare the palace drawing room for the trial of Alex Morden. Annie speaks first:

"What do they want with a table in here, anyway? This isn't a dining-room."

Joseph moved a chair up to the table and he set it carefully at the right distance from the table, and he adjusted it. "They're going to hold a trial," he said. "They're going to try Alexander Morden."

"Molly Morden's husband?"

"Molly Morden's husband."

"For bashing that fellow with a pick?"

"That's right," said Joseph.

"But he's a nice man," Annie said. "They've got no right to try him. He gave Molly a big red dress for her birthday. What right have they got to try Alex?"

"Well," Joseph explained, "he killed this fellow."

"Suppose he did; the fellow ordered Alex around. I heard about it. Alex doesn't like to be ordered. Alex's been an alderman in his time, and his father, too. And Molly Morden makes a nice cake," Annie said charitably. "But her frosting gets too hard. What'll they do with Alex?"

"Shoot him," Joseph said gloomily. (74-75)

And so on in much the same vein. Steinbeck had here fallen into the trap, which he had knowingly and deliberately set himself, of having to explain external action by means of credible dialogue. Only here, it is not credible. Annie's apparent surprise that the invaders should be about to try Alex Morden is hard to accept. After all, she did know that Alex had "bashed that fellow with a pick." In this context, her comments that the invaders have no right to try Alex because he is "a nice man" and "gave Molly a big red dress" (and what is the significance of that "big"?) verge on the ludicrous, as do her asides about Molly's ability to make "a nice cake," but that "her frosting gets too hard." While such irrelevancies are often voiced in moments of stress and tension to hide emotion, Steinbeck does not here succeed in making them ring true. Annie may well be the comic servant of theatrical tradition, but the comedy is strained. In any case, no actor or actress could have made this dialogue sound convincing on the stage, and Steinbeck wisely revised it for the stage version (stage directions omitted):

ANNIE. What's a dining table want in here!

JOSEPH. The Colonel wants it here. They're going to hold some kind of a trial.

ANNIE. Why don't they hold it down at the City Hall where it belongs?

JOSEPH. I don't know. They do crazy things. It's some kind of way they have . . . .

ANNIE. What do they want to have a trial for?

JOSEPH. Well—there's talk. People say there was trouble at the mine. Some kind of a fight.

ANNIE. You mean they're going to try one of *us*?

JOSEPH. That's what they say.

ANNIE. Who?

JOSEPH. Well, they say Alex Morden got in some kind of trouble at the mine.

ANNIE. That's Molly's husband. He never gets in any trouble. He's a good man. What kind of trouble could Alex get into?

JOSEPH. Well, some people say he hit a soldier.

ANNIE. It's a time of trouble. Molly Kenderly wouldn't have married a man who hit people. Alex is a good man. The soldiers must have done something to Alex. (40-41)

This is far more persuasive than the corresponding conversation in the novel. Steinbeck has already established that the townspeople, in those early days of the occupation, had not even begun to consider the necessity of a system of reliable underground communication to replace casual rumor. Until the killing of Captain Bentick, the townspeople, although sullen under enemy rule, had been comparatively docile, still stunned by the newly-established reality of their predicament. They were not even sure where Mayor Orden stood vis-à-vis the invader. After all, the once-popular Mr. Corell had shown himself sympathetic to the enemy cause and, as a result, had already suffered an isolated physical attack by a person or persons unknown. Alex Morden's spontaneous revolt, although carried out in a fit of anger and by no means premeditated, is the catalyst that unifies the town, and his subsequent fate fires the spirit of active resistance. But before the trial all is vagueness and rumor, and the fact that Alex killed the enemy officer has not become generally known throughout the community. There is, in the play text, a logical progression of question and answer between Annie and Joseph, of the gradual realization by Annie of the seriousness of what has happened, that is entirely absent from the somewhat ineffective passage in the novel.

As with the book, the reviews of the play tended to be rather mixed and to stir the same sort of conflicting passions.[5] John Gassner, writing in *Current History*, considered the Nazis in the play to be "painfully unrepresentative," with all but one of the officers seemingly "so mild as to lead one to wonder how they could have conquered nation after nation and perpetrated the verified brutalities of Warsaw" (230). He also complained that the audience is compelled to find sympathy with the Nazis, by being made aware "of their pathos of bewilderment, longing for home, and desire to be liked and accepted" (230). In *Commonweal*, David Burnham argued that Colonel Lanser is "an insufficient symbol of what Steinbeck meant to attack" (14). *Newsweek* found the play "deficient in impact and plausibility" ("Steinbeck's Faith" 72). On the other hand, Brooks Atkinson in the *New York Times* praised it as "a remarkably convincing play because it is honest in its heart" (22).

It would probably be true to say that the play stands or falls by the performances of its two main characters, Colonel Lanser and Mayor Orden. It is the dramatic tension between these two men that provides the main *raison d'être* of the whole work. However, it seems that the casting of these two roles in the Broadway production was unfortunate. That fine actor, Otto Kruger, playing Colonel Lanser, could not come to grips with the character, and obviously played the part without a great deal of conviction, while Ralph Morgan, playing Mayor Orden, came over, in the words of the *Newsweek* reviewer, as "a bewildered, sentimental old dodderer" ("Steinbeck's Faith" 73). Immediately following its Broadway run of approximately two months, the play enjoyed a successful road show with a somewhat different cast. Since then, however, it has never been revived in the United States "nor," as Robert E. Morsberger has commented, "is it likely to be" (284).

III: THE MOVIE

There can be no denying that the play version of *The Moon Is Down*, for all its faults, is, textually if not dramatically, an improvement over the novel, and that the screen version, in its turn, was certainly more effective in those wartime days than the play. The comparisons arguably are invidious, since Steinbeck did not write the film script and was given no ultimate control over it. However, he was delighted when he learned that Nunnally Johnson, who had done so superb a job of translating *The Grapes of Wrath* into cinematic terms, had been selected for the task. Indeed, when, as Benson records, Johnson asked the author "if he wanted him to take any particular line or . . . had any ideas about how the story should be developed for the screen," Steinbeck had apparently sufficient confidence in Johnson's professionalism and integrity simply to tell him: "Tamper with it" (410). When in October, 1942, Johnson showed him the completed script, Steinbeck's verdict was that it was "very fine," and he declared that it would make "a wonderful picture" (Letter to Williams). He reported to his literary agent, Elizabeth Otis, that Johnson had "changed nothing," but had "added a number of external scenes to accentuate the cold and the hatred" (Letter).

Steinbeck was invited to the Twentieth Century-Fox studios during the latter part of November, and shown the sets of the town, originally designed and built to represent a Welsh mining village for the recently completed John Ford movie, *How Green Was My Valley*, based on Richard Llewellyn's bestselling novel.[6] Steinbeck was evidently delighted with all he saw. "Very fine. Beautiful job," he enthused (Letter to Otis). The following month, he was invited back to view the rushes of the few scenes that had been shot. Afterwards, he wrote to Johnson, again expressing his pleasure at the manner in which his original play had been opened up. "There is no question," he wrote, "that pictures are a better medium for this story than the stage ever was" (qtd. in "Brighter

'Moon'"). He told Elizabeth Otis in December: "It is a really beautiful job and there is a curious three dimensional quality in it. It is something like the best English and before the war German pictures, you know a sustained mood" (Letter).

Although Steinbeck seemed to be content that Johnson had "changed nothing," the screenwriter had in fact changed a considerable amount. By the time Johnson began work on the script, America had been almost a year at war with Germany, and there was no longer any necessity to practice circumspection in the way Steinbeck had felt constrained to do while writing the novel. Accordingly, there was no attempt on Johnson's part to disguise the setting of the movie as other than Norway and the identity of the invaders as other than the Germans. The swastika is shown flying over the Mayor's palace shortly after the occupation of the town has been effected, and in the nearby park the German military band is playing "We're Sailing Against England." Much of Steinbeck's subtlety could now also be thrown out of the window. The more damning the portrayal of the Nazis, the greater the explicitness of the brutality to which they resorted, the better the establishment liked it. The movie, while retaining the main elements of Steinbeck's story, centered more on the plight and courage of the mayor and his people than on what had widely then been considered in the novel and the play as misguided sympathy for the German soldiery.

If Johnson retained extensive slabs of Steinbeck's dialogue, he also introduced many new scenes and much additional dialogue of his own. Whereas both the novel and the play begin after the invasion has become a *fait accompli*, the movie opens on board a German cruiser with a scene in which a naval staff man briefs Colonel Lanser and his officers on the arrangements Corell has organized to ensure the successful and trouble-free occupation of the little town. In the town itself, Corell and the mayor are seeing off the local militia, consisting of twelve young soldiers, together with their families, on a coach trip to a field six miles from town, where Corell has arranged a target practice and beer picnic. Subsequently, the transport planes, the descending paratroopers, and the killing of exactly half the militia force are all graphically shown.

If the characters of Mayor Orden and Doctor Winter undergo little, if any, change, Colonel Lanser and his officers (Lieutenant Tonder always a possible exception) become the despotic and brutal oppressors of popular conception. The harshness of the regime they intend to impose is manifest from the very beginning, when the Colonel's initial encounter with Orden and Winter is continually interrupted by Joseph as he tries to cope with a potentially awkward situation in the kitchen. In the book and the play, after Annie has been arrested for throwing boiling water over one of the enemy soldiers, the Colonel helplessly orders that she should be released, warning Orden that he could have had her locked up or even shot. In the movie, Lanser becomes progressively angrier with Joseph's interruptions, until he completely loses his temper and shouts at Orden that he could have them all shot.

Possibly the most radically changed of all the Germans in Johnson's script is Captain Bentick. In the book and the play, Bentick is presented as a family man, "a lover of dogs and pink children and Christmas" (43), more akin to an English gentleman than a German soldier. In Johnson's script, however, he becomes just another of the typical sadistic Nazi bullies portrayed in the movies of those days. In the novel and the play, it is Captain Loft who provokes Alex Morden's anger and attack, and Bentick is killed solely because he intervenes in an effort to prevent bloodshed. But in the movie it is Bentick alone who enrages Alex when, confronting a group of miners who are refusing to work, he picks out five of the men by the simple expedient of flicking pebbles into the crowd. He then informs the miners that if they continue refusing to work their families will be deprived of food for three whole days. They themselves will always be well fed, for their strength is needed to work the mine but their wives and their children and their mothers will go hungry. Alex raises his voice in protest and, when Bentick spits contemptuously in his face, smashes the captain's skull with an iron bar. After Alex is executed and an unsuccessful attempt is made on Lanser's life, resulting in the wounding of Lieutenant Prackle, the five hostages Bentick so arbitrarily selected are publicly shot, singing the Norwegian national anthem as they die.

There then follow several scenes epitomizing the manner in which the German troops are ostracized by the townspeople, who refuse to talk to them or even to recognize their existence, unless forced to do so. The emphasis is on the character of Lieutenant Tonder, demonstrating how his idealism begins to crack under the strain of so much undisguised but passive hatred. British planes fly over and, guided by lights in the fields below, drop their bombs squarely on the mine. The Anders boys escape to England, their farewell scene with Orden and Winter taking place under cover of darkness on the seashore near the pier where their boat is tied up, thus dispensing with the contrived comings and goings at Molly's house that occur in the book and the play. The four are surprised by a German soldier, but he is overcome from behind and strangled by the bartender from the local inn. The band still plays in the park, but with less assurance now. The bandleader has amended the title of his score to read, "We're *Still* Sailing Against England." Some of the soldiers, equally starved for hard news about the progress of the war as the townspeople, discover the location of a clandestine radio listening post in an old barn, but, instead of arresting the operators and confiscating the wireless set, make a practice of listening in themselves every night through cracks in the barn walls, despite the fact that they are constantly demoralized even more by the reports of the bombing of German cities where their families are.

Following Tonder's murder by Molly Morden and the dropping of the little packages of chocolate and dynamite by the British planes, ten hostages, including Orden and Winter, are taken against the threat of further sabotage. When this measure proves of no avail, Lanser orders that the executions should go ahead. The populace is assembled and forced to witness the mass hanging. The people begin singing the national anthem to give whatever comfort and courage they can to the doomed men. As the hostages mount the steps to the scaffold with its ten nooses, there is a series of explosions. One after the other, the mine, the radio station, and Corell's shop are destroyed. "How did it go about the flies?" Mayor Orden asks Doctor Winter. "The flies have conquered the flypaper," comes the reply. These are the last words the two men are able to exchange. As they and the other eight hostages die together, the sound of the singing of the national anthem becomes louder and louder, and the movie ends in a cinematic apotheosis of patriotic emotion and fervor.

Once again, the reception of the work was mixed. In the eyes of some critics, Steinbeck's discredited treatment of the Nazis had not been satisfactorily eliminated from the movie. While admitting that Steinbeck's Nazis "are harsher in the movie than in the novel or the play," and that Sir Cedric Hardwicke, as Lanser, "looks more like a cold-blooded Junker than like the unmilitary officer described by Steinbeck," the *Time* reviewer declared that the whole premise of the work was based upon questionable psychology and presented "an extraordinarily naive view of the facts of Nazi life" ("The New" 54, 56). In the *Nation*, James Agee roundly condemned the movie for adding to "the growing, already over-ripe vocabulary of democratic claptrap which all but destroys our realization that modest heroism is possible, constant, and implicit in this war" (643). On the other hand, *Newsweek* praised the movie's Colonel Lanser ("a cold, impersonal intelligence") and Henry Travers's portrayal of Mayor Orden ("a gentle, clear-thinking hero of the people"), observing that the film did not "rely on the melodramatics of terror and sabotage to underscore its message," going "beyond overt action to reach to the inner strength of a conquered people" ("Brighter 'Moon'" 88). The *New York Times* critic, Bosley Crowther, thought the movie "far and away the best conception of the human and moral issues involved when the Nazis took over a free country that the screen has yet manifested."

It is difficult today—and especially for those who did not live through the war years—to appreciate fully the depths of the emotions aroused by this one work. Arguably, *The Moon Is Down* was never, at the time of its appearance, widely accepted in America for what it was. What the majority of American readers, playgoers, and movie audiences wanted was precisely what James Agee so passionately criticized, those, in Joseph R. Millichap's words, "reassuring, patriotic melodramas" (75) in which superhuman acts of courage are enacted and in which the issues between good and evil are presented in clear-cut, psychologically simplified terms, as in such movies as *The Commandos Strike at Dawn* and *Edge of Darkness*, both of which were set in occupied Norway and released at more or less the same time as the movie version of *The Moon Is Down*. The best that can be said is that the movie did go some way toward satisfying popular demand, by at least observing and accepting the change of climate since the book's publication twelve months or so before.

The movie can thus be said to have had a more *immediate* visual and emotional impact than either the play or the novel. In the broadest sense, while it remained true to the basics of Steinbeck's story, its didactic content and its more simplistic approach to the representation of good and evil (i.e. patriot and invader) undoubtedly was better propaganda for serving up to the masses in wartime. The play, on the other hand, would appear to have had considerably less impact on a national basis either as art or propaganda, despite many revised and improved passages of dialogue. The book, although less immediately convincing than the movie, had its own impact at the time, not merely on a nationwide but also on a worldwide basis, for the printed word could be circulated whereas cans of film could not. The book, in any case, with its basic allegoric nature, as Steinbeck had conceived it, has ultimately proved to be the most enduring, if not altogether as a great work of art, then certainly as an impassioned statement for all time and for all peoples of the world of man's unconquerable spirit in the face of dark adversity.

Notes

[1] According to Steinbeck, he originally intended that the book should be set in an American town occupied by foreign forces, but his bosses at the Foreign Information Service vetoed the idea on the grounds that such a work would be damaging to morale in the USA.

[2] Steinbeck is said to have completed the final draft of the book on 7 December 1941, the very day the Japanese bombed Pearl Harbor.

[3] See Coers for the best and fullest account of these European clandestine printings of *The Moon Is Down*.

[4]The mantle of anonymity was preserved in the play presentation. Steinbeck's stage directions for the invaders' uniforms is quite specific on this point: "Throughout, the uniforms of both soldiers and officers are plain as possible. Rank can be indicated by small colored tabs at the collar, but little else. Helmets should be a variation on any obvious shape which will identify these as being soldiers of any known nation" (4).

[5]For an excellent account of the Broadway presentation of the play and its critical reception, see French.

[6]In the circumstances, it is perhaps unfortunate that John Ford did not also direct *The Moon Is Down*.

Works Cited

Agee, James. "The Moon Is Down." *Nation* 1 May 1943: 642-43.

Anon. "Steinbeck's Faith." *Newsweek* 20 Apr. 1942: 72.

_____. "New Play in Manhattan." *Time* 20 Apr. 1942: 36.

_____. "The New Pictures." *Time* 5 Apr. 1943: 54, 56.

_____. "Brighter 'Moon.'" *Newsweek* 5 Apr. 1943: 86, 88.

Atkinson, Brooks. "The Play." *New York Times* 8 Apr. 1942: 22.

Benson, Jackson. *The True Adventures of John Steinbeck, Writer.* New York: Viking, 1984.

Burnham, David. "The Moon Is Down." *Commonweal* 24 Apr. 1942: 14-15.

Coers, Donald V. *John Steinbeck as Propagandist:* The Moon Is Down *Goes to War.* Tuscaloosa: U of Alabama P, 1991.

Crowther, Bosley. "The Longer View." *New York Times* 4 Apr. 1943, sec. 2: 3.

Fadiman, Clifton. "Books: Two Ways to Win the War." *New Yorker* 7 Mar. 1942: 59-60.

Fensch, Thomas. *Steinbeck and Covici: The Story of a Friendship.* Middlebury: Eriksson, 1979.

French, Warren. "*The Moon Is Down*: John Steinbeck's 'Times.'" *Steinbeck Quarterly* II (1978): 77-87.

Gassner, John. "'The Moon Is Down' As a Play." *Current History* May 1942: 228-32.

Millichap, Joseph R. *Steinbeck and Film.* New York: Ungar, 1983.

Morsberger, Robert E. "Steinbeck and the Stage" in *The Short Novels of John Steinbeck: Critical Essays with a Checklist to Steinbeck Criticism.* Ed. Jackson J. Benson. Durham: Duke UP, 1990.

Steinbeck, John. Letter to Annie Laurie Williams. 15 Oct. 1942.

_____. Letter to Elizabeth Otis. n.d. [Oct. 1942]. Department of Special Collections. Stanford University.

_____. Letter to Elizabeth Otis. n.d. [Nov. 1942]. Department of Special Collections. Stanford University.

_____. Letter to Elizabeth Otis. 8 Dec. 1943. Department of Special Collections. Stanford University.

_____. *The Moon Is Down.* New York: Viking, 1942.

_____. *The Moon Is Down: Play in Two Parts.* New York: Viking, 1942.

_____. "Reflections on a Lunar Eclipse." *New York Herald Tribune Book Week* 6 Oct. 1963: 3.

_____. *Steinbeck: A Life in Letters.* Ed. Elaine Steinbeck and Robert Wallsten. New York: Viking, 1975.

Thurber, James. "What Price Conquest?" *New Republic* 16 Mar. 1942: 370.

Three Strong Women in Steinbeck's The Moon Is Down

Eiko Shiraga

The three women in *The Moon Is Down* offer a revealing study in Steinbeck's concept of female characters. Despite their distinctive differences in personality, all three serve traditional roles as European women, two as wives and another as cook. As such they provide a comforting sense of continuity and established order during the distressful upheavals of military defeat and occupation. But they also serve political functions, doing their part in one way or another, sometimes subtly, sometimes overtly, to challenge or subvert the new political order imposed on the town by the invaders. In so doing, they are very much involved in—indeed, vital to—the resistance movement which develops in their defeated town. Thus Steinbeck's presentation of these women is at once conventional and unorthodox: while they are ordinarily bound to traditional supportive roles, they are immediately capable of extraordinary action and valor when it is essential to the preservation of their society.

Sarah Orden functions primarily as the wife of Mayor Orden, the hero of this novel. She plays an active role as traditional European housewife—a woman loving, practical, shrewd, and maternal toward her husband. An expert homemaker, she looks after her dependent husband—personally and domestically: "No little appetite or pain, no carelessness or meanness in him escaped her . . ." (7). She helps him dress properly not only because he tends to be slovenly without her but also because she wants him to look dignified and superior to the barbarian invaders (4). This task represents her instinctive womanly protest against the invaders. In spite of the political crisis, she holds the struggling mayor by the neck and trims the hair out of his ears as if she totally dismisses the intimidating armed intruders (4). Judging from the conversation between Joseph, the mayor's servant, and Dr. Winter, we can recognize that Mayor Orden would not dare allow the job of trimming to be done except by his wife, who "mothers" him. Sarah also provides the novel with a comic relief at this point—a much needed one—at a time of political tension and crisis.

An active and practical person as well as the commander-in-chief at home, Sarah often lacks her husband's imagination and creativity. As Steinbeck's narrator reveals, "Only once or twice in her life had she ever understood all of him . . ."; and ". . . no thought or dream or longing in him ever reached her" (7). However, by supporting and caring for her husband all her married life, she constantly manages him so that he can

95

devote himself totally to his citizens' welfare without the disruption of personal, domestic, or practical chores. Although she does not rate her husband too highly as a family man or a practical man, she respects him instinctively as the town's political leader. Furthermore, Sarah intuitively understands her husband's needs and his citizens' needs so well that she helps Mayor Orden carry out his public duties. She is, in fact, willing to accept any assignment, no matter how large or small. These include dangerous and even awkward tasks her husband asks her to do—such as staying in bed with Joseph to let the mayor sneak out of the house to contact the underground fighters without being detected by the enemy. (This particular act offers yet another episode of comic relief.) As the first lady of the city, Sarah indeed comforts the weak, the lonely, and the oppressed, whenever possible. The narrator says, "She had learned not to confuse the Mayor with her husband" (10). When Mayor Orden faces execution by refusing collaboration with the invaders, she manifests her utmost concern for him as the leader of the people:

> And then the bedroom door opened and Madame came out, carrying the Mayor's chain of office in her hand. She said, "You forgot this." ... [A]nd he stooped his head and Madame slipped the chain of office over his head, and he said, "Thank you, dear." (112)

This action symbolically displays her love and her respect for her husband as the mayor; she supports him totally in war and peace. We can imagine that, thanks to her support, Mayor Orden is able to face death with courage and dignity. Sarah is always behind the mayor, who believes in freedom and democracy and who preserves his integrity and his hope for a brighter future, as he refuses to become a collaborator to save his own neck.

Finally, Sarah serves as a chorus to her husband and his beliefs. For instance, the narrator states: ". . . several times in her life she had seen the stars" (7). This description reveals that she shares glory and depression, success and failure, and joy and sorrow with her husband. Furthermore, she supports the mayor's leadership in organizing a resistance movement against the enemy. When Alexander Morden is executed, Sarah would prefer not to visit Molly, because she has "a hundred things" to do. But the mayor convinces her otherwise. "Yes . . . Yes, I will," she quickly agrees (46). Sarah, contrary to her own desires, thus becomes conscious of her husband's political and moral commitments and willingly accepts his imperative.

Like Sarah, Annie, the mayor's cook, participates in the mayor's resistance against the invaders. She, too, functions as a champion of resistance, fearlessly but cautiously supporting the mayor's leadership.

According to Steinbeck's narrator, "Annie was always a little angry . . ." (39), but her personal anger begins to reflect the public outrage of her people after the enemy battalion's invasion in effect imprisons every citizen. Mayor Orden highly values Annie as a source of essential information: "I don't know what I'd do without her . . . . She gets everywhere, she sees and hears everything" (83). Madame Orden, too, admits her dependency upon Annie's resourcefulness: "The people are down listening to the music. Annie told me" (9-10). A little later, Joseph tells Mayor Orden and Doctor Winter, "I heard—that is, Annie heard—" (10). And then Joseph reports, "Six men were killed, sir, by the machine guns. Annie heard three were wounded and captured" (11). When Annie visits Molly Morden with the mayor, she reports what she has just observed: "There's a soldier coming up the path. He looks like the soldier that was here before. There was a soldier here with Molly before" (86).

As the mayor's critical eyes and ears, she accurately reports what she has heard and observed; at the same time, she acts thoughtfully for her people against the invaders. Her actions often have political significance: Annie carries a little cake or meat for Molly when she visits with her and the mayor. Because the townspeople do not have much to eat then, her gift of food is a generous gesture of friendship and concern, but also a defiant political act: Annie proudly says to Molly, "I stole it from the colonel's plate. It's meat" (73). Eventually Annie becomes Orden's agent and spy—his most resourceful resistance fighter. At one point he asks Annie to stand guard while he and Doctor Winter meet at Molly's house with Will and Tom Anders just before the brothers' escape to England to join the international resistance movement: "He [Orden] turned to Annie . . . . 'Give us one knock for the patrol, one when it's gone, and two for danger'" (82). Annie's fearlessness and fury as well as her commitment to assist Mayor Orden in his resistance activities remind us of her gradual transformation from the mayor's cook to a first-class patriot—a magnificent fighter with a fiery spirit, an inspiration to her fellow citizens, and a comfort to Mayor Orden.

Steinbeck's characterization of Annie as a passionate patriot is suggested several times when she is described as angry and red-eyed (14, 17, 39, and 73). She is indeed a woman of action, as shown when she throws boiling water at some invaders who come to her back door. Unintimidated, she thus expresses the fury of her fellow citizens against the invaders while providing more comic relief as well as emotional purgation. "Annie was always a little angry . . . . Indeed, what for years had been considered simply a bad disposition was suddenly become a patriotic emotion" (39).

When Colonel Lanser finally arrests both Mayor Orden and Dr.

Winter, the mayor asks Annie to console his wife: "Annie, I want you to stay with Madame as long as she needs you"(114). Thus Annie proves to be the kind of person the mayor finds indispensable and trustworthy in this time of crisis.

Annie, like Sarah, functions as the mayor's chorus, but in that capacity she functions more capably and aggressively than the Mayor's wife. Annie is the unabashed voice of the resistance. She articulates Mayor Orden's fury, frustration, and determination to defend his citizens at any cost. Annie exemplifies, through her defiant spirit, the private citizen's fury that eventually prevails in the town. She foreshadows the growing public anger that will become overwhelming, as Tetsumaro Hayashi suggests (12-23).

Molly Morden also proves a capable resistance fighter, one just as determined and committed as Sarah Orden and Annie, but she plays an even more aggressive role than either of the other two women. Out of vengeance, she kills Lieutenant Tonder, one of the invaders, who wants to make love to her. (Tonder is unaware that she is the wife of Alex Morden, whom the lieutenant has executed.) The narrator describes Molly Morden as "pretty and young and neat. Her golden hair was done up on the top of her head and a blue bow was in her hair" (72). Given this description, it is hard to imagine—at least initially—that she is the kind of person capable of killing anyone, even her enemy. But her determination is fueled by her desire to avenge her beloved husband's untimely death. When Alex is arrested by the occupation forces and accused of murdering Captain Bentick, Molly visits Mayor Orden to defend her husband: "He's a quick-tempered man, but he's never broken a law. He's a respected man" (44). Molly's assessment of Alex is honest, but loving. Even the tart-tongued Annie calls Alex a nice man (40). When Molly discovers that Mayor Orden has no power to save Alex's life, she gradually becomes stronger and braver, without being conscious of her change, and begins to serve as a quiet but committed resistance fighter, while helping Mayor Orden to avenge her husband's death in a larger mission. Mayor Orden comes to trust Molly as a dedicated partisan. He chooses her house to meet with the Anders boys to plot their successful escape to England (74).

It is shortly after this secret meeting that Lieutenant Tonder visits Molly. When Tonder sees her, he begins to express his despair and loneliness. As he confesses his amorous feelings for her, he says, "I'm lonely to the point of illness. I'm lonely in the quiet and the hatred." And he also pleads, "Can't we talk, just a little bit?" (75). And he dedicates to her as his own the poem he has plagiarized from Heine. Just as the poem is false, so is his love. Though Molly immediately exposes the fact that he did not write the poem, she and Tonder are soon laughing together, as this episode humanizes and relaxes the relationship, tense as it may have been at the beginning: "He stopped laughing just as suddenly and a bleakness came into his eyes. 'I haven't laughed like that since forever'" (77).

This incident shows these two young people outside the context of military action simply as human beings—they are candid, sensitive, and lonely. If they had not been at war, and if Lieutenant Tonder had not participated in Alex's execution, they might have become intimate friends. Here Steinbeck reveals the irony and pathos of the war and occupation. Molly asks Lieutenant Tonder, "Do you want to go to bed with me, Lieutenant?... You are a civilized man," she says. "You know that love-making is more full and whole and delightful if there is liking, too.... My price is two sausages" (78). As these conversations reveal, lovelessness, loneliness, distrust, hatred, fear, depravity, and frigidity serve as repeated images in *The Moon Is Down*. Molly says to him, "You want to call it something else? You don't want a whore" (79). Lieutenant Tonder cries, "Please don't hate me. I'm only a lieutenant. I didn't ask to come here. You didn't ask to be my enemy. I'm only a man, not a conquering man" (79). He asks her only for love, friendship, and trust, but she can't accept him. When his hand rests on her shoulder (79), Molly says to him, "... [Y]ou took him [Alex] out and you shot him" (80).

Molly Morden, like Sarah and Annie, also functions as the mayor's chorus, but she has a special role. Like the other two women, she is thoughtful, active, and resourceful, but she reflects the concept of youthful love at the same time. The narrator says that she is a beautiful young woman with golden hair. Ironically, Lieutenant Tonder wants her to talk to him and wants to make love to her without knowing her to be one of the resistance fighters and the widow of a man he has executed. Molly loves Alex with all her heart not only as her husband but also as a patriot who fought for freedom and independence for his country in defiance of his enemy. It is impossible for Molly to love Lieutenant Tonder, the enemy, no matter how lonely and how tempted she might be. She cannot be kind to a man who has recently killed her beloved husband. The pathos of the situation is that two lonely human beings have to pretend to love while circumstances compel them to hate. Such a predicament conveys the spiritual depravity and alienation caused by the war. The narrator explains Molly's dilemma and determination: "... [S]he was holding them [the scissors] like a knife, and her eyes were horrified.... Her voice was strained and sweet. She called, 'I'm coming, Lieutenant, I'm coming!'" (87). Although she is tempted sexually, Molly still chooses to kill Lieutenant Tonder to avenge her husband's death, and thus proves a gallant resistance fighter. She controls her emotional needs and performs her mission.

Tetsumaro Hayashi has observed that "Steinbeck ends *The Moon Is Down* with an implicit but affirmative prediction: 'The sun shall rise again'" (12) even though the play-novel reveals a dark, fallen world. The novel greatly inspired and comforted fighting men and women in Europe—especially the anti-Nazi resistance fighters during World War II. *The Moon Is Down* proved to be a highly effective propaganda novel, as Donald V. Coers has testified:

> . . . [F]ew books have demonstrated more triumphantly the power of ideas against brute military strength, and few books in recent times have spoken with such reassurance to so many people of different countries and cultures . . . . *The Moon Is Down* was an inspiriting statement of faith that despite the darkness of their hour, freedom and decency would return. That power to inspire . . . remains today its signal distinction. (138)

Even if *The Moon Is Down* is merely a propaganda novel, it still reveals truths of the human heart, and it seriously explores how human beings should live in the face of overwhelming political and moral crises like those in occupied Europe during World War II. Mayor Orden exemplifies the proper course of action, enjoying the wholehearted support of three women: Sarah Orden, Annie, and Molly Morden, who enforce the themes of love, courage, integrity, outrage, and commitment. Thus Steinbeck gives these three female characters significant dramatic functions in *The Moon Is Down*. They achieve heroic stature through their intense involvement in the war and their audacious confrontation with the enemy. As "indestructible women" they represent oneness with the mayor's defiance against enemy oppression and dictatorship in *The Moon Is Down*.

Works Cited

Coers, Donald V. *John Steinbeck as Propagandist:* The Moon Is Down *Goes to War*. Tuscaloosa: U of Alabama P, 1991.

Hayashi, Tetsumaro. *Steinbeck's World War II Fiction,* The Moon Is Down: *Three Explications*. Steinbeck Essay Series, No. 1. Muncie: Steinbeck Research Institute, 1986.

Steinbeck, John. *The Moon Is Down*. 1942. New York: Bantam, 1973.

"The Boat-Shaped Mind": Steinbeck's Sense of Language as Discourse in Cannery Row and Sea of Cortez

Kevin Hearle

There is an understandable tendency among readers and critics to focus on John Steinbeck's formidable talent for describing actual places; however, any reading which analyzes Steinbeck's works as if they were primarily descriptive risks reducing those works to masterfully executed social documents. This essay is instead an attempt to read *Sea of Cortez* and *Cannery Row* as highly self-conscious works which are profoundly concerned with the power of discourse—literary and non-literary—to shape our understanding of the world.

Perhaps because *Cannery Row* opens with the declaration that "Cannery Row . . . is a poem" (111), critics have long acknowledged that it is a book obsessed with language. As Joseph Fontenrose points out, the Word dominates *Cannery Row*, giving it form and impetus. Specifically, Fontenrose (101-08) interprets the Word—which he notes is clearly derived from the biblical Logos, the Word made flesh—as being the instrument of the author, creating order out of chaos, and he gives as evidence the beginning of the second chapter of *Cannery Row*:

> The Word is a symbol and a delight which sucks up men and scenes, trees, plants, factories, and Pekinese. Then the Thing becomes the Word and back to Thing again, but warped and woven into a fantastic pattern. The Word sucks up Cannery Row, digests it and spews it out, and the Row has taken the shimmer of the green world and the sky-reflecting seas. Lee Chong is more than a Chinese grocer. He must be. Perhaps he is evil balanced and suspended by good . . . . (124)

Unfortunately for Fontenrose's argument, the relationship between Thing and Word here is neither as neat and tidy nor as sacral as his model of chaos into order or word into flesh would suggest. For one thing, Fontenrose's essentially realist model for the mimetic relationship between originating subject and resultant artistic reproduction is clearly not what Steinbeck is proposing. Instead, Steinbeck inverts the formula of the biblical Logos; therefore, since Cannery Row was, after all, a real place before it was ever a book, he delineates the metamorphosis of the flesh made word. Furthermore, the Word's transformation of the Thing "warp[s]" the flesh of existence "into a fantastic pattern," and this transformation is opposed grammatically to Fontenrose's simple chaos-into-order model by the conjunction "but." Then, in the next sentence, the metaphoric result of the transformation is that the world of the transformed Cannery Row is both beautifully shimmering and disgustingly fecal. As an extended metaphor for the process by which language represents the world, this metamorphic movement from food/place to feces/page highlights both language's basis in metaphor and its transfiguring power.

Furthermore, because this is a book, and because people think about the world in language, Steinbeck's narrator tells us that Lee Chong "must be" more than a fact; language will interpret him. "Perhaps" there will be an element of truth in that interpretation, but, to the extent that the truth of an interpretation will always be judged in the language of the interpretation, any interpretation will always be, by definition, contingent.

What Fontenrose's model ultimately fails to account for then is that for human authors, the creation of order is always, to some extent, prior to them and fictional. Each language is a conceptualization of the universe, one system among many possible systems, for breaking the world down into nameable, and therefore mentally manipulable, parts (Bakhtin 269-75).

If such a thing is possible, Steinbeck's self-consciousness about language is an even more intrinsic part of *Sea of Cortez*[1] (originally published in 1941) than it is of *Cannery Row*, which came after it (originally published in 1945). Although *Sea of Cortez* continues to be read primarily as both the most significant statement of Steinbeck's and Ed Ricketts's philosophy of non-teleological thinking, and as a realistic nonfiction account of a scientific expedition to the Gulf of California, Steinbeck's understanding of the power of discourse to shape human consciousness is palpable in *Sea of Cortez*.

The first two sentences of the Introduction establish "design" as the central problem of the work: "The design of a book is the pattern of a reality controlled and shaped by the mind of the writer. This is completely understood about poetry or fiction, but it is too seldom realized about books of fact."

At first, this idea of the author's mind as the force controlling the book seems to be contradicted in the very next paragraph:

> We have a book to write about the Gulf of California. We could do one of several things about its design. But we have decided to let it form itself: its boundaries a boat and a sea; its duration a six weeks' charter time; its subject everything we could see and think and even imagine; its limits—our own without reservation. (1)

This is not, however, as it first seems to be, a declaration that the book will be "natural" or "unstructured." Rather, as an analysis of its images reveals, it is a declaration that reality for each of us is "controlled and shaped" by the language we speak. As Louis Owens illustrates in *John Steinbeck's Re-Vision of America*, the ocean is a recurring symbol in literature in general and specifically in Steinbeck's works for the unconscious (159-63), and, in chapter 4 of *Sea of Cortez*, that symbology is explicit: "If one ask for a description of the unconscious, even the answer-symbol will usually be in terms of a dark water into which the light descends only a short distance" (31). Therefore, since the sea is one of the boundaries of the book, it seems reasonable to assume that Steinbeck's unconscious bounds *Sea of Cortez*.

Tracking down the symbology of the other boundary, the boat, leads us back again to language: "This is not mysticism, but identification; man, building this greatest and most personal of all tools, has in turn received a boat-shaped mind, and the boat, a man-shaped soul" (17). Ostensibly, this is about boats, but clearly language is the "greatest and most personal of all tools"; the tool which allows us to travel over, and not to drown in, the unconscious; and the tool which shapes our minds and is shaped by us in return.

Steinbeck plays off this boat imagery in both *Sea of Cortez* and in *Cannery Row*.[2] Steinbeck's use of Rimbaud is an important example. Rimbaud's drunken boat in "Le Bateau ivre" sought to achieve "le deréglèment de tous les sens," the goal which Rimbaud had stated as his larger poetic project in his "Lettres dites 'du Voyant.'" Rimbaud's recurring use of synaesthesia in lines such as "les rousseurs amères de l'amour," the repetition of "je sais" in conjunction with what are normally called sensory experiences, and the line "Et j'ai vu quelquefois ce que l'homme a cru voir!" all point to the deregulation of all the senses which Rimbaud called for in his epistolary manifesto.[3]

In *Cannery Row*, the references to Rimbaud appear in the section devoted to Henri, the painter who "regularly revolt[s] against outworn techniques and materials," and who "[o]ne season . . . threw out perspective" (244). Henri is like Steinbeck at the time he wrote *Cannery Row* in that he is an artist and that "he had been married twice and promoted a number of semipermanent liaisons" (245-46). More importantly, Henri is a boat builder and Hazel's fear that Henri might be crazy because he keeps changing the boat establishes a link between boat and mind much like that which Steinbeck delineated in *Sea of Cortez*. Furthermore, both Doc's "one great fear—that of getting his head wet" (138)— and his explanation for Henri's repeatedly starting over on the boat each time it nears completion—that "Henri loves boats but he's afraid of the ocean" (147)—reinforce the link between the language/boat and the fearsome ocean of the unconscious which Steinbeck sets up in *Sea of Cortez*:

> Among others, as even among ourselves, the giving of a name establishes a familiarity which renders the thing impotent. It is interesting to see how some scientists and philosophers, who are an emotional and fearful group, are able to protect themselves against fear. In a modern scene, when the horizons stretch out and your philosopher is likely to fall off the world like a Dark Ages mariner, he can save himself by establishing a taboo-box which he may call "mysticism" or "supernaturalism" or "radicalism." Into this box he can throw all those thoughts which frighten him and thus be safe from them. (56)

To top it all off, each time a wife or girlfriend leaves Henri, he gets drunk and "read[s] Rimbaud aloud with a very bad accent" (246).

Steinbeck's many references to the prodigious amounts of drinking they did on the *Western Flyer* (13, 24, 171) may thus be more than mere boasting. They appear to allude to the simultaneous desire to experience, and fear of experiencing—along with Arthur Rimbaud of "le deréglèment de tous les sens"—the world directly as the world itself, and not as the world mediated by language.

Mikhail Bakhtin makes a crucial distinction between "internally persuasive discourse" and "authoritative discourse" (342-48). Authoritative discourse, even though it originates outside a speaker's individual consciousness, provides categories for thought, and is thus like the "good hypothesis" which when elegantly completed is difficult to renounce even when it proves to be demonstrably false (*Sea* 182-84). Internally persuasive discourse is language which the speaker has made personal by testing its ideological and social limits.

Throughout *Sea of Cortez* there are cautionary tales about just such hardening of the discourses as occurs when someone accepts an authoritative discourse as "truth." In one humorous example, Steinbeck demonstrates his consciousness that, because discourses are by nature hegemonic, they will come into conflict with one another. Sparky Enea, a member of the crew, rejects the scientific name for a fish and calls it a skipjack, because he is uncomfortable with the idea of eating a "*Katsuwonus pelamis*" (51) for breakfast.

The problem, then, is to remain as open as possible to experience as experience, to break through the restrictions of any single discourse[4] (*Sea* 1-3), and to constantly remake language and thought itself. To accomplish this, "Henri never want[s] to finish his boat." Nor does he want to fix its identity by naming it, so, when asked, Henri tells people that he will "name it when it [is] finished" (*Cannery* 245). Like Henri when faced by this dilemma, Steinbeck and Ricketts understand that they must be suspicious of the very categories provided by language, and, more specifically, of the scientific system, taxonomy, for naming things:

> ... as one watches the little animals, definite words describing them are likely to grow hazy and less definite, and as species merges into species, the whole idea of definite independent species begins to waver, and a scale-like concept of animal variations comes to take its place. The whole taxonomic method in biology is clumsy and un-wieldy .... (208-09)

Repeatedly, *Sea of Cortez* makes clear how difficult it is to experience the world free of names and other limiting categories established by discourse:

> It is very easy to grow tired at collecting; the period of a low tide is about all men can endure. At first the rocks are bright and every moving animal makes his mark on the attention. The picture is wide and colored and beautiful. But after an hour and a half the attention centers weary, the colors fade, and the field is likely to narrow to an individual animal. Here one may observe his own world narrowed down until interest and, with it, observation, flicker and go out. And what if with age this weariness become permanent and observation dim out and not recover? (87)

Because the written word is virtually permanent, the categories provided by written discourse are even harder to escape than are the categories provided by spoken discourse. The fixity of written language is also inherently in conflict with a universe which is in constant flux. Thus it makes sense that most of the examples Steinbeck gives of the problem of rigid categories in language are about discrepancies between the written word and the "real" world. For instance, Steinbeck's descrip-tion of the penalties set down in the ship's charter for the *Western Flyer's* trip to the gulf and back emphasizes both the limitations and the rigidity of that particular legal document (9-10 and 19-20). His description of *The Coast Pilot* is also illustrative of the problem of authoritative discourse in a world of flux:

> This is a good careful description by men whose main drive is toward accuracy, and they must be driven frantic as man and tide and wave undermine their work ....
> These coast pilots are constantly exasperated; they are not happy

men. When anything happens they are blamed, and their writing takes on an austere tone because of it. No matter how hard they work, the restlessness of nature and the carelessness of man are always two jumps ahead of them. (108-09)

If anything, the difficulties inherent in the attempt to reconcile language with reality are even more poignantly revealed in the figure of Tony Berry, the captain. Tony, Steinbeck makes clear, is a realist who, because of his love for "truth" and his unswerving belief in the fixity of both that concept and of reality, does not easily accept change. The Gulf, however, as depicted by Steinbeck, is in many ways an "unreal" place constantly in flux. It is, in short, a place dominated by exactly "[t]he whole relational thinking of modern physics," which Tony finds obscene (20):

> Tony grew restive when the mirage was working, for here right and wrong fought before his very eyes, and how could one tell which was error? It is very well to say, "The land is here and what blots it out is a curious illusion caused by light and air and moisture," but if one is steering a boat, he must sail by what he sees, and if air and light and moisture—three realities—plot together and perpetrate a lie, what is a realistic man to believe? Tony did not like the mirage at all. (84)

Tony is without a doubt the realistic man of the passage, and even Steinbeck's acknowledgement of the power that Tony's certainty provides him in most situations—"His qualities made him a good master" (20)—is undercut. Clearly, Tony needs to act decisively, and because his knowledge is usually sufficient to allow him to make solid judgments, Tony's certainty about the nature of the world serves him well; however, "a good master" also has the connotation of master and slave. Tony, with his need for immutable "truth," is in one sense a slave of authority—he needs things to go by the book.

Lest we miss this conflict between the rigidity of written language and the flux of reality, Steinbeck also interpolates the story of the diarist who, having read about a city in Panama before visiting it, describes his visit to the city he had read about—despite the fact that the city had been destroyed in an earthquake and rebuilt at a different location (75). Furthermore, Steinbeck mentions previous visitors to the Gulf—young adventurers, romantics, and naturalists with rigidly defined specialties (5)—whose focus made it hard for them to see anything other than what they had come to see.

The problem then for any author who aspires to writing the "truth," to writing "non-fiction," is how to write against language, how to open it up to new conceptualizations of the world. As Mikhail Bakhtin expressed it in "Discourse in the Novel":

> Indeed, any concrete discourse (utterance) finds the object at which it was directed already as it were overlain with qualifications, open to dispute, charged with value, already enveloped in an obscuring mist—or, on the contrary, by the "light" of alien words that have already been spoken about it. It is entangled, shot through with shared thoughts, points of view, alien value judgments and accents. (276)

So-called "non-teleological thinking," (*Log* 135-55) with its rejection of cause-and-effect relationships and of definitive "answers" as simplistic, and with its self-awareness of its limitations, is the compromise solution which Steinbeck and Ricketts developed in reaction to the twin problems of limitation by discourse and limited attention spans. Non-teleological thinking for them is a process and not a result (*Log* xli).

Because the only truth is totality, and totality is beyond the scope of human attention, non-teleological thinking can make no claim to "truth," but neither does it allow its practitioners to delude themselves with the pretense of ultimate knowledge. What knowledge non-teleological thinking does provide is always provisional and aware of its limited scope. Also, because it is aware of the extent to which the processes it uses give form to its experience, non-teleological thinking tries to be multifarious in its methodologies. As a philosophy, it is discontinuous, multi-discursive, performative, and vigilantly aware of the structuring force of language.

The result of all this questioning—all this rewriting and rethinking of language, and this re-representing and re-viewing of reality—is first off the creation of a healthy anxiety about both representation and any too simple notion of reality. Ultimately, if the conceptualization of the world, that system of categories provided by any language, is merely a convenient fiction shared by the speakers of that language, and if those same conceptualizations—which we inherit as we learn to speak—shape our thinking about the world, what sort of knowledge can we claim to have about "reality," and what can terms such as "non-fiction" or "realism" possibly mean?

To answer that requires a return to Steinbeck's beginning of *Sea of Cortez*: "The design of a book is the pattern of a reality controlled and shaped by the mind of the writer. This is completely understood about poetry or fiction, but it is too seldom realized about books of fact." In short, this book, which readers begin reading as a piece of nonfiction, if read carefully—with strict attention to what Steinbeck has to say about the nature of language—ultimately forces readers to question whether or not there is any such thing as a "book of fact."

Although this withdrawal of even the possibility of certainty may seem frightening, Steinbeck forces attentive readers to ask themselves which is better—to live in a comfortably static delusion, or to live in a world which constantly challenges them to understand existence on its own terms. In *Sea of Cortez*, Steinbeck, like Rimbaud's boat as it floats off to sea, argues convincingly for a life of challenge.

In *Cannery Row*, however, Steinbeck seems to take a less optimistic, but more playful, view of language than he does in *Sea of Cortez*. In *Cannery Row*, his attitude seems closer to that of Rimbaud's boat on its return from the sea. From its beginning, the very existence of "Le Bateau ivre" as a text written mostly in the past tense (or as a fictively "oral" story told in the past tense) suggests that the attempt to experience the world directly, unmediated by language or any system of perception, will not be successful. The pastness of the narrative functions as a reminder that a totally distended being with all of its senses deregulated or deranged would have difficulty communicating at all, much less stringing together a narrative; therefore, the poem, by existing, negates the possibility of the ultimate success of its "deréglèment" project. Whatever truth there might be outside of language is irrecoverable, and *Cannery Row* is, after all, "a poem" (111).

Perhaps out of disgust for just this problem of the essential fictionality of language, Doc says in *Cannery Row*, "I guess everything that comes out of the human mouth is poison" (162). In fact, truth and language do not go well together in either *Sea of Cortez* or *Cannery Row*. In *Sea of Cortez*, as an explanation for their need to make up for the local Indians a plausible story for their expedition (102-03), Steinbeck tells a story which the narrator of *Cannery Row* repeats in slightly different words: one time when Doc walked from Chicago to Florida his attempts along the way to convince people of his real reason for the trip were met with such suspicion that, eventually, he began lying. "He said he was doing it on a bet—that he stood to win a hundred dollars. Everyone liked him then and believed him." The narrator moralizes, "Doc still loved true things but he knew it was not a general love and it could be a very dangerous mistress" (*Cannery* 213-14).

Still, language, for all its fictionality, is far from being a universally negative force in *Cannery Row*. Doc's relationship with Hazel, for instance, is a good example of how the conceptual ordering which language provides is useful. After briefly mentioning that he helps Doc collect specimens in the tidepools, and that he lives in the Palace Flophouse, Steinbeck's narrator tells us, "Hazel got his name in as haphazard a way as his life was ever afterward" (142). Thus, at first,

Steinbeck simply associates inattention to proper naming to Hazel's mental weakness. A bit later on, however, the narrator adds, "Hazel loved to hear conversation but he didn't listen to words—just to the tone of conversation. He asked questions, not to hear the answers but simply to continue the flow" (142-43).

Finally, and more importantly, Steinbeck suggests a more direct, perhaps almost cause-and-effect, relationship between Hazel's limited linguistic ability and his retardation:

> While he [Hazel] was looking for a question Doc asked one. Hazel hated that, it meant casting about in his mind for an answer and casting about in Hazel's mind was like wandering alone in a deserted museum. Hazel's mind was choked with uncatalogued exhibits. He never forgot anything but he never bothered to arrange his memories. (144)

Because language is the mind's cataloguing system (Bakhtin 291-92), the system which allows literate people to break down the continuum of existence into manipulable and therefore analyzable parts, and because Hazel's grasp of language is inadequate, his thinking is random or chaotic.

In this episode, Steinbeck again gives evidence of the subtlety of his understanding of language. In particular, he derives humor from the difference in modes of thinking between primarily oral and primarily chirographic or typographic cultures (Ong) by pairing the presumably illiterate Hazel (142) with the highly literate Doc. Hazel understands words, but he doesn't think analytically. He is unable to conceptually separate things from their physical contexts and then manipulate relationships between things in his mind. In fact, Hazel isn't trying to learn or communicate conceptually; his purpose in using language is strictly to establish contact with another person, so the meaning of the questions he asks repeatedly is unimportant. Doc, on the other hand, is highly analytical and uses language so purposefully to derive and to communicate meaning (143) that he cannot conceive of any other purpose—including, especially, a phatic purpose such as Hazel's—for asking and answering questions. Small wonder that loneliness, especially Doc's, is one of the novel's prevailing themes.

Doc's loneliness, both real and purported, provides the book with much of its plot structure. Upon moving into the Palace Flophouse at the end of the first chapter, Mack and the boys observe Doc going to Lee Chong's for beer. Mack says, "'That Doc is a fine fellow. We ought to do something for him'" (123). The rest of the book is woven around the attempts of the denizens of the Palace Flophouse to do something nice for Doc. And even though many of the incidents are humorous, this is not a comedy in the classical sense, because Doc does not get the girl at the end.

What Doc does get is the consolation of language and art. Despite the profusion of musical references—Count Basie (235), the melody Doc hears when he discovers the drowned beauty (219-21), three pieces by Monteverdi (240, 295), Benny Goodman trios (294), and two Gregorian chants (305)—the most obvious example of Doc being consoled by art is his recital of the Sanskrit poem "Black Marigolds" at the novel's conclusion.

Perhaps, however, the most important allusions to works of art in *Cannery Row* are those to Steinbeck's own earlier works. Joseph Fontenrose (108) long ago noted the similarities between Mac in *In Dubious Battle* and Mack in *Cannery Row*, but that is far from the sole example of Steinbeck's borrowing from Steinbeck in *Cannery Row*. For example, Gay does not make it to frogdom's epic battle with Mack and company because he gets mixed up in a bar fight with Sparky Enea and Tiny Colletti (179), two of the crew members from the *Sea of Cortez* voyage. The water snake from *Of Mice and Men* (7) reappears in *Cannery Row* as multiple water snakes with "heads held up like little periscopes" (187). Similarly, the paean to the Model T in *Cannery Row* (172-80, 184) especially its conversion to a truck, and the ready availability of replacement parts—are taken almost whole cloth from *The Grapes of Wrath* (95, 137, 241-53). Even the non-plot-centered chapters, which Steinbeck described in a letter as "those little inner chapters in *Cannery Row*" (Benson 2), serve a somewhat analogous purpose to the intercalary chapters of *The Grapes of Wrath*. *Cannery Row* is thus an assemblage of Steinbeck's fictions about the world.

Just as importantly, Steinbeck undercuts some of the very theories set forth in *Sea of Cortez*. Most of Doc's discussion with Richard Frost (251-54) about Mack and the boys being the "true philosophers" because "[t]hey can satisfy their appetites without calling them something else" is a redaction of Steinbeck's treatment of what he calls the "ethical paradox" in *Sea of Cortez* (97-98), that supposedly "good" qualities are not those which are rewarded by human society or nature.

Doc's idea about Mack's and the boys' not needing to rationalize their appetites is also, in this instance, demonstrably false. Mack and the boys decide that they should do something nice for Doc only after they notice him making one of his many trips to Lee Chong's for beer (123). Later, as they are planning the first party, Mack, admitting to himself that they will drink far more per person than will Doc, realizes that the party is more for their benefit than for Doc's (190-91). And even though he berates himself, "God damn it. I hate a liar," that this is merely another form of rationalization is clear from the way it echoes the language Mack uses during the previous episode with William the pimp. In that incident, Mack says, "But God damn it, I hate a pimp!" The narrator immediately comments on Mack's outburst, "Now this was obviously untrue although William didn't know that" (129). Mack is a liar, especially when he says that he hates a liar.

Despite what Doc thinks, rationalization is one of Mack's most fully developed talents. What's more, this rationalization is in opposition to the sort of continual observing, hypothesizing, and re-hypothesizing in which Doc engages. Thus, to the extent that Doc's assertion about Mack and the boys is true, that "they survive in this particular world better than other people" (251), it seems that Doc's efforts to be constantly open to experience as experience may be one of those virtues which go largely unrewarded.

Finally, *Cannery Row* is a comic novel composed of parts of other novels. And, in its assertion of the fictionality of even the most realistic of those versions of the world, Steinbeck's novel is, like Rimbaud's "Le Bateau ivre" (Fowlie 32), also ultimately a lament for a time or place in which it may have been possible to experience the world directly. Alone in his lab, Doc ends the book by reciting from the Sanskrit poem "Black Marigolds" a passage in which the poet acknowledges his experience of "the hot taste of life" and "[t]he whitest pouring of eternal light" (306). It is a wonderful passage, exemplifying the beauty of which language is capable; however, it is also, like "Le Bateau ivre," completely in the past tense.

The best Doc can hope for from language is beautiful consolation. And the Steinbeck who wrote all those works parodied and pasted together into *Cannery Row* has no more cause for hope than does Doc. *Cannery Row* is thus Steinbeck's funny, bittersweet reply to *Sea of Cortez*'s adventurous optimism about the continual challenge posed by the relationship between language and the world.

Notes

[1]Because the frequently reprinted *The Log from the* Sea of Cortez (first published by Viking in 1951) contains all of the narrative portions from the now difficult to find *Sea of Cortez* (published by Viking in 1941), all page references herein are to the readily available 1984 Viking Penquin edition of *The Log*.

[2]Although I disagree with its conclusion about the self-parody in *Sweet Thursday* being unique in Steinbeck's work, Owens's "Critics" is important for what it suggests about inter-textuality in Steinbeck's works.

[3]These titles and phrases translate into English as, respectively, "The Drunken Boat," "the de-regulation of the senses," "Letters Spoken to 'Seer,'" "the bitter

rednesses of love," "I know," and "And I saw sometimes that which the man believed he had seen."

[4]Steinbeck *Log* 5; and Marx 319-25. Leo Marx notes that Mark Twain had a related dilemma: he needed to find a language to describe the Mississippi which combined the factuality of the riverboat captain with the aesthetic sense of the young adventurer.

Works Cited

Bakhtin, Mikhail M. *The Dialogic Imagination: Four Essays.* Caryl Emerson and Michael Holquist, trans. Austin: U of Texas P, 1981.

Benson, Jackson J. *Steinbeck's* Cannery Row: *A Reconsideration.* Steinbeck Essay Series No. 4. Muncie: Steinbeck Research Institute, 1991.

Fontenrose, Joseph. *John Steinbeck: An Introduction and Interpretation.* New York: Holt, 1963.

Fowlie, Wallace. *Rimbaud.* Chicago: U of Chicago P, 1967.

Marx, Leo. *The Machine in the Garden.* New York: Oxford U P, 1967.

Ong, Walter J. *Orality and Literacy: The Technologizing of the Word.* London: Methuen, 1982.

Owens, Louis. "Critics and Common Denominators: Steinbeck's *Sweet Thursday.*" *The Short Novels of John Steinbeck: Critical Essays with a Checklist to Steinbeck Criticism.* Ed. Jackson J. Benson. Durham: Duke UP, 1990. 195-203.
_____. *John Steinbeck's Re-Vision of America.* Athens: U of Georgia P, 1985.

Rimbaud, Arthur. "Le Bateau ivre" *Poésies/Une saison en enfer/Illuminations.* Paris: Edition Gallimard, 1984.

Steinbeck, John. *The Grapes of Wrath.* New York: Viking, 1939.
_____. *In Dubious Battle.* 1936. New York: Penguin, 1987.
_____. *The Log from the* Sea of Cortez. 1951. New York: Penguin,1984.
_____. *Of Mice and Men/Cannery Row.* 1937. 1945. New York: Penguin, 1987.
_____. *Sweet Thursday.* New York: Viking, 1954.

Passages of Descent and Initiation: Juana as the "Other" Hero of The Pearl

Debra K. S. Barker

"My heart knows the truth, I speak truth, friends: whoever prays to the Only Spirit gives his precious heart to him. And isn't that beyond? And on earth are we born not twice? Yes, it's true. We live in the Place Unknown within the sky. And there alone is happiness."
—Song XVI, *Cantares Mexicano: Songs of the Aztecs*

In 1940, while visiting the Gulf of California, John Steinbeck was given the story of *The Pearl* by the Mexican Indians living there. In his retelling of this Indian legend, Steinbeck not only creates a story that has resonated powerfully in the American literary canon: he has preserved and passed on cultural and mythic elements that support the interpretive valencies of not only Kino's and Juana's roles in the story, but also that of the pearl and the quest for the real treasure of an individual's life. *The Pearl* is a story about a man who finds a pearl and nearly loses his soul; but it is also a story about initiation, death, sacrifice, and the heroism of a woman who confronts and overcomes death.

Juana, as a woman and a Native American, participates in an archetypal rite of passage which, although differing somewhat from the one Kino undergoes, nevertheless corresponds with his in suffering and loss, earning her scrutiny as another type of fully participating actor in the mythic story of the hero's journey. As Carol Pearson and Katherine Pope observe, "Until the heroic experience of all people—racial minorities and the poor as well as women—has been thoroughly explored, the myth of the hero will always be incomplete and inaccurate" (*Female Hero* 5).

Until very recently, critical attention to Juana's character in *The Pearl* has been cursory in comparison to that devoted to Kino, who is generally viewed as the one who grapples with the central conflict of the narrative and is transformed by his experience. When critics have discussed Juana, they have tended to view her as a type, categorizing her with Steinbeck's noble women: Ma Joad of *The Grapes of Wrath*, Rama of *To a God Unknown*, and Mary of *The Winter of Our Discontent*, for instance. Classifying Juana as a "good woman," Peter Lisca argues that Steinbeck creates narrowly confined roles for his female characters. In her study on Steinbeck's representation of women, Sandra Falkenberg singles out Juana as both "dynamic and memorable," worthy of "close study and critical attention" (1). John Timmerman and Mimi Gladstein, however, have devoted extensive attention to Juana. Gladstein makes the case that Juana is the "heroine" of *The Pearl*, symbolizing "the positive and nurturing qualities of woman" (50). Stronger spiritually and more determined than Kino, Juana is nevertheless drawn as a flat character whose status in the story is more symbolic than interactive or dynamic. Gladstein asserts that she is "a composite of all the best qualities of the archetypal feminine" (52). Also viewing Juana from a Jungian perspective, John Timmerman argues, rightfully, that Juana indeed has a role in the narrative and that her role has been "overlooked or misunderstood" ("The Shadow" 154). Timmerman regards Juana as a kind of figurative acolyte, an embodiment of the anima emanation which serves to bring Kino into reconciliation with the shadow, thus empowering him as he realizes "psychological harmony" with the story's denouement (160).

Even while complimenting Juana, readers nevertheless persist in marginalizing her as a supporting character whose status in the narrative is more symbolic than dynamic and whose experience still warrants less attention than Kino's. Further, no American critics have approached the character of Juana as a Native American woman whose experiences bear examination from a critical viewpoint decentered from past Euramerican perspectives.[1]

Numerous scholars have agreed that Steinbeck was drawn to the order of archetypal symbolic structures that can be found not only in Native American narrative conventions but also in the mythic forms investigated by Carl Jung. In his discussion of *The Pearl*, Peter Lisca explores Steinbeck's "persistent interest in man's mythopoeic heritage," citing Harry Slochower's observation that Steinbeck draws upon myth as a source of "the prototypes of human fate" (qtd. in Lisca 230).

In a letter to Pascal Covici, his editor at Viking Press, Steinbeck expressed his ongoing involvement with not only Jungian theory, particularly the notion of the collective unconscious, but also the use and application of Jungian patterns to illuminate human behavior. Steinbeck writes, "I have even gone into Jung's interpretation of the myth in a modern psychological sense. I rather think it has been necessary" (qtd. in DeMott 62).

John Timmerman suggests that Steinbeck's interest in Jungian theory informs the inception of *The Pearl*, and numerous other critics have likewise presented evidence of Jung's influence upon Steinbeck's representation of the mythic dimension of a range of his characters' inner lives ("Shadow").[2] Robert DeMott confirms Steinbeck's continuing reading of Jungian theory, noting that throughout his writing career, from

Murder at Full Moon to *America and Americans,* Steinbeck "drew on Jung's writings and theories for ritual actions, individual and collective psychological characterizations, natural symbolism and totemic imagery" (156). According to DeMott, Steinbeck not only owned and read Joseph Campbell's *The Hero with a Thousand Faces,* which was published two years after *The Pearl*: he also talked with Campbell on numerous occasions over the years and most particularly during the writing of *To a God Unknown.* In addition to myth and spirituality, one of the subjects Campbell and Steinbeck discussed, Campbell related to DeMott, was "the interpretation and use of symbolic forms" (138), one of the most common being the hero's passage into illumination, in Campbell's words, "the nuclear moment when, while still alive, he found and opened the road to the light beyond the dark walls of our living death" (259).[3]

Across cultures and throughout time, one of the central myths articulating the course of human fates is that of initiation, specifically the rite of "disenchantment," a metaphysical passage entailing not only the disintegration of identity but the shattering of the initiate's belief system. Various American Indian tribes, the Hopi people in particular, have ritualistically subjected their young people to this passage, during which the initiate is brought to realize that previously held beliefs and views of reality have been illusory or misrepresentative.

Hurled from the spiritual stasis of innocence into the travail of experience, Juana survives the ultimate initiation experience, transforming into a new being, a powerful character whose role is far more significant than readers have previously recognized. Two particularly important tableaus, when juxtaposed, reveal not only a qualitative change in the dynamics of Kino and Juana's relationship, but also the extent to which Juana's character has grown.

With the first tableau Steinbeck draws of Juana and Kino's relationship, Juana appears as a submissive figure trailing after her husband with a devotion nearly dog-like. Indeed, the narrator's choice of verbs suggests a subordinate status that is less than human. When they venture into La Paz to meet with the pearl dealers, for instance, Juana follows Kino, "trotting after him," (504); later, after he beats her, the narrator describes her as "creeping" along the beach after him (509). Then as they flee La Paz, we are told that her feet "pad" behind him (514).

In the second tableau, Juana's elevation to a status equal to Kino's is twice signalled in the final scene in the story, where the narrator mentions that as the two return to La Paz with their murdered infant, they "were not walking in single file, Kino ahead and Juana behind, as usual, but side by side" (526). In this emotionally charged scene, the narrator also reveals not only that Juana seems "removed from human

115

experience," but that her ordeal has scarred and aged both her face and her spirit: "Her face was hard and lined and leathery with fatigue . . ." (526).

This final scene stands as one of the story's most potent in terms of psychic weight, resonant with the soul-ache of profound bereavement. The scene, with its focus upon both Juana's stoicism and the equal footing with which the two return to their community, prompts us to consider that although Kino is represented as the protagonist and nominal hero of the story, Juana nevertheless undergoes a trial equal to or perhaps more momentous than his.

Critics have failed to explain the fact that Juana and Kino reenter the village walking side by side, rather than in single file, even though this is the first instance in the story in which we see the couple doing so. Readers have likewise failed to construe the nature of her trial or the significance of Juana's physical transformation. Upon several occasions the narrator takes special note of how Juana (but not Kino) has aged as a result of her ordeal: she goes out into the world a young girl—youthful, vital, and strong—yet returns an old woman.

In his synopsis of the narrative, Stanley J. Krause calls to mind both the elliptical structure and thematic imperative of classical tragedy: *The Pearl* is a story of "consuming greed" which concludes with "the stirring up of violent emotions, moral recognition, and a need of cleansing" after the pearl has aroused the baser natures of those who have coveted it (7-8). The central conflict of tragedy also necessarily entails the hero's confrontation with the danger of moral disaster before he or she becomes transformed, then initiated into a higher state of wisdom. Although it is Kino who must grapple directly with his moral crisis, Juana is the one who is called upon to transcend local and material concerns to come to terms with pressing metaphysical ones, the synchronism of good and evil, life and death. The narrator tells us that as assailants circle their hut, Kino protects his pearl while she sings "the melody of the family" to foil "the Song of Evil" (506). While Kino desires to leave the village to avoid the theft of his treasure, Juana reminds him of the inexorable law that will later obtain to their family: "A man can be killed. Let us throw the pearl back into the sea" (507). Clearly, Juana and Kino themselves represent the axiological dialectic of the narrative, assuming moral positions with the material ranged against the spiritual. Indeed, in his analysis of *The Pearl*, John Timmerman underscores the "spiritual dimension" of the conflict: "The spiritual significance rises from the story and extends beyond it rather than being imposed by the author" (*Steinbeck's Fiction* 194).

A carefully articulated definition of the nature of the type of heroism that Juana represents can be found in Carol Pearson's and Katherine

116

Pope's taxonomy of female heroes and heroines. Heroines include "The Virgin," "The Mistress," and "The Helpmate," the last of which corresponds to Joseph Campbell's category of "earth mother" (*Who* 2). The female heroes are "The Artist," "The Warrior," and "The Sage." An important difference between the two typologies lies with the self-definition of the female character: generally the heroine is "defined primarily in relationship to a man" (3). Passive, supportive, as well as one-dimensional, the heroine remains a stereotype, a flat character who neither asserts her will, nor reinvents herself within the confines of her role.

In the course of the narrative conflict Juana evolves from the role of "Helpmate" to that of "The Sage," a figure elevated to the status of hero because she possesses "wisdom beyond that of the culture." The culture, however, restricts her to "passive heroine roles," even though she "understands the world" and may be fully capable of contending with strife (*Who* 146). Such is certainly the case in Juana's circumscribed world, which is not only a colonized one but patriarchal as well.

Within the role she sustains with Kino, that of wife and helpmate, Juana nevertheless seizes numerous opportunities to assert her powerful will, spiritual vision, and enduring capacity to transcend her own ego to place the needs of her family first. All these traits distinguish her as not only a Hero-Sage, but as one who has syncretized her tribal culture with a modern, Christian one. Ironically, she is yet unaware of her power, deferring to Kino's position as her husband and later to the authority of the white doctor whose medicine she has been taught to believe is more potent than her own. It is Juana, for instance, who reacts quickly to suck the scorpion's poison from Coyotito's shoulder, then invoke the aid of the Christian God, as well as her older ones, with prayers and ceremonies. When they go out to dive for pearls, Juana makes "the magic of prayer, her face set rigid and her muscles hard to force the luck, to tear the luck out of the gods' hands" (483). The narrator notes the irony in the success of Juana's prayer: "She had not prayed directly for the recovery of the baby—she had prayed that they might find a pearl with which to hire the doctor to cure the baby . . ." (482).

As she witnesses Kino's moral deterioration, growing more alarmed as his obsession with the pearl threatens to consume him, she finally begs him to renounce the jewel: "It will destroy us all," Juana prophesies. "Even our son" (496). With Kino's rejection of her entreaties, she performs another ceremony, lighting a candle and crooning the old songs, seeking to bring the sacred into ascendancy within the realm of the secular to foil the evil forces of man and nature operating upon the ordinary world of existence.

As Hero-Sage, Juana possesses a spiritual identification with the natural world that affords her a special insight into its power. She does not have to be told about the trees in the desert that blind and bleed, bringing bad luck. Likewise, she soon recognizes the ineffable power exerted by the pearl, a jewel of the sea which archetypally suggests the emotional depths of the unconscious. When the venom of greed poisons the natures of those from whom they have sought help, she instinctively questions the real value of the pearl in relation to all they must sacrifice for it. Juana says, "Perhaps the dealers were right and the pearl has no value. Perhaps this has all been an illusion" (515).

In *Images and Symbols: Studies in Religious Symbolism*, Mircea Eliade articulates the symbolic value that pearls have held for indigenous cultures in both North and Meso-America, as well as in Asia and Europe, noting that pearls had been associated with the "sacred powers...concentrated in the Waters, in the Moon and in Woman" (125). Because of a perceived metaphorical correspondence between female sexual organs and sea shells, as well as the fetus and the pearl, pearls came to be viewed as "an emblem of absolute *reality*." Consequently, shells and pearls were incorporated into the ceremonies celebrating experiences of passage undergone by members of the community: birth, initiation, marriage, and death. According to Eliade, the indigenous people of both North and South America used pearls and shells in funeral rites (144). Interestingly enough, in other ritualistic contexts, pearls were used to cure cases of madness and melancholy, as well as poisoning (145-46).

Over time, however, the original "metaphysical meaning" of pearls has pejorated with the commercial value they have gained as ornaments. Eliade points out that "archetypal images keep their metaphysical valencies intact in spite of later 'concrete' re-valorisations" (144-48). Accordingly, the powerful symbolism of pearls has been recovered and sustained within Western religious traditions, particularly in the Gnostic scriptures, as pearls in their sacred aspect came to be associated with the purity of Christ and the salvation of God (148-49).

In its profane aspect the pearl of Steinbeck's tale evokes the latent materialism of Kino's character, while also stirring the potent forces of the greed and violence within the natures of those obsessed with wrenching the treasure from Kino's grasp. First singing the song of hope, promise, and security for Kino and Juana's future, the pearl comes to sibilate the music of evil and untold suffering. By the end of the story Kino finally recognizes "the music of the pearl" as "distorted" and "insane." As Stanley Krause points out, Kino's own moment of recognition of Juana's prescience is dramatized by his first offering to her the chance to cast the pearl back into the Gulf (6).

Pearson and Pope observe that in the case of the Hero-Sage, the female hero often goes unrecognized by the primary male figure in her life who "epitomizes the blindness of the patriarchy to female wisdom and strength" (*Female Hero* 243). The narrator of *The Pearl* acknowledges both Kino's blindness and Juana's strength: "Sometimes the quality of woman, the reason, the caution, the sense of preservation, could cut through Kino's manness and save them all" (508). Throughout the story, Kino ignores Juana's insistence that the pearl is the source of the evil that threatens their lives; and no more powerfully is Kino's blindness illustrated than when he beats and kicks her after coming upon her as she attempts to throw the pearl into the sea. Echoing Tetsumaro Hayashi's observation of Juana's instinctive wisdom in allowing Kino's plan to run its course to its tragic conclusion (86), Pearson and Pope note that the Sage-Hero is keenly aware of "the spiritual dimension of life" since she "ministers to the family's physical needs" and is "more keenly aware of transience and death than a man may be" (*Who* 146).

Transience and death are clearly important motifs of the story, as is that of the journey or quest. In *The Pearl* the journey is forced upon Juana and Kino; but as Joseph Campbell notes, the heroes of a quest are sometimes reluctant to surrender the known and familiar for the unknown future. Frequently, quests entail descent experiences during which the questor actually or symbolically dies and then is reborn or resurrected, as in the case of Jonah, the prophet Mohammed, or the Bear Man of Cherokee legends who resurrects in the spring. What heroes inevitably undergo during this process is the dissolution of identity, the sacrificing of the old self for a new one.

In *The Hero with a Thousand Faces*, Joseph Campbell divides the journey of the hero into three stages: the departure, the initiation, and the return. The departure of Juana and Kino is prompted by the assailants who have burned their home and destroyed their canoe, leaving them no choice but to flee their village to seek material salvation in the capital city. Steinbeck comments, in a phrase reminiscent of the book of Genesis, they "went out into the world" (513). Crossing a wasteland, they travel a nightmare where "the evils of the night" surround them, where trees bleed and blind those who dare touch them, where toads like tiny "dragons" stand guard. Everywhere the natural world represents an experiential zone of danger, pain, and horror.

The initiation of Juana takes place in a mountain cave where she and Coyotito hide while Kino attempts to ambush the trackers. Holding her child, the narrator tells us, "Juana whispered her combination of prayer and magic, her Hail Marys and her ancient intercession, against the black unhuman things" (523). Caves and mountains are traditionally feminine, archetypal symbols of passage. More importantly, mountains, as topographical regions of ascension, suggest points of epiphany, according to Northrop Frye. It is here where "the cyclical world of nature" and the "apocalyptic" realm meet (203). Although he mentions neither Juana's ordeal nor the story's cave as a site of transformation, John M. Ditsky does note in "Music from a Dark Cave: Organic Form in Steinbeck's Fiction" that the cave generally serves as an "earth-womb" where one may prepare oneself "for eventual reappearance or . . . for death" (63).

Caves, as womb symbols, suggest the threshold conjoining one state to the next, what Campbell refers to as the "sphere of rebirth . . . symbolized in the worldwide womb image of the belly of the whale. The hero, instead of conquering or conciliating the power of the threshold, is swallowed into the unknown, and would appear to have died" (90). Rather than endure her own physical death or dismemberment (as have other heroes, such as Osiris or Christ, for instance), Juana must suffer the loss of the child of her body as a stray bullet fired from below shoots off the top of Coyotito's head. It is here where she ventures to that numinous point of the interpenetration of life and death. After bringing the child into the world and then later snatching him from death by sucking the scorpion poison from his shoulder, Juana—acting as a type of metaphysical midwife—attends to the infant as he again crosses the threshold between the worlds of being and non-being.

In the last stage of the journey, the return, Juana and Kino go back to their village, profoundly bereft not only of the thing they loved most, their child, but also of their innocence and their dreams. Northrop Frye places quest stories like Juana's into the second phase of tragedy. It is, he says,

> the tragedy of innocence in the sense of inexperience, usually involving young people . . . . In many tragedies of this type the central character survives, so that the action closes with some adjustment to a new and more mature experience. (220)

Frye also notes that in such stories the survivors are frequently adults who are "educated through the death of a child" (220). For Juana the trial has meant her confrontation and acceptance of the fundamental truths about life and the human condition: the ineluctability of evil and death. Meanwhile, she has also attended Kino in his own passage into maturity, watching him move from the boyish arrogance of untested innocence to the bitter acceptance of his own cupidity.

With the return of the hero ensues what Campbell calls the hero's "recognition," in which his or her "true character is revealed" (329), after which the hero is drawn back into the matrix of his or her community. As feminist critics, Carol Pearson and Katherine Pope view the recognition and acceptance of the notion of a female hero as tantamount to a declaration of optimism in a world of modern literature, devoid of myth and full of male anti-heroes who feel increasingly more helpless in what they perceive to be a fragmented universe.

Pearson and Pope argue that the female heroes, on the other hand, effect a transformation from passivity to action "to reveal their true, powerful, and heroic identities" (*Female Hero* 13). Juana's "heroic identities" are realized with a spiritual transformation that brings her to a kind of apotheosis and a transcendence that affords her a point of view from which she has apprehended eternal truths that lie beyond the temporal field of human experience. The narrator speculates that it is as if she had "gone through pain and had come out on the other side"; he observes that Juana's "wide eyes stared inward on herself. She was as remote and as removed as Heaven" (526). With the paradox of the inwardness that is as remote as Heaven, the narrator expresses the numinous quality of Juana's awakening of consciousness. She looks inward because she knows that the source of evil lies not in pearls but, rather, in the human heart.

With the simile "as Heaven," Steinbeck suggests apotheosis and Juana's ascension to a higher, more divine order of consciousness. The myth of apotheosis, as it relates to self-realization, entails the liberation of the individual from roles which may confine his or her nature. In Annis Pratt's words, the culmination of rebirth journeys "create[s] transformed, androgynous, and powerful human personalities out of socially devalued beings..." (142). For Juana the crisis of the pearl and the death of her son help transform her into an acknowledged equal partner in her marriage as she evolves from Help-mate to Hero. Thus, the concluding tableau of the story points to Juana's recognition of her rebirth as she takes her place alongside Kino when they re-enter the village. Clearly, the profound nature of her suffering has elevated her in both spiritual and secular respects.

Sensing an "almost magical protection about them," the townspeople run to meet them, yet fall silent at the dramatic appearance of the bereft couple carrying "two towers of darkness with them" (526). With the return to the community comes the return to order and the renunciation of the pearl as Juana bequeaths to Kino the opportunity to hurl it back into its watery origins, where, the narrator says, "... the music of the pearl drifted to a whisper and disappeared" (527).

With the conclusion of the parable the narrator recalls, "Everyone in La Paz remembers the return of the family .... It is an event that happened to everyone" (526). This pronouncement suggests that Kino and Juana's story has since become woven into the fabric of the community's history. In native cultures, the story of the individual becomes the story of the group, indelibly inscribed upon the tribal imagination. The couple's great attempt and tragic failure to transcend their poverty, achieve their dreams, and escape the ubiquitous greed that sucked them into a maelstrom of panic, violence, and death has ultimately robbed them of not only their innocence, but also the real treasure of their lives, their baby son.

Meeting them at the city's edge, the townspeople see reflected in Kino's and Juana's faces the dreams and nightmares of the community. In pointing out that the event of the couple's return "happened to everyone" (526), the narrator suggests the collective participation in the scapegoat phenomenon. In her study of the scapegoat archetype, Jungian analyst Sylvia Brinton Perera points out that the scapegoat "serves a transpersonal, atonement purpose that is felt to be essential for the sustenance of the group's life and well-being" (49). To the group, Kino and Juana represent an object lesson in the way humankind victimizes itself; and to a certain extent Juana's role is that of the scapegoat with a primary source of dignity rooted in profound suffering, analogous to that of the Virgin Mary, the primary *Mater Dolorosa*.

Steinbeck stresses the necessity of suffering, as well as joy, in order to live more fully and enlarge our capacity to embrace humanity. In *Sea of Cortez* he observes that "it is through struggle and sorrow that people are able to participate in one another"; otherwise, he says, we would be "heartless" (117). It is the song of the enlightened heart and of the heroic spirit that the parable of *The Pearl* ultimately sings, recognizing not only the mystery of the journey of life but also the courage of the sojourner.

Notes

[1]Scant critical attention has been directed to Steinbeck's representation of Indian people throughout his works. See Britch and Lewis.

Interestingly enough, Steinbeck apparently realized the importance of framing the film version of *The Pearl* with music derived from the Aztec roots of Juana's and Kino's culture. In a letter to Elizabeth Otis, he writes, "These themes are ancient Indian music long preceding the Conquest. And I think they are beautiful" (*Life* 281).

[2]See also May; Lewis, "Jungian Psychology"; and Stone.

[3]For an account of the friendship that grew between John Steinbeck, Ed Ricketts, and Joseph Campbell during the early 1930s in Carmel and Monterey, see Larsen and Larsen.

Works Cited

Britch, Carroll, and Cliff Lewis. "Shadow of the Indian in the Fiction of John Steinbeck." *Rediscovering Steinbeck: Revisionist Views of His Art, Politics and Intellect.* Ed. Cliff Lewis and Carroll Britch. Lewiston: Mellen, 1989. 127-54.

Campbell, Joseph. *The Hero with a Thousand Faces.* Princeton: Princeton UP, 1949.

DeMott, Robert J. *Steinbeck's Reading: A Catalogue of Books Owned and Borrowed.* New York: Garland, 1984.

Ditsky, John M. "Music from a Dark Cave: Organic Form in Steinbeck's Fiction." *Journal of Narrative Technique* 1 (1971): 59-67.

Eliade, Mircea. *Images and Symbols: Studies in Religious Symbolism.* Trans. Philip Marret. New York: Sheed, 1961.

Falkenberg, Sandra. "A Study of Female Characterization in Steinbeck's *The Pearl.*" *Steinbeck Quarterly* 8 (1975): 50-56.

Fontenrose, Joseph. *John Steinbeck: A Critical Essay.* Grand Rapids: Eerdmans, 1970.

Frye, Northrop. *Anatomy of Criticism: Four Essays.* Princeton: Princeton UP, 1957.

Gladstein, Mimi Reisel. "Steinbeck's Juana: A Woman of Worth." *Steinbeck Quarterly* 9 (1979): 49-52.

Hayashi, Tetsumaro. "*The Pearl* as the Novel of Disengagement." *Steinbeck Quarterly* 7 (1974): 84-88.

Krause, Stanley J. "*The Pearl* and 'Hadleyburg': From Desire to Renunciation." *Steinbeck Quarterly* 7 (1974): 3-18.

Larsen, Stephen, and Robin Larsen. *A Fire in the Mind: The Life of Joseph Campbell.* New York: Doubleday, 1991.

Lewis, Clifford. "Jungian Psychology and the Artistic Design of John Steinbeck." *Steinbeck Quarterly* 10 (1977): 84-97.

Lisca, Peter. *The Wide World of John Steinbeck.* New Brunswick: Rutgers UP, 1958.

May, Charles E. "Myth and Mystery in Steinbeck's 'The Snake': A Jungian View." *Criticism* 15 (1973): 322-35.

Pearson, Carol, and Katherine Pope. *The Female Hero in American and British Literature.* New York: Bowker, 1981.

_____. *Who Am I This Time?: Female Portraits in British and American Literature.* New York: McGraw, 1983.

Perera, Sylvia Brinton. *The Scapegoat Complex: Toward a Mythology of Shadow and Guilt.* Toronto: Inner City, 1986.

Pratt, Annis. *Archetypal Patterns in Women's Fiction.* Bloomington: Indiana UP, 1981.

Steinbeck, John. *The Pearl. The Short Novels of John Steinbeck.* New York: Viking, 1963. 473-527.

_____. *Sea of Cortez.* New York: Viking, 1941.

_____. *Steinbeck: A Life in Letters.* Ed. Elaine Steinbeck and Robert Wallsten. New York: Viking, 1975.

Stone, Donal. "Steinbeck, Jung, and *The Winter of Our Discontent.*" *Steinbeck Quarterly* 11 (1978): 87-96.

Timmerman, John H. *John Steinbeck's Fiction: The Aesthetics of the Road Taken*. Norman: U of Oklahoma P, 1986.

_____. "The Shadow and the Pearl: Jungian Patterns in *The Pearl*." *The Short Novels of John Steinbeck: Critical Essays with a Checklist to Steinbeck Criticism*. Ed. Jackson J. Benson. Durham: Duke UP, 1990. 143-61.

The Wayward Bus: *Misogyny or Sexual Selection?*

Brian Railsback

John Steinbeck indicated that he wrote with several levels of meaning intended; he noted "five layers" in *The Grapes of Wrath* and "four levels of statement" in *Sea of Cortez* (Fensch 20, 31). As subsequent criticism has shown, his works can indeed be understood on many levels, from realism to allegory. However, the most consistent and original level of meaning in his work is his scientific, biological message. Steinbeck wants to understand the human as a species, as an *animal*; this fundamental and unsettling desire runs beneath the sometimes contradictory philosophy and politics of his work like a subterranean river. "It is not observed that I find it valid to understand man as an animal before I am prepared to know him as a man," writes Steinbeck in an oft-quoted response to his critics; "It is charged that I have somehow outraged members of my species by considering them part of a species at all" ("Postscript" 307). With such a perception of the human being, we should not be surprised that he was influenced by the work of the naturalist who brought this species view to the world in the nineteenth century: Charles Darwin.

Steinbeck probably read *The Origin of Species*, and the novelist certainly reviewed Darwin's journal of the *Beagle* voyage, which provided the naturalist with the evidence necessary for the theory of evolution (see DeMott 32 and Railsback). Thanks to Robert DeMott's *Steinbeck's Reading: A Catalogue of Books Owned and Borrowed*, we know that Steinbeck also would have been exposed to many Darwinian concepts from his reading of such evolutionists as Henri Bergson, John Elof Boodin, and Jan Christian Smuts. In *The Log From the* Sea of Cortez, Steinbeck praises Darwin as a naturalist and a man. The novelist hoped that his and Ed Ricketts's expedition aboard the *Western Flyer* would resemble the naturalist's: "In a way, ours is the older method, somewhat like that of Darwin on the *Beagle*" (61). Steinbeck's Darwinian view of *Homo sapiens* is most apparent in works like *The Grapes of Wrath* or *In Dubious Battle*, where the civilized veneer of landowners or the political labels of strike organizers fade against the brutal reality of animalistic struggles for territory.

Steinbeck applies Darwinian concepts of competition and survival to violence and war, creating a disturbing picture of the human as animal. The novelist extends this conception of *Homo sapiens* into the exalted sphere of love, just as Darwin did three quarters of a century before. Because of Darwin's and Steinbeck's biological perspective, their consideration of sex is cold and brutal. The naturalist's theory of sexual selection in *The Descent of Man* and the novelist's dramatization of that theory in *The Wayward Bus* invite criticism. Steinbeck's portrayals of male and female relations have earned him the label of misogynist. However, as in all things with this author, before we label him, we must consider the scientific implications of his work.

The most serious examination of Steinbeck's misogyny occurs in "*The Wayward Bus*: Steinbeck's Misogynistic Manifesto?," by Bobbi Gonzales and Mimi Gladstein. This essay, although a challenging and engaging one, operates from the debatable thesis that the novel is misogynistic because of Steinbeck's personal troubles at the time he wrote it, during his difficult marriage to Gwyndolyn Conger. The biographical facts simply do not support the notion that Steinbeck wrote the novel as some pointed attack on his wife and women in general. As Gonzales and Gladstein acknowledge, *The Wayward Bus* was dedicated to Gwyn, and their "relationship seemed satisfactory and secure for, during the process of writing the book, their second son John was born" (Gonzales 157). Indeed, in a letter written while he was working on the book, Steinbeck reported that Gwyn liked what she had read of the novel and, along with Pat Covici, she was the only one to have seen any of it (Benson 582). How could she miss even a veiled attack in a manuscript being written by her husband? This book also came out in the same year as *The Pearl* (1947), in which we find Steinbeck's creation of Juana. As Gladstein writes in an article for the monograph *Steinbeck's Women*, Juana is "After Ma Joad . . . the most positively depicted woman in Steinbeck's works" (49). Following the divorce in 1948 (a year after *Bus* was published), while Steinbeck was most bitter, he began the screenplay for *Viva Zapata!* In 1949, he also began work on *Burning Bright* (published in 1950). Sandra Beatty finds the women in these productions—Josefa in *Zapata* and Mordeen in *Bright*—to be individual and complex creations with some of the most positive characteristics portrayed in Steinbeck's women. Whatever animosity Steinbeck felt toward women apparently evaporated quickly (a process certainly hastened by his meeting Elaine Scott, his third wife, in the spring of 1949).

During the late summer and early fall of 1948, when Steinbeck was living a self-described nightmare at the cottage in Pacific Grove, and when Mildred Lyman of McIntosh and Otis noted his strange views about women (and his letters during the period do reveal misogynistic attitudes), Steinbeck seems to have refused to let the venom get into his work. In a letter to Joe and Charlotte Jackson, Steinbeck tells that he wrote a "completely evil" story that was very effective—but he burned it right away (*Life* 336-37). Perhaps this story was his misogynistic manifesto; in any event, he knew it to be unsuitable. As for the letters, where he vented his fury to his friends, we should recall that these were never meant for publication. Like the wicked story he wrote and destroyed, they represent the kind of rage typical of anyone dealt a bitter divorce and the death of a close friend (Ed Ricketts was killed in an accident in May, 1948). Despite the tension between John and Gwyn during their four years together, little evidence suggests that Steinbeck chose *The Wayward Bus* to be his misogynistic manifesto.

Yet the Gonzales/Gladstein article raises some important questions. What can we make of *The Wayward Bus*, where "women are seen by the men in their lives as serving only one purpose: they are sex objects, objectified to the extreme, there to satisfy a basic animal drive" and where "None of the sexual couplings in the novel is contextualized in a way that could be characterized as loving" (Gonzales 159)? There is a streak of brutality in Steinbeck's darker view of male/female relationships, but it is an extension of his biological view of *Homo sapiens*. We must look at the biological substructure of what he does before we pass judgment; in matters of sex, particularly in *The Wayward Bus*, his views parallel Charles Darwin's.

Although no evidence suggests Steinbeck read Darwin's *The Descent of Man*, in which the naturalist discusses his theory of sexual selection, the novelist could have learned of it from Smuts's summary in *Holism and Evolution* or from the brief sketch in *The Origin of Species*. Steinbeck's thinking on the subject might have been further refined by his reading Robert Briffault, who of course was well steeped in the theories of Charles Darwin (DeMott lists Briffault's *The Making of Humanity* and *The Mothers: The Matriarchal Theory of Social Origins* among books read by Steinbeck). Looking today at Darwin's biological view of sex, we would find it objectionable—its dramatization in Steinbeck's fiction can be downright disturbing.

In the typical Darwinian process, the naturalist discusses his theory of sexual selection as it pertains to all species, including *Homo sapiens*. His theory extends competition to sexual matters, so the most successfully competitive male will dominate other males and win the most desirable female (most likely to produce offspring). In generation after generation, the strongest of the species will win the right of procreation. Since the burden of attracting and winning a female falls upon the male, selection will have the most profound effect on him. Darwin thus explains why in so many species the male has the greatest size, the most strength, and the most profound adornment. Arriving at humans in his discussion, Darwin writes, "There can be little doubt that the greater size and strength of man, in comparison with woman, together with his broader shoulders, more developed muscles, rugged outline of body, his greater courage and pugnacity, are all due in chief part to inheritance from his half-human male ancestors" (872). In his consideration of the effects of sexual selection on humans, Darwin's writing seems never more open to debate. He feels that sexual selection has played an important role in what he describes as the differing mental powers of men and women. The naturalist finds man's mental capacity generally to be superior to woman's, due to the sharpening of competition, so that the "chief distinction in the intellectual powers of the two sexes is shewn by man's attaining to a higher eminence, in whatever he takes up, than can woman" (873).

This conception of man and woman is at times demonstrated in Steinbeck's writing. For Darwin, as well as Steinbeck, man is the competitor, the striver, while woman is the vessel of compassion, the maternal life preserver. Perhaps this view explains why, as Peter Lisca, Beatty, and Gladstein have observed, Steinbeck's women tend to be either prostitutes or mothers. Although a very narrow perception of women, it does not come from a misogynist determination, but rather from some seriously flawed inductive reasoning. And, as in the cases of Elisa Allen of "The Chrysanthemums" or Curly's wife in *Of Mice and Men*, the limitations of these "natural" roles are poignantly recognized by the author.

The best place to find Steinbeck's expression of the sexual human is *The Wayward Bus*, a novel conjuring up his darker view of *Homo sapiens*, to be sure, but hardly a misogynistic manifesto. What *In Dubious Battle* is to conflict, *The Wayward Bus* is to sex. Wrapped tightly in civilized lies, the characters practice a cultivated denial of sex or they are duped—even victimized—by the primped-up commercial hype of this biological act. In a spring environment charged with fecundity, the bus takes a wrong turn, stalls in the mud, and the repressed animal desires of a group of people are loosed in a primitive setting. Both men and women represent points on a scale; those who know the illusion they have been living rank highest, those who cannot fall low, little better than frustrated beasts. Steinbeck examines these characters, made neurotic by a culture that glosses a biological reality, and sees what becomes of them when the artificial governors have been removed. This stark portrayal of the naked *Homo sapiens* is certainly neither romantic nor beautiful.

Like *In Dubious Battle*, *The Wayward Bus* is unpleasant—as Steinbeck knew it to be. Before writing the book Steinbeck thought he would create something like *Don Quixote*, about "a cosmic bus holding sparks and back firing into the Milky Way . . . *The Wayward Bus* will be a pleasant thing" (*Life* 284). His opinion of the novel changed after its completion, and his comment about it to friend Jack Wagner nearly two years later echoes that of his ugly strike novel: "I hope you will like it although 'like' is not the word to use. You nor anyone can't *like* it. But at least I think it is effective" (*Life* 296). If, as Gonzales and Gladstein assert, *The*

Wayward Bus is an ugly look at "Everywoman," it is an equally unflattering look at Every*man*. Steinbeck spares neither sex.

Gonzales and Gladstein rightly observe that Juan Chicoy is "The touchstone of masculinity in the novel" (166). Although past his prime (about 50), he remains in good physical shape, he is the driver of the bus, and he is in control of his own sexuality. While "a fine, steady man," Juan is probably the least grand among those whom we might identify as Steinbeck's heroes. Like everyone else in the novel, Juan is frustrated and, though a good mechanic and a good enough man, he lacks the vision to do much about his situation. Juan is trapped, like his wife, Alice, in Rebel Corners, and it will be his sentence to run the bus on its route year after year. Juan's compassion is also limited in scope, partly demonstrated by the cold way he regards Alice, whom he has conditioned to enjoy his beatings. Clearly, the Chicoys function on a primitive level which Steinbeck has never portrayed as the most admirable place for his characters. Juan plans to escape Rebel Corners, and he thinks of stranding the bus on the muddy road, perhaps just walking away from it forever. He tries to get away, goes as far as a barn down the road, and finds—like Pat Humbert of *The Pastures of Heaven*—that his course is utterly circumscribed. He does have control over his sexual impulses, understands them, and therefore places high on the scale of sexual selection—rather like a seasoned stallion.

If Juan and Alice were the only characters of *The Wayward Bus*, it might indeed be a misogynistic manifesto. However, there are women in the book who equal Juan, if not surpass him, in potential and sexual power. Juan eventually seduces Mildred Pritchard, but not without her reciprocal selection of him. Steinbeck describes Mildred as young, strong, and intelligent. She has a healthy sexual appetite, which she is not afraid to satisfy (she has "consummated" two affairs). Mildred is still largely inexperienced, has "variable" convictions, although "She had undertaken causes and usually good ones" (44). Youthful, healthy, and open, Mildred is one of the few characters in the novel whose life has not settled into a pattern. Disgusted with her parent's quarrel, she walks down the road, in the same direction as Juan, with the same idea: "Suppose Mildred didn't come back? Suppose she walked on and caught a ride and disappeared..." (176). Upon meeting, Juan and Mildred engage in some perfunctory love-making, a mockery of all the trumped up preliminaries in movies and magazines: "Aren't you going to make a pass at me?" Mildred asks; "Yes, I guess so," Juan responds (182). To make things look acceptable, Mildred asks to be forced a little—although both know such forcing is not necessary. They have selected each other for the act, absurdly go through some theater, and then fulfill their desires in one of Steinbeck's typically primitive settings: a barn, next to an abandoned farmhouse given up to the weeds. Mildred knows the whole little affair was half-wrapped in fantasy and romance but she comes away clean and unaffected: "I wish it could go on a little more . . . but I know it can't. Good-by, Juan" (198). Juan and Mildred use each other and know it; both seem satisfied. She leaves free and, in a sense, still becoming; Juan goes back to his bus.

For sheer sexual power, Camille Oaks is the strongest character in the novel; ironically, she is a victim of her own strength, a victim of competition and selection. As Gonzales and Gladstein have already observed, "Steinbeck's explication of Camille is a case study of Darwinian naturalism" (162). Men react to her as if they unconsciously sense pheromones at her approach. Gonzales and Gladstein rightfully note that although "Camille is beautiful, sexually desirable, and intelligent, all of the men in the book treat her as nothing more than a sop for their sex drives" (163). Her relationships with men are marred by the intensity of the sexual selection process her desirability causes: "Men fought each other viciously when she was about. They fought like terriers" (74). Yet she exercises her power, for she has strength and intelligence. Louie, the Greyhound bus driver, is the mouthpiece for all misogynists, and clearly Steinbeck does not portray him as a hero. His character is established immediately, after he cheats a reward for a lost wallet from George, a black swamper. Louie tries all of his pathetic wiles on Camille, but she knows by experience every move he will make. He tries to unsettle her with stares, but her eyes match his; she will not look meekly away. Juan assesses her, but quickly realizes he is too old and she is more than his equal; Camille is too self-possessed to be affected by him.

Camille is adept at ornamentation. Her exaggeration of those attributes that the culture deems beautiful is reminiscent of Darwin's observation of the pains primitive tribes take to augment physical attractiveness by conforming to a standard. Darwin also notes that among the civilized cultures external appearance plays a great part in sexual selection (as it does among the other animals). Darwin writes: "The general truth . . . [is] that man admires and often tries to exaggerate whatever characters nature may have given" (889). Among primitive peoples, such attempts at adornment involve mutilations (piercings, scars, etc.), while of advanced cultures he notes, "In the fashions of our own dress we see exactly the same principle and the same desire to carry every point to an extreme" (889). Louie tries to set a fashion trend by growing the nail on his little finger to an extraordinary length; Steinbeck makes a point similar to Darwin's with the bus driver's absurd attempt.

Camille's prowess with the game of adornments (which she has given in to; for a time she tried severe dress to put men off but failed) demonstrates Steinbeck's awareness of an oppressive cultural standard. Camille, who has decided to take advantage of her position, and performs at stag parties for easy money, is a victim of a society lost in advertising and the image of the poster girl. She happens to look like the exaggerated calendar women hanging in the diner who are depicted as

> ... improbable girls with pumped-up breasts and no hips—blondes, brunettes and redheads, but always with this bust development, so that a visitor of another species might judge from the preoccupation of artist and audience that the seat of procreation lay in the mammaries. (3)

We can see in such works as *The Winter Of Our Discontent* or *America and Americans* that Steinbeck despises the whole advertising veneer; as his friend Webster Street said, "I think he hated dishonesty of any kind, you know—hypocrisy, particularly things like advertising and campaigning and that kind of thing" (Street 122). Certainly Steinbeck's sketch of the self-destructive, failed advertising man who came between Camille and her friend Loraine confirms his dim view of the profession. That an advertising man should cause trouble for Camille is ironic, for men like him have created the mold this hapless woman happens to fit. Men hound Camille because they are amazed to see the commercial standard of adornment alive in their midst (a sophisticated perspective reminiscent of Naomi Wolf's view in *The Beauty Myth*). Camille wants to live a normal life, perhaps raise a family (conceived in her imagination, ironically, from "advertising in the women's magazines") (74). She is a forced practitioner in a male system not of her design; nevertheless, by knowing the system well and by being tough, she has achieved a muted control over her own sexuality.

Norma, being rather plain in physical form and personality, lacks the dynamism of Juan, Mildred, or Camille. Although she has a hopeless desire to be discovered as a star, she can survive: "Her high, long-legged dreams were one thing, but she could take care of herself too" (62). Under Camille's tutelage, Norma spruces up, conforms more expertly to the picture of physical attractiveness. Her transformation arouses the interest of Pimples, who, along with everyone else in the novel but Ernest Horton, loses his inhibitions once the bus is mired in the mud. Norma tries to reason with him, but finally "Her work-hardened muscles set rigidly" and she beats Pimples away with her fists (204). Here, sexual selection goes both ways; the undesirable Pimples may seize his woman with wolf-like rapacity, only to find that she is not his at all, and never will be.

Elliot and Bernice Pritchard are obviously loathed by the author; they represent the middle-class respectability and hypocrisy that Steinbeck made a career of attacking. Both live in an artificial world and, unlike Juan or Mildred, cannot recognize a natural impulse nor act upon it.

Elliot tries to pick up Camille, half believing his own lie that he wants to hire her as a receptionist, and fumbles when she holds up the truth to him—that he's looking for a mistress. Confronted with this fact, "he felt naked before this girl" (194). She also confronts him with his sleazy lust, his staring at her body during a performance for The Octagon International: "I don't know what you get out of it and I don't want to know" (195). Camille reveals the beast in Elliot, and he cannot stand the truth.

Bernice also denies reality, trying desperately to make her marriage appear perfect. A physiological problem that makes her unable to enjoy sex has made her slowly manipulate her husband, strangling his natural desire which, considering the weakness of his character, has not been hard to do. Gonzales and Gladstein write they are "sure Steinbeck means for readers to be pleased when Elliot Pritchard, driven by his interchange with Camille to a recognition of his sexual needs, walks into the cave where his wife lay, and brutally asserts his marital rights" (165). However, this scene is perhaps one of the most pathetic of Steinbeck's many depictions of characters who drop the artificial masks of civilization and entirely lose control of themselves. Elliot's rape of his wife, enacted in the cave—another of Steinbeck's primitive arenas—demonstrates the wretched state of people who live lies, denying or withholding natural desire until they are driven to acts of desperation. Once Elliot stalks off, Bernice mutilates herself in animal fury—rubbing dirt into the bloody scratches she has made on her face.

Alice Chicoy is on the wrong end of the spectrum of sexual selection; she feels ugly, past her prime, and fears that she will lose Juan to a more desirable or youthful female. Gonzales and Gladstein suggest that Steinbeck devotes chapter 11 to her merely because he "is bent on reducing this woman to her most vile state" (169). Yet Alice is not singled out; we shall soon see Pimples, Elliot, and Bernice in their most vile states as well. One good reason for chapter 11 is that alone, Alice must face the truth about herself: that she is weak, old, and afraid of her mortality. We also see her try to use alcohol to hide from these realities. The lonely lunchroom is for Alice what the cave is for the Pritchards or what the back of the bus is for Pimples—the place for veneers to drop, for the true self to emerge. Alice tries to live in denial during "her day," but even drink and imaginary drinking buddies cannot stave off the horrifying image of her dying mother (116). She skips from this to her own physical aging and tries desperately to defy the truth: "'I'm getting along—That's a god-damned lie,' she shouted, 'I'm as good as I ever was'" (116). She plunges into more Old Grandad, and then tries cosmetics to put some youth into her face. We get her side of life at Rebel Corners: a life in an isolated lunchroom, married to a man with whom she must "walk on eggs all the time to keep . . . happy" (119). The smallness of her world, the circumscribed limits which she feels so painfully, are all magnified by her drunken pursuit of a housefly. Alice passes out, which is what she wanted all along, and the fly dips "his flat proboscis into the sweet, sticky wine" (122). Gonzales and Gladstein believe Steinbeck uses this "sassy fly" to thumb his nose at wives; if so, what a symbol in which to embody male *machismo*! This fly can hardly be seen in a positive light, especially when flies have been linked so carefully to Pimples, easily the most disgusting character in the novel. Alice cannot face old age and waning sexual desirability any better than Elliot can face his repressed sexual desire, Bernice her lack of desire, or Pimples his inability to succeed sexually.

Two male characters represent the lowest of the sexual/biological scale in *The Wayward Bus*. Pimples is the fly, one of Steinbeck's grotesques, a man who tries to satisfy his cravings—be they for a woman or for a custard cream pie—with the delicacy of an insect. Van Brunt, like Alice, feels his years and fears the helplessness and deterioration age brought his parent (the father, in this case). Minor strokes fuel his anger. Feeling his gathering weakness, like Alice, he lashes out at others with hatred. His illness has robbed him of the ability to control his emotions, including his sexual desires: "The stroke had knocked the cap off one set of his inhibitions . . . . He was pantingly drawn toward young women, even little girls" (200). Both Pimples and Van Brunt are ugly, arguably uglier than Alice, and the two men are completely enslaved to their bodies. Pimples, hardly better than a fly, follows his appetite or his hormones. Van Brunt is a victim of his own clogged arteries and dying brain cells.

The Wayward Bus, as harsh a view of *Homo sapiens* as *In Dubious Battle*, most fully extends Steinbeck's biological perspective into human sexual relations. The novel is a grotesque portrayal of Darwin's theory of sexual selection, made all the more distressing because of the repression and perversion of sex by a warped society. The characters are coldly measured by their control over biological reality. The better people understand their desires. Juan and Mildred meet in a barn, satiate their needs, and play at romance until they both know the game is over. Camille Oaks sees the sexual power plays of society for what they are, and she knows the role her body and the men around her have forced her to play. Norma believes in the romantic pap of Hollywood movies, but she also possesses a toughness to face reality, to face the grotesque, when it reaches out to grab her. Elliot and Bernice Pritchard wrap themselves in the lies of middle-class respectability, and when the truth of their own sexual power game appears in a cave, they scurry to deny what they see. Alice and Van Brunt live in a waning physical world; as their bodies run down, the fear of their mortality possesses them. Pimples is disfigured, undesirable, but is so base in his nature he is little better than the fly Steinbeck has made him. *The Wayward Bus* is meant to be a slap in the face, but certainly not just for women. Rather, it attacks the inherent weakness of a society that has gone Hollywood, that has tried to cover up biological reality with make-up, booze, or a handsome business suit.

Works Cited

Beatty, Sandra. "Steinbeck's Play-Women: A Study of the Female Presence in *Of Mice and Men, Burning Bright, The Moon Is Down,* and *Viva Zapata!*" Hayashi 7-16.

Benson, Jackson J. *The True Adventures of John Steinbeck, Writer.* New York: Viking, 1984.

Briffault, Robert. *The Making of Humanity.* 1919. London: Allen , 1928.

_____. *The Mothers: The Matriarchal Theory of Social Origins.* New York: Macmillan, 1931.

Darwin, Charles. *The Origin of Species and The Descent of Man.* 1859 and 1871. New York: The Modern Library, n.d.

DeMott, Robert. *Steinbeck's Reading: A Catalogue of Books Owned and Borrowed.* New York: Garland, 1984.

Fensch, Thomas. *Steinbeck and Covici: The Story of a Friendship.* Middlebury: Eriksson, 1979.

Gonzales, Bobbi, and Mimi Gladstein. "*The Wayward Bus*: Steinbeck's Misogynistic Manifesto?" *Rediscovering Steinbeck—Revisionist Views of His Art, Politics and Intellect.* Ed. Cliff Lewis and Carroll Britch. Lewiston: Mellen, 1989. 157-73.

Gladstein, Mimi Reisel. "Steinbeck's Juana: A Woman of Worth." Hayashi 49-52.

Hayashi, Tetsumaro, ed. *Steinbeck's Women: Essays in Criticism.* Steinbeck Monograph Series, No. 9. Muncie: Steinbeck Society, 1979.

Lisca, Peter. *The Wide World of John Steinbeck.* New Brunswick: Rutgers UP, 1958.

Railsback, Brian. "Darwin and Steinbeck: The 'Older Method' and *Sea of Cortez.*" *Steinbeck Quarterly* 23 (1990): 27-34.

Smuts, Jan Christian. *Holism and Evolution.* New York: Macmillan, 1926.

Steinbeck, John. *America and Americans.* New York: Viking, 1966.

_____. "A Postscript From Steinbeck." *Steinbeck and His Critics: A Record of Twenty-five Years.* Ed. E. W. Tedlock and C. V. Wicker. 1957. Albuquerque: U of New Mexico P, 1969. 307-08.

_____. *Burning Bright.* 1950. New York: Penguin, 1979.

_____. *In Dubious Battle.* 1936. New York: Penguin, 1979.

_____. *The Grapes of Wrath.* 1939. New York: Viking, 1976.

_____. *The Log from the* Sea of Cortez. 1951. New York: Penguin, 1975.

_____. *The Pearl*. 1947. New York: Penguin, 1986.

_____. *Steinbeck: A Life in Letters*. Ed. Elaine Steinbeck and Robert Wallsten. 1975. New York: Penguin, 1986.

_____. *The Wayward Bus*. 1947. New York: Penguin, 1979.

_____. *The Winter of Our Discontent*. 1961. New York: Penguin, 1986.

_____. *Zapata: The Little Tiger*. London: Heinemann, 1991.

Street, Webster. "Remembering John Steinbeck." *San Jose Studies* 1 (1975): 109-27.

Wolf, Naomi. *The Beauty Myth*. New York: Morrow, 1991.

Work, *Blood, and* The Wayward Bus

John Ditsky

I

In John Steinbeck's *The Grapes of Wrath* journals, *Working Days*, there appears this revealing passage:

> I can't stop. But oh! if I only had lots of time. I need to settle down some. Burned my pen finger with a match the other day and the blister comes right where the pen fits. And it hurts like hell and my handwriting reaches new heights of badness because of it . . . . How did I ever get started on this writing business anyway? To work. (68)

In one sense, there is little remarkable here to anyone racing against a writing deadline who also suffers some injury to a pen-holding or type-writing finger. On the other hand, so to speak, to have been put into such a position is perhaps to feel that some malign deity of writing has made a special and perverse point of assaulting the writer at the point where direct contact with the work itself is made. Moreover, this instance is but one of the many examples of the aches and pains Steinbeck complains of in forcing himself through the act of writing his novel. Hurt becomes the writer's badge, emblem, escutcheon.

The sexual dimension of Steinbeck's work seems patent enough. Certainly he seems to have regarded writing as a masculine act, whoever performs it—though by no means is it necessarily a male prerogative. In these same *Grapes* journals, the complaining male artist creates and gripes, while his wife Carol does the housework—and the typing of his manuscript. Writing is thus presumably masculine and active, typing feminine and passive. This cleavage between the worlds of male and female activity, sharpest in this example from the writer's life, is also present in his work, especially in some of the stories from *The Long Valley*. But nowhere is this sexual sundering more sharply presented than in the novel *The Wayward Bus*. There, while Alice Chicoy rises and begins to putter around in her domain, the lunchroom, Juan Chicoy and his helper Pimples Carson continue their work on the bus:

> The two men worked together well. Each understood what was to be done. Each did his piece. Pimples lay on his back too, tightening the housing nuts, and in the teamwork a good feeling came to him.
> Juan strained a tight forearm against a nut and his wrench slipped

and he took skin and flesh off his knuckle. The blood ran thick and black out of his greasy hand. He put the knuckle in his mouth and sucked it and made a line of grease around his mouth.

"Hurt it bad?" Pimples asked.

"No, it's good luck, I guess. You can't finish a job without blood. That's what my old man used to say." He sucked the blood again and already the flow was lessening. (24-25)

With respect to this establishment of affinity between Juan and Pimples, it would be well to remember what Jackson J. Benson wrote some time ago about the resemblance between Steinbeck and Mark Twain:

> ... Steinbeck's and Twain's characters gain distinction not by wealth or birth, but by demonstrating strength of character, common sense, and the ability to handle practical problems. The ideal is the man of skill, the riverboat pilot or the auto mechanic. Both writers, in the western tradition, concentrate on a masculine society. Neither deals much with romantic love, except to satirize it, and ideal love is most often achieved between men. (Benson 4-5)

The separation of the worlds of men and women is never clearer in Steinbeck's work than in the present novel, and in the scene being discussed. Moreover, the communion of work between the two men is further emphasized as this scene comes to an end. Pimples achieves an assertion of manhood when, borne along by his good feelings for Juan, he gets the latter to agree to call him "Kit," a recognition of his passage from adolescence to manhood. Juan, having ingested his own blood, agrees to the confirming.

It might be considered sexist to dwell much longer on this scene, but anyone who has ever spilled blood in working on machinery will understand the peculiar mix of sorrow and pride that comes with the experience. (Conversely, many a male has felt unmanned by the failure of his machine, or by his inability to control its workings.) Surely, it might have been Alice who cut herself on the coffee machine, just as it might have been Carol Steinbeck who injured her typing finger. Nonetheless, if the creative act for Steinbeck is masculine, it is also frequently accompanied by suffering in the name of work, and this notion can be traced throughout much of his fiction and nonfiction, though the present study will deal largely with *The Wayward Bus*. There, Juan Chicoy is a prime example of the transmission of the roles of maker and namer—and redeemer—to the created and "named." Obviously, such considerations are extremely pertinent to Steinbeck's conceptions of the role and burden of the artist. Given this terminological frame, these conceptions

137

deal with the presence of the spark of the divine—even if it is of a self-actualized sort. A conflation of the creative and the divine, the symbolic functions of gender, and the notion of work as suffering, occur in *The Wayward Bus* in large part as a result of the operation of naming, but the implications of this circumstance are relevant to other works as well.

One remembers, of course, that in Anglo-Saxon the same term was used for the creating God and also for the wordsmith: "shaper," or "maker." One thinks, perhaps, of the famous letter Steinbeck wrote to Pat Covici from Cuernavaca on 12 July 1945, when he was first toying with the idea for *The Wayward Bus*—and still intending to set it in Mexico:

> ... my bus is something large in my mind. It is a cosmic bus holding sparks ... and turning the corner of Betelgeuse without a hand signal. And Juan Chicoy the driver is all the god the fathers you ever saw driving a six-cylinder broken down, battered world through time and space. If I can do it well *The Wayward Bus* will be a pleasant thing. (*Life* 284)

Around the same time, Steinbeck thought he "saw" his first name written in clouds across the face of the moon, and from the same vantage point (*Life* 285). In the scene quoted from above, the novel lifts its gaze skyward to observe a day's dawning, and of course it does so again at the conclusion, toward the stars above the passengers' destination of San Juan de la Cruz. Clearly this is a book that wonders about portents, written by an agnostic writer whose thoughts were nevertheless out in the cosmos (while managing to suggest the "substance" of the sorts of film normally, of late, released during the summer season). And Juan's mother was, like John Steinbeck's, identifiably Irish, which will be considered below.

This letter's reference to Juan's symbolic identity has been much noted, but little delved into. It will be seen at once that the bus equals the world. But evidently its driver is not in total control if the bus is in fact "wayward" or wandering. Moreover, for all the effort and time the author expected to expend on this project, there remains the question of his attitude: the fact that what he envisaged is something of an animated cartoon, a "pleasant thing." Falling into the trap of treating the book simply as allegory, and either discerning its "meaning" or demeaning it accordingly, readers of *The Wayward Bus* might once again have missed its author's typical whimsy, even when the "cosmic" is involved. And what to make of that peculiar phrase, "all the god the fathers you ever saw"? How many does one normally "see"? Or imagine? Perhaps a person might see—or imagine—one the way he might see his name written across the moon.

Something seems to have happened to *The Wayward Bus* on its way to the market, for not only was the locale altered, but Juan Chicoy somehow got to be rather less than a "god" in the process, just as the bus's slogan, *"el Gran Poder de Jesus"* [accentless, sic, in text], a respectable Caribbean name for a vehicle, got turned into the sappily postwar-American "Sweetheart." More interesting is the process by which "all the god the fathers" became a parody of Christ, to judge from his obvious and portentous initials, and in the operation saw his great power reduced to pap, as if to so reduce the bus mascot, the Virgin, to commercial pabulum. Worth noting is Steinbeck's description of the metal Virgin of Guadalupe perched on Juan's dashboard:

> Her rays were gold and her robe was blue and she stood on the new moon, which was supported by cherubs. This was Juan Chicoy's connection with eternity. It had little to do with religion as connected with the church and dogma, and much to do with religion as memory and feeling. This dark Virgin was his mother and the dim house where she, speaking Spanish with a little brogue, had nursed him. For his mother had made the Virgin of Guadalupe her own personal goddess. Out had gone St. Patrick and St. Bridget and the ten thousand pale virgins of the North, and into her had entered this dark one who had blood in her veins and a close connection with people. (20)

Note that once again, Steinbeck makes the Virgin Juan's mother's "goddess," with a small initial. Note also that the Virgin's stature is being carefully separated from the trappings of institutional religion; this Virgin stands for "memory and feeling," and also for a dark Lawrencian blood force not possessed by St. Ursula or any other of the "ten thousand pale virgins of the North," presumably also *"el Norte."* This Virgin had "entered" into his mother—the syntax is vague—as the Holy Spirit entered into Mary on the occasion of the Annunciation. But what is being worshiped here is clearly the dark blood force of sheer maternity.

What is missing from Steinbeck's description of Juan's statuette, but what is also implicit—and known to the writer—is the Virgin's miraculous use of roses to establish her claim on the attention of Juan Diego, the peasant to whom she appeared. Any tourist visiting Mexico City today can travel a conveyor belt past what is supposedly the cloak Juan Diego filled with roses at the Virgin's instruction and then took to his bishop—in the process creating his nation's outstanding religious icon. The Virgin, rayed in gold, appears on the rough cactus-fiber cloak of the Indian Juan Diego, a cloak that, at her instruction, he had previously filled with "... roses of Castile fresh and lovely growing in a place where roses could not grow and blooming in a frosty month when roses do not bloom" ("Miracle" 59-60). Steinbeck wrote those lines in the deliberately naive "The Miracle of Tepayac," a creation of the same days when *The Wayward Bus* was being finished. The tones of the story and the novel are at superficial odds. What is missing in the novel are the roses— presumably, not "Sweetheart" roses—that bridge the gap between some sort of father and a pair of Juans.

Or a trio of Juans, who go off on their separate missions. Juan Diego becomes the unwitting founder of a cult of faith. Juan Chicoy enjoys a bit of dubious dalliance, and then heads home (presumably) and resumes his domestic routine with his Alice, who has been defeated by a fly. Meanwhile, John Steinbeck turns to the rigors of preparing to write his second "big" novel, *East of Eden*. But in a novel full of apparent admonitions from nature, beginning with the flooding and including cliffside warnings to repent, it is significant that there is nothing quite like Juan Diego's roses present. That is to say, there is no element of the miraculous in a book so rife with religious referents. Of course, the miraculous would have only capped the string of deceptively pathetic fallacies and given its characters reassurance that the author wishes to deny them. Yet the Virgin of Guadalupe remains the novel's icon, a version of its standard image prominent on the original dust jacket just below the cosmic word *"Bus."* But as noted, the author's usage makes it clear that this is no more the "Mother of God" being addressed by Juan Chicoy than it is a figure of fecundity, as much Eve as Mary, and though fertile, giving birth to no Savior.

"Chicoy" is a highly unusual Hispanic or *mestizo* surname, and one has no easy way of explaining why that *y* is there. A colleague who is a specialist in Spanish names suggests that "Chicoy" would be of Mayan origin,[1] which would make Juan Chicoy a long way from home indeed. (Juan Diego, conversely, would likely have been of Aztecan stock.) The text does nothing to explain why a person with such a genealogy should have had a letter added to the word for "boy." Of course, at precisely the spot in the novel at which the editorializing narrator mentions Juan Chicoy's parentage, he notes that Alice "was insanely in love with him and a little afraid of him too, because he was a man, and there aren't very many of them . . . in the world, as everyone finds out sooner or later" (6). In this sense, and in a way that would make for little logic outside of the pages of a novel, Juan can be said to combine in his name the dual aspects of his heritage: he is *chico*, to be sure, but he is also the Real McCoy.

But the absence of the miraculous in *The Wayward Bus* may remind us of even a fourth Juan, the Juan Diego who is the protagonist of the Steinbeck film *The Forgotten Village*, conceived of slightly earlier and also set in Mexico. There, the namesake's function seems clearly intended and ironic: miracles are brought about, in the Steinbeckian view, less by faith than by the enlightened human mind engaged in an inquiring pursuit of knowledge. *The Wayward Bus* seems at first rife with clues as to "meanings," but in the end seems to work by means of indirection. The traditional religious referents Steinbeck employs are used in ironic or "irreligious" ways, and this requires the reader to attend to the manner in which Steinbeck's Juans/Johns come to a focal point in the redemptive power of the maternal, epitomized in the Virgin but by no means limited to her.

II

This open-ended novel reminds us that in terms of the theory of the Fortunate Fall, Mary's function is to redeem through her motherhood the descendants of Eve. Earlier Steinbeck criticism was given to dithering about supposedly allegorical, religious elements: this stood for that; therefore; etc. It was seldom if ever conceded that Steinbeck, as a non-believer, would hardly have intended conventional, straightforward religious allusions in his work. Rather, he seemed bent on implying universal meanings his friend Joseph Campbell would have approved of. His Virgin, worn by *The Wayward Bus* like a scapular, is no biblical figure, or figurine. She is a fertility goddess, an emblem of the creative act. She might have come off a shelf at Freud's apartment at 19 Berggasse. Juan Chicoy uses her to bounce ideas off, the way Steinbeck used his journal.

Juan's dashboard Virgin thus becomes motherhood itself, "his mother and the dim house where she, speaking Spanish with a little brogue, had nursed him." She is the Dark Lady of his unwritten sonnets, an ironic reminder of what sexuality is meant to accomplish. Themes of sterility and/or what Eugene O'Neill would have termed "misbegotten" children haunt Steinbeck's work during this period, this rough decade of the 1940s, and it is not unlikely that they also reflect the writer's misgivings about his work at that time. Juan Chicoy's vain attempt to control the workings of the female is ultimately issueless; he is much more successful when anointing the innards of his bus's engine with his bodily fluids. The point being made here is that the Virgin is as much Eve as she is the Virgin, and as for that, she is primarily no virgin at all.

Steinbeck, consciously and unconsciously, developed the essential male-female relationship as a way of mirroring his art, both thematically and stylistically. In this sense, the "female" includes darkness, fecundity, and both house and language. The male, correspondingly and by implication, must mean light, fertilization, intrusion, and a barbarian

141

grappling with speech. Think of how, among some Slavic tribes, the word for "German" also corresponds with that for "speechless," "unable to speak," no small comment on the impression the sound of that language is apt to make on ears used to softer, less guttural sounds. The half-German Steinbeck also struggled for speech like some Billy Budd, and succeeded only in the presence of the female—a gentling influence not present on Billy's man-o'-war. His wordspinning Irish half can thus be seen as imprisoned in a mute and male German jail. But his fictional self, Juan, has recourse to a mothering force that speaks "with a little brogue." As driver of his bus, he is in charge of a "she," a "her," bent on doing her will, even when she is boarded and driven. The point to be made here is that like its famous successor, *The Wayward Bus* contains elements that are not only biblical but Edenic, and like its famous predecessor its floodtime is fraught with potentiality and new beginnings, whether or not they are achieved.

If the Virgin can be both the Mother of God and also Eve, I would suggest, Juan Chicoy can be one of the "god the fathers"—lower case—as well as the Christ figure he seems to parody by his misapplied initials. By the same token, he is "Adamic," of the earth, and founder of the line his Father created and that the Son would redeem—given the repentance urged by the signs in nature, the most spectacular of which in the Bible is the Flood. The theologian Phyllis Trible has aptly cited as the second sin recorded in the Bible Adam's naming of Eve (Gen. 3:20); for by that act he turned on his assigned equal and, by giving her a name, reduced her to the status of the animals that it had been his prior if specified hobby to designate as this or that.[2] Thus the Original Sin, by which humankind acquired moral consciousness, is immediately followed by a sexist discrimination that has haunted the species forever, but that is intrinsically related to the creative act.

Doubtless *The Wayward Bus* suffered some sort of sea-change on its way from rural Mexico to California. But in that process, is it likely that Juan could have descended as he did from "all the god the fathers you ever saw" to being a character whose only claim on Christhood is his initials? Hardly. On the one hand, the novel—heretofore often read, painstakingly, laboriously, as allegory, could be read as making tongue-in-cheek biblical references, and spoofs. On the other, the author could be making some heavyhanded and inept allusions that simply don't work. Steering our bus right down the middle of the road—a dangerous place to be, come to think of it—suggests that Juan's tenuous control over the destiny of his passengers may be in fact a takeoff on the 18th-century notion of the indifferent watchmaker God, or at least an ineffectual 20th-century version. What remains paramount here is Juan's concern for his vacillating vehicle, not his passengers. Passengers come and go, with no divinity to shape their ends. Vehicles must be made to rattle on forever— with baling wire if necessary—like passenger cars in Cuba.

Similarly, the vehicle is the major concern of John Steinbeck. His art is his baby, his lady, his muse. For it he would shed blood and suffer; for it alone. Only this sense of Juan as a paradigm for the artist himself explains Steinbeck's otherwise confusing mixing of references to God the Father and also to Jesus Christ—if indeed that is what they are. The two are conflated in the passage quoted above, when Pimples asks whether Juan has hurt himself badly, and Juan identifies his injury as "good luck." By offering his flesh and his blood to his redemptive task, Juan is fulfilling the instruction of his "old man," and in the process standing in his father's place. In being about his father's business, Juan Chicoy "saves" his beloved, his errant vehicle, his Sweetheart, his Rocinante.

III

All this may be merely critically "ingenious," an interpreting of what in Steinbeck the author may have simply been a muddle of religious referents not meant to be taken consistently or steadily. On the other hand, Steinbeck takes evident pains in his opening chapter to lay down for us the history of Rebel Corners—needlessly, indeed, since his story requires no historical context dragging in the American Civil War, especially given its highly contemporary—late '40s—ambience. There was, indeed, a Rebel something-or-other just south of Salinas until very recently; a gas station-cum-eatery, whatever. But Steinbeck fills in the historical details so portentously, given the fact that he had already taken a novel's title from Milton, that it is almost as if he had deliberately outfitted his landscape so as to fool the unwary graduate student.

Steinbeck's own father's business may have been business, as Coolidge said of America generally, but the writer himself incorporated both fatherhood and sonhood in a single autonomous person. With perhaps the conspicuous exception of Louis Owens, the critics of *The Wayward Bus* have insisted on reading the work as though it were a carpet with a figure in it to be puzzled out before the whole can be appreciated. The importance of apprenticeship is laid down early on in the novel, and in a clearly gender-discriminated sense. There is little to fault Steinbeck the author for here, for one can find the same world reflected in kinescopes from the late '40s. Subtler are the uses to which Steinbeck, like any good dramatist, puts gender significance. Norma, under the tutelage of both Alice and Camille, learns two different ways of presenting herself to the world, the domestic and the cosmetic. Pimples is taught how to focus his secretions in a higher cause. *The Wayward Bus* can be read as a treatise on the difficulty of getting the sexes together. A book without babies, it is also a manual on procreation.

For *The Wayward Bus* seems to allude, however playfully, to myths by which males perform the creational acts. God makes the world in six days; God plays the midwife as Adam gives birth to Eve; Jesus Christ saves the world of men and women by the sacrifice of his flesh and blood, duly consumed by his followers like the matzohs and sweet Jewish wine that the Eucharist commemorates, and that the characters of *The Wayward Bus* satirize with their addictions to pastries and sweets. Juan Chicoy sheds his blood and gives his flesh for his "Sweetheart," alias "*el Gran Poder de Jesus*." John Steinbeck suffered a variety of physical complaints in the name of art, even—presumably—for that "pleasant thing," *The Wayward Bus*. In these creative acts, the "male" gives birth to the "female."

A 1975 article on this novel makes a connection worth repeating here, though little has transpired to make the link any more secure than it was then (Ditsky). In the listing of California towns and cities, there follow (after "Salinas") some dozens bearing the Spanish names for Roman Catholic saints, many of these places the original mission towns on which Californian culture was founded. There is no "San Juan de la Cruz" on any such list; and yet *The Wayward Bus* ends in this putative utopia. Moreover, though the action begins a specific number of miles south of "San Ysidro," the real San Ysidro is only slightly north of the Mexican border. If John Steinbeck had wanted simple religious allusion, he might have chosen the name of the town near Salinas, San Juan Bautista, which has the added cachet of being seated on a major fault line. Instead, he chose to invent a town named after a mystic and writer whose name might be resolved to "Holy J.C.," though San Juan Capistrano would have done much the same trick. No one has yet proved that Steinbeck owned or read the historical St. John of the Cross; obviously, however, the writer knew who he was.

And what he was. While one would love to have found a reference to Jesus's great power in rereading St. John of the Cross, it has not been possible to do so. But there are lines from poems that in addressing the relationship of Father and Son, God and Virgin, seem almost pertinently and germanely Steinbeckian. This is from "Romance I":

In the beginning of all things
The Word lived in the Lord at rest.
And His felicity in Him
Was from infinity possessed . . . .

   •   •   •

Even so has God conceived Him
And conceived Him always so,
Ever giving Him the substance
As He gave it long ago . . . .

   •   •   •

As the loved-one in the lover
Each in the other's heart resided . . . . (Campbell 65)

The co-eternity of Father and Son is a matter of theological argument few other poets have tackled; but here, quoted in its entirety—again in Roy Campbell's felicitous translation—is a poem John Steinbeck might have written in his guise as St. John of the Crossroads:

With the divinest Word, the Virgin
Made pregnant, down the road
Comes walking, if you'll grant her
A room in your abode. (Campbell 107)

IV

Or a seat on your bus. John Steinbeck's conflation of pagan and Christian elements in *The Wayward Bus* seems patent enough. It remains to suggest that in other works, these principles can be seen at work— or that these principles of work can be seen. For instance, the negative fruits of work deprivation, or of appropriate reward for work, can be seen in such disparate novels as *In Dubious Battle* and *The Winter of Our Discontent*. The female as ideal appears in *Cup of Gold*, but also in *East of Eden*. A revisionist view of the paisano novels might be established on the basis of the apparent fact that males, deprived of female contact, turn towards an irresponsible, Peter Pan-like existence. And so on. Most radical of all might be a reading of *The Grapes of Wrath* in terms of how the males, deprived of the satisfactions of work but allowed its pains, are watched by the females for signs of flagging in their mission, and then eventually supplanted by creative innovation, role-change, on the part of the women

Surely no better, if unwitting, encapsulation of the Steinbeckian position of the nature of the creative act and its connection with religious allusion can be found than the opening speech by Thomas à Becket in T. S. Eliot's *Murder in the Cathedral*. In it, the Crucifixion—the Passion, as it is often termed—is deemed a creative act, one which the laity cannot fully understand, preoccupied as they must be with the problems of mere survival. The shedding of blood is, miraculously, also a positive act by which a redemption is accomplished; the laity are the Women of Canterbury, here standing in for the Women of Jerusalem, female generically because that is the Hebrew usage, whether or not Steinbeck knew as much when he made extensive use of the referent in *The Winter of Our Discontent*:

> THOMAS. Peace. And let them be, in their exaltation.
> They speak better than they know, and beyond your
>   understanding.
> They know and do not know, what it is to act or suffer.
> They know and do not know, that action is suffering
> And suffering is action. Neither does the agent suffer
> Nor the patient act. But both are fixed
> In an eternal action, an eternal patience
> To which all must consent that it may be willed
> And which all must suffer that they may will it,
> That the pattern may subsist, for the pattern is the action
> And the suffering, that the wheel may turn and still
> Be forever still. (Eliot 17)

These lines, which range from Zen acceptance to Christian usage to a universality of belief that Joseph Campbell might have approved of, have perhaps not been applied to Steinbeck before. They seem enormously relevant now, even if only as codicil.

Note that they expect that a "pattern may subsist," a way of saying that a permanent and organically right expression might come to be, naturally, out of materials worked upon by a creative spirit that can be characterized as a Godhead that subsumes its creative function into an appropriate passivity that is His Son: a fitting sacrifice drained of bodily fluids (John 19:34) as if it were a lamb being prepared for ritual sacrifice. Thus the creativity resides in the willingness to suffer. The passage also expects an eternal Yin/Yang to be going on, sexually or not, between the willing and the consenting, a distinction that in the end must come to "nothing." To act, to create, is also somewhere along the line to expect to have to bleed, and then to expect a permanent stillness. The revolving wheels of bus (and coffee urn) somehow manage to take their places in space, bringing *The Wayward Bus* to rest at a point of "eternal action."

But this is perhaps only the tip of the proverbial iceberg. *The Wayward Bus*, chronologically almost central in Steinbeck's canon, seems to be a major statement on the vital relationship between writer and work, and on the possibility that such a relationship can be truly subjective. Clearly enough, the writer believed in the universality of myth as the expression of the deepest human yearnings. Almost as clearly, he uses the commitment of the heart's blood to define the gender-infused occupation of human creativity. Such creativity certainly includes the artistic, by which inclusion Steinbeck displays no proclivity for raising the creative artist to some lofty station above the mass of toiling humankind. In the end, writing is simply hard work, and the writer not willing to shed blood in the creative act is hardly worthy of the name.

Notes

[1] I am indebted to colleague Prof. Paul V. Cassano for this information.

[2] I am indebted to the independent scholar William E. Oyler for this reference.

Works Cited

Benson, Jackson J. "John Steinbeck's *Cannery Row*: A Reconsideration. *Western American Literature* 12 (1977): 11-40. Rpt. as Steinbeck Essay Series, No. 4. Muncie: Steinbeck Research Institute, 1991. 1-29.

Campbell, Roy, trans. *St.John of the Cross Poems*. Baltimore: Penguin, 1960.

Ditsky, John. "*The Wayward Bus*: Love and Time in America." *San Jose Studies* 1 (1975): 89-101. Rpt. in *Steinbeck's Travel Literature: Essays in Criticism*. Ed. Tetsumaro Hayashi. Steinbeck Monograph Series, No. 10. Muncie: Steinbeck Society, 1980. 61-75.

Eliot, T. S. *Murder in the Cathedral. The Complete Plays of T. S. Eliot*. New York: Harcourt, 1967.

Nakayama, Kiyoshi, ed. *Uncollected Stories of John Steinbeck*. Tokyo: Nan'un-do, 1986.

Owens, Louis. *John Steinbeck's Re-Vision of America*. Athens: U of Georgia P, 1985. 58-69.

Steinbeck, John. "The Miracle of Tepayac." *Collier's* 122 (1948): 22-23. Rpt. in *Uncollected Stories of John Steinbeck*. Ed. Kiyoshi Nakayama. Tokyo: Nan'un-do, 1986. 52-61.

_____. *Steinbeck: A Life in Letters*. Ed. Elaine Steinbeck and Robert Wallsten. New York: Viking, 1975.

_____. *The Wayward Bus*. New York: Viking, 1947.

_____. *Working Days: The Journals of* The Grapes of Wrath, *1938-1941*. Ed. Robert DeMott. New York: Viking, 1989.

Trible, Phyllis. "Eve and Adam: Genesis 2-3 Reread." Rpt. in *Womanspirit Rising*. Ed. Carol P. Christ and Judith Plaskow. San Francisco: Harper, 1979. 74-83.

Charting East of Eden: *A Bibliographical Survey*

Robert DeMott

"It isn't simple at all," said Lee. "It's desperately complicated. But at the end there's light." —East of Eden *(chapter 22)*

Although *The Grapes of Wrath* is acknowledged as John Steinbeck's masterpiece, he always considered *East of Eden* to be his "big" book, for which he felt all the others were merely "practice," as he told several of his friends and confidants in the years prior to its writing in 1951. His stake in the book was enormous for a number of reasons, not the least of them because it represented a dramatic change in his fictional method. Steinbeck abandoned the reigning mode of modern critical realism (exemplified by Hemingway's fiction), with its emphasis on verisimilitude and seamless unity. Instead, in the manner of Fielding's *Tom Jones*, Melville's *Moby-Dick*, and Gide's *The Counterfeiters* (three works Steinbeck explicitly praised), he created an open, reflexive form that allowed for autobiographical intrusions, personal editorial digressions, and even alternating points of view. Judging from such recent novels as Toni Morrison's *The Bluest Eye* (1973) and Tobias Wolff's *The Barracks Thief* (1984), to name two powerful and critically acclaimed examples, our age is far more comfortable with technical maneuvers that mix first and third person perspectives. But this is now and that was then: from the outset, Steinbeck feared critics might not agree with his new departure (when The Viking Press actually published *Eden* in September, 1952, it was 90,000 words shorter than his capacious original; to this day, few people have read the initial draft, with its haunting salutariness, its recurring paternal addresses on reality and illusion to the novelist's young sons, Thom and John). In a humorous, self-deprecating response to a *Saturday Review* inquiry in the summer of 1952 (not published until February 27, 1954), Steinbeck predicted the reviews of *Eden* in "advance":

The New Yorker . . . will never forgive me for not being Proust. God! If I could only write in French and have a bad translation I would get a good review there. Monastic *Time* will turn out the pin-striped monks who will intone, "IT IS A GOOD BOOK BUT IT FAILS." . . . The *Chicago Tribune* will have confused me with England to my benefit and the Hearst papers will spell my name Steinberg and review my latest volume of cartoons. And last—the intense young men with receding hairlines who are too smart to do a daily Piece—they will save (I think they call them interpretations) for a book. They will find me *passé* . . . . (8)

A few of Steinbeck's judgments proved true for that time and that place. In *The New Yorker*, high-toned Anthony West said, "Mr. Steinbeck has written a precise equivalent of those nineteenth-century melodramas in which the villains could always be recognized because they waxed their moustaches" (125). *Time's* reviewer, true to form, claimed Steinbeck had "done some of his best writing in *East of Eden* . . . . But whether as a novel about pioneers in a new country or just as men and women working out their private, earthly fates, *East of Eden* is too blundering and ill-defined to make its story point" (110). For the Hearst chain, which Steinbeck long considered his enemy, Clark Kinnaird's thumbnail impression of *Eden*, syndicated in the *Parade of Books* section in the Sunday pictorial weekly magazine of such papers as the *Chicago Herald American* and *Pittsburgh Sun Telegraph*, was typical: "While it is a major achievement for Steinbeck . . . and one with more popular appeal than any recent work of his, it suffers by comparison with Hemingway's latest [*The Old Man and the Sea*]." The Hearst papers were silent on one topic, however, because no one discovered that their recently deceased founder, William Randolph Hearst (1863-1951), was the subject of Steinbeck's scathing criticism in chapter 34 of *Eden* ("When this man died the nation rang with praise and, just beneath, with gladness that he was dead" [414]).

However sweet revenge was, sweeter yet must have been Steinbeck's considerate treatment at the hands of some contemporaries. For example, even the *Chicago Tribune* reviewer, Paul Engle, admired *Eden* ". . . for the sweep and range of its conception and the variety of its human qualities" (3). On the front page of the *New York Herald Tribune Book Review*, Joseph Wood Krutch hailed the novel, prophesying that the ". . . merits of so ambitious and absorbing a book are sure to be widely and hotly debated" (1). In *Saturday Review*, Harvey Curtis Webster began "Out of the New-born Sun" by stating that, while "*East of Eden* isn't a great novel according to the strict conventions of formal purity so widely accepted today . . . it will take almost equal quantities of pride and stupidity to deny that it is one of the best novels of the past ten years and the best book John Steinbeck has written since *The Grapes of Wrath*" (11). Webster's praise was reinforced by the magazine's cover illustration. An out-sized Steinbeck (shown from the neck up) appears foregrounded against rolling agricultural fields; as the writer gazes out under a furrowed brow, he seems to transcend the natural landscape from which he drew inspiration.

And yet despite these prominent hurrahs, Steinbeck's *Saturday Review* predictions can be regarded as fairly acccurate gauges to the mixed critical and scholarly reaction to *East of Eden* during most of the past four decades. (Indeed, *East of Eden* as a kind of "magnificent failure," or what Warren French in 1961 called a "Patchwork leviathan" [152], is a persistent refrain in this critical literature.) In fact, Steinbeck's huge novel proved so vexing to some of his contemporaries that one writer, Mark Schorer, who boldly praised *Eden* as Steinbeck's "best" novel in his *New York Times Book Review* front-page review, "A Dark and Violent Steinbeck Novel," later completely reversed his opinion and regretted ever having published the review at all. (Ironically, Schorer had written the ground-breaking essay on modern literary process in 1948, "Technique as Discovery.") In his 1952 review for *New Republic*, Arthur Mizener, taking a direct cue from Edmund Wilson's notoriously influential 1940 *New Republic* critique-turned-book, *The Boys in the Back Room* (1941), claimed:

> There is evidence even in *East of Eden* of what is quite clear from Steinbeck's earlier work, that so long as he sticks to animals and children and to situations he can see and to some purpose from the point of view of his almost biological feeling for the continuity of life he can release his considerable talent and sensitivity which are naturally his.... Let us hope that some day he will go back to the Long Valley he really knows and maybe even find Jody Tifin [*sic*] there. (23)

Mizener, who seems not to have read the novel very carefully, would later denounce the propriety of Steinbeck's Nobel Prize award with a *New York Times* essay, "Does a Moral Vision of the Thirties Deserve a Nobel Prize?" Meantime, the "basic premise" of R. W. B. Lewis's "John Steinbeck: The Fitful Daemon" (1959) was the "badness of *East of Eden*," which he pronounced "a literary disaster" (123; 132). Here, too, is a significant irony—another example of giving with one hand while taking away with the other. In this essay, Lewis, famous for his earlier book, *The American Adam: Innocence, Tragedy, and Tradition in the Nineteenth Century* (1955), devalued Steinbeck's version of the Adamic mythos in *Eden*. Lewis's comments about the "contemporary situation" of American fiction in the epilogue of *American Adam*—he mentions *The Great Gatsby*, "The Bear," *Invisible Man*, *The Catcher in the Rye*, and *The Adventures of Augie March* as examples of the Adamic tradition "in a comic or tragic perspective by . . . novelists who have escaped . . . the arrested development of innocence and the premature old age of an absorption with sin"—might have provided a natural framework for his later discussion of the fifty-year-old Steinbeck's *East of Eden*. But Lewis's 1959 essay signified no such continuity, and one is left wondering why and how the rules of the game always seemed to change when Steinbeck came up to bat. "Critics," Steinbeck once told his editor, Pascal Covici, "are building their own structures which have little reference to mine."

Schorer's vacillation and Mizener's and Lewis's outright disapproval seem in retrospect not only to sum up the reactions of privileged establishment critics in general, but also to have exerted an authoritarian presence, for Roger Sale's "Stubborn Steinbeck," a 1980 *New York Review of Books* essay-review (on Thomas Kiernan's woeful biography, *The Intricate Music*, and Penguin reprints of *The Wayward Bus* and *Eden*), proved that entrenched attitudes among literary sophisticates (based more on personal taste than the critic admits) die hard. "Though there is a place called Steinbeck country," Sale says, and

> though there are "ideas" we can now call Steinbeck's themes, he seems a writer without a source of strength. For years he thought he had a subject, a big book about the Salinas valley that only he could write. But all that came out of this was *East of Eden*, a bloated, pretentious, and uncertain book. (10)

In his introduction to *John Steinbeck* in Chelsea House's Modern Critical Views series (1987), Harold Bloom claimed that *Eden* does not even bear rereading. Karen Hopkins's succinct reaction still speaks directly to the issue of mandarin condescension: "There is something disturbing about the criticism of . . . *East of Eden*" (63).

II

Yet I say "most of the past four decades" because many recent commentaries on the novel—beginning with John Ditsky's influential revisionist monograph, *Essays on* East of Eden (1977), and continuing in selected instances through Hopkins's spirited defense (1978); Martha Cox's presentation of "Steinbeck's Family Portraits: The Hamiltons," in a special *Eden* issue of *Steinbeck Quarterly* (1981); John Timmerman's "Harvest of the Earth: *East of Eden*," chapter 8 of his informative *John Steinbeck's Fiction* (1986); and Roy S. Simmonds's keynote address, "'And Still the Box Is Not Full': Steinbeck's *East of Eden*," delivered at Steinbeck Festival XI, in Salinas, California, in August 1990 (printed in revised form in *San Jose Studies* in 1992)—show evidence of taking seriously Steinbeck's opinion of the novel's "big" achievement, and of weighing the importance his transformed artistic sensibility had upon *Eden*'s moment, method, and material. Although I do not intend to present the entire history of critical trends on *East of Eden* (good starting places are Richard Peterson's 1979 chapter in Tetsumaro Hayashi's *A Study Guide to John Steinbeck,* Daniel Buerger's essay in the 1981 "Mapping *East of Eden"* issue of *Steinbeck Quarterly,* and Charles Etheridge's 1993 overview of changing attitudes toward Steinbeck's naturalism, in Donald Noble's *The Steinbeck Question),* it may prove instructive, as a prelude to the accompanying bibliographic list, to mention that, like Schorer, one of our generation's leading Steinbeck critics also shifted his attitude toward *East of Eden.* This time, however, the change was efficacious, signifying that Steinbeck has become increasingly relevant rather than *passé.*

Louis Owens's change of tune about *East of Eden* can be considered a trope for this current trend toward re-evaluating Steinbeck's novel in a positive light and for considering the book—among many other possibilities—as a postmodernist creation or metafictional construct. Owens's first book, *John Steinbeck's Re-Vision of America* (1985), took a derivative stance toward *East of Eden,* heavily dependent upon the 1950s ambivalence about Steinbeck in general, and about *Eden* in particular. This rigorous strain of formalist criticism, which emphasized wit, irony, dispassion, authorial effacement, and autonomous form, necessitated qualifications in regard to Steinbeck's work. This divided opinion characterized Peter Lisca's often intemperate New Critical appraisal of *East of Eden* in his otherwise valuable and pioneering *The Wide World of John Steinbeck* (1958), and it was also to be found in the accounts of *Eden* by Warren French (1961), Joseph Fontenrose (1963), and Howard Levant (1974). Lisca condemned the book because he found that the elements of "greatness" which some critics had discerned ". . . might have been brought to fulfillment in a subtle fusion of *East of Eden's* imposing theme and its more credible human beings and events—a fusion which is not accomplished in the novel" (273-74). Like Lisca, Owens was unappreciative of the novel's experimental elements, denouncing Steinbeck for failing "unmistakably" (141) and having "lost his way" in the wilderness of conflicting structure and thought (155).

Owens's insistence in *Re-Vision* that *East of Eden* can only be analyzed as an objective product has changed drastically. This may be a result of the tolerant critical trends and shifting sensibilities that affect us all in the academy, not the least of them our revised notions of the nature of literary representation. Just as the cover portrait of Steinbeck on the September 20, 1952, issue of *Saturday Review* (mentioned above) might once have been taken only as a statement of the novelist's mimetic posture toward the Salinas Valley, so from our vantage point forty years later, the picture can also be "read" as a testimony not to authorial ennoblement or sovereignty, but to authorial indeterminacy (it is possible to detect a questioning, hesitant look in Steinbeck's heavily shadowed face); or, in a larger way, the cover art can be interpreted as an icon of Steinbeck's post World War II situation as a literary con man, a perpetrator of fictive illusion.

Such transformations in the way we think about writing and the critical act has conditioned a greater willingness to embrace Steinbeck's own statements about his artistic intentions and interests. These appear in fugitive items, such as "Un Grand Romancier de Notre Temps," his appreciation of *The Counterfeiters* published in a special *La Nouvelle Revue Française* issue, "Hommage à André Gide," in November, 1951 ("*The Counterfeiters* is one of the greatest books that I have read.... Gide knew how to write, because his mind knew how to explore .... Because he thought what he wanted to and gave form to his curiosities"), and in interviews assembled in *Conversations with John Steinbeck* ("I felt that I could tell *East of Eden* better by being in it myself," he told Charles Mercer in 1953 [57]), but especially in *Journal of a Novel: The* East of Eden *Letters*, the revealing daily record of his writing process. (Here, too, new possibilities are emerging: consider Jackson Benson's biography, *The True Adventures of John Steinbeck, Writer*, which claimed *Eden* "seems destined to be read and remain a part of our literature for some time to come," yet its "unconscious" companion, *Journal of a Novel*, "may be" a "greater" book [691]; and Nancy Zane's essay—the first of its kind—on the *Journal* as an independent Romantic text.)

In three overlapping essays (in 1989, 1990, and 1993) Louis Owens has focused his attention on *East of Eden* as a processive construct and a self-conscious fiction, aspects far more congenial to understanding the dynamics of Steinbeck's complicated effort in narrative form and characterization than the blueprint methods of earlier criticism. Indeed, in the first revisionist statement, "The Story of a Writing," Owens, echoing Steinbeck, self-consciously announced: "When I said, in my recent study of Steinbeck's fiction [*Re-Vision*], that *East of Eden* fails 'unmistakably,' it seemed to me that it was so. Now I have bent close with a glass over the fine print of the novel and reread the footnotes, and I wonder if it is true" (60). Later, in "The Mirror and the Vamp," in James Barbour's and Tom Quirk's *Writing the American Classics* (1990), Owens confessed, "*East of Eden* is a more subtle and complex construction than we are at first prepared to believe" (256).

Others feel that way, too. In his 1975 revision of *John Steinbeck*, Warren French, taking a cue from Lawrence William Jones's earlier study of fabular form, addressed *Eden* as a "cosmogony" (141). By considering Steinbeck's late fictions to be "dramas of consciousness," French's influence is still being felt. In a valuable essay on *Eden*'s postmodernist qualities, Steven Mulder established the ways Steinbeck's novel not only anticipates, but participates in, metafictional discourse, the slippery transactions between domains of fictiveness and reality that define what might loosely be called the postmodernist "moment," the place where, in Roland Barthes's terms, "readers" become "writers" (116). Besides intense interest in the poetics of Steinbeck's narrative processes and the intertextuality of novel and journal, recent critics have been engaging similarly pressing topics including the controversial and conflicting role of women and minority characters in his novel (Beatty, Bedford, Gladstein, Hayashi, Timmerman), the importance of the first manuscript version in understanding Steinbeck's intentions and original scope (Govoni, Nakayama, Simmonds), the mirroring of literal and symbolic landscapes and environment (Owens, Turner), the examination of his myriad literary, linguistic, historical, and personal sources (Gribben, Kawata, Quinones, Yarmus), and the adaptations of his novel into cinematic forms (Morsberger, Rathgeb).

In short, however, although recent analysis of *East of Eden* has become responsible and responsive, the definitive word on many topics is yet to be written. Even that fundamental staple of biographical interpretation—Steinbeck's unquestioned privileging of his maternal line, the Hamiltons—has obscured his debt to his other family, the paternal Steinbeck line, whose gruesome experiences in Jaffa in the 1850s throw some startling light on *Eden*'s characters. It is not too much to claim that, after more than four decades, the frontiers of critical exploration are just beginning to open. As John Ditsky, a pathfinder in this wilderness, said in *Essays on* East of Eden: "A negative acknowledgement is also due: to the man's many detractors who condemn what they have rarely ever read, my thanks for leaving so much to be said" (vi).

The sane application of contemporary critical theory is another conspicuously neglected area in Steinbeck studies where much indeed is yet to be said. Outside of Karen Hopkins's energetic (and often neglected) advocacy of *Eden*, one rarely hears invoked the names of Roland Barthes, Jacques Derrida, Michel Foucault, Jacques Lacan or others, foreign or domestic, though in fact understanding the thrust of contemporary theory—about such highly charged terms as "author," "subjectivity," "gender," "culture," and "representation," to name a few key concepts—would be especially pertinent to *Eden*, a book which, at least in part, subverts normative fictional presentation and interrogates attributes of western humanism by offering an historiographic vision of American experience.

To complicate matters, Steinbeck's project, which turned radically from constructing phalanxes (as evinced, say, in *The Grapes of Wrath*) toward negotiating contexts of individualism in *East of Eden*, was influenced not only by his 1948 divorce from his second wife, and the death that same year of his soul mate Edward F. Ricketts, but also by the larger implications of American intellectual response to the Cold War and our entrance into the Korean conflict. The writer's desire to metaphorize the ironic quest for a unique American character is especially germane to all future contextual discussions of *East of Eden*, as David Wyatt suggests in his New Historical introduction to Penguin's Twentieth-Century Classics series reprint (xviii-xix), which situates Steinbeck amid the myriad conflicting cultural forces of his time. Given Steinbeck's interest in the fictiveness of history and the performative nature of narrative consciousness, an analysis of Steinbeck's construction, or authoring, of himself (as both recorder and participant, subject and object) in that national drama ought to be in order. Further, *East of Eden* cries out for Bakhtinian discourse analysis, or a dialogic investigation, for "heteroglossia," the linked multiplicity of social voices, is a key feature of this polyphonic text. In any case, while we have come far in our appreciation of the work, its special qualities, its animating peculiarities and curiosities, will allow it to elude us unless we learn more about Steinbeck's conception of language, history, and referentiality. Louis Owens struck the proper note when he conceded, in his 1993 essay, "Steinbeck's *East of Eden*," that the novel still "may be the most misunderstood of all of Steinbeck's creations" (85).

Thirty years ago John Milton proclaimed to the Western History Association Conference in Oklahoma City that "*East of Eden* will one day be seen as a major western novel" (72). Indeed, despite (or perhaps because of) its rifts, swerves, ruptures, and dissonances, *Eden* has come increasingly to stand as a major Steinbeck text, though it might eventually prove to be major for reasons quite different than those promulgated three decades ago. Nearly everything has changed since 1964, and—in the aftermath of those cataclysmic influences on the way we conduct literary business—whether *Eden* will ever be considered a truly great novel or even the most representative Steinbeck text are questions unanswerable now. Some theorists would consider questions of transcendent greatness, of writerly genius and achievement, to be spurious categories and hence no longer part of the critical conversation, though for the sake of a healthy, ongoing debate it seems to me that the question of origins can never be fully abandoned.

East of Eden, which has never been out of print, continues to gain respect: Penguin Books has added several Steinbeck novels in their Twentieth-Century Classics series (each with an informative introduction by a contemporary scholar), including these standards—*The Pastures of Heaven, In Dubious Battle, The Grapes of Wrath, Of Mice and Men, The Red Pony, Cannery Row*, and *The Pearl*—and one former maverick, *East of Eden*, introduced capably, as I have already noted, by Wyatt. The Library of America, publisher of uniform editions of America's most important writers, has launched a multi-volume Steinbeck project with *East of Eden* slated for volume 3. (Still needed, however, at least for serious scholars and Steinbeck aficionados, is a facsimile edition of the autograph manuscript, with its alternating sections of the daily journal and the unabridged text of the novel; or, at the very least, an edition of both novel and journal bound as one, something like the complete edition of Gide's *The Counterfeiters*, which Steinbeck so admired.) Roy Simmonds predicted in his keynote address in Salinas that the critical and scholarly "limelight will slowly but surely shift from *The Grapes of Wrath* toward *East of Eden*," and there is no denying that the past decade has witnessed increasing critical interest in and sophisticated commentary on the novel. Indeed, *Eden* has recently become the Steinbeck text of choice in discussions of American writing: besides Barbour's and Quirk's *Writing the American Classics*, see also Frederick Turner's *Spirit of Place*, David Wyatt's *The Fall into Eden*, and Ricardo Quinones's *The Changes of Cain*. All of them demonstrate *Eden*'s richness and resonant possibilities. Finally, after 40 years of debate, what goes around, comes around: it turns out to be neither sinful nor shameful that, in Harvey Curtis Webster's prescient view, Steinbeck ". . . never learned or cared to learn the lesson of Henry James . . ." (11).

III

Looking over the following entries, I am struck by the impact Ted Hayashi's *Steinbeck Quarterly*, his Steinbeck Monograph Series, and his Study Guides have exerted in the revisionist effort. *Eden*'s moral character and spiritual quality, its writerly conundrums and existential riddles, and its lovingly portrayed Oriental philosopher, Lee, seem to have spoken to Hayashi more deeply than any other Steinbeck novel; as a result, no other person has instigated (if necessary, like Lee, by sweet-talking, prodding, pleading, or cajoling) so much new writing and thinking about *East of Eden*. After a quarter century of continuous publication, the *Quarterly* has ceased, but thanks to Professor Hayashi, whatever *Eden*'s final reputation becomes, at least it will have had a conscientious and energetic airing. Even Steinbeck could not have asked for a more intelligent appraisal of Lee, "explicating the author's allegorical lesson—his gospel—to the reader," than Hayashi's 1992 *San Jose Studies* essay, which rings exactly the right kind of grace note to all of our endeavors.

Amid this abundance and promise of good things to come, however, it is easy to forget that a convenient bibliography of primary and secondary writings is always a most desirable and worthwhile thing, for it provides a chart of the journey, a map of the landscape—a lesson Ted Hayashi taught us in 1967 when he published *John Steinbeck: A Concise Bibliography (1930-1965)*. His comprehensive bibliography (the first of its kind) ushered in an era of change by serving notice that studying Steinbeck could no longer be a "simple" matter, and might, in fact, prove to be "desperately complicated" (he has several times updated and revised his book). Obviously, then, honoring Hayashi's editorial skills and his presence as a scholarly gadfly in the Steinbeck community is incomplete without a deep bow in the direction of his bibliographical achievements.

In that vein, I offer the following English language checklist to facilitate continued discourse and serious investigation of *East of Eden*. Like Melville's Confidence-Man, this list has appeared in several alternate guises. It was initially compiled in abbreviated form as a Xeroxed handout for students in my classes at Ohio University and San Jose State University; then, expanded further, for distribution to participants and guests at the Third International Steinbeck Congress held in Honolulu, May 29-30, 1990 (which featured papers on *East of Eden* by Kiyoshi Nakayama and Ikuko Kawata printed in *John Steinbeck: Asian Perspectives*) and at Steinbeck Festival XI, a 1990 conference devoted to a forum on *East of Eden* (which featured papers by John Ditsky, Mimi Gladstein, Tetsumaro Hayashi, Robert Morsberger, Louis Owens, and Roy Simmonds, and a special address, "Adam's Wound," by the late John Steinbeck IV); and most recently, as a contribution to *Steinbeck Quarterly* (1992). The following checklist (substantially revised and updated from all previous versions) follows MLA documentary form in nearly all regards, except for journal dating, where I cite in parentheses the specific month or season(s) of publication, a method which I prefer to less differentiable numerals. Although it is not exhaustive, this bibliography attempts to cover the range and variety of writing on *East of Eden*, including material devoted solely to the novel, as well as to a sampling of important general essays (Jackson Benson's "John Steinbeck: Novelist as Scientist," John Ditsky's "Music from a Dark Cave," and his "Rowing from Eden: Closure in the Later Steinbeck Fiction," and John H. Timmerman's "John Steinbeck's Use of the Bible" are four examples) whose theoretical or practical bearings relate directly to the novel. These too are part of the evolving picture, where, as Steinbeck once said, "everything is an index of everything else."

I. Primary Sources

Note: The related manuscripts of *East of Eden,* housed at the Harry Ransom Humanities Research Center, University of Texas, Austin, Texas, are composed of the 540-page holograph first-draft manuscript, written in a 10 3/4 x 14 inch, lined ledger book (which also includes Steinbeck's concurrent daily commentary later excerpted as *Journal of a Novel*), and more than 900 pages of typescripts, including emendations, deletions, discards, and extensive revisions. Two handwritten personal diaries for 1951, as yet unpublished, are held by the Pierpont Morgan Library, New York City.

A. Texts

Steinbeck, John. "The Sons of Cyrus Trask." *Collier's* 12 July 1952: [14] 15, 38-41.
[Pre-publication excerpt from chapter 3, sections 1-4, and chapter 4, section 1, which differs significantly on many points from the novel's text; reprinted in British *Liliput* 31 (November-December 1952): 89-102.]

_____. *East of Eden.* New York: Viking, 1952.
[Published September in a limited, signed edition of 1500 copies—750 for private distribution—in brown paperboard slipcase, and a trade edition of 112,621 copies with colored pictorial dust jacket; British edition published in London, November (1952) by William Heinemann.]

_____. *Chapter Thirty-Four From the Novel* East of Eden *By John Steinbeck.* Bronxville, New York: Privately Printed by Valenti Angelo, 1952.
[Limited edition chapbook of 125 copies with variant titles.]

_____. *Journal of a Novel: The* East of Eden *Letters.* New York: Viking, 1969.
[Posthumous publication of Steinbeck's daily journal—29 January 1951 to 1 November 1951—addressed to his editor, Pascal Covici, during composition of the novel. Limited edition of 600 copies, in blue slipcase, specially bound with facsimiles of the original manuscript, and a trade edition in brown dust jacket; paperback edition available from Penguin Books.]

_____. *East of Eden.* Introd. David Wyatt. New York: Penguin , 1992.

[Paperback reprint of original Viking Press text, with 23-page introduction; the inaugural Steinbeck volume in Viking Penguin's "Twentieth-Century Classics" Series.]

B. Correspondence, Interviews, and Related Documents

Fensch, Thomas. *Steinbeck and Covici: The Story of a Friendship*. Middlebury: Eriksson, 1979. 143-94.
[Some repetition of entries in *Journal of a Novel* and letters in *Steinbeck:
A Life in Letters*, but valuable for Covici's correspondence and for
corrected texts of some Steinbeck letters.]

Steinbeck, John. [Comments on *East of Eden* and on hand-carved box for
Pascal Covici.] In Laura Z. Hobson, "Trade Winds," *Saturday Review*
30 Aug. 1952: 4.

_____. [Note on importance of *East of Eden* to his career.] In Bernard
Kalb, "The Author," *Saturday Review* 20 Sept. 1952: 11.
["Once . . . I read and wept over reviews. Then, one time I put the
criticisms all together and found that they canceled each other out and
left me non-existent. . . . I feel a little numb about this book. . . . I think
everything else I have written has been, in a sense, practice for this.
I'm fifty years old. If *'East of Eden'* isn't good, then I've been wasting
my time. It has in it everything I have been able to learn about my art
or craft or profession in all these years. Do you know, I want terribly
for people to read it and to like it. I'll be miserable if they don't." This
issue of *Saturday Review* features Steinbeck on its cover.]

_____. [Bilingual letter prefacing Greek translation of *East of Eden*.]
Thessalonika: A. N. Suropoulis, [1953?].
["To have my work published in Greece is at once a pleasing and
frightening thing . . . . To the literature of the world, Greece is the
mother. Perhaps this book is a wandering child come home to visit
. . . ."]

_____. [Excerpted letter predicting *East of Eden*'s reviews.] *Saturday
Review* 27 Feb.1954: 8.

_____. *Steinbeck: A Life in Letters*. Ed. Elaine Steinbeck and Robert
Wallsten. New York: Viking, 1975. 417-40.

_____. "John Steinbeck." Preface by Nathaniel Benchley. *Writers at Work*. The Paris Review *Interviews*. Fourth Series. Ed. George Plimpton. New York: Viking, 1976. 179-207.
[Not a typical *Paris Review* interview on the "Art of Fiction," but a topical selection from *Journal of a Novel* and *Steinbeck: A Life in Letters*, arranged by George Plimpton and Frank Crowther.]

_____. *Conversations with John Steinbeck*. Ed. Thomas Fensch. Jackson: UP of Mississippi, 1988. 49-63.
[Reprinted brief interviews and informal talks with Steinbeck, conducted by various people from 1948 through 1955, entirely or in part about *East of Eden*.]

II. Secondary Sources

A. Selected Contemporary Reviews

Bloomfield, Paul. *Manchester Guardian* 5 Dec. 1952: 4.

Brunn, Robert R. *Christian Science Monitor* 25 Sept. 1952: 15.

Engle, Paul. *Chicago Sunday Tribune* 21 Sept. 1952: 3.

Gurko, Leo. "Steinbeck's Later Fiction." *Nation* 20 Sept. 1952: 235-36.

Hughes, Riley. *Catholic World* 176 (Nov. 1952): 150-51.

"It Started in a Garden." *Time* 22 Sept. 1952: 110.

Jackson, Joseph Henry. *San Francisco Chronicle* 21 Sept. 1952: 20.

Kinnaird, Clark. *Chicago Herald American Sunday Pictorial Review* 28 Sept. 1952: [8].

Krutch, Joseph Wood. "John Steinbeck's Dramatic Tale of Three Generations." *New York Herald Tribune Book Review* 21 Sept. 1952: 1. Rpt. in *Steinbeck and His Critics: A Record of Twenty-five Years*. Ed. E.W. Tedlock and C.V. Wicker. Albuquerque: U of New Mexico P, 1957. 302-05. Rpt. in *Dictionary of Literary Biography: Documentary Series, An Illustrated Guide*, Volume 2. Ed. Margaret A. Van Antwert. Detroit: Gale, 1982. 314-17.

"Larger Than Life." *Times Literary Supplement* 5 Dec. 1952: 789.

Magny, Claude-Edmond. "Magny on Steinbeck." Trans. Louise Varese. *Perspectives USA* 5 (Fall 1953): 146-52.

Mizener, Arthur. "In the Land of Nod." *New Republic* 6 Oct. 1952: 22-23.

Phillips, William. "Male-ism and Moralism: Hemingway and Steinbeck." *American Mercury* 75 (Autumn 1952): 93-98.

Pickrel, Paul. *Yale Review* 42 (Autumn 1952): viii-x.

Prescott, Orville. *New York Times* 19 Sept. 1952: 21.

Rolo, Charles. "The Peripatetic Reviewer." *Atlantic* 190 (Oct. 1952): 94.

Schorer, Mark. "A Dark and Violent Steinbeck Novel." *New York Times Book Review* 21 Sept. 1952: 1; 22.

Scott, J. D. "New Novels." *New Statesman and Nation* 44 (1952): 698-99.

Smith, Eleanor T. *Library Journal* 77 (Aug. 1952): 1303.

Webster, Harvey Curtis. "Out of the New-born Sun." *Saturday Review* 20 Sept. 1952: 11-12.

West, Anthony. "California Moonshine." *New Yorker* 20 Sept. 1952: 121-22; 125.

B. Bibliographical Resources

Beebe, Maurice, and Jackson R. Bryer. "Criticism of John Steinbeck: A Selected Checklist." *Modern Fiction Studies* 11 (Spring 1965): 95-96.

DeMott, Robert. "*East of Eden*: A Bibliographical Checklist." *Steinbeck Quarterly* 25 (Winter-Spring 1992): 14-28.

French, Warren. "John Steinbeck." *Sixteen Modern American Authors: A Survey of Research and Criticism.* Ed. Jackson R. Bryer. New York: Norton, 1963. 383, 514, 517, 519, 526.

_____. "John Steinbeck." *Sixteen Modern American Authors. Volume 2: A Survey of Criticism Since 1972.* Ed. Jackson R. Bryer. Durham: Duke U P, 1990. 607-09.

Goldstone, Adrian, and John R. Payne. *John Steinbeck: A Bibliographical Catalogue of the Adrian H. Goldstone Collection.* Austin: Humanities Research Center, 1974. 75-78.

Gross, John, and Lee Richard Hayman, eds. *John Steinbeck: A Guide to the Collection of the Salinas Public Library.* Salinas: Salinas Public Library, 1979. 45.

Harmon, Robert B. *The Collectible John Steinbeck: A Practical Guide.* Jefferson: McFarland, 1986. 43-47.

_____. *Steinbeck Editions: A Bibliographic Checklist.* San Jose: Bibliographic Research Services, 1992. 12-15.

Hayashi, Tetsumaro. *John Steinbeck: A Concise Bibliography (1930-1965).* Metuchen: Scarecrow, 1967. Passim.

_____. *A New Steinbeck Bibliography, 1929-1971.* Metuchen: Scarecrow, 1973. Passim.

_____. *A New Steinbeck Bibliography: 1971-1981.* Introd. Robert DeMott. Metuchen: Scarecrow, 1983. Passim.

Morrow, Bradford. *John Steinbeck: A Collection of Books and Manuscripts Formed by H. Valentine of Pacific Grove, California.* Foreword by John R. Payne. Santa Barbara: Bradford Morrow, 1980. 55-57.

Payne, John R. "John Steinbeck in the Humanities Research Center, The University of Texas at Austin." *Steinbeck Quarterly* 11 (Summer-Fall 1978): 100-02. Rpt. in *A Handbook for Steinbeck Collectors, Librarians, and Scholars.* Ed. Tetsumaro Hayashi. Steinbeck Monograph Series, No. 11. Muncie: Steinbeck Society, 1981. 33-34.

Timmerman, John H. "John Steinbeck's Use of the Bible: A Descriptive Bibliography of the Critical Tradition." *Steinbeck Quarterly* 21 (Winter-Spring 1988): 24-39.

Todd, William B. *John Steinbeck: An Exhibition of American and Foreign*

Editions. Austin: Humanities Research Center/U of Texas, 1963. 26-27.

Woodward, Robert H. *The Steinbeck Research Center at San Jose State University: A Descriptive Catalogue*. Foreword by Robert DeMott. San Jose: San Jose State U, 1985. 51-53. Also spec. issue of *San Jose Studies* 11 (Winter 1985): 51-53.

C. Biography and Background

Astro, Richard. *John Steinbeck and Edward F. Ricketts: The Shaping of a Novelist*. Minneapolis: U of Minnesota P, 1973. 193; 207-12.

_____. "John Steinbeck." *American Novelists, 1910-1945. Part 3: Mari Sandoz-Stark Young. Dictionary of Literary Biography*, Volume 9. Ed. James J. Martine. Detroit: Gale, 1981. 62-64.

Benson, Jackson J. *The True Adventures of John Steinbeck, Writer*. New York: Viking, 1984. 666-68; 700-03; 731-34.

_____. *Looking for Steinbeck's Ghost*. Norman: U of Oklahoma P, 1988. 11, 27, 95, 183, 195-96, 223-24.

Cox, Martha Heasley. "In Search of John Steinbeck: His People and His Land." *San Jose Studies* 1 (Nov. 1975): 41; 45-47.

_____. "Steinbeck's Family Portraits: The Hamiltons." *Mapping* East of Eden. Ed. Robert DeMott. Spec. issue of *Steinbeck Quarterly* 14 (Winter-Spring 1981): 23-32.

_____. "John Steinbeck." *Dictionary of Literary Biography: Documentary Series, An Illustrated Guide*, Volume 2. Ed. Margaret A. Van Antwert. Detroit: Gale, 1982. 314-19.

DeMott, Robert. "Steinbeck's Other Family: New Light on *East of Eden*." *Steinbeck Newsletter* 7 (Winter 1994): 1-4.

Kiernan, Thomas. *The Intricate Music: A Biography of John Steinbeck*. Boston: Little, 1979. 295-301.

D. Criticial Analysis

Atkinson, Rebecca L. "Steinbeck's *East of Eden.*" *Explicator* 48 (Spring 1990): 216-17.

Beatty, Sandra. " A Study of Female Characterization in Steinbeck's Fiction." *Steinbeck Quarterly* 8 (Spring 1975): 50-56. Rpt. in *Steinbeck's Women: Essays in Criticism*. Ed. Tetsumaro Hayashi. Introd. Richard Peterson. Steinbeck Monograph Series, No. 9. Muncie: Steinbeck Society, 1979. 1-6.

Bedford, Richard C. "Steinbeck's Uses of the Oriental." *Steinbeck Quarterly* 18 (Winter-Spring 1980): 5-19.

Benson, Jackson J. "John Steinbeck: Novelist as Scientist." *Steinbeck and the Sea*. Ed. Richard Astro and Joel Hedgpeth. Corvallis: Oregon State U Sea Grant College Program (Apr. 1975): 15-28. Rpt. in *Novel* 10 (Spring 1977): 248-64. Rpt. in *John Steinbeck*. Ed. Harold Bloom. New York: Chelsea, 1987. 103-23.

Brown, Joyce C. "Steinbeck's *East of Eden.*" *Explicator* 38 (Fall 1979): 11-12.

Buerger, Daniel. "'History' and Fiction in *East of Eden* Criticism." *Mapping* East of Eden. Ed. Robert DeMott. Spec. issue of *Steinbeck Quarterly* 14 (Winter-Spring 1981): 6-14.

Burningham, Bradd. "Relation, Vision, and Tracking the Welsh Rats in *East of Eden* and *The Winter of Our Discontent.*" *Steinbeck Quarterly* 15 (Summer-Fall 1982): 77-90.

Covici, Pascal, Jr. "From Commitment to Choice: Double Vision and the Problem of Vitality for John Steinbeck." *The Fifties: Fiction, Poetry, Drama*. Ed. Warren French. Deland: Edwards, 1970. 63-72.

DeMott, Robert. "The Interior Distances of John Steinbeck." *Steinbeck Quarterly* 12 (Summer-Fall 1979): 86-99.

_____. "Mapping *East of Eden.*" *Mapping* East of Eden. Ed. Robert De-Mott. Spec. issue of *Steinbeck Quarterly* 14 (Winter-Spring 1981): 4-5.

_____. "'Culling All Books': Steinbeck's Reading and *East of Eden.*"

Mapping East of Eden. Ed. Robert DeMott. Spec. issue of *Steinbeck Quarterly* 14 (Winter-Spring 1981): 40-51.

_____. "Cathy Ames and Lady Godiva: A Contribution to *East of Eden*'s Background." *Steinbeck Quarterly* 14 (Summer-Fall 1981): 72-83.

_____. "'A Great Black Book': *East of Eden* and *Gunn's New Family Physician*." *American Studies* 22 (Fall 1981): 41-57. Rpt. as "Steinbeck's *East of Eden* and *Gunn's New Family Physician*," *Book Club of California Quarterly News-Letter* 51 (Spring 1986): 31-48. Rpt. slightly altered as "Creative Reading/Creative Writing: The Presence of Dr. Gunn's *New Family Physician* in Steinbeck's *East of Eden*." *Rediscovering Steinbeck—Revisionist Views of His Art, Politics and Intellect.* Ed. Cliff Lewis and Carroll Britch. Lewiston: Mellen, 1989. 35-57.

_____. *Steinbeck's Reading: A Catalogue of Books Owned and Borrowed.* New York: Garland, 1984. xxxii-xliii.

_____. "'Of Ink and Heart's Blood': Adventures in Reading *East of Eden*." *Connecticut Review* 14 (Spring 1992): 9-21.

Ditsky, John. "Music from a Dark Cave: Organic Form in Steinbeck's Fiction." *The Journal of Narrative Technique* 1 (Jan. 1971): 59-66.

_____. *Essays on* East of Eden. Steinbeck Monograph Series, No. 7. Muncie: Steinbeck Society, 1977.

_____. "The 'East' in *East of Eden*." *John Steinbeck: East and West.* Ed. Tetsumaro Hayashi, Yasuo Hashiguchi, and Richard F. Peterson. Introd. Warren French. Steinbeck Monograph Series, No. 8. Muncie: Steinbeck Society, 1978. 61-70.

_____. *John Steinbeck: Life, Work, And Criticism.* Fredericton: York, 1985. 10-11, 21, 23, 25, 30.

_____. "'I' in *Eden*: The Narrational Voice in Steinbeck." *Kyushu American Literature* 27 (Sept. 1986): 57-69.

_____. "Rowing from Eden: Closure in the Later Steinbeck Fiction." *North Dakota Quarterly* 60 (Summer 1992): 87-100.

Etheridge, Charles L. "Changing Attitudes Towards Steinbeck's Naturalism and the Changing Reputation of *East of Eden*: A Survey of

Criticism Since 1974." *The Steinbeck Question: New Essays in Criticism.*
Ed. Donald R. Noble. Troy: Whitston, 1993. 250-59.

Everest, Beth, and Judy Wedeles. "The Neglected Rib: Women in *East of Eden.*" *Steinbeck Quarterly* 21 (Winter-Spring 1988): 13-23.

Farrell, Keith. *John Steinbeck: The Voice of the Land.* New York: Evans, 1986. 145-55.

Fontenrose, Joseph. *John Steinbeck: An Introduction and Interpretation.* New York: Barnes, 1963. 118-27.

French, Warren. *John Steinbeck.* New York: Twayne, 1961. 152-56.

——. *John Steinbeck.* Rev. ed. Boston: Hall, 1975. 141-52.

Frohock, W. M. *The Novel of Violence in America.* 2nd ed. Dallas: Southern Methodist U P, 1957. 141-43.

Fuller, Edmund. *Man in Modern Fiction.* New York: Random, 1958. 20-31.

Geismar, Maxwell. *American Moderns: From Rebellion to Conformity.* New York: Hill, 1958. 164-67.

Gladstein, Mimi Reisel. *The Indestructible Woman in Faulkner, Hemingway, and Steinbeck.* Ann Arbor: UMI, 1986. 75-100. Partly rpt. as "Abra: The Indestructible Woman in *East of Eden.*" *John Steinbeck.* Ed. Harold Bloom. New York: Chelsea, 1987. 151-53.

——. "The Strong Female Principle of Good or Evil: The Women of *East of Eden.*" *Steinbeck Quarterly* 24 (Winter-Spring 1991): 30-40.

Govoni, Mark. "'Symbols for the Wordlessness': A Study of John Steinbeck's *East of Eden.*" Diss. Ohio U, 1978.

——. "'Symbols for the Wordlessness': The Original Manuscript of *East of Eden.*" *Mapping* East of Eden. Ed. Robert DeMott. Spec. issue of *Steinbeck Quarterly* 14 (Winter-Spring 1981): 14-23.

Gribben, John. "Steinbeck's *East of Eden* and Milton's *Paradise Lost*: A Discussion of 'Timshel.'" *Steinbeck's Literary Dimension: A Guide to*

Comparative Studies. Ed. Tetsumaro Hayashi. Metuchen: Scarecrow, 1973. 94-104.

Hayashi, Tetsumaro. "'The Chinese Servant' in *East of Eden*." *San Jose Studies* 18 (Winter 1992): 52-60.

_____. "Steinbeck's Moral Vision in *East of Eden*." *Studies in Foreign Languages and Literatures* 25 (Winter 1989): 87-104.

Heavlin, Barbara A. "Steinbeck's Exploration of Good and Evil: Structural and Thematic Unity in *East of Eden*." *Steinbeck Quarterly* 26 (Summer-Fall 1993): 90-100.

Hopkins, Karen J. "Steinbeck's *East of Eden*: A Defense." *Itinerary: Criticism: Essays on California Writers*. Ed. Charles L. Crow. Bowling Green: Bowling Green State U P, 1978. 63-78.

Jain, Sunita. *Steinbeck's Concept of Man*. New Delhi: New Statesman, 1979. 82-92. Rpt. in *Indian Response to Steinbeck. Essays Presented to Warren French*. Ed. R.K. Sharma. Foreword by Yasuo Hashiguchi. Jaipur: Rachana Prakashan, 1984. 271-76.

Jones, Lawrence William. *John Steinbeck as Fabulist*. Ed. Marston La-France. Steinbeck Monograph Series, No. 3. Muncie: Steinbeck Society, 1973. 25-28.

Kawata, Ikuko. "'Timshel': Steinbeck's Message through the Hebrew Original." *John Steinbeck: Asian Perspectives*. Ed. Kiyoshi Nakayama, Scott Pugh, and Shigeharu Yano. Osaka: Osaka Kyoiku Tosho, 1992. 73-87.

Kazan, Elia. *A Life*. New York: Knopf, 1988. 534-39. [On filming *East of Eden*.]

Levant, Howard. *The Novels of John Steinbeck: A Critical Study*. Introd. Warren French. Columbia: U of Missouri P, 1974. 234-58.

Lewis, Clifford. "John Steinbeck: Architect of the Unconscious." Diss. U of Texas, 1972. 252-66.

Lewis, R. W. B. "John Steinbeck: The Fitful Daemon." *The Young Rebel in American Literature*. Ed. Carl Bode. London: Heinemann, 1959. 121-

41. Rpt. in *Steinbeck: A Collection of Critical Essays*. Ed. Robert Murray Davis. Englewood Cliffs: Prentice, 1972. 163-75.

Lisca, Peter. *The Wide World of John Steinbeck*. New Brunswick: Rutgers U P, 1958. 261-75.

_____. *John Steinbeck: Nature and Myth*. New York: Crowell, 1978. 161-78.

McCarthy, Paul. *John Steinbeck*. New York: Ungar, 1979. 116-24.

McDaniel, Barbara. "Alienation in *East of Eden*: The 'Chart of the Soul.'" *Mapping* East of Eden. Ed. Robert DeMott. Spec. issue of *Steinbeck Quarterly* 14 (Winter-Spring 1981): 32-39.

Marks, Lester. *Thematic Design in The Novels of John Steinbeck*. The Hague: Mouton, 1969. 114-31. Rpt. as "*East of Eden*: 'Thou Mayest.'" *Steinbeck Quarterly* 4 (Winter 1971): 3-18.

Martin, Stoddard. *California Writers: Jack London, John Steinbeck, The Tough Guys*. 1983. Boston: St. Martin's, 1984. 110-17.

Millichap, Joseph. *Steinbeck and Film*. New York: Ungar, 1983. 137-52.

Milton, John R. "The Novel in the American West." *Western Writing*. Ed. Gerald W. Haslam. Albuquerque: U of New Mexico P, 1974. 72.

Morsberger, Robert E. "Steinbeck's Happy Hookers." *Steinbeck Quarterly* 9 (Summer-Fall 1976): 110-113. Rpt. in *Steinbeck's Women: Essays in Criticism*. Ed. Tetsumaro Hayashi. Introd. Richard F. Peterson. Steinbeck Monograph Series, No. 9. Muncie: Steinbeck Society, 1979. 43-46.

_____. "*East of Eden* on Film." *Steinbeck Quarterly* 25 (Winter-Spring 1992): 28-42.

Mulder, Steven. "The Reader's Story: *East of Eden* as Postmodernist Metafiction." *Steinbeck Quarterly* 25 (Summer-Fall 1992): 109-18.

Nakayama, Kiyoshi. "Steinbeck's Creative Development of an Ending: *East of Eden*." *John Steinbeck: Asian Perspectives*. Ed. Kiyoshi Nakayama, Scott Pugh, and Shigeharu Yano. Osaka: Osaka Kyoiku Tosho, 1992. 193-298.

Owens, Louis. *John Steinbeck's Re-Vision of America*. Athens: U of Georgia P, 1985. 140-55.

_____. "The Story of a Writing: Narrative Structure in *East of Eden*." *Rediscovering Steinbeck—Revisionist Views of His Art, Politics and Intellect*. Ed. Cliff Lewis and Carrol Britch. Lewiston: Mellen, 1989. 60-76.

_____. "The Mirror and the Vamp: Invention, Reflection, and Bad, Bad Cathy Trask in *East of Eden*." *Writing the American Classics*. Ed. James Barbour and Tom Quirk. Chapel Hill: U of North Carolina P, 1990. 235-57.

_____. "A Garden of My Land: Landscape and Dreamscape in John Steinbeck's Fiction." *Steinbeck Quarterly* 23 (Summer-Fall 1990): 78-88.

_____. "Steinbeck's *East of Eden* (1952)." *A New Study Guide to Steinbeck's Major Works, With Critical Explications*. Ed. Tetsumaro Hayashi. Introd. Reloy Garcia. Metuchen: Scarecrow, 1993. 66-89.

Pearson, Pauline, and Mary Jean S. Gamble. East of Eden *Film Notes*. Salinas: John Steinbeck Library, 1987.

Peterson, Richard. "*East of Eden*." *A Study Guide to Steinbeck, Part II*. Ed. Tetsumaro Hayashi. Introd. Reloy Garcia. Metuchen: Scarecrow, 1979. 63-86.

Pratt, John Clark. *John Steinbeck*. Grand Rapids: Eerdmans, 1970. 24-32.

Quinones, Ricardo J. "The New American Cain: *East of Eden* and Other Works of Post World-War II America." *The Changes of Cain: Violence and the Lost Brother in Cain and Abel Literature*. Princeton: Princeton UP, 1991. 134-44.

Rathgeb, Douglas. "Kazan as Auteur: The Undiscovered *East of Eden*." *Literature/Film Quarterly* 16.1 (1988): 31-38.

_____. "The Four Faces of Cal Trask: Steinbeck's Troubled Hero and James Dean." *Steinbeck Newsletter* 6 (Winter 1993): 8-9.

Sale, Roger. "Stubborn Steinbeck." *The New York Review of Books* 20 Mar. 1980: 10-12.

Satyanarayana, M. R. *John Steinbeck: A Study of the Theme of Compassion*. Hyderabad: Osmania U P, 1977. 112-24.

Shimomura, Noburo. *A Study of John Steinbeck: Mysticism in His Novels*. Tokyo: Hokuseido, 1982. 152-85.

Simmonds, Roy S. *Steinbeck's Literary Achievement*. Steinbeck Monograph Series, No. 6. Muncie: Steinbeck Society, 1976. Passim.

_____. "Cathy Ames and Rhoda Penmark: Two Child Monsters." *Mississippi Quarterly* 39 (Spring 1986): 91-101. Rpt. in *Steinbeck's Literary Dimension: A Guide to Comparative Studies Series II*. Ed. Tetsumaro Hayashi. Metuchen: Scarecrow, 1991. 102-13.

_____. "'And Still the Box Is Not Full': Steinbeck's *East of Eden*." *San Jose Studies* 18 (Fall 1992): 56-71.

Sreenivasan, K. "*East of Eden*: Steinbeck's Testament of Faith." *John Steinbeck: A Study of His Novels*. Trivandrum: College Book House, 1980. 144-58. Rpt. in *Indian Response to Steinbeck: Essays Presented to Warren French*. Ed. R. K. Sharma. Foreword by Yasuo Hashiguchi. Jaipur: Rachana Prakashan, 1984. 258-70.

Timmerman, John. *John Steinbeck's Fiction: The Aesthetics of the Road Taken*. Norman: U of Oklahoma P, 1986. 210-47.

Turner, Frederick. "The Valley of the World: John Steinbeck's *East of Eden*." *Spirit of Place: The Making of an American Dream*. San Francisco: Sierra Club, 1989. 249-82.

Watt, F. W. *Steinbeck*. New York: Grove, 1962. 93-99.

Wyatt, David. "Steinbeck's Lost Gardens." *The Fall into Eden: Landscape and Imagination in California*. New York: Cambridge U P, 1986. 131-32.

Yano, Shigeharu. *The Current of Steinbeck's World*. Tokyo: Seibido, 1978. 148-64.

Zane, Nancy. "The Romantic Impulse in Steinbeck's *Journal of a Novel: The* East of Eden *Letters*." *Steinbeck's Posthumous Work: Essays in Criticism*. Ed. Tetsumaro Hayashi and Thomas J. Moore. Introd.

Reloy Garcia. Steinbeck Monograph Series, No. 14. Muncie: Steinbeck Society, 1989. 1-12.

Sweet Thursday *Revisited:*
An Excursion in Suggestiveness

Robert DeMott

"I am not a great writer but I am a competent one. And I am an experimental one."—Steinbeck, in an unpublished 1946 diary

"It's quite a performance. I bet some of it is even true, and if it wasn't, it is now." —Steinbeck's encomium for Gypsy Rose Lee's memoir, Gypsy *(1957)*

I

In the fall of 1969, Ted Hayashi wrote from Muncie, Indiana, inviting me to participate in a Steinbeck conference he was co-organizing with Richard Astro at Oregon State University. Slated for April, 1970, it would be only the second Steinbeck conference ever convened (the first, which both Ted and I attended, was a thirtieth anniversary celebration of *The Grapes of Wrath* organized by John Seelye a year earlier at the University of Connecticut). Fresh out of graduate school, I was trying to turn my dissertation on the creative process in Thoreau's major writings into a book. At the same time, I was trying to suppress the growing realization that, except for being a well-intentioned and nominally intriguing topic, the dissertation was straight-laced and pedantic, and would probably be a boring read. When the summons came from Hayashi, toward the end of my first quarter of full-time teaching at Ohio University, I put down Thoreau (for good as it turned out) and picked up Steinbeck's just-published *Journal of a Novel: The* East of Eden *Letters.* Borrowing from Steinbeck's writing journal, as well as from some of my Thoreau *cum* Georges Poulet/Gaston Bachelard inspired theories, and armed with a recent reading of Richard Brautigan's avant-garde fiction and Allen Ginsberg's poetry and prose (part of my eventual title came from his essay on legalizing marijuana), I opened a hermeneutic path into *Sweet Thursday,* a novel I felt had taken undeservedly hard knocks from formalist critics who held sway in academic circles during the 1950s and 1960s.

The result was "Steinbeck and the Creative Process: First Manifesto to End the Bringdown Against *Sweet Thursday,*" a meta-critical divagation temperamentally at home in that age of rampant iconoclasm, and which—true to its era—raised more questions than it answered. The essay's tenuousness and irreverent tone—its breezy affectivity and hip talk of *Sweet Thursday* being a parable of the artist, a "novel about the writing of a novel"—owes partly to the fact that I labored on it in the dead of an unusually cold Appalachian winter in a rented house that, I learned too late, had a faulty furnace—a coal burner ineptly converted to burn fuel oil. Between dives into the cellar to coax the ancient beast back to life, I worked in the owner's window-lined study laboriously writing and typing in woolen gloves and heavy clothes. Like Doc in the novel I was attending to, I couldn't sustain my concentration long enough to develop my argument in a more systematic manner, and so the essay became susceptible to its context, but was not wholly constructed by it (the legitimacy of some post-structuralist beliefs aside, common sense tells us that such makings never are wholly unmixed, a point I believe Steinbeck's disposition toward writerly habits supports). As a result, I abandoned many pretenses of objectivity while the essay became a performative piece about a self-displaying text, a way of "using something to cover up something else," in Mack's definition of "substitution," which appears in chapter 9 of *Sweet Thursday* (64).

There are few more excrutiating events than rereading one's own early writing, but as I realize now (without, I hope, being shamelessly vain) the informal voice of "Steinbeck and the Creative Process" fit the conversational format and ebullient dialogue of the Corvallis conference, though since being printed in Astro and Hayashi's *Steinbeck: The Man and His Work* its silences, rifts, and lacunae seemed to have grown more—rather than less—blatant. It would be impossible to redress all its shortcomings—nor, at this late date, would I care to (absences have a way of becoming part of the permanent record, and both objectivity and dispassion remain, for me, anyway, elusive and dubious goals). Yet I am grateful for this second chance not only to elaborate a few old points about Steinbeck's controversial little book, *Sweet Thursday*, but to resurrect briefly a forgotten public debate on its merits (a 1954 television broadcast), suggest an important vector of popular culture influence (Al Capp's *Li'l Abner* comic strip), and arrive, without being too fanciful or precious, at a new trope of relevancy (Steinbeck's portable typewriter) in the following circuitous revisitation to his still underrated fable of the life in art.

While this essay performs a personal function by forestalling the closure of my lifelong professional friendship with Professor Hayashi, it also proves, as Thoreau knew, that it's possible to catch two fish with one hook. Indeed, returning to this novel after such a long hiatus strikes me as fitting, because doing so has once again been occasioned by Ted Hayashi. That alone creates a happy gesture of personal Pietas. But revisiting also constitutes a renewed arc of connection, which both refines and postpones an inevitable end that began in the later 1960s when we hit it off as graduate students at Kent State University, where I first glimpsed through Ted (and through my mentor, Howard Vincent) the intriguing possibility that critical discourse could be enhanced by personal engagement and appreciative intervention. In that it also circles toward a meeting many years later with Steinbeck's elder son, Thom, from whom I received, temporarily at least, his father's favorite typewriter (which became a metaphor for a way of looking at the senior Steinbeck's creative drive), the landscape of this essay inscribes an intersubjective ground (Hawthorn 85), a moving geography of inner and outer voices, private and public presences, selves and texts.

II

From the outset, the conversation surrounding *Sweet Thursday* was heated and antagonistic, as the following account by Pascal Covici demonstrates. One evening in early August, 1954, Covici, John Steinbeck's loyal friend and his editor at Viking Press, turned on the television set at his brother-in-law's house in New Rochelle, New York, to watch a show called "The Author Meets the Critics." The topic that night was Steinbeck's *Sweet Thursday*, published in June and already selling by the box load. Steinbeck was living in Paris with his wife, Elaine, and his two sons, Thom and John IV, that summer, and so could not appear on the program. The critics, however, according to Covici's previously unpublished August 9, 1954, letter to Steinbeck, were represented by chief discussants Lewis Gannett and Joseph Bennett.

Gannett, the book critic for the venerable New York *Herald Tribune*, and a longtime friend and supporter of Steinbeck's, took an affirmative position toward the novel. Bennett, a founding editor of the upstart *Hudson Review*, argued negatively. Bennett's "salubrious" opinion that *Sweet Thursday* was "dull, repetitious and phony" met with extreme resistance from Gannett and the other panelists, who defended the novel for its "delightful" wit and humor. The moderator, perhaps sympathetic to Bennett's plight, broadened the topic to include the overall importance of Steinbeck's contribution to contemporary American literature. According to Covici, Bennett asserted that Steinbeck had managed to produce some "worthwhile" fiction only when he was "angry," as in *In Dubious Battle* and *The Grapes of Wrath*. Steinbeck, however, was not one of the truly significant American novelists, but was merely a commercially successful writer who had skillfully learned how to "appeal to the largest public" audience possible. Gannett took the long view, arguing that Steinbeck had earned his recent success by virtue of his initial obscurity, his long years of hard work, and his willingness to experiment with the novel genre. Apparently, his persuasiveness carried the day, for at the end of his correspondence, Covici reassured Steinbeck that Bennett's "harangues" were unconvincing, and would do nothing to injure the novel's reputation: ". . . the book keeps on selling!"

There is truth on each side of this debate, just as there is misapprehension and intolerance. Bennett's rigorous intellectualism and Covici's glib commercialism both represent passionate positions, but reductive ones, too, which impede understanding. Covici never was a consistently brilliant appreciator of fiction's technical properties, and may even have done Steinbeck a disservice during his career by pushing the marketable aspects of the novelist's work above all else. On the other hand, Steinbeck was a professional writer, a man who supported his family and earned his living by writing, so his being financially successful at his chosen vocation need not automatically have qualified as a cause for shame. Ironically, Bennett, quick to wave the avant-garde flag, seems to have missed the contemporaneity of *Sweet Thursday*, especially its artistic playfulness and self-reflexivity, its internalization of the American frontier theme, and its fabular dimensions. Steinbeck's text seems to have appeared too soon in our critical history to have been amply tolerated; in some ways, it belongs more comfortably to the nineties than to the fifties. At the very least, even though Bennett, Gannett, and Covici were unable to recognize it, Steinbeck exposed the American reading public to an early example of experimental meta-fiction, on the order of what Linda Hutcheon has called a "self-referring or autorepresentational" text (xii).

Historically—as the Bennett-Gannett fiasco symbolizes—*Sweet Thursday*'s reputation has always been unsettled. Even though many newspaper and magazine reviews were extremely critical, the book sold prodigiously: on one day alone—June 15, 1954—Viking sold 2000 copies; in another letter to Steinbeck written the following day (this also heretofore unpublished), Covici predicted it would top 100,000 for the year. Unimpressed by such abundance, *Time's* anonymous reviewer castigated *Sweet Thursday* as "a turkey with visibly Saroyanesque stuffings. But where Saroyan might have clothed the book's characters and incidents with comic reality, Steinbeck merely comic-strips them of all reality and even of much interest" (121). In *The New Yorker*, Brendan Gill called the novel "labored" (71). And in the *New York Times*, Carlos Baker judged *Sweet Thursday* as "gaily inconsequential" (4), while Robert H. Boyle told *Commonweal* readers it was "a grade-B potboiler" (351).

A few contemporary notices, however, reached a moderately balanced assessment, leavening disapproval, bewilderment, or reservation with optimism. Milton Rugoff covered *Sweet Thursday* for the *Herald*

Tribune's Book Review, situating it in the "ancient and honorable tradition" of "low comedy"; Steinbeck saves the book from corniness, he says, by the "up-bubbling notes of rowdy humor, and the occasional broad satiric thrusts . . ." (1). *Saturday Review*'s Harvey Curtis Webster announced that ". . . Steinbeck can become as great an American writer as we've had in our century (I thought so when I read 'East of Eden'); at other times, it appears that he is a gifted writer who can never control his fiction sufficiently to write a first-rate book. 'Sweet Thursday' makes one feel betwixt and between" (11). Hugh Holman, writing in *The New Republic*, struck a rarely heard revisionary note:

> I think we have been wrong about Steinbeck. We have let his social indignation, his verisimilitude of language, his interest in marine biology lead us to judge him as a naturalist. . . . Steinbeck is . . . a social critic . . . occasionally angry but more often delighted with the joys that life on its lowest levels presents. I think *Sweet Thursday* implicitly asks its readers to take its author on such terms. If these terms are less than we thought we had reason to hope for from *The Grapes of Wrath*, they are still worthy of respect. (20)

Despite Holman's prophetic warning, however, with few exceptions scholarly opinion of *Sweet Thursday* is, Roy Simmonds claims, "unfavorable and at best lukewarm" (141). Everyone agrees that *Thursday* is not among Steinbeck's premier efforts, but there has been so much disagreement over the locus of the book's apparent flaws, its numerous aporia (does it fail in technique, characterization, gender coding, philosophy, or tone?), that even that minority cadre, including Astro, Holman, Howard Levant, Charles Metzger, and myself, who have found the book worth attention, cannot agree on the basis of our attraction. Moreover, during the past fifteen years, since Roy Simmonds surveyed the scene, serious interest in *Sweet Thursday* has been nearly nonexistent. Brian St. Pierre and David Wyatt say nothing of it in their books on the California aspects of Steinbeck's career. Paul McCarthy's monograph mentions the novel only in passing (19, 21, 24, 125), and even Jackson Benson's scrupulously detailed biography, *The True Adventures of John Steinbeck*, has little on *Thursday* itself, though it does provide a factual context for the book's background and its inception as a musical comedy in 1953 called "Bear Flag" (740-45). Louis Owens's 1985 thematic study of Steinbeck's Western fiction, *John Steinbeck's Re-Vision of America*, perpetuates a line of objection to the novel that extends all the way from Joseph Bennett, through critical monographs by Peter Lisca, Warren French, Joseph Fontenrose, and on to Stoddard Martin. Owens finds the novel contemptuous and dismisses it out of hand. His judgment is founded on his belief that the novel rejects "the most meaningful symbol in Steinbeck's fiction and Western culture: the Christian sacrifice" (196), though it is hard to imagine how such a caveat can be considered a universally applicable norm for judging twentieth-century fiction. More intriguing—but no less caustic—is the recent political argument on male authority/female portrayal in *Sweet Thursday* raised by feminist critic Mimi Reisel Gladstein, who exposes Steinbeck's "time-worn sexist cliches"("Missing" 92).

Amid such looming dissensus, John Timmerman went against the grain. In *John Steinbeck's Fiction*, he advanced a positive view of *Sweet Thursday* based squarely on Wylie Sypher's theory of comedy, and offered a convincing analysis of the novel as a literary "farce" (174-80). Meantime, what goes around, comes around: in an essay written for Jackson Benson's collection, *The Short Novels of John Steinbeck*, Louis Owens apparently rethought *Sweet Thursday*, and now considers it "an investigation into the role of the artist as author" (200). His tune has a suspiciously familiar ring to it, but makes good reading anyway when paired with another chapter in Benson's anthology, Mimi Gladstein's considered attempt—partly gender-driven, partly formalistic—to explain *Thursday*'s "enjoyable" but manipulative enigmas ("Straining" 244-48).

So if the opinions of Bennett and Covici represent mutually exclusive positions on *Thursday*, then perhaps Gannett's synthesism is the one to recommend. Criticism, his view suggests, is an act of understanding, a tolerance for what actually exists in a work of fiction, rather than a lament for what it lacks. This perspectival stance jibed with Steinbeck's own theories on writerly texts and readerly participation at this juncture of his career. Steinbeck's announcement in "Critics, Critics, Burning Bright" that an "experiment, which at first seems outrageous to the critic and the reader who have not been through the process of its development, may become interesting and valid when it is inspected a second and third time" (47), and his "wish" in *East of Eden*—"that when my reader has finished . . . he will have a sense of belonging . . . ." (*Journal* 61), by which he invited his reader to actively enter the process of fictionality—carried over to "Mack's Contribution," the original 156-line Introduction to *Sweet Thursday*. Mack, reacting to some unflattering reviews of *Cannery Row* and sounding much like a modern Huck Finn, claims to "have laid out a lot of time on critics," and wonders whether they all read the same book: "Some of them don't listen while they read, I guess," he states, because they are more interested in assigning handy catchwords to a work—"overambitious," "romantic," "naturalistic doggavation"—than in "understanding" (Galley I). In the truncated forty-seven line version which became *Sweet Thursday*'s published

Prologue, Mack's pointed suggestions about chapter headings, character descriptions, and loose-limbed hooptedoodle (ix-x) are laid out as matters of personal preference, not as punitive markers, and they are eventually incorporated in the novel to undercut aesthetic distance and to initiate the audience's "belonging."

Most importantly, Steinbeck is in on the con game, part of its web of decentered intrigue. *Sweet Thursday*'s affective and constitutive implications—its multiple layers of meaning, its "reality below reality" (133), its rambunctious tone, and its wilful blurring of historical reality/actual persons with invented scenarios/made-up actions (marginalized characters in an earlier *roman-à-clef* discuss a novel they appeared in; its real-life author follows their advice in a fictional sequel in which they once again appear as dramatic participants)—took precedence over traditional, directed representational means. At this juncture, before looking more closely at *Sweet Thursday* in the next section, it is worth recalling Steinbeck's 1959 letter to Elia Kazan, for it summarizes his radical epistemological project of the 1950s: "Externality is a mirror that reflects back to our mind the world our mind has created of the raw materials. But a mirror is a piece of silvered glass. There is a back to it. If you scratch off the silvering, you can see through the mirror to the other worlds on the other side. I know that many people do not want to break through. I do, passionately, hungrily" (*Life* 625).

III

Although his critics and literary historians do not agree on much else, nearly all concur that John Steinbeck staked out two major themes in his fictional career: the California experience, including the westering process and the ironic vision of Eden; and the phalanx, or group-man, theory of social and familial organization. Just about everything Steinbeck wrote touches one or both of these compelling concepts; they run so deep in the first twenty years of his career that one or the other (or both) inform his conceptions of character, setting, plot, style, and theme. When allied with his non-teleological philosophy and omniscient narrative technique, these aspects became recognizable signatures of the Steinbeck novel from the early 1930s through the late 1940s. Steinbeck's harshest critics (Edmund Wilson and Arthur Mizener, for instance) expected Steinbeck to play some variation of this music over and over again, an expectation he refused to fulfill because of his periodic dissatisfaction with the "clumsy" novel form (*Life* 194).

But if Steinbeck's proletarian narratives have a social necessity and documentary integrity that urges us to think of them as whole-cloth fabric, his late fictions can equally profit from being grouped as products of necessity and integrity, too, though of an aesthetic order and literary sensibility removed from documentary realism. Steinbeck's shift radiates from a confession in his June 8, 1949, letter to novelist John O'Hara, in which he relinquishes his earlier mode: "I believe one thing powerfully—that the only creative thing our species has is the individual, lonely mind . . . . The group ungoverned by individual thinking is a horrible destructive principle" (*Life* 359). Following this breakthrough, Steinbeck composed four experiments: the play-novelette *Burning Bright* (1950), the filmscript *Viva Zapata!* (1952), the epic *East of Eden* (1952), and the comic *Sweet Thursday* (1954). While these intensely personal books still carry elements of Edenic mythos and phalanx organization, and while they also evince a moral quality which can be said to perform a social or cultural function, overall they comprise a different order of fictionality from their predecessors. By calling attention to their own literariness through allusions, language play, scriptable referentiality, and artful framing devices, they demonstrate Steinbeck's turn toward an incipient postmodernism, a condition of openness where the act of writing in all its paradoxical manifestations becomes its own valid end (Clayton 10). "If a writer likes to write," he claimed in 1950,

> he will find satisfaction in endless experiment with his medium. He will improvise techniques, arrangements of scenes, rhythms of words, and rhythms of thought. He will constantly investigate and try combinations new to him, sometimes utilizing an old method for a new idea and vice versa. Some of his experiments will inevitably be unsuccessful but he must try them anyway if his interest be alive. This experimentation is not criminal . . . but it is necessary if the writer be not moribund. ("Critics" 47)

The result of Steinbeck's (r)evolution has been the source of much notorious and uncompromising critical reaction to his work after *Cannery Row*. However, the canonical critical ground rules of formalism do not always apply to the later Steinbeck, whose writing moved farther away from naturalism and closer toward fabulation, parable (Jones 3), and magical realism; with his new-found prerogative, Steinbeck veered from the documentary novel toward a self-revealing scriptive art. In light of this dramatic swerve, I propose that in his late career he discovered nothing less than a third major theme, which I call "The Creative." This set of values was motivated by autobiographical consciousness, individual choice, redemptive love, domestic themes, and, of course, artistic experimentation, all of which enabled Steinbeck to explore a new narratological world after 1950.

Sweet Thursday was consciously proposed as a tonal, thematic counterbalance to the "weight" of *East of Eden* (*Life* 472). It is a boisterous sequel (with the same geographical location and many of the same characters) to Steinbeck's more famous *Cannery Row*, which appeared nine years earlier (treating Monterey's pre-War era). *Thursday* takes up the post-World War II life of Doc (based on Steinbeck's soul mate, Edward F. Ricketts, who had died in a car-train crash on Drake Avenue in May, 1948); it emphasizes Doc's difficulties in reestablishing his Western Biological Laboratory on Monterey's Cannery Row, including his viccisitudes with a scholarly treatise, his rocky off-again, on-again relationship with a tough-talking, golden-hearted hooker-turned-waitress named Suzy. It also features the burlesque-like antics of the Row's Palace Flophouse denizens (Mack, Hazel, and others) and Fauna, the madame of the Bear Flag, who—playing Cupid for Doc and Suzy—want to insure a happy romantic ending.

As this brief precis suggests, when approached from a rigid analytical position, *Sweet Thursday* can be considered sentimental (like most other hookers at Fauna's Bear Flag brothel, Suzy's indelible goodness erases her stigma as a prostitute), reductive (Doc imagines he cannot be happy without a woman to complete his identity), slapstick (events and characterizations have a cartoon-like quality), and improbable (the plot hinges on concidences and convenient superficialities). Such flaws have made the book an easy target for snipers. But to arrive at the deeper significance of this fiction, questions of character motivation, realism, agency, and gender portrayal need to be willingly suspended here (and may even be beside the point). Rather, *Sweet Thursday* is important for what it reveals of Steinbeck's aesthetic and philosophical sea-changes, and for his attitude toward the necessity of fictive experimentation in the unsettling wake of a postwar depletion that affected all levels of the Row's socio-economic, philosophical, aesthetic, personal, and linguistic existence. Old ways of doing business no longer obtain for Doc, for inhabitants of the Row, or for the narrator and author (implied or otherwise): "discontent," he writes, is "the lever of change" (21). *Sweet Thursday*, then, is Steinbeck's effort at accomplishing what "has not been done a million times before" (23) in American writing.

Steinbeck understood the corrosive nature of disaffection. There was a span in his career, beginning in mid-1948, when he was cut adrift from accustomed moorings by the death of Ed Ricketts and by his divorce from Gwyn (his second wife and the mother of his two children). On and off for over a year, mired in his own enervation, misogyny, and self-pity, Steinbeck's self-identity as a writer seemed splintered, fragmented, even fraudulent. After *The Pearl* and *The Wayward Bus*, both published in 1947, this customarily resilient writer found it increasingly difficult to settle on his next project (the many versions of *Zapata*, for instance, the false starts on *East of Eden*, as well as the several unwritten plays he planned during this period). Steinbeck's personal disarray and emotional discontentedness, coupled with his awakening reaction to America's Cold War intellectual climate, which called into question the currency of social(ist) visions (Schaub 25-26), set him willy-nilly on a road toward an end he could not yet envision, but whose allurements he could not refuse. In the feverish and sometimes blind searches of that period he underwent deep readjustments toward many things, not the least of them his own fictive art. In his relationship with his third wife, Elaine, whom he met in May, 1949, and married in December, 1950, Steinbeck discovered healing powers in love and domestic attachment which in turn had a direct, exponential bearing on his work energy and anticipation (*Life* 397) and, by his own admission, may have saved him from suicide (Personal Diary 1951). Eventually, as if to validate that recovery by repeating it, Steinbeck raised his own emotional and creative processes to the level of subject, at once self-generating and historically determined. Once he entered that thorny realm he probably realized he knew it as well as anything else, which is perhaps why he considered *Sweet Thursday* "a little self-indulgent" (*Life* 473). In writing Doc trying to write, Steinbeck turned out to be narrating nothing less than the symbolic story of his own emotional rescue and artistic refashioning. In the process Steinbeck did not destroy Doc (Lisca 282) but replaced him with himself; in recasting his portrait of the artist, he did so on an entirely personal scale.

That Steinbeck took so much pleasure in writing this blissful, ludic novel should not, I think, be held against him. As a person who labored with words day in and day out, year after year, he often spoke of his need for his task to be "fun." "There is a school of thought among writers which says that if you enjoy writing something it is automatically no good and should be thrown out. I can't agree with this," he told Elizabeth Otis, his agent, and the dedicatee of *Sweet Thursday*, on September 14, 1953 (*Life* 472). If *Cannery Row* represented the way things were, he explained two months later, then *Sweet Thursday* became the way things "might have" been (474). The two propositions ("[t]he one can be as true as the other") are necessary for a holistic view of the novelist's mind, and for an understanding of what the spirit of Ed Ricketts meant to Steinbeck, who didn't "seem . . . able to get over his death" (474). Thus, only by embracing comedy and tragedy, realism and fabulation, the inarticulate "transcendental sadness" of *Cannery Row* and the "frabjous" expression of joy of *Sweet Thursday*, could Steinbeck lay to rest the ghost of Ed Ricketts, which, by this time, had become the ghost of Steinbeck himself. In giving himself to revisionary impulses, Steinbeck presented his new

Doc not as an unapproachable mythic hero, a practitioner of rigorous non-teleology, or an enigmatic isolato, but as a man—like the newly renovated Steinbeck—who was once again connected to quotidian life, to the local human community, and to author and readers, by common links—the search for meaningfulness, the potentially saving grace of love, and the ongoing struggle of the creative consciousness toward articulation:

> For hours on end he [Doc] sat at his desk with a yellow pad before him and his needle-sharp pencils lined up. Sometimes his wastebasket was full of crushed, scribbled pages, and at others not even a doodle went down. Then he would move to the aquarium and stare into it. And his voices howled and cried and moaned. "Write!" said his top voice, and "Search!" sang his middle voice, and his lowest voice sighed, "Lonesome! Lonesome!" He did not go down without a stuggle. He resurrected old love affairs, he swam deep in music, he read the *Sorrows of Werther*; but the voices would not leave him. The beckoning yellow pages became his enemies. (*Sweet* 58)

Though I obviously still endorse the premise that *Sweet Thursday* is a novel about the creative process, because it foregrounds the struggle of individual consciousness in (and through) language, I am inclined to regard Steinbeck's attitude toward the key artist figure in a less totalizing way than I did twenty-five years ago; that is, less as a result of Doc's masterful, isolated genius (his figurate role in *Cannery Row*) than as a workaday, representative negotiator between public and private realms: "When trouble came to Doc," Steinbeck notes, "it was everybody's trouble" (58). In chapter 6, "The Creative Cross," Doc's tribulations in researching and writing his proposed scholarly essay, "Symptoms in Some Cephalopods Approximating Apoplexy" (32), mirror aspects of Steinbeck's preparatory stages in his own creative regime and his usual pre-writing jitters and inability to concentrate, and reflect as well Steinbeck's wrenching artistic and personal upheavals of the late 1940s. Embedded in Steinbeck's comic treatment of Doc's trials of mind and heart is a felt psychological validity and sense of emotional immediacy. Steinbeck's new artistry lay in striking a balance between the old desire for the sovereignty of the imagination and the new awareness of contextual facticity, the ineluctability of quotidian demands. In *Sweet Thursday* this pragmatic balance took the form of a comedic stance toward the artist's traditionally elitist position. Steinbeck does not entertain the death of the author (that would erase his own reason for being), but he does give us a restrained view of Doc's performance, suggesting that success lies as much in the marshalling of conjunctive forces and ambient fortune as it does in the completion of the writing project. Paradoxically, even though Doc is freighted with Steinbeck's self-projection and autobiographical angst, there is also a telling difference in ends, because the form Steinbeck adopts for *Sweet Thursday* takes on a life of its own, "gives form to its own curiosities," as he said of André Gide's *The Counterfeiters*, and veers away from the kind of objective, autonomous document a practicing scientist would be expected to produce.

Revising, Steinbeck must have realized as he reread and reprocessed the Doc of *Cannery Row* and "About Ed Ricketts," was not a tidy allegorical process; rather, it was a way of re-entering a slippery emotional place that was no less a part of the makeup of "reality" than the physicality of his present moment. Thus "Sweet Thursday" functions as a double signifier, at once private and public utterance, reference and object, process and product, text and work. The name refers to a "magic kind of day" (122) when all manner of unanticipated, fissionable, random events occur on Cannery Row (to which Steinbeck devotes three contiguous, titled chapters—19, 20, 21—at the midpoint of his novel, and one—39—at the very end). Then, refracted, *Sweet Thursday* becomes the title of the book Steinbeck brings into being, which operates in turn as a textual looking glass that reflects, distorts, enlarges, and/or magnifies the implicit ethereality and quantum activities of the "magic day" by borrowing a sense of its own disruptive form from the carnival quality of life on the Row.

That inherent duality, that fluid interchangeability, which is encoded in the title, also functions as a symbol for Steinbeck's imaginative concerns. When Fauna tells Joe Elegant, "'When a man says words he believes them, even if he thinks he is lying'" (134), she is suggesting that language (not only experience) is a reality, and a seductive one at that. Philosophically and aesthetically, after 1949 Steinbeck wrote out of a belief in the preeminence of individual—rather than group—creativity, but he did so in such a way that his expressivism was also a critique of realism, and the issue of origination was open to authorial skepticism. The moral center he wrote toward in his late works was, like Cannery Row itself, not so much a sacred ground as it was a negotiable site of contingency and indeterminacy. For good reason, then, Steinbeck names chapter 10 "There's a Hole in Reality Through Which We Can Look if We Wish," for in its pointed artificiality, in its intertextuality, his fiction partially dismantles (but does not completely explode) the authority implicit or embedded in traditional authorship and in narrative propriety. It demonstrates that in the random, seesaw poetic form of *Sweet Thursday*, he was able to bring both the narrative plot and the process of reflexive commentary into a single work, which has the spontaneity of appearing to be made up on the spot, to undercut its own profound pretensions, and to deconstruct the rules and format of its own invention and ontology: "There are people who will say that this whole account is a lie, but a thing isn't necessarily a lie even if it didn't necessarily happen" (57). In such instances as various characters' use of malapropisms, and in Mack's humorous use of Latin phrases and exalted language, *Sweet Thursday* interrogates the representational qualities of language (and class) at the same time it validates the fluctuating process by which such mysteries emerge without ever being fully concluded. That characters as diverse as Doc, Joe Elegant, the Bear Flag's cook, who is writing a Freudian novel called *The Pi Root of Oedipus*, and Fauna, who not only writes horoscopes but authors Suzy's conduct and manners ("I should write a book . . . ." "If She Could, I Could" [143]), all wrestle with compositional acts and problems of inscription invites us to consider seriously Steinbeck's perception that the tangled wilderness of language (whether of speech, writing, body gesture, or masquerade dress) is one of the few frontiers left to us in a discontented, apocalyptic age.

IV

To the degree that the divorced Steinbeck was often an absentee parent to his boys, his writing in *East of Eden* (the original manuscript was addressed explicitly to his sons) and in *Sweet Thursday* represents surrogate ways of being a father, alternate means of assuaging his guilt and easing their dislocation by making them participants in his fictional landscape. (Two short stories from this era, "His Father" and "The Affair at 7, Rue de M——," are drawn directly from Steinbeck's family life.) While young boys could hardly be expected to read, much less understand, the philosophical *East of Eden* (Thom was 8, John IV was 6 when it appeared), *Sweet Thursday* was another matter, for with it he wrote a humorous book that not only profited from being read aloud to children, but also explained in a comedic and self-deprecating manner what it was that their father did every day with sharpened pencils and yellow note pads.

In enacting this mysterious concept of "work," *Sweet Thursday* gains its exaggerated propriety from self-conscious adaptations of fictive reality, including Steinbeck's own prior writings (*Tortilla Flat* and especially *Cannery Row*), and from parallel, engendering artifices. As I have detailed in *Steinbeck's Reading*, Steinbeck often read to write. *Sweet Thursday* is no exception. In the populist echoes, and in the literary parodies, mimicries, puns, wordplays and allusions to The Bible, *The Little Flowers of Saint Francis*, the Welsh *Mabinogian*, Coleridge's "Kubla

Khan," Lewis Carroll's "Jabberwocky" and "The Walrus and the Carpenter" from *Through the Looking Glass*, Robert Louis Stevenson's *Child's Garden of Verses*, to list but a few, *Sweet Thursday* is enriched by Steinbeck's eclectic browsing in favorite works. Perhaps more than anything else, however, Steinbeck's avowed reading of Al Capp's enormously popular, extremely inventive *Li'l Abner* comic strip, which he and his family followed assiduously in newspapers at home and abroad, propelled *Sweet Thursday* toward what New Historicists might consider its contextual thickness and tonality (Hawthorn 118-19). "Yes, comic strips," he told Sydney Fields in 1955. "I read them avidly. Especially *Li'l Abner*. Al Capp is a great social satirist. Comic strips might be the real literature of our time. We'll never know what literature is until we're gone" (*Conversations* 59). New Historicism and cultural materialism aside, what more natural way to find common ground between a stoic father and his rambunctious sons than by employing the familiar language and gestures of their milieu—comic books?

I have long been an advocate of Steinbeck's ephemeral writings ("Introduction" 3-4). Far from being marginal documents, his introductions, prefaces, dust jacket blurbs, and testimonials actually illuminate his own art. In 1953, the same year he was working on "Bear Flag," the musical precursor of *Sweet Thursday*, Steinbeck introduced Capp's book-length collection, *The World of Li'l Abner*. Steinbeck did not habitually provide encomia or introductions to the work of other writers, but when he did it was for a strong reason (*Your Only Weapon* [v]). As with many of Steinbeck's lesser-known or fugitive items, this six-page brief reveals much about his creative bearings, influences, and purposes. Beneath his jaunty, tongue-in-cheek tone there are numerous revelations which bear directly on *Sweet Thursday*'s zany style and technique. To state it simply, *Sweet Thursday* is Steinbeck's attempt at writing a literary comic book, his conscious attempt "to get into Capp's act" ([ii]).

Steinbeck theorizes that Al Capp "May very possibly be the best writer in the world today . . . the best satirist since Laurence Sterne." From a patrician point of view Steinbeck's reasoning might not at first seem convincing, and yet, while his proofs reveal some very large leaps of faith, given Steinbeck's interest in pictorialism, his populist beliefs, and his aggressively non-academic disposition, this argument is not entirely fallacious either and should not be dismissed out of hand. Steinbeck asserts that, like Dante, who redefined the established traditions of literature in his time by writing in Italian rather than in Latin, Capp, too, is a pioneer, perhaps even a visionary. The literature of the future, he claims, might eventually depart from the "stuffy" adherence to "the written and printed word in poetry, drama, and the novel," and eventually include popular forms of cultural discourse such as the comic book, Capp's *métier*. Steinbeck asks:

> How in hell do we know what literature is? Well, one of the . . . diagnostics of literature should be, it seems to me, that it is read, that it amuses, moves, instructs, changes and criticizes people. And who in the world does that more than Capp? . . . Who knows what literature is? The literature of the Cro Magnon is painted on the walls of the caves of Altamira. Who knows but that the literature of the future will be projected on clouds? Our present argument that literature is the written and printed word . . . has no very eternal basis in fact. Such literature has not been with us very long, and there is nothing to indicate that it will continue . . . . If people don't read it, it just isn't going to be literature. ([i; iv])

The key point of Steinbeck's prophetic thesis is less shocking to a reader in the mid-1990s—accustomed as we are to issues of contingency and indeterminacy caused by recent theoretical debates over the existence of a uniform canon, shared texts, and the autonomy of representation— than it was forty years ago (Eagleton 1-4). Indeed, in an age that has ushered in interactive media forms, including virtual reality and hypertexts, the comic book as a literary form appears now to be rather tame.

Nevertheless, in Capp's ability to "invent" an entire world in Dogpatch, to give it memorable characters, recognizable form, and unique spoken language, he created just that quality of aesthetic "participation" Steinbeck aimed for in all his fictions, in which the reader completed his or her own arc of a subjective transaction. The unbridled license to make up in any way that fits the artist's or the medium's immediate, compulsive demands—not those of a critical blueprint—are what Capp and Steinbeck share. Indeed, Steinbeck's description of the key elements of the *Li'l Abner* strip can be applied to *Sweet Thursday*: its plot has a "fine crazy consistency" of (il)logic, it satirizes the "entrenched nonsense" of blind human striving, respectable middle-class life, and normal male/female courting rituals; it constructs an entire fictive world in the Palace Flophouse and its larger domain, Cannery Row itself (where, like Capp's Dogpatch, realistic outside rules of aesthetics and morality do not necessarily apply); and it contains suitably exaggerated situations (Capp's Sadie Hawkins Day and Steinbeck's annual return of monarch butterflies to Pacific Grove, and The Great Roque War), as well as characters whose names are distinctive, colorful, and unique (Steinbeck's Whitey No. 1, Whitey No. 2, and Jesus and Mary Rivas; Capp's Hairless Joe, and Moonbeam McSwine, for example). In Hazel's absurd run for the presidency of the United States, we catch Steinbeck's echoes of Zoot Suit Yokum's improbable presidential nomination in 1944 (Capp 47).

Moreover, in its optimistic, life-affirming treatment of the roller-coaster love affair between Doc and Suzy, Steinbeck playfully echoes not only his own affair with Elaine, but the courtship and marriage of the recalcitrant Li'l Abner and bountiful Daisy Mae. There are numerous examples of passages, such as the one in chapter 16, where Mack believes he can heal the psychosomatic diseases of rich women, that not only pay homage to Capp (there are echoes in Mack's proposal of Marryin' Sam's "perspectus" for expensive weddings), but that also underscore Steinbeck's own self-mimicking method, his application of Capp's satiric "tweak with equal pressure on all classes, all groups," and his appreciation for the "resounding prose" of Capp's folk dialogue. Mack boasts:

> ". . . first I'd hire me a deaf-and-dumb assistant. His job is just to set and listen and look worried. Then I'd get me a bottle of Epsom salts and I'd put in a pretty little screwcap thing and I'd call it Moondust. I'd charge about thirty dollars a teaspoonful, and you got to come to my office to get it. Then I'd invent me a machine you strap the dame in. It's all chrome and it lights colored lights every minute or so. It costs the dame twelve dollars a half-hour and it puts her through the motions she'd do over a scrub board. I'd cure them! And I'd make a fortune too. Of course they'd get sick right away again, so I'd have something else, like mixed sleeping pills and wake-up pills that keeps you right where you was when you started." (102)

Perhaps more than anything else, however, there is a scene in chapter 28 that I think serves as a synecdoche in language, execution, and purpose for Capp's influence. In "Where Alfred the Sacred River Ran" (all *Sweet Thursday*'s chapters have similarly parodic or incongruent titles, very much like Capp's bold-faced commentary and frame headings in his comic strip; the chapters themselves are short and easily apprehended, like cartoon strip panels, which is one of the features Mack called for in his Prologue), Steinbeck describes the action of a wild party, and Doc's reaction to it, in a way that can best be understood if we imagine ourselves to be reading a comic strip or cartoon, blissfully participating in its "preposterous" archi-text-ure. It is necessary to quote at length from the following scene, a masquerade on the theme of "Snow White and The Seven Dwarfs," to suggest the flavor and dimensions of Steinbeck's recitation:

> A fog of unreality like a dream feeling was not in him but all around him. He went inside the Palace and saw the dwarfs and monsters and the preposterous Hazel all lighted by the flickering lanterns. None of

187

it seemed the fabric of sweet reality . . . .

Anyone untrained in tom-wallagers might well have been startled . . . . Eddie waltzed to the rumba music, his arms embracing an invisible partner. Wide Ida lay on the floor Indian wrestling with Whitey No. 2, at each try displaying acres of pink panties, while a wild conga line of dwarfs and animals milled about . . . .

Mack and Doc were swept into the conga line. To Doc the room began to revolve slowly and then to rise and fall like the deck of a stately ship in a groundswell. The music roared and tinkled. Hazel beat out rhythm on the stove with his sword until Johnny, aiming carefully, got a bull's eye on Hazel. Hazel leaped in the air and came down on the oven door, scattering crushed ice all over the floor. One of the guests had got wedged in the grandfather clock. From the outside the Palace Flophouse seemed to swell and subside like rising bread. (196-97)

This festive carnival passage (Ames 21-25), which occurs in what Mack calls a "veritable fairyland" (189), is one of Steinbeck's most pleasurable fictive moments. It revels in a sense of fancifulness, in a luxurious staging and fluid movement that joins sacred and profane experience in startling ways. Steinbeck's reversals of gender expectations, and his conscious abdication of the "fabric of sweet reality" account for the bizarre, ridiculous swelling house, the instances of cross-dressing and masquerade impersonation, the unpredictable loops and digressions of the novel's structure, his abandonment of overtly linear, "literary," progression in favor of a quantum randomness, and for his one-dimensional (but not necessarily simplistic) characterizations. All in all, it is an example of his belief that "Technique should grow out of theme" (*Life* 521).

Furthermore, Steinbeck's postwar change of aesthetic sensibility made an enormous difference between his treatment of Doc, whose "transcendent sadness" and essential loneliness closed *Cannery Row*, and this portrayal which ends with the partially incapacitated, but romantically redeemed, Doc riding off with Suzy (she is driving) into the sunset of a day that was "of purple and gold, the proud colors of the Salinas High School." Steinbeck continues: "A squadron of baby angels maneuvered at twelve hundred feet, holding a pink cloud on which the word J-O-Y flashed on and off. A seagull with a broken wing took off and flew straight up into the air, squawking, 'Joy! Joy!'" (268). It is a moment that lends *Sweet Thursday* the same quality Steinbeck found in *The World of Li'l Abner*: "such effective good nature that we seem to have thought of it ourselves" ([ii]). Love, considered both seriously and as a form of play, Steinbeck suggests, heals the split between language and life, self and world, parent and children, text and audience.

Recognizing the supremacy of such playful fictive invention under-scores that for the late Steinbeck authoring was not a thoroughly mimetic task, a representational rendering of shared social reality; it was the creation of a reality all its own, a reality once set down in or arising from language that created its own set of interpretative valuations, and whose norms, values, and ground rules changed from work to work, so that even to speak of the novelist's fictive task of creating a world in *East of Eden* would not be to describe the same created world in *Sweet Thursday*, published only two years after *Eden*, and also set in a remembered California. Far from being a tired failure because he abandoned critical realism after *The Grapes of Wrath*, Steinbeck was a prophetic Postmodernist, a journeyer in the literary fun house, a traveler in the land behind the mirror of art, a mirror which in *Sweet Thursday* had become nearly silverless, so that we see his hand at work, calling attention to the house he is building, insistently redeeming it from "mechanical convention" by "unmasking" the originating system (Hutcheon 24). Thus the old thinking, with its imposition of preordained critical hegemonies of harmony, unity, distance, mimesis, for instance, simply will not work with a textual construct like *Sweet Thursday*, or for that matter, much of what Steinbeck wrote in the last phase of his career. Authoring these texts, he authored himself anew, and vice-versa.

The pejorative *Time* magazine review, which I quoted earlier, was only partly—and unintentionally—correct in its assessment of *Sweet Thursday*. Indeed, Steinbeck did "comic-strip" his characters of reality, but that, I suggest, was his desire; far from being proof of his decline into an undifferentiated Saroyanesque landscape, his appropriation of Al Capp's free-form inventiveness, vivid technique, exaggerated scenarios, and "dreadful folk poetry" helped further in the novel what Steinbeck saw in *Li'l Abner*—a "hilarious picture of our ridiculous selves" ([ii]). Even that most significant of late Steinbeckian topics—the role of the artist—came in for its share of satire; rather than elevating it to a vaunted, culturally unassailable position, Steinbeck demystifies it by emphasiz-ing the pre-writing process, the elusive valences of language, and the necessity for human bonding, rather than the austere finished result (Doc has yet to write his essay as the book ends). In lifting the veil to expose the process of fictionalizing the fictionalizing process, Steinbeck saves *Sweet Thursday* from being masturbatory or egregiously narcissis-tic by its parodic tone and functionally inspired purpose. "Don't think of literary form," he advised famous humorist Fred Allen. "Let it get out as it wants to . . . . The form will develop in the telling. Don't make the telling follow a form" (Foreword n.p.). In seeking its own trajectory, *Sweet Thursday* turns out to be, on closer inspection, not an overstuffed turkey, but more like that gull which presides over the conclusion—earthbound on occasion, but still capable of some startling flights of fancy. Pascal Covici was correct—the novel sold with abandon—and while its commercial success justified Covici's smug faith in Steinbeck, just as it fueled Bennett's scorn, there is, as with all Steinbeck's late work, a mediating ground, an aesthetic/emotional context, a cultural current, a text behind the text that provides an enabling evaluative presence.

V

"You fix the day and hour," Steinbeck says in *Sweet Thursday*, "by some incident that happened to yourself" (121). In the fall of 1984, midway in the second semester of my visiting appointment at San Jose State University as Director of the Steinbeck Research Center, I called on Thom Steinbeck, the novelist's elder son, in Carmel Highlands. I meant only to deliver a Xeroxed mock-up of *Your Only Weapon Is Your Work*, a limited edition pamphlet publication of a 1957 letter Steinbeck had written to Dennis Murphy, the son of a longtime Steinbeck family friend, and himself author of a highly acclaimed novel, *The Sergeant* (which Steinbeck had directed first toward Elizabeth Otis, who in turn successfully placed it with Viking Press). The day, however, quickly turned into something more. We spent that afternoon lounging on the deck of his splendid rented house, taking in its view of sheltering pines, craggy bluffs, and beyond them the sparkle and flash of the Pacific Ocean north of Big Sur. For a transplanted easterner the locale provided a spectacular glimpse of a remnant of the old Pacific coast frontier, the intimidating unpeopled landscape of Robinson Jeffers's poems and Steinbeck's "Flight," and, on a different scale, "the foreign and fancy purlieus" where, in *Sweet Thursday*, Whitey No. 1 peddled raffle tickets for the Palace Flophouse sale. For several hours Thom and I talked and drank wine—much wine, as I recall—which undoubtedly helped create the glow of camaraderie in that luminous time and place. We were contemporaries—a year apart in age—and our sense of having shared generational experiences and opinions seemed pronounced that afternoon.

Of course, we spoke often of his father and I remember vividly how Thom talked in that specially tinged, offhand and amazed way that children of the celebrated and famous have of communicating their conflicted sense of acceptance and estrangement, honor and renunciation, pride and embarrassment in their legacy. The afternoon was interrupted by at least two long-distance telephone calls from Thom's younger brother, John IV, and while these hiatuses stopped the flow of our talk for a while, each time Thom came back he was fueled with new energy, new reminiscences, often circling around tales of his father reading aloud to them, and his exasperation at their short attention spans. While I was not actively seeking gossip, I admit I was not averse to such inside news, though I was also leary of its implications, and the burden of complicity or degree of co-option it might create in the future. But such knowledge is always double-edged and serves unanticipated ends: listening to stories of Thom's childhood following his parents' divorce, I glimpsed something of the cause of his father's paternal attachment to Dennis Murphy, who became, for a while anyway, a surrogate son for what might not have been the best of reasons.

As much as anything else that afternoon I was painfully aware that even with firsthand information I was being offered in moments of spirited fellow-feeling, I could not know this man's father, John Steinbeck, whom I had spent so many years studying, in anything but a partial way, refracted through the bias of my own sensibility, the lens of my own being. Perhaps, I thought, I really had failed the test of perspectival criticism after all, and had fallen a long way from the level of a Lewis Gannett, or, in my own time, a Jackson Benson, who had more than anyone else I knew given Steinbeck's life and career the fairest assessment. And yet if such musings made Steinbeck less a monument, less a cultural icon, to me, I wasn't sure that I was willing to trade places with my host either, who, with his brother, knew even more than I the burden of shadows cast by the dead. Sometimes, I figured, it is better to be an everlasting outsider, inventing reasons for the reasons, rather than having to live them.

In the course of that afternoon, though, in addition to regaling me with raucous tales and anecdotes, Thom showed me Steinbeck family memorabilia, and we briefly entertained the possibility of my purchasing some items for the Steinbeck Center at a later date. (Almost a year later I bought a number of 8 mm home movies for the Center, including rare footage of Steinbeck and Ricketts's Sea of Cortez collecting trip.) As I was about to leave for Los Gatos, Thom said he had something he wanted me to have. I told him I was representing the Research Center and could not accept a gift for myself, though I could and would—gladly—receive one on behalf of San Jose State. He agreed, then hauled out a 1950s vintage portable typewriter, which he opened for my inspection. It was a Hermes, aptly named for the messenger of the gods, and himself a deity who embodied plural functions—god of invention, god of thievery, and god of roads and travel—in short, the god of process. "This was my father's," he said. "I want you to have it."

But only after reaching home that night did I notice the most intriguing part of the gift: on the back of the typewriter's grey cover Steinbeck had scratched indelibly with a pin, or knife, or maybe a nail, these words: "The Beast Within." I think that it was his way—part humorous, part deadly serious—of personalizing an otherwise somber-looking mechanical device, giving a name and an identity to one of those technological gadgets that the inventor side of him dearly loved and remained fascinated by throughout his life. In its ideal state the typewriter (and its kin) abetted the writer's imagination, processed his arc of reality, helped turn emergent material, whatever its source, into fictive form, and—not to put too purple a shade on this—gave shape, weight, palpability to experience in/of language: "The discipline of the written word punishes both stupidity and dishonesty," he told Pascal Covici, Jr. "A writer lives in awe of words for they can be cruel or kind, and they can change their meanings right in front of you" (*Life* 523). As a mediating trope, so to speak, for transmission of shifting words, the typewriter paradoxically distorts, transforms, and modifies in order to clarify and illumine; although it is not an "appendage," an "umbilical connection" like the more comfortable pencil Steinbeck often preferred, it still operates in the same way as a focussing "tool" (*Life* 624), like his later use of the dictaphone, that tends outward as well as inward, facilitating (and in some cases creating) his view of the world. The important thing, however, is the process of looking and of immersion implied in writing—the pen(cil) or knife or nail or typewriter key scratch on the surface of a papery medium—that records what it means to have been alive in the magnificent constellation of inner and outer experience. "After all," Doc says, "I guess it doesn't matter whether you look down or up—as long as you look" (*Sweet* 273).

In my moment of obsessive identification, the tiny machine came alive as a cumulative metaphor for the entire complex of Steinbeck's working life, an artifice situated on a horizon somewhere between expressivism and determined construction. On one hand, it represents process: the constant tyranny of being driven by "ancient" human compulsions toward expression (*Life* 523) and the daily, obsessive financial need to write (which made him frequently moody, selfish, inward-looking in a way no doubt only those who lived in his life—his wives, children, and stepchild, for instance—could fully ascertain and in a perverse way were fully qualified to judge). On the other hand, it symbolizes product: the indescribable and fleeting moments of success when a work was published and commercially viable, and then nominally at least put behind him as he went on restlessly to the next project. "To finish is sadness to a writer—a little death. He puts the last word down and it is done. But it isn't really done. The story goes on and leaves the writer behind, for no story is ever done" (*Life* 523).

The unfinished story surfaces in unforeseen ways, even when you

think it is done, including its intrusion into this fragmentary attempt at synthesis and integration, when Steinbeck rewrites Ed Ricketts by reimagining Doc as himself, when he revises Capp's act by reinventing the comic book for his children, when I revisit the scene of my revisionism, and all of us—fathers and sons, current lovers and ex-spouses, past mentors and abiding friends—drive, so to speak, toward La Jolla, where all things seem to resolve into metaphoric simplicity and intuitive clarity: "This is the greatest mystery of the human mind—the inductive leap. Everything falls into place, irrelevancies relate, dissonance becomes harmony, and nonsense wears a crown of meaning. But the clarifying leap springs from the rich soil of confusion, and the leaper is not unfamiliar with pain" (*Sweet* 28). It is a moment when the machinery, the inventions, the necessary metaphors and tropes of leaping and journeying which so fixed and fascinated Steinbeck during his career—the Joad's Hudson Super Six, the Western Flyer, The Word, Juan Chicoy's broken-down bus, Olive Hamilton's airplane ride, the telescope that Mack and the boys present Doc at the conclusion of *Sweet Thursday* (he actually needed a microscope), his Hermes typewriter, his truck camper Rocinante, even the hieroglyphic *timshel*, and the surreal, topsy-turvy architecture of Al Capp's Dogpatch—all begin moving evocatively in roughly the same direction to fuel the transforming "drama of magic and alchemy" by which Steinbeck entered fascinating worlds of resonant language and rich experience, where, because the old strictures no longer applied, he felt obliged to make "new rules" of artistic conduct, propriety, and deportment (*Life* 532). Steinbeck's gift—much underrated in the final phase of his career—was his ability to make each book a different kind of "life experience" (*Journal* 61) by sending back reports from all the creative venues he entered—whether it was the tidepool, human speech and language, or the conflicted labyrinth of the heart. Maybe after all critical commentary subsides, after the process and nature of writing itself has been redefined yet again according to whatever the future current fashion will be, then what has gone around will come around, and John Steinbeck will prove to have been on the right road all along, the rest of us dust swirls in the spokes of his wheels.

Works Cited

Ames, Christopher. *The Life of the Party: Festive Vision in Modern Fiction*. Athens: U of Georgia P, 1991.

Astro, Richard. "Steinbeck's Bittersweet Thursday." *Steinbeck Quarterly* 4 (1971): 36-47. Rpt. in Benson, ed. 204-15.

_____, and Tetsumaro Hayashi, eds. *Steinbeck: The Man and His Work*. Corvallis: Oregon State UP, 1971.

"Back to the Riffraff." *Time* 14 June 1954: 120-21.

Baker, Carlos. "After Lousy Wednesday." *New York Times Book Review* 13 June 1954: 4.

Benson, Jackson J. *The True Adventures of John Steinbeck, Writer.* New York: Viking, 1984.

_____, ed. *The Short Novels of John Steinbeck: Critical Essays with a Checklist to Steinbeck Criticism.* Durham: Duke UP, 1990.

Boyle, Robert H. "Boozy Wisdom." *Commonweal* 9 July 1954: 351.

Capp, Al. *The World of Li'l Abner.* Introd. John Steinbeck. Foreword by Charles Chaplin. New York: Ballantine, 1953.

Clayton, Jay. *The Pleasures of Babel: Contemporary American Literature and Theory.* New York: Oxford UP, 1993.

Covici, Pascal. Letter to John Steinbeck. 16 June 1954. Harry Ransom Humanities Research Center, Austin, Texas.

_____ Letter to John Steinbeck. 9 August 1954. Harry Ransom Humanities Research Center, Austin, Texas.

DeMott, Robert. "Introduction." *A New Steinbeck Bibliography: 1971-1981.* By Tetsumaro Hayashi. Metuchen: Scarecrow, 1983. 1-4.

_____. "Steinbeck and the Creative Process: First Manifesto to End the Bringdown against *Sweet Thursday*." Astro and Hayashi 157-78.

_____. *Steinbeck's Reading: A Catalogue of Books Owned and Borrowed.* New York: Garland, 1984.

Eagleton, Terry. *Literary Theory: An Introduction.* Minneapolis: U of Minnesota P, 1983.

Fontenrose, Joseph. *John Steinbeck: An Introduction and Interpretation.* New York: Barnes, 1963.

French, Warren. *John Steinbeck.* New York: Twayne, 1961.

_____. *John Steinbeck.* 2nd ed. rev. Boston: Hall, 1975.

Gill, Brendan. *New Yorker* 10 July 1954: 71.

Gladstein, Mimi Reisel. "Straining for Profundity: Steinbeck's *Burning Bright* and *Sweet Thursday*." Benson, ed. 234-48.

_____. "Missing Women: The Inexplicable Disparity Between Women in Steinbeck's Life and Those in His Fiction." *The Steinbeck Question: New Essays in Criticism.* Ed. Donald R. Noble. Troy: Whitston, 1993. 84-98.

Hawthorn, Jeremy. *A Concise Glossary of Contemporary Literary Theory.* London: Arnold, 1992.

Holman, Hugh. "A Narrow-gauge Dickens." *New Republic* 7 June 1954: 18-20.

Hutcheon, Linda. *Narcissistic Narrative: The Metafictional Paradox.* 1980. London: Methuen, 1984.

Jones, Lawrence William. *John Steinbeck as Fabulist.* Ed. Marston LaFrance. Steinbeck Monograph Series, No. 3. Muncie: Steinbeck Society, 1973.

Levant, Howard. *The Novels of John Steinbeck: A Critical Study.* Columbia: U of Missouri P, 1974.

Lisca, Peter. *The Wide World of John Steinbeck.* New Brunswick: Rutgers UP, 1958. Rpt. with new Afterword. New York: Gordian, 1981.

McCarthy, Paul. *John Steinbeck.* New York: Ungar, 1980.

Martin, Stoddard. *California Writers: Jack London, John Steinbeck, The Tough Guys.* 1983. Boston: St. Martin's, 1984. 67-122.

Metzger, Charles. "Steinbeck's Version of the Pastoral." *Modern Fiction Studies* 6 (1960): 115-24. Rpt. in Benson, ed. 185-95.

Murphy, Dennis. *The Sergeant*. New York: Viking, 1958.

Owens, Louis. *John Steinbeck's Re-Vision of America*. Athens: U of Georgia P, 1985.

_____. "Critics and Common Denominators." Benson, ed. 195-203.

Rugoff, Milton. "Business as Usual, and Fun, Too, on John Steinbeck's Cannery Row." *New York Herald Tribune Books* 13 June 1954: 1.

St. Pierre, Brian. *John Steinbeck: The California Years*. San Francisco: Chronicle, 1983.

Schaub, Thomas Hill. *American Fiction in the Cold War*. Madison: U of Wisconsin P, 1991.

Simmonds, Roy S. "Steinbeck's *Sweet Thursday*." *A Study Guide to Steinbeck, Part II*. Ed. Tetsumaro Hayashi. Metuchen: Scarecrow, 1979. 139-64.

Steinbeck, John. *Burning Bright*. New York: Viking, 1950.

_____. *Cannery Row*. New York: Viking, 1945.

_____. *Conversations with John Steinbeck*. Ed. Thomas Fensch. Jackson: UP of Mississippi, 1988.

_____. "Critics, Critics, Burning Bright." *Saturday Review* 11 November 1950: 20-21. Rpt. in *Steinbeck and His Critics: A Record of Twenty-five Years*. Ed. E. W. Tedlock and C. V. Wicker. Albuquerque: U of New Mexico P, 1957. 43-47.

_____. Dust Jacket Encomium. *Gypsy: A Memoir*. By Gypsy Rose Lee. New York: Harper, 1957.

_____. *East of Eden*. New York: Viking, 1952.

_____. "His Father." *Reader's Digest* 55. 329 (1949): 19-21.

_____. Introduction. *The World of Li'l Abner*. By Al Capp. [i-vi].

_____. Introduction. Mack's Contribution. Unrevised galley proofs of *Sweet Thursday*. MS. 776642. Harry Ransom Humanities Research Center, Austin, Texas.

_____. *Journal of a Novel: The* East of Eden *Letters*. New York: Viking, 1969.

_____. Letter to Fred Allen. Qtd. in Foreword. *Much Ado About Me*. By Fred Allen. Boston: Little, 1956. n.p.

_____. Personal Diary, 1946. MA 4685. The Pierpont Morgan Library, New York.

_____. Personal Diary, 1951. MA 4689. The Pierpont Morgan Library, New York.

_____. *Steinbeck: A Life in Letters*. Ed. Elaine Steinbeck and Robert Wallsten. New York: Viking, 1975.

_____. *Sweet Thursday*. New York: Viking, 1954.

_____. "The Affair at 7, Rue de M——." *Harper's Bazaar* 2921 (1955): 112, 202, 213.

_____. "*Un Grand Romancier de Notre Temps*. "Hommage à André Gide 1869-1951." Spec. issue of *La Nouvelle Revue Francaise* (Nov. 1951): [30].

_____. *Your Only Weapon Is Your Work: A Letter by John Steinbeck to Dennis Murphy*. Ed. Robert DeMott. San Jose: Steinbeck Research Center, 1985.

Timmerman, John. *John Steinbeck's Fiction: The Aesthetics of the Road Taken*. Norman: U of Oklahoma P, 1986.

Webster, Harvey Curtis. "'Cannery Row' Continued." *Saturday Review* 12 June 1953: 11.

Wyatt, David. *The Fall into Eden: Landscape and Imagination in California.* New York: Cambridge UP, 1986. 124-57.

Citizen Cain: Ethan Hawley's Double Identity in The Winter of Our Discontent

Michael Meyer

In "Talismanic Patterns in the Novels of John Steinbeck," Todd Lieber notes that at the heart of Steinbeck's work is the conviction that the

> writing most worth doing is that which can penetrate to the sources of human thought and behavior and present in the form of some objective correlative the archetypal and mythopoeic knowledge that lies deep in the mystery of human existence. (275)

For Steinbeck, this correlative was often rooted in the Biblical allusions that "form the warp and woof of plot and character development in many of his major works" (Timmerman 272). Yet Steinbeck's use of Bible stories and Christian symbolism is often unorthodox, splicing together Old Testament and New Testament references to suggest paradoxical complexities and differing interpretations.

For example, Peter Lisca comments in *John Steinbeck: Nature and Myth* that "the young communist, Jim Nolan, serves Steinbeck not only as a Satan figure, the corrupter of mankind, but also as a Savior, a type of Christ "(75). Similarly, Stoddard Martin notes that critics of *The Grapes of Wrath* have identified the preacher Casy with Christ, John the Baptist, and Aaron while Tom Joad has been associated with St. Peter, the apostle Paul, and Moses (71). Finally Ray Griffith notes that "mixtures of gray tones are more frequent in Steinbeck than stark black and stark white . . . resulting in an outlook that is tantamount to dual duality" (20).

Assuming these analyses are accurate, Steinbeck's syncretic merging of allusions[1] suggests that a complex task of unraveling awaits readers who decide to delve beneath the surface of Steinbeck's allegorical texts. Unfortunately, most critics have deplored what they consider Steinbeck's blatant associations of characters with specific Biblical archetypes. For example, Martin states that the incorporation of religious allusions in *East of Eden* is not

> as deft and subtle as his use of the Arthurian myth in *Tortilla* [*Flat*] or the Everyman framework in *Wayward Bus*. The naming of the Trasks by 'A' or 'C' according to where they stand in the good-evil dialectic is a transparent device which contributes to the book's over-wrought Manicheanism. (208)

However, once Steinbeck's syncretic methodology is discovered, quite the reverse is shown to be true. Steinbeck's Biblical images are far from transparent and simple and surely require a good deal of thought before they can be explicated.

Although the allegorical quality of Steinbeck's last novel, *The Winter of Our Discontent*, has been duly noted by critics, most commentaries have centered on the bipartite arrangement of the novel and the holidays that frame the action of each part: Easter and the Fourth of July. Thus the Christological and socio-political symbols used by Steinbeck have been analyzed and criticized as being overstated and perhaps too obvious.[2] Yet since Steinbeck yoked New Testament and Old Testament allusions in *The Grapes of Wrath*, *To a God Unknown*, and *East of Eden*, it is more than likely that there are other Biblical allusions to mine in Steinbeck's final novel than would at first appear. Given Steinbeck's previous preoccupation with the Cain and Abel myth in *East of Eden* and his assertion that it is "perhaps the greatest story of all—the story of good and evil, of strength and weakness, of love and hate, of beauty and ugliness . . ." demonstrating "how these doubles are inseparable—how neither can exist without the other . . ." (*Journal* 2), it should not be surprising that this particular myth resurfaces for one last examination in *The Winter of Our Discontent*. "What a strange story it is and how it haunts one," Steinbeck says in *Journal of a Novel*. ". . . [W]ithout this story—or rather a sense of it—psychiatrists would have nothing to do . . . . [T]his one story is the basis of all human neurosis—and if you take the fall along with it, you have the total of the psychic troubles that can happen to a human" (139).

In his retelling of the myth, Steinbeck deliberately reminds the reader of the Manichean distinction between good and evil, a theological construct that involves two roots and three moments and that suggests the impossibility of absolutes. One root is light, a kingdom of peace and goodness, while the other is darkness, a time of turmoil and evil. These two roots were separate in a past moment according to Mani's theory, but in the present times they no longer exist as unique entities but rather have formed a strange mixture of light and darkness. Steinbeck presents his protagonist in the novel, Ethan Allen Hawley, in a similarly ambiguous tone, his major dilemma being his inability to distinguish between good and evil within a modern society. Although Steinbeck acknowledges that Ethan will ultimately have to choose which of the two brothers (Cain or Abel) will serve as his role model for life, when the reader first meets him, Steinbeck's heroic anti-hero is presented ironically as a composite of both archetypes. As the plot progresses, the Cain story is romanced and given many faces having to do with conquest, domination, and power; however, Steinbeck also examines the Abel traits of unity, concord, and cooperation, presenting them as valid options for the modern age. Thus, while the evils of betrayal, murder, greed, adultery, and theft are portrayed in their current modes, brotherhood and morality are also advocated as potential solutions for fratricidal conflict. Ultimately, the novel issues a warning to American citizens who had become perversely fascinated with evil. In order to bring about the third moment anticipated in Manichean theology when the two kingdoms would again separate, Americans must eschew evil and consciously choose good. There is no doubt that the message of *The Winter of Our Discontent* reiterates Steinbeck's *timshel* doctrine, which was originally presented in *East of Eden*: all men, even Cains, have choices; they are not predestined to act one way or another. Consequently, modern-day Cains have redemptive potential.

Ricardo Quinones has demonstrated this potential in his study *The Changes of Cain: Violence and The Lost Brother in Cain and Abel Literature* by pointing out how the Biblical myth may have either a positive or negative reading depending upon the time frame of its use. Quinones notes that "the remarkable quality of the story this book will tell is that Cain, so potently and insistently subversive of the ideals of unity and the community will himself become a figure of regeneration" (5). Later in his introduction, Quinones points out that Cain in the modern age becomes "the quester, the metaphysical rebel, the force in search of new ideas and new modes of being" while there is "progressive pejoration of the qualities of Abel," who now is seen as "subservient . . . stagnant," and "conservative" (19).

Quinones states:

The essential drama that the Cain-Abel theme represents in the modern world is that between a questioning, dissatisfied, probing critical intelligence, keenly aware of division and somehow in search of a better order, and a non-aspirant Abel, who by virtue of some personal accommodation or by simple resignation is more accepting of the contradictions of life. (13)

While Steinbeck depicts an America torn between early moral values that were "absolute" and the shifting standards which were associated with the twentieth century, his characters, especially Ethan, experience the four stages of the Cain drama as it is analyzed by Quinones: division, tragic differentiation, arbitrariness of preference, and the reactions of violence, envy, and mystery. Quinones theorizes that Steinbeck understood that the Cain-Abel story had become an American type abundantly suited to its history (143).[3] Specifically, he posits the probability that in the early Biblical Puritan tradition, Americans had seen themselves as Abels, obedient individuals who found God's favor in the new world. However, as America continued to develop, it became evident that Cain had become the icon and role model of a new society as more and more of its citizens saw aggression and violence as a necessity for advancement and success. As Steinbeck observed in *The Log From the Sea of Cortez*, "in our structure of society, the so-called and considered good qualities are invariable concomitants of failure, while the bad ones are the cornerstones of success" (97-98).

Perhaps the structure of the novel is one indication of Steinbeck's attempt to combine Old Testament theology with that of the New Testament. The ten chapters that comprise Part I could easily relate to the ten commandments and could represent the rigid law of the Old Testament, a law which in New Baytown has given way to new rules of conduct, those of greed and immorality; similarly, the twelve chapters included in Part II may represent the New Testament and the potential for positive change and reform, possibilities which exist despite the bleak events that occur in its pages.

The first section of the book begins on Good Friday and ends on Easter Tuesday. During this brief time period, Steinbeck brings his protagonist, Hawley (suggesting a New England pronunciation of "holy"), to a confrontation between his two natures, natures embodied symbolically in the images of a revengeful and aggressive Cain and a victimized, passive Abel. Steinbeck suggests this dichotomy by recounting Ethan's dual ancestry: pirates on one side of his family and Puritans on the other (*Winter* 7, 10). Up to the time the novel begins, Ethan has served as an Abel, a passive victim whose fortunes have fallen as more aggressive Cains have asserted their claims on society. The power of money and the threat of aggression have overcome the weak, and Ethan's mild-mannered ethical actions have served only to drive him into debt and despair. It is becoming increasingly clear to Ethan that maintaining an Abel role will bring him neither happiness nor success. As a result, he begins to examine his positive actions and his clean reputation in an effort to decide whether his attempt to be good is worth it. The other option is, of course, to capitulate, following his Cain tendencies and worshipping power, prestige, and acknowledgment as the new American gods while ignoring the moral beliefs on which America supposedly was founded.

Steinbeck cleverly presents these Old Testament allusions in a complex interwoven pattern with New Testament stories, especially elements from the Gospels. As readers examine the Christological imagery so evident in the plot's structure (especially allusions to the Crucifixion and the Resurrection), it is important to remember that the Abel figure in the Old Testament was considered the earliest precursor of Christ.

The Biblical character is portrayed as a guiltless victim, and his death at the hands of his brother is the first blood sacrifice, prefiguring redemption's high cost, Christ's death on the cross. As a result of Cain's crime, Abel's blood calls out to God for vengeance, while, on the other hand, the death of Christ pleads for mercy and forgiveness for the human sins that demand his crucifixion. Ironically, the novel depicts Ethan's pure Abel-like self dying on Good Friday in an imitation of Christ's sacrifice. Yet the text also suggests a reversal, for Ethan/Abel has reached a turning point, a crisis that motivates him to deny his primitive commitment to Yahweh and to convert to the materialistic world's values.

Eventually, the symbolic "death" of Ethan's positive nature as Abel and his rebirth as Cain creates an effect that intersects with the New Testament's theology of salvation and reverses the outcome of Christ's literal death on the cross. Christ's sacrifice is efficacious: it brings eternal salvation for the sinner. But Ethan as Cain realizes that such a sacrifice produces only suffering and pain for the self: Christ-like Abels work toward their own demise. Consequently, based on selfish motivations, he decides to change roles, to become the victimizer rather than victim. While Christ dies to eradicate sin, Ethan's sinless self (his Abel alter-ego) dies. For a true worldly "life" to occur, Ethan as Cain understands that he must subdue his moral nature and his adherence to God's principles; instead of his tendency to evil, his violent espousal of worldly values must be reborn. In this Easter season, Ethan/Cain ironically buries the new man/Abel, the resurrected image of Christ, in deliberate opposition to the advice of Scripture (2 Cor. 4:16 and 5:17). Instead he resurrects the old self—the "old man" of the scriptures who is evil and depraved and who is inclined toward defiance of God rather than adherence to His law. As Quinones points out, the Cain-Abel myth "persists in showing the dramas of people brought to a crossroads, where some kind of radical action is required involving either the community or the self" (14). While outwardly remaining his old self, Ethan/Abel paradoxically begins to take on the characteristics of his brother Cain. Unfortunately, by acting in a manner opposed to his moral center, he will also ironically serve as his own destroyer.

In the first chapter Steinbeck spends a great deal of time delineating the worldly temptations which Ethan/Abel faces. He must confront the devious bank president, Mr. Baker; the town whore, Margie Young-Hunt; and the nefarious wholesaler, Mr. Biggers, of B.B.D. & D. Wholesalers. While many critics have drawn attention to the obvious parallel of Christ's temptation in the wilderness,[4] few have noted that the dilemma Ethan confronts is one that also confronts Cain: choosing between following Yahweh's commandments or attaining the more appealing worldly offerings of the devil, the world and the flesh. Cain must decide whether to destroy brotherhood in order to gain selfhood. As Quinones reminds readers: "The physical slaying of the brother assures the coming into being of the self" (19). In order to attain such individuation, Ethan must opt to be destructive, must evaluate whether he is willing to pay the high price of guilt in order to obtain the differentiation he so desires. He must choose whether to submit to his own self-centeredness and egotism and commit murder or whether to obey a moral code despite the seemingly arbitrary lack of recognition he receives for such an action.

For a while Ethan remains a composite Cain/Abel figure in the novel, vacillating between his moral legacy of goodness and uprightness (the Hawley/Edenic heritage) and at the same time struggling with the realization that Adam and Eve's sin has changed the complexion of mankind's relationship to God. With all humanity now marked by the stain of original sin, Ethan perceives that the future belongs to those who utilize the corruption around them to their own benefit. Despite Ethan's "religious" tendencies, which he associates with his Great Aunt Deborah, he realizes that in direct contrast to the Biblical story of Cain and Abel, no higher power has singled him out for praise for his ethics; instead his moral code has brought about his downfall. It is no wonder then that Ethan bridles at his failure and his slow descent into insolvency, while foreigners like his boss, Marullo, with less moral sense than he, are successful.

As the syncretic Cain and Abel character, Ethan expects God to honor his life as a thank offering which is equal to that of his brothers, the other residents of New Baytown. He even attempts to define absolutes of good and evil that will promote such fairness. However, in typical Steinbeckian ironic counterpoint, Ethan observes that the Biblical myth is reversed: good is devalued, and evil is idealized. Thus, worldly claims are shown to hold precedence over spiritual values, a fact that is confirmed by the actions of Marullo and the salesman, Mr. Biggers, whose aggressive Cain-like acts have spiraled them to the top of society. When Ethan acknowledges that God is arbitrary in his preference for those who follow the path of Cain, he begins to see that there is common sense in converting completely to a Cain-role and protesting God's seeming unfairness by joining in the destruction of less fortunate, weaker Abels.

When he shares the ethical dilemmas he has observed in his work with his friend Joey Morphy, a teller at the local bank, Ethan has another opportunity to observe that moral concerns are not shared by others. Instead, Morphy advocates money and prosperity as appropriate American gods, and Ethan is again forced to ponder whether ethical actions are foolish. Since acceptance and success are no longer based on adherence to right, moral Abels may be out of date. Morphy's capitulation is the last straw for Ethan, who more than ever identifies with Cain (as well as with Jesus) in his lament that God has forsaken him (*Winter* 32). Thus Cain-like isolation marks the last hours of Ethan's work day, and, as he carries home his heavy grocery bags and his guilt, he must face imminent capitulation to evil. Further evidence of Ethan's transformation from Abel to Cain may be found in the loneliness his character experiences at this point in the novel. Ethan is pictured on long solitary walks where he contemplates the injustice of his situation and mentally bemoans his fate.

In his subsequent visit to his "Place," a cave about four feet wide and five feet deep carved into the harbor, Ethan continues his isolation, mulling over whether or not to pursue the transformation. "It's big changes take me there—big changes," says Ethan (*Winter* 51), implying his decision has already been made. Later, while deciding his future, he interrogates himself, "Could I incline to want what I didn't want?" (54). Such a question poses the dichotomy in Ethan's personality, and he must decide which self will be allowed to predominate. When he emerges from this tomb-like structure, he has the potential for an Abel victory, which parallels Christ's resurrection, but he can also choose to ignore "God-given" rules and succumb to the way of the world.

At this point, instead of examining his soul, it is significant that Ethan rather takes stock of his earthly situation and his desire for some type of success, either monetary or emotional. After contemplating the rewards of Cain-like actions, Ethan ironically meets his best friend, Danny Taylor, on his way home. Steinbeck deliberately points out that Ethan and Danny are blood brothers, having carved a similar heart on their arms as youngsters (*Winter* 286). This interchange of blood is classified by Quinones as a habitual way of asserting a fraternal commitment of risk and sharing, one to another (4). Yet Ethan sees Danny rather as a way to recapture power and social prestige, recognizing his alcoholism as a fatal flaw that could eventually be exploited to Ethan's monetary advantage. Danny thus becomes an unsuspecting Abel figure, and his future death at Ethan's hands is predictably foreshadowed despite Ethan's outward show of concern and caring for his person. For example, as part of a soliloquy in chapter 3, Ethan confesses his deep feelings for Danny as he says:

> I should be able to help him. I've tried, but he won't let me. Danny is as near to a brother as I ever had, same age and growing up, same weight and strength. Maybe my guilt comes because I am my brother's keeper and I have not saved him. (*Winter* 48)

Later Ethan echoes this typically Cain-like comment when he tells Mr. Baker of his dream about Danny: "Once we were closer than brothers. I had no brother. I guess we were brothers in a way. I don't carry it out, of course, but I feel I should be my brother Danny's keeper" (*Winter* 121).

Danny represents a new type of Abel, a "good" man who has been ruined both physically and mentally by the modern age and who has suffered at the hands of greedy and jealous Cains. He is Quinones's single-minded, simplistic individual, ill-equipped for life in the world (138). As such a stereotype, Danny allows Ethan to take advantage of him and to repeat his insincere claims of concern for his welfare. After upbraiding Danny for his overindulgent drinking, Ethan repeats his belief in their brotherhood but significantly chooses the past tense to express it. "You *were* my brother, Danny," Ethan says. Then he adds almost in an afterthought: "You still are. I'll do anything in the world to help you" (emphasis mine, *Winter* 56). However, Ethan's sincerity toward Danny is surely in question after this interchange since he has already considered the benefits he would receive if Danny should die. It is also important to note that when Ethan is greeted by others as he approaches his home, he appears to them as a marked/changed man. Again the Cain parallel resurfaces. Ethan has chosen to follow the Cain-sign, seeking success even though it may lead to his own destruction.

Not surprisingly, very few residents of New Baytown are shocked by Ethan's changes since as a modern Cain he maintains the facade of respectability and makes his motives appear pure rather than tainted. Critic Deborah Schneer in her discussion of *The Grapes of Wrath* calls attention to Steinbeck's use of the mental process known in psychoanalytic discourse as "splitting." Schneer defines splitting as

> the mental activity by which people project and introject aspects of themselves and the external world, thereby keeping what feels right and good, safe and separate from what feels dangerous and destructive. Splitting indicates polarization. Good and bad cannot be integrated. One side is devalued, the other idealized. (107)

Splitting is precisely what Ethan is practicing here, rationalizing his sinful acts and, like Cain, attempting to fool himself into believing he is only an innocent observer rather than an active participant in his brother's downfall.

Ultimately, Ethan comes to believe his own duplicitous defense of his indulgence in evil and continues his descent into hell. His first decision is to proceed with his plan to destroy Danny in order to get control of his land. Unlike Cain's direct murder of Abel, Ethan decides to use a more modern roundabout method, one which will not hold him directly responsible. He offers to lend Danny $1000 of his own money in hopes that Danny's alcoholism will prove fatal. Then Ethan will sell Danny's property, given as collateral for the loan, for a large profit, and the location will be developed as the city airport.

However, since evil has multiplied in a modern age, one destruction of a brother is not sufficient for a present-day Cain. Therefore, Ethan also arranges the destruction of his boss, the Sicilian immigrant, Marullo, by revealing that he is an illegal alien. The action results in Marullo's deportation and assures Ethan's restoration as owner of the grocery store, a position he initially lost through virtuous rather than deceptive marketing. In this second betrayal, the new Cain again attains dominance by non-violence, but the destruction of his brother remains the same. Marullo will not only lose the store, but his deportation will end his life for all intents and purposes.

Chapter 6 provides Ethan's analysis of the dark side of his subconscious that fosters such evil acts. Here Ethan relates still another brother story, the death of his wife's sibling, Dennis, from an infected thyroid. As Dennis succumbs to his illness, Ethan describes feeling as if "a monster swam up out of the dark water" (*Winter* 99), promoting his desire to tear apart his bedridden brother-in-law, whose weakness is his only defect. Reflecting back on the time, Ethan relates the following: "I hated him. I wanted to kill him, to bite out his throat. My jaw muscles tightened and I think my lips fleered back like a wolf's at the kill" (99). Shortly after, he muses that

> events and experiences nudged and jostled me in a direction contrary to my normal one or the one I had come to think was normal—the ... failure, the man without real hope or drive ... caged by habits and attitudes I thought of as being moral, even virtuous. And it may be that I had a smugness about being what I called a "Good Man." (100)

Nonetheless, Ethan continues to defend his newly acquired Cain role, concluding that morality is a defect that needs to be overcome. Cain acts are, he decides, ultimately beneficial, a reaction that emphasizes the changing American response to betrayal, violence, and greed. Chapter 7 then reinforces Ethan's predisposition to violence by mentioning his reaction to killing during the war. "No man ... ever had less murder in his heart than I," Ethan says. "The times, the moment, demanded that I slaughter human beings and I did" (*Winter* 116). A similar parallel is related as Ethan recounts the story of the rabbits in his backyard. "A man can get used to anything," he relates, "Slaughtering or undertaking or even execution; rack and pincers must be just a job when one gets used to it" (130). By the middle of the book, then, the Cain myth has become one of the novel's central metaphors, reasserting Steinbeck's belief that jealousy, envy, and avarice have become the moral norms of today's world and reminding contemporary Americans of the consequences of their decision—that to be a Cain is not so bad after all. As Quinones states in his study, the figure of Cain has shifted from its original meaning: "When one brother rises, as Abel does in the predominately Christian era, the other falls; but in the romantic and postromantic era[s], it is Cain who attempts to rise and Abel who most certainly falls" (13). Ethan's emphasis on his own recognition rather than caring for the other can also be attributed to the rising worship of success and materialism in America that Steinbeck witnessed during his career as an author. These typical American traits are also related to the original myth since they stress Cain's preoccupation with the recognition of self and the necessity of being number one. When the store replaces the church as the new American congregation and its crafty owner Marullo becomes the symbol of the corruption brought about by the almighty dollar, material values are exalted over spiritual ones. According to Ethan's pal, Joey Morphy, the bank also metamorphoses, becoming the new "holy of holies," complete with "mystic numbers" for the safe, and its customers stand in awe outside the rail, like humble communicants waiting for the "sacrament" (*Winter* 221). "Then the time lock springs and Father Baker genuflects and opens the safe, and we all bow down to the Great God currency," says Morphy (150). This worship is in direct contrast to the primitive thank offerings of grain and animal flesh in the original Biblical tale and suggests a rejection of the need for approval from a Higher Being; instead, man himself becomes the ultimate arbiter of worth and that worth is measured in material goods, wealth, and possessions rather than by acknowledgment or acceptance by other individuals, let alone an Almighty Being.

Another change in spiritual values is evident in Ethan's refusal to acknowledge that his childhood has resulted in his body's being in the shape of a cross (*Winter* 115).[5] Instead, he recognizes that in today's society he can rationalize his evil and make it appear to be good. Like Mr. Baker, he realizes it is possible to "raise a moral reason for doing what [one] wanted to do anyway" (201). He also begins to understand that although he has a process in motion, believing he can control it at every turn and even stop it when he wants to, his role is not only that of the mover but also that of the moved. As a Cain figure he has committed murder, has aggressively pursued the material desires he lacked as an Abel; however, in the process, he has lost his moral center and wounded his soul.

Though the loss is momentarily painful, the pain can be alleviated by projecting the bad and directing blame for it elsewhere. Several quotations from the text illustrate the power of Ethan's continued use of the previously mentioned psychological trait of splitting. For example, Ethan convinces himself that honorable men are not crooked but merely clever (*Winter* 211). In other comments, Ethan proclaims the following: "Strength and success are above morality, above criticism" (211). "No crime is committed unless a criminal is caught" (211). "If individuals do something long enough, they stop thinking of it as wrong" (239), and a crime is "something someone else commits" (291). By looking at Cain's sin as if it is a very small offense, Ethan follows in the steps of New Baytown's town fathers, who "abolished part of the Decalogue and kept the rest. And when one . . . had what he . . . wanted, he resumed his virtue as easily as changing his shirt . . . " (104-05).

Ethan justifies his acts primarily by using the argument that the end justifies the means. Thus he reasons that even though all the rules might be abolished for a short period of time in order to obtain a single selfish objective, they can be reassumed later. "It has to be faced," says Ethan, "in business and politics a man must carve and maul his way through men to get to be King of the Mountain. Once there, he can be good and kind—but he must get there first" (*Winter* 173).

However, when Ethan must come to terms with his own son's lack of ethics and his plagiarism in the "I love America" contest, he begins to recognize that unless action is taken, the sins of the fathers will be visited upon the children. As a result, the marked race of Cain will continue in the next generation in even greater measure. Allen's act of aggression against his sister Ellen after she reveals his cheating (307) is yet another reminder of the potential for fratricide when individuals place the needs of self before the needs of community. In the words of David Bakan, such agentic actions create a "rising sense of emptiness, meaninglessness, and absurdity" (14). This event also provides Ethan with yet more evidence of what it means to be Cain—to trade " . . . a habit of conduct and attitude for comfort and dignity and a cushion of security" (*Winter* 226).

Overwhelmed by his Cain-sign, Ethan observes his guilt beginning to rise. As he notes on page 227: "Danny's scribbled papers hurt like a sorrow, and Marullo's grateful eyes." As the book draws to a close, it becomes more and more difficult for Ethan to practice splitting and to rationalize his crime. His argument that no one would be hurt because "it was not a crime against men, only against money" (241) is shown to be a shallow excuse. Ethan's self-assurance about the validity of his change becomes more and more questionable as his inner dialogue continues. The ethical act of Marullo (restoring Ethan's ownership of the store) is yet another reason for re-evaluation. Marullo's act is based on his belief that Ethan's racket is Honesty, a value he once held dear. His confidence in Ethan's moral core begins an inner-questioning in

Steinbeck's protagonist about whether he wishes to be responsible for "letting the light go out." Though he continues to deny his inherited attraction to ethics, Ethan's reaction to his son's plagiarism and to Marullo's misplaced confidence offers hope that he will return to his former Abel state.

In her final conversation with Hawley, Margie Young-Hunt assesses his potential to remain a Cain. "'I'm betting ten generations of Hawleys are going to kick your ass around the block,' she says, 'and when they leave you off you'll have your own wet rope and salt to rub in the wounds'" (*Winter* 302). According to Margie, Ethan just might break the rules of "me-first" and turn honest. Certainly, the final chapter suggests that her assessment of Ethan's limited potential to remain evil has merit, for Hawley does express regret and momentarily considers suicide as an apt punishment for his Cain act. Eventually, however, he settles for acknowledging his own corruption and his failures and concentrating on changing the future generation by aiding his daughter Ellen. Ethan's commitment to help her keep her "light" shining reflects Steinbeck's belief that

> . . . any man . . . when he comes to maturity has a very deep sense that he will not win the Quest . . . . He knows he has fallen short and all his excellences, his courage, his courtesy, in his own mind cannot balance his vices and errors, his stupidities . . . . The self-character cannot win the Quest, but his son can, his spotless son, the son of his seed and his blood who has his virtues but has not his faults. (*Acts of King Arthur* Appendix 364)

Yet Steinbeck was not content merely to portray the Cain myth in the primary story of Ethan Hawley. He suggests literary parallels as well,[6] parallels which also reinforce labeling the novel as a revisionist expression of the Cain myth. For example, the novel's title is taken from the opening soliloquy of Shakespeare's *Richard III* and is spoken by the title character himself. Richard says:

> Now is the winter of our discontent / Made glorious summer by this sun of York; / And all the clouds that loured upon our house / In the deep bosom of the ocean buried. / And therefore, to entertain these fair well spoken days, / I am determined to prove a villain / And hate the idle pleasures of these days. / Plots have I laid, inductions dangerous, / by drunken prophecies, libels, and dreams, / To set my brother Clarence and the king / In deadly hate the one against the other. (Act I, Sc. I, 11. 1-4, 29-35)[7]

In this speech, Richard himself is revealed as another paradoxical Cain symbol. Outwardly he appears to be the helpful servant of his brothers, King Edward IV and the Duke of Clarence, but he is jealous of their power and prestige in England. Cleverly, Richard (just like Ethan) conceals his real attitude and pretends to care for his siblings, claiming he desires only their health and prosperity rather than their demise. Although the Biblical account of the first murder does not reveal that Cain had any previous quarrel with Abel, Cain is similar to Richard because he too is unable to deal with the obvious favoritism his brothers enjoy and so plots their deaths. Richard's ascension to power and the throne also takes place after he feels slighted and unfairly treated. On the other hand, Richard's crafty and wily plots are quite unlike the abrupt violence brought about by Cain. Instead, they are subtle and stealthy like Ethan's. For example, Richard uses "inductions dangerous" and "drunken prophecies, libels and dreams" to set his two siblings "in deadly hate the one against the other." Reloy Garcia points out that

> Just as Shakespeare's hero-villain, Richard, degenerates in the conflict with his brother, from a cold Machiavellian plotter to an emotional sinner who derives pleasure from pain and evil, so too does Ethan degenerate in conflict with his "brother," Danny Taylor, over the "kingdom" of Taylor's Meadow. (244)

Richard is the epitome of duplicity, and the parallelism to Ethan and the shifting Cain myth is surely deliberate.

However, the discontent with morality and the attraction to evil portrayed in *Richard III* is not Ethan's alone but is rampant in his society. For example, the uneasiness of Ethan's family with poverty, the unfulfilled greed of Mr. Baker, and the unsatisfied lust of Margie Young-Hunt all relate to the title of the novel and the allusion to the Shakespearean history play. Thus Steinbeck's contention in *Journal of a Novel* that the Cain myth "with its implications has made a deeper mark in people than any other" story is shown to have merit (120). Such discontent is shown to be Cain-like and will eventually lead to a rejection of the restrictions of the past and obligations to society in order to attain a brighter future for the self. Shakespeare's mock heroic parallel in *Richard III* ironically reveals that it is not only a modern world where values have been turned topsy-turvy. Sadly, as long as humans have existed, greed, duplicity, and aggression have struggled to replace virtue and morality as the absolute values of society. Thus, if Richard's duplicity and trickery elicit at least some admiration from observers, there is evidence that even in this early era, Cain acts were becoming acceptable.

Another literary referent used by Steinbeck is the Arthurian legend and the Grail Quest. This story also contains a parallel to Cain in its rivalry between brothers and in its presentation of the values of communion as opposed to agency. In the late 1950s Steinbeck had begun research for an updated version of Malory's *Morte Darthur*, so this material was heavy on his mind. Steinbeck also stated in letters to Elizabeth Otis, his literary agent, that "Arthur" was perhaps the most important influence on his childhood and that he felt the legend, like the Cain myth, was timeless. Arthur, the perfect king, has established a utopia and received recognition as an individual Abel who has been blessed by God. On the other hand, Steinbeck presents Lancelot as a Cain hero-villain, one who places his own self-concern over his brother's welfare but yet one who is not completely evil and who has the possibility for redemption. In another transformation of the traditional negative or monstrous Cain, Steinbeck's Lancelot character is the finest knight of the Round Table. However, though he is well-respected like Ethan and known for his goodness, he ironically becomes a source of destruction, the one who initiates Arthur's fall from innocence and injects sin into his utopia. Although Arthur's ultimate destruction is caused by his nephew, Mordred, his brother in arms, Lancelot, is the primary cause of his demise as a perfect ruler since his envy of Arthur's relationship with Guinevere eventually motivates a destructive affair. According to Joseph Fontenrose, this detail may also be related to the Cain myth since there has been speculation by Biblical scholars that Cain's anger toward his brother was in part motivated by a rivalry with Abel over which brother would marry the other's twin sister.[8] Perhaps Ethan's sexual attraction to Margie Young-Hunt repeats this element of the Cain myth as he is consistently tempted by his desire to please himself rather than to be concerned about others.

The other allusions to the Arthurian legend in the novel are primarily related to Ethan's membership in the Knights Templar. When Ethan's son Allen asks to use his father's Knights Templar sword, the knight's hat, complete with plume, has yellowed, indicating the moral decay and evil nature of its owner. Thus Ethan is associated with Lancelot, whose jealousy of Arthur brought down a whole realm. It is precisely the fear that this national destruction will be repeated in a modern age that motivates Steinbeck. Ethan merely serves as an emblem of the dilemma faced by all Americans as they ponder difficult moral choices.

Finally, the Hawley talisman, a translucent stone which has the power to renew and reform, suggests an Arthurian parallel to the Holy Grail. Steinbeck also utilizes this talisman to suggest a potential revitalization or rebirth of a new Cain. Like the anticipated resurgence of the degraded Arthur after the Holy Grail is restored to him, there is potential for Ethan's renewal even in this most tragic of stories. Steinbeck's protagonist illustrates his belief that Cain figures can be restored, can struggle to maintain the power of light over the power of darkness and can return to Abel-consciousness. They may not attain these positive goals personally, but they can endeavor to make sure that moral truths do not disappear entirely for future generations.

Like Malory's Arthur, Ethan is continuously threatened by materialism, greed, and selfishness; his heritage of truth, justice, and honesty is in question. Like Arthur, Ethan also falls from an original Abel state. Renewal can occur only with the resurgence of a new sense of morality; only then can a restored Camelot (Paradise, Eden) be attained. This promise of moral regeneration is seen primarily in the characters of Marullo and Ethan's daughter, Ellen, who both believe in the power of good to triumph over evil.[9] Moreover, this renewal takes on added historical meaning when the reader realizes that the novel's composition coincided with the 1960s, an era often associated with the Kennedy presidency as a return to Camelot, where knightly actions would right wrongs by means of potent deeds and legislation.

A close examination of *The Winter of Our Discontent* gives evidence of a complex presentation of the Cain and Abel myth and its ambiguities. Steinbeck seems fascinated by the fact that unleashing the perversities of evil could result in an atrocious but positive liberation. Yet, as Quinones would attest, Steinbeck's transformation of Ethan Hawley into a revitalized and reformed Cain figure makes sense. Cains can be repatriated and re-integrated into productiveness, can recreate themselves as new and morally sound citizens of an ethical community.

Steinbeck once wrote to Elizabeth Otis of the Arthur saga that "[s]o many scholars have spent so much time trying to establish whether Arthur existed ... that they have lost track of the single truth that he exists over and over" (*Acts* 357). The same can be said of the Cain myth, whose "extraordinary longevity and variousness of ... appeal" makes it stand apart (Quinones 3). The ancient myth

bears in its background the dream of the human family, the pastoralism of the heart, a vision of unity and concord and cooperation so basic that it can only be summarized in the unconscious innocence of siblings ... yet cutting across this unity it [also] brings difference, discord, and division ... a shattering reminder of the fragility of the human compact. (Quinones 3)

Steinbeck's rearrangement of the myth's meaning establishes an understandable pattern for the here and now. As Quinones states: "Of our authors, it is perhaps Steinbeck who captures the pathos of this moment best" (12), the pained anguish over the mystery of the offering itself, the careless indifference it represents and the terror of the rejection or invalidation it symbolizes. In his retelling, he addresses "a breach in existence, a fracture at the heart of things" (Quinones 3). Repairing that breach and healing that fracture are surely Steinbeck's moral goals in his last novel. He is forever attempting to find his way back into the Garden of Eden. As *The Winter of Our Discontent* merges the wavering images of Cain and Abel, the trembling balance of ethics brought about by Ethan's fluctuation between his Cain and Abel role models forms a subtle warning to America. Steinbeck's protagonist seeks not the static polarity of opposites but rather the delicate dynamic equilibrium of life.

Notes

[1]See Pratt for a detailed analysis of how Steinbeck uses this technique in his writing.

[2] The Christologic allusions are discussed by Lisca 181-83; Garcia 244, 249-59; Fontenrose 134, 136; Owens 201, 205; and Timmerman 259-61.

[3] See Quinones, chapter 7, "The New American Cain," for expansion of this hypothesis. Especially relevant are pages 135, 139, and 142. According to the author, Cain represents the American people and "America is thus itself made from symbolic slayings, from shedding of the past, from disruption, from all the sacrifices that accommodation to the new requires" (143). Also relevant are the notes to this chapter on pages 267-69.

[4] See especially discussions by Lisca 182 and Garcia 250 for this analog.

[5] Elsewhere, however, Steinbeck stresses the ambiguous nature of Ethan and acknowledges that Abel influences still remain in his character. For example, Ethan admits the depth of his belief in the Christian ethic by his comments about his Aunt Deborah's influence on his perception of the Passion and Resurrection (15, 42, 60) and through his confession about being moved by Psalm 23 (115). In addition, his quoting of the Passion story to the canned goods in the store and to Margie Young-Hunt (15, 22) gives evidence that his moral core has not entirely eroded.

[6]Timmerman comes closest to an understanding of Steinbeck's interworking of Biblical and literary borrowing when he notes that "the focus of the text is on man-centered conniving rather than Christ-centered salvation" (259) and that the story represents a "moral center from which men have strayed" (260). He does not, however, connect the varied strands as presenting parallel arguments nor does he connect them with the Cain myth.

[7]Ethan quotes this passage at the end of part I of the novel (178) and alludes to it again in part II (280-81 and 295).

[8]This idea is shown in Fontenrose 122.

[9]The references to maintaining light (good) are interrelated with Grail symbolism. They occur in chapter 15 (255-56), chapter 16 (260), and chapter 22

(311). Marullo, though like Ethan transformed into a corrupt Cain, also has Abel tendencies. He even impresses the immigration agent by his espousal of good and his desire to preserve a moral code or "light." Similarly, Ellen, perhaps symbolically named after Elaine, The Grail Mistress or Guardian, provides the book with a moral and ethical center. She also transfers the Hawley talisman to Ethan in his time of deep despair and thus prevents his suicide and, by providing him with hope, suggests a potential triumph over Cain and a return to Abel-like virtue.

Works Cited

Bakan, David. *The Duality of Human Existence*. Boston: Beacon, 1966.

Fontenrose, Joseph. *John Steinbeck: An Introduction and Interpretation*. New York: Barnes, 1963.

Garcia, Reloy. "Steinbeck's *The Winter of Our Discontent*." *A Study Guide to Steinbeck: A Handbook to His Major Works*. Ed. Tetsumaro Hayashi. Metuchen: Scarecrow, 1974. 244-57.

Griffith, Ray. "Dissonant Symphony: Multi-Level Duality in the Fiction of John Steinbeck." Diss. Loyola U (Chicago), 1972.

Levant, Howard. *The Novels of John Steinbeck: A Critical Study*. Columbia: U of Missouri P, 1974.

Lieber, Todd. "Talismanic Patterns in the Novels of John Steinbeck," *American Literature* 44 (1972), 262-75.

Lisca, Peter. *John Steinbeck: Nature and Myth*. New York: Harper, 1978.

Martin, Stoddard. *California Writers: Jack London, John Steinbeck, The Tough Guys*. New York: St. Martin's, 1984.

Owens, Louis. *John Steinbeck's Re-Vision of America*. Athens: U Georgia P, 1985.

Pratt, John Clark. *John Steinbeck: A Critical Essay*. Grand Rapids: Eerdmanns, 1970.

Quinones, Ricardo J. *The Changes of Cain: Violence and The Lost Brother in Cain and Abel Literature*. Princeton: Princeton UP, 1991.

Schneer, Deborah. "A Psychoanalytic Reading," *San Jose Studies* 16 (1990): 107-16.

Steinbeck, John. *The Acts of King Arthur and His Noble Knights*. Ed. Chase Horton. 1976. New York: Ballantine, 1977.

_____. *Journal of a Novel: The* East of Eden *Letters*. 1969. New York: Bantam, 1970.

_____. *The Log from the* Sea of Cortez. 1951. New York: Penguin, 1976.

_____. *The Winter of Our Discontent*. 1961. New York: Penguin, 1982.

Timmerman, John H. *John Steinbeck's Fiction: The Aesthetics of the Road Taken*. Norman: U of Oklahoma P, 1986.

Reading Steinbeck (Re)-Reading America:
Travels with Charley *and* America and Americans

Geralyn Strecker

Travels with Charley and *America and Americans* are John Steinbeck's final works of nonfiction. The former is the narrative account of a cross-country trip the author took in the fall of 1960 with his French poodle Charley, the latter a series of nine essays plus a foreword and afterword, exploring different facets of America. Both works have the people and places of the United States as their subjects, yet critics have noticed that each has a distinct vision. James Woodress sees two different Steinbecks in the author's later career: "One Steinbeck is the older version of the artist-social critic who wrote *The Grapes of Wrath*, and the other is the pot-boiling journalist" (386). Although Woodress's assessment of *Travels with Charley* is not favorable, his two Steinbecks accurately describe *Travels with Charley* and *America and Americans* respectively. As an account of a fiction writer's journey, the earlier work is colored by his use of narrative and personal description. *America and Americans*, however, is a journalistic essay and more objective in its approach. John Ditsky makes a similar distinction, suggesting that *Travels with Charley* is non-teleological and *America and Americans* is "a teleology of nationhood" (56). The earlier work takes America as it comes without any regard for order, except geographic, but the later categorizes and tries to explain how America and Americans came to be the way they are. Robert S. Hughes sees a more patterned approach in the later work as well: "Although in some ways *America and Americans* is a pastiche of Steinbeck's earlier writings, it represents a more thorough attempt than does *Travels with Charley* to analyze the nation and its people" (87). Richard F. Peterson accounts for the analytical nature of *America and Americans* by arguing that Steinbeck employs the same biological theory in this work that he used in *Sea of Cortez*. What is missing in criticism of *Travels with Charley* and *America and Americans* is the application of contemporary literary theory, which is appropriate for these works since throughout *Travels with Charley* Steinbeck's exploration of how individuals encountering America participate in the creation of meaning often resembles reader-response theories of how readers experience texts. Theorists such as Louise Rosenblatt and Wolfgang Iser offer intriguing ways to approach Steinbeck's work.

In *The Reader, the Text, the Poem*, Rosenblatt defines two types of reading—aesthetic and efferent—which parallel the critics' perceptions of Steinbeck's vision. The aesthetic reader looks only for beauty, but the efferent reader expects to take practical knowledge away from his reading. These types are not exclusive; one person may practice both, but one will be dominant. Steinbeck is primarily an aesthetic reader in *Travels with Charley* with an artistic appreciation for the country without any driving concern for order. In *America and Americans*, he is an efferent reader, looking for patterns, order (teleology), and scientific knowledge about his country and its people. Another segment of Rosenblatt's theory explores the relationship between reader, text, and poem, in which the reader is the observer, the text what is observed, and the poem what is created through play between reader and text. This relationship is more thoroughly defined by Iser in *The Implied Reader*. According to Iser's reader-response theory, a person brings his past experience to the text, and as he reads, values from the text become part of his experience. After reading a word, the reader adds its value to that experience, which colors the reader's expectations for the next word. Meaning then does not occur at the word itself, but in the space between words. The reader's anticipation and retrospection of the values also color the meaning. Since words alone do not have meaning, the reader is to some extent free to make meaning from values (words) he reads. Each reader brings a unique experience to the text; therefore, meaning cannot be exact—it remains virtual. Within a text's "virtual dimension" of meaning (280), an infinite number of meanings can be experienced by different readers (or the same reader at different times). Rosenblatt's and Iser's theories provide a new means of understanding how Steinbeck experiences America in *Travels with Charley* and *America and Americans*.

Steinbeck's text in both works is America, and he realizes that his reading of America is unique to his own experience, influenced by factors in his life at any given time. Each trip is different; he writes: "A trip . . . is an entity, different from all other journeys. It has personality, temperament, individuality, uniqueness. A journey is a person in itself; no two are alike" (*Travels* 4). Anticipating Iser's theory that an individual's experiences shape his interpretation of a text/object/place, Steinbeck recognizes that how a person perceives a trip is partly determined by his past experience—along with his physical baggage, he brings to a trip all things he has previously experienced. And just as Steinbeck uses other baggage on the trip, he also applies his experience to create meaning from what he sees. Steinbeck explains his theory in *Travels with Charley*:

I've always admired those reporters who can descend on an area, talk to key people, ask key questions, take samplings of opinions, and then set down an orderly report very like a road map. I envy this technique and at the same time do not trust it as a mirror of reality. I feel that there are too many realities. What I set down here is true until someone else passes that way and rearranges the world in his own style. In literary criticism the critic has no choice but to make over the victim of his attention into something the size and shape of himself.

And in this report I do not fool myself into thinking I am dealing with constants. (69)

He then illustrates his theory by describing a specific instance when two people experience a place differently:

A long time ago I was in the ancient city of Prague and at the same time Joseph Alsop, the justly famous critic of places and events, was there. He talked to informed people, officials, ambassadors; he read reports, even the fine print and figures, while I in my slipshod manner roved about with actors, gypsies, vagabonds. Joe and I flew home to America in the same plane, and on the way he told me about Prague, and his Prague had no relation to the city I had seen and heard. It just wasn't the same place, and yet each of us was honest, neither one a liar, both pretty good observers by any standard, and we brought home two cities, two truths. For this reason I cannot commend this account as an America that you will find. (69-70)

In these passages, Steinbeck admits his interpretations of America and Americans will differ from anyone else's (here what he calls "the size and shape of himself" and later "the macrocosm of microcosm me"). As "the justly famous critic of places and events," Alsop went to Prague anticipating his encounters with "informed people, officials, [and] ambassadors." Traveling in a "slipshod manner" with his own unique expectations, Steinbeck witnesses Prague differently, even meeting a different set of characters: "actors, gypsies, [and] vagabonds." This situation also ideally illustrates Iser's theory that readers from dissimilar backgrounds behold texts differently. According to Iser, neither Steinbeck's nor Alsop's experience of Prague is *the* correct reading— each is just one of the infinite number of possibilities within Prague's "virtual dimension" of meaning as a text. Steinbeck wants us to see *Travels with Charley* and *America and Americans* in the same way—as *his* version rather than the "true" America.

Steinbeck also acknowledges that his own interpretations of people and places are not impervious to influence, but will vary depending on his mood. In *Travels with Charley* he writes: ". . . our morning eyes describe a different world than do our afternoon eyes, and surely our wearied evening eyes can report only a weary evening world" (70). His view of America varies throughout the day: in the morning he is most often refreshed and hopeful, but after a long day's journey he becomes tired and pessimistic. This cycle can be extended metaphorically to fit the journey as a whole: early in the trip he is hopeful, but less than half-way through he becomes tired, bored, and homesick. He takes short cuts, skips places, and hurries toward home. This weariness is the result of many factors—loneliness of being away from his wife Elaine, bore-dom with the tedious routine his travel has become, poor nutrition from food warmed in cans, and disappointment that the America he finds is not what he expected. Steinbeck began his travels on September 23, 1960, and on September 27 in a letter to Elaine from Deer Isle, Maine, he wrote: ". . . the roads are very long. It's a big damn country. And I find I get tired in the behind over two hundred miles" (*Life* 679). Steinbeck's exhaustion metaphor can be extended even further to apply to his life. At the time of "Operation Windmills" (the trip chronicled in *Travels with Charley*), Steinbeck was fifty-eight years old and had the previous December experienced a serious illness. Knowing he was in the later years of his life and growing tired, he wrote to his editor Elizabeth Otis: ". . . what I am proposing is not a little trip or reporting, but a frantic last attempt to save my life and the integrity of my creative pulse" (*Life* 669). Faced with his own mortality, Steinbeck was apt to see the world in a dark light.

Other factors at the time of the trip affected his response to America as well. The Steinbecks had the year before spent several months in England (from late February to October, 1959), John had suffered his "stroke" on 3 December 1959, and from "about the first of March" (Benson 870) to "the middle of July" (Benson 880) 1960 he had written *The Winter of Our Discontent*. Critic Robert S. Hughes suggests that Adlai Stevenson's failure in 1960 to secure the Democratic nomination for president also contributed to Steinbeck's low spirits and his dissatisfac-tion with America. Regardless of which factor was key in his decision to take the trip, Steinbeck designed his journey for a purpose—to re-connect himself with America and its people.

Steinbeck's experience of America during "Operation Windmills" (itself a "reading" of Cervantes and Robert Louis Stevenson's *Travels with a Donkey*) is not arbitrary—he deliberately selects his "text." This happens in part when he chooses to travel in a truck-camper which he names after Don Quixote's famous steed Rocinante. Concerned about his safety and health, friends want Steinbeck to travel by public transpor-tation, but he does not want to meet only people riding on buses and staying at roadside motels. In a letter to Elizabeth Otis he writes of travelers: "They are not *home* and they are not themselves. There is a change that takes place in a man or a woman in transit" (*Life* 668). Steinbeck wants to observe Americans in their natural environments—

as with his experiments in marine biology.

Steinbeck deliberately selects the states he will visit. He rejects suggestions to take a sampling of certain states and writes to Otis: "... I want the thing in context against its own background—one place in relation to another" (*Life* 669). He wants to see America "in context," and in planning his route from Long Island, up to Maine, and then over to California, he chooses to read the country cover to cover, shore to shore. Following this order, Steinbeck also anticipates another of Iser's theories—that relationships between adjoining sentences, or in Steinbeck's case places, affect the way we perceive those places. Iser's "intentional correlative" between words/sentences/places is one way in which an author controls or directs the reader's creation of meaning. During Steinbeck's journey, the "intentional correlation" exists in the "subtle connections" between villages, cities, states, or rest stops. No one can tell him what those connections are: he must experience them for himself. Correlation between places/events is most apparent after Steinbeck witnesses white "Cheerleaders" jeering at black students entering a recently desegregated New Orleans school. We see an abrupt change in his mood when a man asks him: "Are you traveling for pleasure?" Steinbeck responds: "I was until today. I saw the Cheerleaders" (*Travels* 231). Steinbeck's experience of America would not have been the same if he had visited New Orleans before seeing the splendor of places like Vermont and Montana.

To keep his trip "pure," Steinbeck avoids tourist areas. He stops at Niagara Falls and Yellowstone but recognizes that these are not natural representations of American landscape. He writes:

> I must confess to a laxness in the matter of National Parks. I haven't visited many of them. Perhaps this is because they enclose the unique, the spectacular, the astounding—the greatest waterfall, the deepest canyon, the highest cliff, the most stupendous works of man or nature .... For it is my opinion that we enclose and celebrate the freaks of our nation and of our civilization. Yellowstone National Park is no more representative of America than is Disneyland. (*Travels* 145)

According to critic Joseph Dewey, "national parks are on par with Charley's careful grooming" (25). Grooming the land into parks artificially restricts our experience of them by showcasing the good and concealing the bad. Steinbeck wants to see the good and bad America has to offer, not an edited text.

Another aspect of reader-response theory comes into play when we consider that Steinbeck had previously been to some of these places but not to others. Some places he found by accident, while others were planned stops—places he had always wanted to visit (Vermont in autumn, Niagara Falls, Wisconsin, Fargo) or places friends insisted were vital to his trip (Deer Isle, Maine). His response to the aesthetic beauty of autumn leaves in Vermont is especially interesting:

> In Salinas, California, where I grew up, although we had some frost the climate was cool and foggy. When we saw colored pictures of a Vermont autumn forest it was another fairy thing and we frankly didn't believe it . . . . To find not only that this bedlam of color was true but that the pictures were pale and inaccurate translations, was to me startling. I can't even imagine the forest colors when I am not seeing them. (*Travels* 34-35)

Vermont surpassed Steinbeck's anticipation, so in retrospection, he was awestricken. However, this reaction to autumn's splendor is not reserved only for first-time viewers. A woman in New Hampshire tells Steinbeck: "It is a glory . . . and can't be remembered, so that it always comes as a surprise" (*Travels* 35). Steinbeck's first fall trip to Vermont is unequivocally positive, but his assessments of other new places vary. His experience of Fargo, North Dakota, is nothing like what he had anticipated. He writes:

> Curious how a place unvisited can take such hold on the mind so that the very name sets up a ringing. To me such a place was Fargo, North Dakota. Perhaps its first impact is in the name Wells-Fargo, but my interest certainly goes beyond that. If you will take a map of the United States and fold it in the middle . . . right in the crease will be Fargo. . . . But beyond this, Fargo to me is brother to the fabulous places of the earth. . . . From my earliest memory, if it was a cold day, Fargo was the coldest place on the continent. If heat was the subject, then at that time the papers listed Fargo as hotter than any place else, or wetter or drier, or deeper in snow. (*Travels* 121-22)

Despite Steinbeck's great expectations, Fargo turns out to be unspectacular; in fact, he drives past on the interstate without stopping.

Although he has been away for some time, Steinbeck expects familiar places to be as he had last seen them. Returning to the West Coast he remarks: "This Seattle had no relation to the one I remembered" (*Travels* 162). The city had grown so much that once familiar country roads were now foreign four-lane freeways. He had a similar response to Salinas, California, which he remembered as a small town of 4,000 people. Now he finds a population of 104,000 fast on its way to 204,000. In Monterey, many of his old friends are dead, and those still alive are not as he had remembered them. He writes of leaving a favorite bar: "The double door swung to behind me. I was on Alvarado Street, slashed with neon light—and around me it was nothing but strangers" (*Travels* 181). Instead of enjoying his return to old haunts, he discovers the truth to Thomas Wolfe's adage: "You can't go home again." But Steinbeck also admits that all of the changes are not for the worse:

> In my flurry of nostalgic spite, I have done the Monterey Peninsula a disservice. It is a beautiful place, clean, well run, and progressive. The beaches are clean where once they festered with fish guts and flies. The canneries which once put up a sickening stench are gone, their places filled with restaurants, antique shops, and the like. They fish for tourists now, not pilchards, and that species they are not likely to wipe out. (*Travels* 182)

Although beautiful, Monterey disappoints Steinbeck because it does not match his expectation. Here, he wants to see filth. Seattle, Salinas, and Monterey had changed over several years, but a more immediate example of his reaction to familiar places is his experience of scenery in Maine. Leaving the state, Steinbeck is in a hurry to get on with his trip, so he retraces his route along roads he had taken going into Maine. Although his path had been full of expectations and fall colors on his way into Maine, it is dreary and dull on his way out, partly because the leaves are beginning to fall, but also because he is already growing tired of the trip and is bored by the too-soon rerun of scenery.

An intriguing contrast to Steinbeck's perception of America is Charley's experience of the trip. Along country roads, Charley sees America as a dog: "There Charley could with his delicate exploring nose read his own particular literature on bushes and tree trunks and leave his message there, perhaps as important in endless time as these pen scratches I put down on perishable paper" (*Travels* 97-98). When they stop in Montana to pay homage to Custer and Sitting Bull at Little Big Horn, Steinbeck removes his hat while Charley salutes by lifting his leg, which he did "with great respect" (*Travels* 143). Charley's perception differs from the author's, not only because he is a dog, but also because of his different background. This may sound silly, but Steinbeck takes time to inform us that his canine companion is "an old French gentleman ... born in Bercy on the outskirts of Paris and trained in France, and while he knows a little poodle-English, he responds quickly only to commands in French" (*Travels* 8). Charley's view of America then is not only canine but French, so he sees the country differently, marking trees and bushes along the way (a skill at which "he has no peer" [*Travels* 24]). Charley appreciates different things than does Steinbeck—female dogs, fine shrubs, good veterinarians—and dislikes some parts of the trip which Steinbeck finds favorable. While the author visits with his wife during a stop in Chicago, Charley reluctantly stays in a kennel. Afterwards, Charley is overjoyed to be back on the road, but Steinbeck writes to Elaine of the scenery and foods of Wisconsin: "I'm too well fed after the weekend to take advantage of it" (*Life* 685).

The most obvious difference between Steinbeck's and Charley's points of view occurs in Oregon. Although the man beholds the great redwoods as "godlike thing[s]" and imagines them a "dog's dream of heaven in the highest . . . the tree of all trees . . . the end of the Quest" (*Travels* 70), Charley will have nothing to do with them and instead relieves himself on a hazlenut bush. He cannot appreciate the redwoods like Steinbeck—"He doesn't raise his head high enough to see the branches to prove it's a tree" (*Travels* 170). Furthermore, although the trees have a great place in Steinbeck's memory, they are not part of the dog's previous experience. Steinbeck anticipates seeing them throughout the early part of his trip, but Charley is unaware of their existence. Steinbeck's disappointment will dampen any future association the author might have with redwoods. In fact, in the brief chapter following this disappointment, Steinbeck is filled with melancholy, equating himself with the old trees vanishing from the Earth.

Charley's company affects the America Steinbeck sees by providing companionship and acting as an ambassador to bridge the gap between Steinbeck and other Americans, but the dog's presence also creates problems. Having a dog necessitates that Steinbeck change his itinerary: he originally wanted to pass through Canada, but because of livestock regulations (no vaccination records), he cannot visit Canada as planned. Instead, he sees Buffalo, Erie, Cleveland, and other industrial cities on the shore of Lake Erie. Steinbeck's unpleasant encounter at the Canadian border poisons his mood, and rather than stopping to explore these cities, he speeds past without looking. He writes of the highway between Buffalo and Cleveland which we now call Interstate 90:

These great roads are wonderful for moving goods but not for inspection of a countryside. You are bound to the wheel and your eyes to the car ahead and to the rear-view mirror for the car behind and the side mirror for the car or truck about to pass, and at the same time you must read all the signs for fear you may miss some instructions or orders. (*Travels* 81)

People and events change our mood on a trip, but traffic and signs along major highways monopolize our attention and prevent us from seeing America. Steinbeck comments on the text that road signs offer travellers:

> ...each state had also its individual prose style, made sharply evident in its highway signs. Crossing state lines one is aware of this change of language. The New England states use a terse form of instruction, a tight-lipped, laconic style sheet, wasting no words and few letters. New York State shouts at you the whole time. Do this. Do that. Squeeze left. Squeeze right. Every few feet an imperious command. In Ohio the signs are more benign. They offer friendly advice, and are more like suggestions. Some states use a turgid style which can get you lost with the greatest ease. There are states which tell you what you may expect to find in the way of road conditions ahead, while others let you find out for yourself. Nearly all have abandoned the adverb for the adjective. Drive Slow. Drive Safe. (*Travels* 72)

Steinbeck does, however, note one similarity in road signs:

> In one matter all states agree—each one admits it is the finest of all and announces that fact in huge letters as you cross the state line. Among nearly forty I didn't see a single state that hadn't a good word to say for itself. It seemed a little indelicate. It might be better to let visitors find out for themselves. (*Travels* 39)

While Steinbeck's reading of signs does have some effect on the journey (what roads he takes, where he stops), Charley's sniffing signs along the road usually does not, except when in Yellowstone National Park his reaction to the bears causes Steinbeck's hasty retreat from the park. Later, Charley's illness affects the journey by dampening Steinbeck's mood, perhaps because he sees in Charley something that could just as easily have happened to himself, as his friends feared. In any case, the dog's illness gives Steinbeck an excuse to further rush the trip.

Charley's status as a foreigner perceiving America in *Travels with Charley* makes an interesting but peculiar transition into *America and Americans*, a work which Steinbeck wrote because:

> For centuries America and the Americans have been the target for opinions—Asian, African, and European.... Americans have allowed these foreign opinions the value set on them by their authors. For our own part, we have denounced, scolded, celebrated, and lied about facets and bits and pieces of our own country and countrymen; but I know of no native work of inspection of our whole nation and its citizens by a blowed-in-the-glass American.... (*America* 7)

This passage echoes *Travels with Charley*, where Steinbeck writes: "In Europe it is a popular sport to describe what the Americans are like . . . . Traveling about, I early learned the difference between an American and the Americans. They are so far apart that they might be opposites" (215). Again, Steinbeck recognizes that people from other cultures will not see America as an American will. He admits that his interpretation of America in *America and Americans* is unique to his own experience, but realizes that it is also different from his encounter with America in *Travels with Charley*. Steinbeck does not spare anyone, any place, or anything in his critique of America in *America and Americans*. He admits "the text is opinionated" (*America* 7), but the opinions are formed in a journalistic fashion reflecting his current political interests. Although the author's purpose differs between *Travels with Charley* and *America and Americans*, many of the same issues appear in both works.

When Steinbeck wrote these works, America was cresting the great wave of abundance which followed World War II. While society desired goods, Steinbeck stepped back and witnessed the destructive powers of abundance. In *American and Americans* he writes: "[W]e are . . . poisoned with things. Having many things seems to create a desire for more things, more clothes, houses, automobiles" (139-40). In the section titled "Americans and the Land," Steinbeck elaborates on the destructive effects abundance has had on America:

> I have often wondered at the savagery and thoughtlessness with which our early settlers approached this rich continent. They came at it as though it were an enemy. . . . They burned the forests and changed the rainfall; they swept the buffalo from the plains, blasted the streams, set fire to the grass, and ran a reckless scythe through the virgin and noble timber. Perhaps they felt that it was limitless and could never be exhausted and that a man could move on to new wonders endlessly. (127)

As Steinbeck travels across America in "Operation Windmills," he observes that the wilderness is receding and the desert growing. People are flooding cities and leaving trash in their wakes. In *Travels with Charley* he writes: "American cities are like badger holes, ringed with trash—all of them—surrounded by piles of wrecked and rusting automobiles, and almost smothered with rubbish" (25). He echoes this observation in *America and Americans*:

> . . . our rivers are poisoned by reckless dumping of sewage and toxic industrial wastes, the air of our cities is filthy and dangerous to breathe from the belching of uncontrolled products from combustion

of coal, coke, oil, and gasoline. Our towns are girdled with wreckage and the debris of our toys—our automobiles and our packaged pleasures. (127)

He writes of our fascination with packaged foods—bought wrapped in tin and plastic, prepared in disposable pans, and eaten from disposable plates with disposable utensils. But Steinbeck himself is guilty of this sin; at every rest stop he leaves artifacts of abundance (cans, plastic wrap, and paper plates) in garbage cans, marking his passage just as Charley marks his by peeing on bushes and trees. However, man's artifacts are more visible and do not wash away with the first rain. Our highways are lined with the trash left behind by people on the move.

America's view of home has also changed with the growing abundance, and now owning a home is not enough—Americans must be mobile too. Steinbeck sees mobile homes both as a sign of America's separation from roots and as a symptom of an unstable economy, where people are concerned about the here and now, not the past or future. Those who live in trailers are more concerned with not paying property taxes (subverting government), being able to pick up and move their residence (although no one ever does), and being able to upgrade their homes. Through conversations with mobile home owners, Steinbeck learns that trailer manufacturers have somehow inspired owners with the need to upgrade their homes every few years just as they would the family car. Purchasing "the new model" gives a family status and sense of progress, as well as variety to cure (and fuel) their restlessness. Steinbeck is struck by this distancing from traditional "home" values where a family's house was something to be built and preserved for future generations. He discusses trailers in both *Travels with Charley* and *America and Americans*, but his focus in each is determined by the purpose of his writing. During "Operation Windmills" he experiences trailer parks firsthand when he stops to camp and talk to trailer owners; in *America and Americans* his examination is more scientifically objective— he describes trailers as he would the shell of a turtle, an evolutionary adaptation to changing conditions.

Along with abundance and mobility comes another symptom of acquisition—the homogenizing of the American people. In both works, Steinbeck realizes that we are not a nation of many different people, but a nation of a type called "Americans." In *Travels with Charley* he tries to stay on less-travelled roads to experience different types of Americans. After discovering that Americans are in many ways the same (sharing radio, television, and fast food), he more often chooses highways. He makes the same point philosophically in the "*E Pluribus Unum*" chapter of *America and Americans* by tracing the patterns through which various immigrant groups have become Americans:

> ... in one or two, certainly not more than three generations, each ethnic group has clicked into place in the union without losing the *pluribus* .... How all these fragments of the peoples of the world who settled America became one people is not only a mystery but quite contrary to their original wishes and intentions. (14)

Despite the sameness Steinbeck finds in our homes, speech, and pastimes, he still finds difference. In the struggle to acquire and progress towards Americanness, man will always be jealous of other men, and this jealousy is nowhere more visible than in the racism plaguing our country. Leaving Louisiana in *Travels with Charley*, Steinbeck breaks his objective stance by confronting a Southerner who says of the New Orleans Cheerleaders: "Does your heart good to see somebody do their duty" (239). After this statement Steinbeck is unable merely to observe the man as an American. He writes: "I should have grunted and let him read what he wanted in it. But a nasty little worm of anger began to stir in me" (239). He then cuts the interview short by telling the man: "I want to get rid of you. Get out" (240). In response, the man repeatedly screams "Nigger-lover" as Steinbeck drives away. In *America and Americans* Steinbeck steps away from the problem of racism to discuss its origins and causes. In the section "Created Equal," he outlines the history of slavery in America and the effect that peculiar institution has had on American society from the time when it was believed an economic necessity to "Today [when] we believe that slavery is a crime and a sin, as well as being economically unsound under our system" (57). Steinbeck ends this section with his diagnosis of racism:

> ... any attempt to describe the America of today must take into account the issue of racial equality, around which much of our thinking and our present-day attitudes turn. We will not have overcome the trauma that slavery has left on our society, North and South, until we cannot remember whether the man we just spoke to in the street was Negro or white. (66)

For Steinbeck, abundance, urbanization, restlessness, and racism result in confusion. Americans have worked so hard to progress beyond their ancestors that they have lost their sense of direction. In *America and Americans* he writes: "The roads of the past have come to an end and we have not yet discovered a path to the future. I think we will find one, but its direction may be unthinkable to us now. When it does appear, however, and we move on, the path must have direction ..." (142). This sense of being lost is also a major theme in *Travels with Charley—*

Steinbeck sets out on a quest to find America, but he does not succeed. Is he lost, or is America lost? Travelers read America via maps, but roads change faster than maps can be revised, and people who bury their heads in maps never see the true America. Asking others for directions makes little sense because we never know whether the person we ask is lost too. Steinbeck believes that we are all lost in one way or another, and ironically, returning to New York at the end of his journey, he gets lost just a short distance from his house. Even this loss of direction can be explained by Iser's theory. Between places or events, Steinbeck anticipates what will come next. When his expectations are thwarted, a sense of "lostness" results. In his own way, he has predicted the postmodern condition of uneasiness which is a common topic for writers in the 1990s.

In both *Travels with Charley* and *America and Americans*, John Steinbeck sets out to read America. The task is enormous because our nation and its people are not simple texts, nor is Steinbeck a simple reader. In the complex relationship between reader (Steinbeck), text (America and its people), and "poem" (*Travels with Charley* and *America and Americans*), we must remember that America is not equivalent to the "America[s]" Steinbeck writes about in these works. Steinbeck's "America" is unique to his own experience of the country and its people; he interprets them according to what he has previously experienced, for every traveler "rearranges the world in his own style" (*Travels* 69).

Works Cited

Benson, Jackson J. *The True Adventures of John Steinbeck, Writer*. New York: Viking, 1984.

Dewey, Joseph. "'There Was a Seedy Grandeur about the Man': Rebirth and Recovery in *Travels With Charley*." *Steinbeck Quarterly* 24. (1991): 22-30.

Ditsky, John. "Steinbeck's *Travels with Charley*: The Quest that Failed." Hayashi 55-61.

Hayashi, Tetusumaro, ed. *Steinbeck's Travel Literature: Essays in Criticism*. Steinbeck Monograph Series, No. 10. Muncie: Steinbeck Society, 1980.

Hughes, Robert S., Jr. "Steinbeck's *Travels with Charley* and *America and Americans*: 'We have never slipped back—never.'" *Steinbeck Quarterly* 20 (1987): 76-88.

Iser, Wolfgang. *The Implied Reader: Patterns of Communication in Prose Fiction from Bunyan to Beckett*. Baltimore: Johns Hopkins UP, 1974.

Peterson, Richard F. "Mythology of American Life: *America and Americans*." Hayashi 11-21.

Rosenblatt, Louise M. *The Reader, the Text, the Poem: The Transactional Theory of the Literary Work*. Carbondale: Southern Illinois UP, 1978.

Steinbeck, John. *America and Americans*. New York: Viking, 1966.

_____. *Steinbeck: A Life in Letters*. Ed. Elaine Steinbeck and Robert Wallsten. New York: Viking, 1975.

_____. *Travels with Charley: In Search of America*. New York: Viking, 1962.

Woodress, James. "John Steinbeck: Hostage to Fortune." *South Atlantic Quarterly* 63 (1964): 385-97.

America and Americans: *The Arthurian Consummation*

Mimi Reisel Gladstein

Elaine Steinbeck's annoyance was evident. After hearing one speaker too many refer to *America and Americans* as a cocktail table book, she got up to voice her displeasure. That was not, she assured us, how John viewed the book. It was, she explained, an important undertaking for him and he had put much work and thought into the project.[1] Her remonstrance is well founded. Though there has been little critical attention paid it, *America and Americans* yields significant insights for a holistic evaluation of Steinbeck's narrative impulses, both expository and fictional. As the last published work in the man's lifetime, it stands as a capstone and culmination of the career. Nor is its position as cumulative work merely a matter of happenstance. There are signals both in the text and in letters of the time that Steinbeck saw the work as summative of certain themes and motifs in his life and creative production.

Few critical readers of Steinbeck's works have explored the recapitulatory role of *America and Americans* in the Steinbeck oeuvre. An exception is Robert S. Hughes, who, in a clearheaded reappraisal of both *Travels with Charley* and *America and Americans*, analyzes a number of aspects of these works which he considers "a compendium of [Steinbeck's] life, thought, and art" (76), concluding that "except for his published letters," these two works provide "Steinbeck's most intimate record of himself and his art . . ." (86). A few earlier studies have focused on singular aspects of this final work. Richard F. Peterson examines the mythic content, while Roy Simmonds provides the view of a non-American "impressed yet again by the almost unbelievable honesty with which the American nation is prepared to parade its faults before the rest of the world" (25). What other attention the work has received is mostly as part of larger studies. Surprisingly, given its obviously relevant subject, it is not even mentioned in Louis Owens' insightful consideration, his aptly named *John Steinbeck's Re-Vision of America*.

One major issue, a subject that influenced both Steinbeck's life and his art but does not figure in the analyses of any of the critical studies mentioned above, is the matter of Arthur and its import in the writing and text of *America and Americans*. Jackson J. Benson makes the connection in a backhanded way during his discussion of the difficulties Steinbeck had after writing *America and Americans* in trying to get back to and complete his Malory project. Benson suggests that one of the problems may have been that " . . . what he had intended to say in 'The

Matter of Arthur' may have already been said, in a different form, in *America and Americans*" (973). Benson does not provide details, but the implications of his suggestion bear exploration.

There has been no dearth of discussion of Steinbeck's fascination with Arthurian myth and legend. It has been amply considered in both the biographical and critical studies. Steinbeck's letters also provide numerous clues to the significance of Arthurian themes and motifs in his personal and professional life. Most readers of Steinbeck know that Malory's *Morte* was the first literary love of his life and that he recreated his own Arthurian vision in many of the early works.[2] But the impact of Arthur is not limited to the early years, nor is it limited to the fiction. In the time period immediately preceding the writing of *America and Americans*, Steinbeck's interest in matters Arthurian was perhaps stronger than it had been at any other period in his life. The major reason for this was his continuing work, based on both the Caxton edition and the Winchester manuscript, on what he first called a "reduction of Thomas Malory's Morte d'Arthur [*sic*] to simple readable prose . . ." (*Life* 540).

The project had been initiated in the mid-50s and involved much research and time, including trips to Italy and England, as well as a long stay in Somerset in 1959, where, in his own words, he was not only "right smack in the middle of Arthurian country" but "it seems as though we had lived here forever" (*Life* 617). Though completion of the project eluded him and he put it aside to work on other books, still the impact of Arthur on himself and on our culture was never far from his consciousness. In early 1964 he wrote to Jacqueline Kennedy, widow of the recently assassinated President, communicating his lifelong absorption with Malory's *Morte Darthur*: "Since I was nine years old . . . I have been working and studying this recurring cycle" (*Life* 792-93). Steinbeck's personal identification with the Arthurian myth worked to create in him an empathy for John F. Kennedy, whose term of office captured the national fancy as a latter-day type of Camelot. Sensing Mrs. Kennedy's discomfort with his use of the word "myth," he explained its derivation from the Greek "mythos" and its meaning for him as "the doubly true." This exchange with Jacqueline Kennedy took place shortly before the *America and Americans* project was first proposed to him. At its inception the project was to be little more than some text to accompany what had been initially conceived of as mainly a "picture book with captions" (Benson 955). It became much more as Steinbeck warmed to his subject.

Other manifestations of Steinbeck's consistent Arthurian impulses abound. "Joyous Garde" is the name he gave to the workroom he built as his own off-limits hideaway at the home in Sag Harbor (Benson 791). The only chair in the room was identified as the "Siege Perilous." He used Lancelot's final words to Guinevere, "in thee I have myn erthly joye," to inscribe a stepping stone which was part of his swimming pool birthday present to Elaine (Benson 972).

Thus, it can be argued that it was with an unfinished Malory translation or reinterpretation in tow, personal connections to the political Camelot, and a lifelong fascination that Steinbeck began writing the essays that comprise his "book of opinions, unashamed and individual" (*America* 7). Not that there were always distinct divisions created in the times allotted to the Malory project and *America and Americans*. They often inhabited his mind simultaneously. At one point in the writing, Steinbeck was working on the concluding essay for *America and Americans*, "Americans and the Future," and on his Arthurian project at the same time (Benson 971). It should not be unexpected, then, that matters Arthurian and the Matter of Arthur resonate in both the text and the context surrounding the writing of *America and Americans*.

Malory's work takes its title from the demise and death of Arthur and the kingdom he dreamed into existence. The reader's awareness of the ending helps shape response to the stories. *Morte Darthur* is, among other things, the story of loss. As Arthur at the scene of his final battle, his *morte*, had experienced the loss of both kingdom and the majority of his closest knights, so Steinbeck, battling to write what was to be his final text, was coming to terms with the loss of the America (kingdom) he had known and the death of many life companions (closest knights). Dealing with mortality, his own and those of his loved ones, plays like a leitmotif in the background of the major texts of this last period of Steinbeck's life.

One by one, people who had shared his dreams and devilment, his personal equivalents of Arthur's round table, were killed or died unexpectedly. The effects of the loss of Ed Ricketts have been the subject of much critical and biographical speculation. Not as much has been written of the effect on his writing of the loss of Robert Capa, with whom he had collaborated on a book of photographs and essays much like the one he was undertaking in *America and Americans*. The losses of Ricketts and Capa came early. Fresher losses mark the period immediately connected to the writing of this final book. Pascal Covici, whom Steinbeck described as "father, mother, teacher, personal devil and personal god," died in October of 1964. Like the loss of Ricketts and Capa, the loss of Covici was unexpected. 1965 brought the premature death of Adlai Stevenson, whom Steinbeck had supported in two presidential campaigns, and who embodied a host of knightly qualities in Steinbeck's estimation. Whatever the effects of these deaths were personally, they are certainly reflected in the elegiac mood that pervades the later works, particularly *The Winter of Our Discontent* and *Travels with Charley*, and reaches its rapprochement in *America and Americans*.

The loss most closely related to things Arthurian was the death in early 1965 of Mary Steinbeck Dekker, Steinbeck's youngest sister. Mary had been his partner in many of the Arthurian fantasies and escapades of childhood. She accompanied him on a trip to Italy to explore what treasures of Arthurian lore the Vatican Library might hold. One of the earliest decisions he had made in connection with his Malory project was to dedicate the work to her. Her belated knighting in its dedication as Syr Mayrie Stynebec of the Vayle Salynis is a touching reminder of lost opportunity and unfinished personal business.

Steinbeck saw many analogies between his America and the England of Malory's text. He signals these connections in the first paragraph of his first chapter "E Pluribus Unum." He writes: ". . . even stranger is the fact that the unit America has come into being in slightly over four hundred years—almost exactly the same amount of time as that during which England was occupied by the Roman legions" (13). Steinbeck deduces that "America did not exist," but was produced by the coming together of all its peoples just as England was a polyglot of peoples but came into being as a nation with the kingship of Arthur. A long process of work, fear, and bloodshed went into the building of the new breed that is America, a process not dissimilar to the creation of Camelot and the Arthurian kingdom. For England, the Arthurian legend works as a creation myth. In "E Pluribus Unum" Steinbeck writes his own "Genesis" narrative for the United States.

In his research on Malory, Steinbeck continually made connections between Malory's situation and his, between Malory's world and the twentieth century. He wrote Eugene Vinaver: "It does seem to me that our time has more parallels with the fifteenth century than, let us say, the nineteenth century . . ." (Life 592). To Elizabeth Otis and Chase Horton he observed: "He [Malory] was caught as we are now. In forlornness. . . . And out of this devilish welter of change—so like the one today—he tried to create a world of order, a world of virtue governed by forces familiar to him" (Life 576). So, in America and Americans Steinbeck, looking at the "exploding dreams" of a "naive time" that is now over, comments upon the "sullen despair and growing anger and cynicism" he saw around him (136) and tries in his conclusion to predict the country's survival.

Most of all Steinbeck saw Malory's work as a means by which the writer strove to deal with the immorality of his times. For Malory, Arthur was the means to convey an ideal during a period of tumult and change. Throughout America and Americans, Steinbeck juxtaposes our many failures and faults, the immorality of our times, against the vision of America's dreams and ideals. He was particularly concerned with the decay from within, the failure in American character. Among the targets of his pen are American child-rearing practices. After a lengthy description of what he calls "[t]he reign of terror, which is actually a paedarchy" (103), Steinbeck warns of America's failure to "create adults," our extensions of "adolescence far into the future, so that very many Americans have never and can never become adults" (103). Another shortcoming he draws attention to is our failure to deal effectively with the problem of a growing population, caused by scientific and medical advances, of older Americans. He calls it "a great burden of unhappy, unused, unfulfilled people" (104). Interpreting Arthur's relevance today, he wrote, "Arthur must awaken not by any means only to repel the enemy from without but particularly the enemy inside.... Now, next to our own time the 15th century was the most immoral time we know" (*Life* 649). In many ways, *American and Americans* is a lament for lost values, a decrying of the moral collapse Steinbeck saw all around him.

Nowhere is this lament more damning than in the chapter called "Americans and the Land." Steinbeck's ongoing environmental concerns are just now being given appropriate critical attention. *America and Americans* reviews and rearticulates ecological worries that Steinbeck had been expressing for some thirty years. He writes of the "savagery and thoughtlessness with which our early settlers approached this rich continent" (127). His images of forests burned, buffalo slaughtered, streams blasted, grass set fire, and "a reckless scythe" run "through the virgin and noble timber" (127) replicate the images of such diverse works as *Log from the* Sea *of Cortez* and *The Grapes of Wrath*. The sin of environmental "irresponsibility" is detailed in this chapter as Steinbeck invokes pictures of "rivers poisoned ... by reckless dumping of sewage and toxic ... wastes," of towns "girdled with wreckage and the debris of our toys," of "filthy and dangerous" air (127). The language he uses is strong and carries moral condemnation. He pictures settlers "raping the country like invaders" (128) and creating ecological havoc like "overindulged children" (128). He writes not only of the destruction of the land, but also of living creatures: the whales, sea otters, game birds, the passenger pigeon (129). His concern here is "evils" which must be overcome if America and Americans are to survive.

The heart of the Arthurian myth is paradox, and paradox is at the heart of Steinbeck's evaluation of his country. "Americans seem to live and breathe and function by paradox" (*America* 30). One of the key paradoxes in the story of the round table is the function of Lancelot, the flower of knighthood, Arthur's finest knight. He is Arthur's greatest friend and he is his betrayer. He is the embodiment of the knightly ideal of might in the service of right, but he uses his acknowledged dominance in battle to prove untrue that which he knows is true. When Guinevere is rightly accused of adultery, he acts as her champion. "Paradox and

Dream" is the title Steinbeck assigns the second chapter in his survey of America and Americans and in it he analyzes the paradoxical operation of the American Dream in the American psyche. Just as the knightly ideal escapes most of those members of Arthur's Round Table, only Galahad achieving the Grail, so Americans seem always to be striving after an American dream which evaporates when achieved and leaves the seeker unsatisfied. Steinbeck calls our dream "the American Way of Life," concluding that "No one can define it or point to any one person or group who lives it, but it is very real nevertheless.... These dreams describe our vague yearnings toward what we wish we were and hope we may be: wise, just, compassionate, and noble" (34). The aforementioned characteristics read like a listing of traditional knightly qualities.

This might appear as nothing so much as a stretch for analogies were it not that on the same page of this essay, Steinbeck has already drawn attention to the Arthurian paradigm. He claims that the most prevalent of American folk heroes, "the brave and honest sheriff who with courage and a six-gun brings law and order and civic virtue to a Western community," is derived from "the brave mailed knight of chivalry who battled and overcame evil with lance and sword" (34). The stories of our frontier, the Old West, are defined by Steinbeck as our folk literature which, in his words, embodies the dreams of our people. The stories of our frontier are our folk stories, and they are like the ones retold by Malory, stories in which "virtue does not arise out of reason or orderly process of law—it is imposed and maintained by violence" (34).

Steinbeck carries the Arthurian paradigm to provocative extremes, comparing the code of behavior of street gangs with "the tight-knit chivalric code of feudal Europe" (34). He goes on to suggest that the very qualities that lead them to fight, "to rumble," are the qualities that would make them heroes if the nation needed them during wartime. Of particular interest to Steinbeck is the concept of heroes and our need for them. Referring directly to the matter of Arthur he writes: "There must have been a leader like King Arthur; although there is no historical record to prove it, the very strength of the story presumes his existence" (34). Following this train of thought, he decides that whether or not there were gunslinging sheriffs, we would have invented them because of our need for them.

In the above case, the allusions to Arthur are direct; at other places in the text, the influence is less overt, more illusory. The reader of this book of photographs, a nonfiction work written for a contemporary audience, might not expect to encounter the supernatural or magical, but Steinbeck quite unexpectedly provides it. The story is one of Steinbeck's interaction with Jimmy, the chief of an Amerindian tribe. It includes many Arthurian elements. The hero is a chief, the leader of his group; he seeks advice of a Merlin figure, the medicine man of his tribe; and his salvation comes when this "magician" has him seek out a Lady of the Lake. Jimmy, the hero, has been ill, evoking images of the fisher king. The illness does not respond to the ministrations of the doctors in Reno. When normal remedies do not work, as they do not in the story of Arthur, supernatural cures must be sought. Jimmy goes to what Steinbeck calls a "medicine man." This being, who, like Merlin, is representative of a past culture, recommends that Jimmy take a fish and give it to a mermaid. As Steinbeck recounts it, Jimmy tells him:

> ". . . I don't know how to describe it."
> I said, "Was it a person?"
> He said, "In a way; but it was an un-person too."
> I said, "Male or female?"
> He said, "It seemed to be a woman."
> I said, "And she took the fish?"
> And he said, "Yes."
> "And she went into the lake?"
> He said, "I don't know. I turned and walked away."
> "Well," I said, "how is your stomach?"
> He said, "I've had no more trouble with the stomach. It went away right then." (20)

In Malory, Arthur instructs Sir Bedivere to return Excalibur to the Lady of the Lake as the medicine man instructs Jimmy to return the fish to the mermaid. Once that is done, Arthur can rest easy. Jimmy's stomach problem dissolves when he returns the fish to the supernatural creature at the lake.

Another comparison between the Malory text and *America and Americans* is in the structure of its narratives. *Morte Darthur* is a series of stories, each complete within itself, but all contributing to the larger compendium of the coming into being of the Kingdom of Arthur, the flowering of the Round Table and its knights, and the eventual destruction of the brotherhood and kingdom. Hughes calls *America and Americans* "a Steinbeck pastiche" remarking on the lack of "continuous story line" (81). He claims it resembles a "series of colorful, yet provoking editorials" (81).

The Arthurian metaphor in Steinbeck's life and works weaves itself into *America and Americans* in unexpected ways. Malory's version of the destruction of Camelot lays much of the blame at the feet of Guinevere. She is the temptress, the forbidden fruit, at the heart of the loss of the Eden that was Camelot. Not only is the Round Table destroyed and the kingdom rent because of her, but upon witnessing her dead body, the flower of knighthood, Sir Lancelot, quits eating and soon dies. Directly and indirectly, her being creates havoc and death. Later developers of Arthuriana are harsher than Malory in their blaming of Guinevere. Steinbeck, lamenting the faults of "genus Americanus," names his own female culprit *Moma Americana* (89). He develops her image in terms of the black widow, describing her as "related to the arachnids" (88). His portrait of the deadly female of the "genus Americanus" holds the male of the species blameless. He is the pathetic slave to his mating instincts, who will "often dance for hours before the females will submit to mating" (89). "After mating, of course, she eats her spouse" (89). The malevolent view of American women is not new in Steinbeck. Nor is its genesis strictly Arthurian. There is a long Western tradition, both Greek and Hebrew, of laying the fault for all humanity's ills at the foot of woman. A more contemporary source for Steinbeck's "Moma Americana" might be Philip Wylie's *Generation of Vipers* (1942) with its misogynistic definition of "momism" as the disease most enfeebling American men.

In his review of the expository prose of John Steinbeck, Sanford E. Marovitz complained that the "sheer optimism" of Steinbeck's conclusion "is in no way justified by anything in the volume that has come before" (100). His argument has merit. However, when looked at in context of Steinbeck's absorption with the matter of Arthur, the optimistic conclusion is totally in keeping with its Maloryian antecedent. At the end of the *Morte* all seems lost. Mordred has declared himself King in England and many of the people have rallied around him for, in Malory's words, "Alas, this is a great default of us Englishmen, for there may no thing please us for long." Steinbeck faults Americans for similar qualities: "We are a restless, a dissatisfied, a searching people. We bridle and buck under failure, and we go mad with dissatisfaction in the face of success. We spend our time searching for security, and hate it when we get it" (29). Malory's picture of England is not an optimistic one. Gawaine and all but two of Arthur's noble knights are dead, Sir Lucan is dying in the process of lifting Arthur, the pillagers and robbers are looting the dead bodies of the noble knights, but still, amidst all the carnage and death, he manages to insert the positive prediction that Arthur will come again. Steinbeck, too, paints a tragic picture of eroded lands and moral will: "Now we face the danger which in the past has been most destructive to the human: success—plenty, comfort, and ever-increasing leisure. No dynamic people has ever survived these dangers" (*America* 205). Yet for all the dangers, he manages to come to the positive conclusion that for all our failure and wrong paths, "we have never slipped back—never" (205).

One final Arthurian connection. Benson observes that Steinbeck throughout his lifelong absorption with the myth, his naming of things for it, his constant alluding to it, often acted as if the Arthurian myth was "a metaphor for his own life" (804). In terms of *America and Americans*, the metaphor operated both within and without and beyond the text. A final mystical connection: When Arthur's work is done, his last battle fought, he dies surrounded by women, three Queens and dame Nimue. The weeping ladies accompany him as he floats toward Avalon and immortality. So too, with his last book written, Steinbeck was attended on his deathbed by women. There for the final moments were Elaine, Elizabeth Otis, Shirley Fisher, and Dr. Nancy Kester.

Reviewers, at the time of *America and Americans'* publication, were more appreciative of Steinbeck's last work than were subsequent scholars. The *Times Literary Supplement* reviewer acknowledges the beauty of the photographs, but insists, ". . . it is the text that matters." Eric Moon, then editor of *Library Journal*, makes the extravagant claim, given the general perception that one picture is worth 10,000 words, that the 70 pages of Steinbeck's text manage "to capture more of the essentials and the paradoxes of *America and Americans* than all the photographers together." This is high praise as the book contains the work of fifty-five of that era's best photographers. Moon cautions the reader not to be misled by the coffee-table look of the book, an admonition which had generally gone unheeded until Elaine Steinbeck reminded us again of the importance of the text to its author.

Notes

[1]This scene took place during the "Steinbeck and the Environment" Conference on Nantucket Island, May 14 - 17, 1992. Elaine Steinbeck attended all of the presentations during the conference.

[2]The most obvious focus for those who explore the Arthurian element in Steinbeck's fiction is *Tortilla Flat*, where Steinbeck himself calls our attention to the connections. However, others have noted Arthurian elements in *Cup of Gold*, *Of Mice and Men*, and *In Dubious Battle*. All of these works were published before 1939.

Works Cited

Benson, Jackson J. *The True Adventures of John Steinbeck, Writer*. New York: Viking, 1984.

Hughes, Robert S., Jr. "Steinbeck's *Travels with Charley* and *America and Americans*." *Steinbeck Quarterly* 20 (1987): 76-88.

Marovitz, Sanford E. "The Expository Prose of John Steinbeck (Part II)." *Steinbeck Quarterly* 7 (1974): 88-102.

Moon, Eric. Rev. of *America and Americans*, by John Steinbeck. *Library Journal* Dec. 1966: 59-62.

Peterson, Richard F. "The Mythology of American Life: *America and Americans* (1966)."*A Study Guide to Steinbeck: A Handbook to His Major Works.* Ed. Tetsumaro Hayashi. Metuchen: Scarecrow, 1974. 5-18.

Rev. of *America and Americans* , by John Steinbeck. *Times Literary Supplement* 1 Dec. 1966: 1128.

Richter, Conrad. "America Appreciated: Especially New England." Rev. of four books, including *America and Americans* by John Steinbeck. *Harper's* 223 (Nov. 1966):133-34.

Simmonds, Roy S. "'Our land . . . incredibly dear and beautiful': Steinbeck's *America and Americans.*" *Steinbeck Quarterly* 8 (1975): 88-95.

Steinbeck, John. *America and Americans.* New York: Viking , 1966.

_____. *Steinbeck: A Life in Letters.* Ed. Elaine Steinbeck and Robert Wallsten. New York: Viking, 1975.

Part III

Interview

Elaine Steinbeck

"John Believed in **Man**": An Interview with Mrs. John Steinbeck

Donald V. Coers

On the 23rd and 24th of April, 1993, Donald Coers, accompanied by his wife, Mary Jeanne, interviewed Elaine Steinbeck in the Manhattan apartment on East Seventy-Second Street that she and John Steinbeck moved into in 1963. The interview began with the Coers giving Mrs. Steinbeck a box of Godiva chocolates.

DC: Do you like the white or dark chocolate?

ES: Any chocolate, and Godiva is my favorite. You know who that lady Godiva was, don't you? She rode naked through the streets.

DC: Eating chocolates.

ES: Eating chocolates! Did you ever read that poem in *Life in Letters* that John wrote in calypso [style] about Elaine, comparing old style Elaine, the Tennyson "Elaine the fair, Elaine the loveable, Elaine the lily maid of Astolat," to new style Elaine? "New style Elaine, she walked real proud. Got a b-flat baritone c-sharp loud." He always used to laugh at me because I would get real excited and talk loud. He talked very softly and mumbled. I said, "Nobody can understand a word you're saying." Once we found ourselves at a big party—people, people, people. I was out on the edges and I looked over in the middle of the room and saw that John had been caught somewhere. He was big-shouldered so you could always see him, and he looked like he was sick or mad or something so I thought, I've got to get to him, get over there and get him out. And I worked my way, wormed my way through the crowd, and he wasn't sick or mad; he was talking to Truman Capote! You see, they were so close together, there was such a crowd, that they couldn't put any distance between them. Truman was talking *up* to John, and John was talking *down* to Truman!

DC: Let's talk about your Texas background.

ES: Well, I'm a Texan and even though I've lived in New York fifty-three years, I still think of myself as a Texan. And I go back once a year, always. And this I'm very proud of: When I go to Fort Worth I still see all of my chums I went to school with from the second grade on. They're mostly widows now. We're going to meet in Mexico in the fall. Anyway, I have a lot of Texas friends. I was born in Austin, but I never lived there as a child. My father was connected with the University of Texas.

DC: Didn't you tell me once he was an Assistant Professor of English? Was he there when J. Frank Dobie was teaching?

ES: I think this was earlier. I'll be seventy-nine this August [1993], and I don't care who knows it. Anyway, my mother lived in Stephenville, and my father first was a principal of the high school there. Then he went into the independent oil business when Texas was discovering all of the great oil fields. It was a thing that a lot of young Texans did to make their fortunes. It was like going to the Gold Rush, you know. I lived in Stephenville through the first grade and then we moved to Fort Worth. I acted in all the shows; I was very interested in theater. I had a wonderful teacher who opened my life to me with Shakespeare. My father used to imitate me when I would walk around carrying a Shakespeare book and they couldn't get me to come to the table. I lived in Fort Worth until I graduated, and then I left for the University of Texas. My first husband was Zachary Scott. Texans know him; he had a theater named for him in Austin. Zack and I came to New York together in 1939 after he got his degree. Even though many years later Zack and I were divorced, his family and I are still very close. I always go to the Zachary Scott Theater when I go to Austin. One of my sisters is married to an Austinite and I go to see them every year. I show them Europe and they show me America—it's a good deal. We drive in Arizona, and we drive in Texas, and we drive in Colorado.

DC: You also go to Santa Fe fairly frequently, don't you?

ES: I love Santa Fe! In fact, I like the Southwest, and Fort Worth is part of the Southwest so that's why I've got it in my bones. It's still a part of my heart. While we're talking about my life in Texas, let me tell you a funny story. During the Vietnam War President Johnson asked John to go to Vietnam to do some reporting, and John said, "I'll go if I can take Elaine." And so the President gave me a press pass and I got around a lot over there, sometimes with John, sometimes not. On one occasion we were at the top of Laos, and I said to John one evening, knowing he was busy the next day with the military or with literary people or whatever, "Would you mind terribly if I got in a jeep and drove over to the jungle with some Marines to a village where they've never seen a white woman before? And he said, "No, if you're not afraid to, that's o.k." And then he said, "Honey, you won't go fifteen minutes until you've run into somebody that you went to the University of Texas with."

MJC: Funny you should say that. Just a few days ago I was in Austin to hear Hillary Clinton speak and I met a woman who said she knew you at the University. Her name was Colleen Grant.

ES: Sure, sure, Colleen Grant. I remember her. Did you like Hillary?

MJC: I loved her.

ES: Me too. I was in Santa Fe last year when the presidential campaign was going on. One morning I got up early to walk by myself and as I went into the plaza, I saw that there was no traffic there, and a lot of people, so I said to a cop, "What's happening?" He said, "Hillary Clinton is having breakfast with the Governor and his wife and various people and they are going to walk through the plaza." Now, I had not met her. I had been invited to a breakfast here in New York for her, in her honor, and had bought my ticket and then I decided to go West. While I was standing there in the plaza, I noticed a group of women, so I went up and said, "Are you women for Clinton? Can I join you?" And they said, "Sure, come on." I worked my way to the front, toward the street, so that I could get a good look, because I'd never met her, you see. She came along soon and was graciously saying hello to people, and then she got near me and I said, "Was the breakfast in New York fun last week?" And she stopped cold and said, "It was the best political party we've had in the whole campaign so far." I said, "I would have been there except I'm here, but my sister and I helped plan it." Well, she stopped and discussed it. Then she shook hands with all of us. She was just wonderful! I think she's going to do a good job. I've always been political. Zack was also political and very liberated although his family was strictly right wing. Then I married John, and, of course you know from reading *The Grapes of Wrath* where he stood! One of the most interesting things that John and I did while we were married was try twice to get Adlai Stevenson elected. John went to both conventions, and I went with him. He always took me with him, which was wonderful for me. And that's why I know so much about John in all directions, because he always said, "I'll go if Elaine can go." We went to the Democratic Convention when Adlai was nominated. I've always worked with politics in New York, and so I was working for Adlai. I'd phone John from one of the

243

Democratic headquarters and he would be at the house working, and I'd say, "Write a five-minute speech for Hank Fonda to give in Minneapolis." And he'd say, "Yeah, o.k., right now." And I'd say, "Get it done within the hour, so somebody can pick it up." He was always writing speeches.

DC: Tell us what you mentioned in our phone conversation this morning about the speech Steinbeck wrote for the Nobel Prize.

ES: Well, that's something funny. John was thrilled to death to win the Nobel Prize, but then he suddenly realized he would have to give a speech in Stockholm. Some writers can speak, and some can't. John just couldn't, and he mumbled, anyway. And he said, "Oh my Lord, I've got to make a speech in Stockholm." So John wrote Adlai a funny letter, saying, "Adlai, you're indebted to me. I've done a lot for you. I've tried to get you elected" and so forth. "Now all you've got to do is go to Stockholm and make a speech for me." Unfortunately some critics read what he said and took it seriously. That's why you scholars have to be careful about these things. John didn't have to be careful at all, you see. He adored the press when they were being smart. John would say to them, "I have a request for you. I don't request that you give me good write-ups; I request that you be as interesting to me as I am to you." Sometimes I would listen to John talk with the press in foreign countries, and by the time the interview was over he would have found out more about the country we were visiting than they would have found out from him. He was pretty clever, and that's what he enjoyed—the give and take. And sometimes, it was quite true, a lot of people would miss John's humor, and also I've heard John swear at the press. But John was never really mean to the press, although sometimes they provoked him. The British press is the most persistent. When we moved to Bruton, that year we lived in Somerset, the press at first nearly drove us crazy. And the village would help us out. The postmaster would say, "Steinbeck? Oh, yes, that chap did come near here. Whether he's stayed or not, we don't know."

DC: A village conspiracy.

ES: They protected him with a village conspiracy that was wonderful. One day I found a reporter outside of our cottage, and I said, "Get out of our meadow!" And the guy said, "It's all right, Mrs. Steinbeck. I'm *American* press." And I said, "O.k., I can really tell *you* what I think. Get the *hell* out of our meadow!"

DC: Tell us more about your days as a drama major at the University of Texas.

ES: Is this interview about *me*?

DC: We might slip this into a prologue or something.

ES: Well, I had acted in Fort Worth while I was in high school. I played the lead in the senior class play. You may be sure if I hadn't I would have laid myself on the floor and held my breath until my face turned purple! And then I acted all the time I was at the university. Lady Bird Johnson used to say, "Oh, you will just never know what a great actress Elaine was."

DC: Were you and Lady Bird in the same class?

ES: No, she was two years older.

DC: Wasn't Nellie Connally [wife of the late Texas Governor John Connally] there at that time?

ES: Nellie is a little younger than I, but Nellie and John and I are still friends. In fact, Nellie and I acted together. You see, one of the things that was so great about the drama department at the University of Texas was that it was so rich. The university had the best drama faculty, and then they built the auditorium and we had all the best facilities and equipment. And now when I go there to visit—I went to my fiftieth class reunion a few years ago—I see the most glorious places to rehearse theater, and to do theater, and to audition, and I say to the students, "Think of all you young actors; a few of you will get to New York after acting in this magnificent theater. You'll go to a scrubby theater on West Forty-Fourth Street where the toilets don't work and there's not enough light to put on make-up. And the only thing you'll have is that you'll walk onto a stage on Broadway." Anyway, we really had a superior faculty there [at the University of Texas]. A lot of them were from Yale. That was a great, great university for people going into the theater, drama, playwriting, and acting. Zack and I did a lot of plays together. And then we married while he was still in school. I went back to school and took some courses, some art history, and those things. And we also acted in the Austin theater, and in the university theater. In those days, all Broadway shows trouped. So we'd meet all the actors. We'd see them in Austin, then we'd drive to San Antonio and see them again in the same play the next night. We met the Lunts, Alfred Lunt and Lynn Fontanne, just after we had done one of their plays. I had played Miss Fontanne's part. I practically worshipped her, so I was never as embarrassed as one night at a party, in Austin, when Miss Fontanne said, "Where's the little girl who's supposed to be so much better than me?" I nearly died. Anyway, the Lunts had heard so much about Zack and me that they wrote the Theater Guild and said, "There's a very talented young couple down here and they're coming to New York and we think you should see them and give them a chance." We were the only actors I knew who already had jobs when we got to New York. The Theater Guild was one of the big producers at that time, and they also ran the Westport Country Playhouse, which is one of the best of the country summer stock playhouses, and Zack and I decided that one of us should have a salaried job so that our families wouldn't have to support us. We discussed the matter, and I finally said, "Look, Zack, it doesn't mean that I think you are a better actor than I am, but I think that I'm more interested in production than you are, so I'll work twelve months of every year in production." That's where I got my training, and so I was one of the first—one of the very first—women stage managers on Broadway. They just didn't let women do that in those days. I had such good teachers there. My bosses taught me so well. The ones who are alive are still my great friends. Zack had sense enough to take bit parts—any parts. He worked himself up quickly and got sent to Hollywood. So it worked out beautifully for us.

DC: So you were living in Hollywood, then, in the late 1940s?

ES: After I'd been working on *Oklahoma!* for about a year and a half—it was an enormous smash, of course—Zack wanted to see me and Waverly, our daughter. I went out just to see if we could make a go and I stayed awhile. I met John there, as a matter of fact. Anyway, I loved my work in production. I was in casting, and I always had a job. Theater was having a bad time then, but I did some interesting ones. I worked on the Paul Robeson *Othello* [1942-43] with Jose Ferrer as Iago and Uta Hagen as Desdemona. Robeson was a big star then on the concert stage. He's one of my most unforgettable characters. I didn't go on the American Tour with *Othello* because I was already doing *Oklahoma!* by then. I just went on the preliminary and part of the Broadway [run]. And this great star, Robeson—they had trouble getting him a hotel room. Can you believe it? No wonder he went to Russia. He was the most wonderful man in the world to work with. He spoke beautiful English. Once, though, he started a rehearsal of *Othello* and began calling Desdemona: [drawling] "Oh Desmonia!"

and all that. I said, "What are you doing?" And he said, "I decided to rehearse today with a Texas accent just for you." He was playing *Othello* with a Texas accent! And I said, "Well, stop at once. We ain't getting nowhere!" Don't you love it! We did our first tryouts with it. The Harvard theater was in Brattle Hall, and this was in the summer because Paul had some concerts he had to do in the fall before we opened on Broadway. So we were traveling by train from the Brattle Hall Theater at Harvard to the McCarter Theatre at Princeton. We stopped for an hour in a station in New York before we moved, and Paul said as I started to get off the car, "Where are you going?" And I said, "I'm going down to check on the car to see if our costumes and scenery are o.k." And he said, "By yourself?" And I said, "Yes, by myself." And he said, "Will it be safe? I'll go with you." And I said, "Now look here, you are the star of this show and I, a woman, have tried very hard to get this job, and if you come I will kill you. I have to prove that I can do anything by myself." So he said, "O.k., all right, o.k. Damn you women!" He was a wonderful man.

DC: Didn't you come back to live here in New York right before you married Steinbeck?

ES: Yes. When John and I fell in love I said to him, "I've not moved here to California permanently. I'm going back to New York. That's where my work and my life is—and my friends." And I wasn't trained to do anything in the movies, so I was bored the whole time I was there because I didn't have any work. John said, "Well, I'm going back to New York, too." So he came on here, and I then came with my maid, my daughter, and my dog! And we stayed at the Algonquin [Hotel] till I found an apartment. Since 1951 I have lived in this "village" right here [East Seventy-Second Street]. The house John and I lived in is right over there. I lived there for nearly fourteen years and here [in this apartment] for thirty, so I know all of these people who have shops around here. You know them in your "village."

DC: As you know, this interview will be published in a book of essays on Steinbeck's middle and later period—the works written after *The Grapes of Wrath*. You were married to him, of course, during most of that time.

ES: Yes, I lived the last twenty years of John's life with him. I met him early in 1949 and he died late in 1968. He was really very famous when I was married to him. I met him in Pacific Grove. People there more or less left him alone, so I don't think I realized how famous John was until I came to New York. And then when we started travelling, the press met every plane that John was on or every train.

DC: That bothered him, didn't it?

ES: He said until the day he died, "The best thing that Elaine ever did for me was not to be shy and to know how to handle this." Anybody who knows me knows that I'm not shy. I would talk to everybody and get everything warmed up. Then I could just disappear, go out and mind my own business, and he could take it up from there, whether we were standing in the open somewhere or in a hotel room. John could handle it here in New York, but when we were travelling, I always did the warm-up. He was very shy at the beginning.

DC: Let me ask you about one of the frequently voiced ideas of critics and scholars about John Steinbeck: that his writing changed fundamentally several years after *The Grapes of Wrath*. Jackson Benson puts that change ten years or so after *The Grapes of Wrath*, about the time Steinbeck met you in California. Benson says the nature of the change, at least in the major works he would write during the remainder of his career, was from a focus on group behavior to a focus on the social and ethical problems of the individual. What are your views on the perceived change? Was the move from California to New York significant? Was he just wanting to get on with something new?

ES: Oh, I have very definite views about that. When I met him in Pacific Grove, John said, "I can't live here. Why in the hell did I think I could come home? You can't go home again. I've lived in New York. I can't live here." And he said to me, "I'm here because I've got a job writing *Viva Zapata!* and I want to write it near the studio so I can help them put it into screen form." But he also said, "One reason I'm here now is that I'm going to write a book. I've been doing research for it a long time. I've been living under such unhappy circumstances in New York that I haven't been able to write." As Jay Parini [author of an upcoming biography on John Steinbeck] said the other day, "He didn't write well with Gwyn because they were so unhappy all the time, because they were fighting all the time." Anyway, John said, "I still have some research to do out here with the newspaper, in history, about when I was a little boy. I'm going to write a book and put everything in it that I know. I'm going to tell everything I know about my family." Well, I think when he had done that [finished his work on *Zapata!* and the research for his book], even if he hadn't met me ... I don't think John moved back to New York because of me. I think he may have moved *when* he moved because of me, but he had already said he wasn't going to stay, that he couldn't stay anymore [even though] he was delighted with his house in Pacific Grove on Eleventh Street. Once while he was living there he told me, "I felt so good this morning. That old man next door looked across and saw me in the garden, and he said, "You Ernst Steinbeck's son?" "Yes sir, I am." "Been away?" He just loved it. That old man only knew him as Ernst Steinbeck's son. Anyway, I know that he was going to move back here [to New York]. How long can you stay and write about Cannery Row? I don't see why anyone is startled that he moved around. One of the first things I asked John when I first met him was, "When Fitzgerald and Hemingway were abroad, why didn't you go?" And he said, "I didn't have the price of a ticket." And he said, "I'm very glad now that I didn't because I stayed at home and wrote about my own people."

DC: Would you agree with those scholars who say that Steinbeck always insisted on doing what he wanted to do, that he maintained his individualism and didn't look at the critics?

ES: Yes, he did not do what the critics wanted, ever. He never wrote to anybody's formula. Critics faulted him, but he never paid attention to them. He wrote whatever he wanted to write. And I would like to say that I know that's why John did not do more on the Arthurian legend—it's all right to say it now because the people involved are dead. In the first place, John had no idea he was going to die so young. He wouldn't have had a spinal operation the year before if he had known he was going to die. That's one of the hardest things anyone could have gone through, learning to walk again and all that. He had no idea his heart system was going to go out and his heart was going to fail. He certainly meant to finish the Arthurian cycle. His agent, Elizabeth Otis, whom he adored, had never interfered in his writing and neither had his editor, Pascal Covici. The man Elizabeth Otis loved and lived with for many years, Chase Horton, owned the bookstore that supplied John with all of those books, so many books, that he used for Middle English. And suddenly John said to me once when we came back from the year in Somerset, "Elizabeth and Chase have gotten so involved in this. How did I let this happen? I can't work like this. I'm going to stop for awhile." I think he stopped and wrote *The Winter of Our Discontent*. John always meant to go back and finish the Arthurian book. I studied Middle English with him just for fun, and he loved the fact that I did. When we would go to London and visit the British Museum, while he was doing research I'd be reading letters in the display case. And he would pass by me getting a book and he would say, "Having fun?" and I'd say, "I'm reading Queen Elizabeth writing to Queen Mary of Scotland; of course I'm having fun." Anyway, what John had meant to do was this: he had meant to translate the Malory straight as Malory wrote it and then to go back and to fictionalize it, write the Steinbeck version of it. But he simply didn't get around to it. He died; that's the only reason. But he just said, "The people who work with me are getting too involved and they are driving me crazy and I will stop for awhile and write something else and then I'll go back to it quietly and not tell anybody I've gone back to it." That's the truth. These are the things that nobody knows but me, because I lived with him. Then about two years after John died, Elizabeth Otis said, "Let's publish it." She said, "I'd like to publish it and publish his letters to Chase there in the back of the book." I wasn't too with it at the time. I had had a terrible time adjusting to John's death.

DC: So, you're not sure you would make that same decision again?

ES: I'm not sorry; every once in a while somebody loves the book, and it gets better as it goes. Towards the last third of the book John is beginning to have fun and to embroider a little. We had gone down to the coast . . . Southampton . . . no, I can't remember where now, and he begins to write about that because he and I had walked there. And he begins to put his characters into that landscape, and, I think, to have fun. It would have been wonderful.

DC: He certainly has fun with those private jokes he puts in the book—the one, for instance, about Toby Street [Steinbeck's longtime friend], who appears as Sir Tobinus Streat de Montroy.

ES: Oh yes, he was happiest . . . if John had finished that book, nobody could have said that he had gone downhill. Because that's what he wanted to do and that's what I regret more than anything for his sake—that he never got that done. Remember the story I told you about when he was dying?

DC: About the time you spent in Somerset?

ES: He was in bed and I was sitting beside him. I was reading to him —he had the oxygen tubes in his nostrils—and he suddenly said, "What was the best time we had in our twenty years together?" I started to answer, but then I said, "You tell me first." And he said, "No, I'm dying and you'll agree with me." And I kind of laughed and he laughed. I said, "I'll write it on a piece of paper and put it in your hand." And I did. Then I asked him, "What's the best time we've had?" And he said, "The year we spent in Somerset." And I said, "Open your hand." And I had written "Somerset." It's an incredible story for me to remember during the last hours with John. I also remember one day when we were alone in the cottage [in Somerset] and he said, "Elaine, can you hear me?" I said, "Yes, I'm on the stairway." He said, "Can you look out the window toward the garden?" And I said, "I'll go quietly and look out." He said, "I'm writing about Morgan le Fay and I want you to see what's in the garden." There was a raven sitting in the garden and he said, "Maybe that raven knows what I'm writing about. That raven is looking for Morgan le Fay." She always rode with a raven on her wrist, you know. The Arthurian legend was all magic to him. Camelot was just a few miles from us; that's why we were there. Once John took Adlai Stevenson up there around midnight and they thought they heard King Arthur's horses riding by. The best two Americans to be out at Camelot to hear King Arthur's horses riding by are John Steinbeck and Adlai Stevenson. Don't you love it!

DC: [Indicating on a desk a small sword stuck in a glass replica of a stone] Where did that come from?

ES: That's the last present I gave John. Tiffany had it—no, Baccarat. It's "The Sword in the Stone." I got it not long before John died and I said, "Here, this is for your desk." Isn't it beautiful? It's a paper opener. And they only made a few of them. It's very heavy crystal.

DC: It looked like something you might have given him when he was working on *The Acts of King Arthur*.

ES: Well, he was always writing it in his head. But yes, that's why I gave it to him, of course. Out hanging on the wall at Sag Harbor is a sword he always had with which he made his sister Mary "Sir Mary." That's in *Life in Letters*, incidentally. Sometimes I wonder how he anointed her, because he and Mary played all these games. He had two sisters much older than he, and the sister Mary who died a few years before him.

DC: Didn't another sister die just recently?

ES: Beth died just the other day at ninety-eight. She died in October while I was in London.

DC: I remember she was still living when we were out in Salinas [for the Steinbeck Festival] last August.

ES: Beth and John were not much alike [but] they were very much family people. Oh my God, everybody is so surprised I'm very caught up in the Steinbecks. When they marry I go there; when they die, I go. The reason I didn't go to Beth's funeral was that I was in London because of *Kiss of the Spider Woman*. But I had said to John's niece, "If she dies while I'm away, here's the hotel number and phone me." John's sister, Mary, was four years younger than John. Her husband was an officer in the American Air Force, and he had been killed as [the Allies] came up the Italian peninsula taking it back. He was killed by friendly fire. By the time I met John, Mary was a widow and she travelled. She and I were very close. She was nearer my age. You see, John was about thirteen and a half years older than I. And Mary was nearer me in age. We were very compatible. And if we were going abroad, she would meet us somewhere and be with us part of the time and then go on her way. I adored her. She died in the year Churchill died, 1965. We happened to be in Paris then. John was very close to her. They always read the Arthurian legends together and acted them out. John, of course, always thought he was Lancelot. When he built me a little swimming pool in Sag Harbor—he never could keep a secret—and before Christmas and my birthday, by the time it got there, I always knew what he was giving me. One day he said to me, I guess it was in July, "Elaine, for your birthday —" And I said, "I'm not listening. I don't care." And he said, "I have to tell you something about your birthday." And I said, "I'm not going to listen. I'm going to run; I'm going to stop my ears up." He said, "Elaine, there's a bulldozer coming up the street, damn it! Up the road to make you a pool!" So anyway, while they were pouring the cement for the pool, he said, "Pour a little cement right over here on the ground." They did, and he wrote in it, following Lancelot, "Ladye, I take reccorde of God, in thee I have myn erthly joye." And so I looked up and said, "I'd rather have that than the pool."

DC: What problems do you have as both literary executor and the widow of a literary institution?

ES: Oh, I say all the time, "Gosh, wasn't he smart to leave the copyrights to me?" Because I work at it all the time. I literally have had four chances to remarry, three near his death, one about two or three years ago. Once I thought about it for awhile. But in the first place, I guess I'm still in love with John. And then I've learned to live alone and like it, and I'm just too busy with Steinbeck. I'm just so lucky. I can talk about him. I can't write. It makes me angry that people ask me to write things. Just because I lived with a writer doesn't mean I can write. Sometimes someone will say, "Pretend it's a letter." Well, you can't do that. The point is, I can talk about him endlessly as you know, and I can go on the air and do those morning shows, T.V. shows, that I did. When *The Grapes of Wrath* [the 1990 dramatic production at the Cort Theater] was opening here, they had no stars, so they had to use anyone they could get to talk and go on the air, and they had me. I can always talk about him in any vein anybody wants. I want to be perfectly frank with you. I'm having a great deal of fun, but I can't do it too often because I don't want to live in the past that much. I live for John and I live for continuation in my life. I'm so happy I didn't have to move to new surroundings that had no relationship with John. And yet, I would no more talk all day long about John or read all day long about John . . . I couldn't live in the past. That's not normal. So I try to balance it. I go to the theater all the time and I read lots of modern fiction.

DC: Who do you like particularly in modern fiction?

ES: I like [Gabriel] Garcia Marquez very much. I also like Toni Morrison, David McCullough, Anne Tyler, Muriel Spark, and Julian Barnes. But let me finish this: I live a life of a modern woman of my age. I travel a lot. I have a lot of friends, but I'm always available for my job as John's widow. I'd never lived alone before in my life, ever. When I went away to college I lived in a sorority house. I'd never lived alone and at first it was horrible, but I've gotten used to it now. John will always be with me in a certain way, but not in the spooky, ridiculous way. I have one thing that bugs me the most. No matter where I am in this city, when it's around six o' clock I think I ought to rush and get home. I have to remind myself that John's not here waiting for me, which is very strange isn't it?. I still say, "Oh, it's six o' clock. He's surely finished his work and he wants a drink and he wants some conversation, and I want it, too." But when people think they can't criticize John and his work, I think that's ridiculous. Of course, some of it isn't as good as it ought to be. When the *New York Times* said that John shouldn't have won the Nobel Prize, I still think that's absolutely the most miserable thing I've ever heard. And by God, it's one of the reasons I'm so glad he's proving them—they said, "Oh, he's just a regional writer." We were in Sag Harbor when that article came out, and I felt so bad. It was pouring rain and I went out and worked in the garden, and John would stand at the door and say,

"Elaine, please come in. It's all right. We'll live through it." He had found it and read it. He said, "You can't treat me like a child. I've had criticism before." So now I always answer back, and I always say, "Yes, I'm sure you're right; some of the works are not good." But guess who's reading *The Grapes of Wrath*? People in forty languages.

DC: Those critics who lashed out in 1942 at *The Moon Is Down*, claiming that it was counterproductive propaganda, that it would hurt the Allied war effort . . . I'm talking mainly about Clifton Fadiman and James Thurber and Stanley Edgar Hyman—

ES: Oh boy! John said bad things about *them*.

DC: Did he ever have any kind of contact at all with any of them after their attacks?

ES: I don't think so.

DC: I was just curious whether Steinbeck ever discussed the controversy with any of them later, because they never retracted anything.

ES: Oh, no. They never retracted anything even after the war when there were many indications that they had been wrong. All of that was stupid. They called him a traitor. John never had a kind word to say for them. I always loved Thurber's writing. But I've never said a good thing about Thurber since I found out about his attack on John. I think it [the attack] was the stupidest thing in the world. Even when they found out how important the book was, how valuable it was to the underground [in Nazi-occupied Europe during World War II], they never retracted a thing, no, not at all.

DC: The odd thing about the attacks was that they were so mean-spirited.

ES: There are a lot of people who didn't like John. I first thought in the back of my head that John must be paranoid when he began to tell me why he went to the war as a correspondent instead of in the service. He started telling me how he kept trying to get in the service. J. Edgar Hoover was behind all this. When the Freedom of Information Act was passed, I immediately sent away for all the papers on John. Everything John suspected was exactly true. J. Edgar Hoover kept saying, "You cannot let him go in any service. He's a communist. He wrote *The Grapes of Wrath*." And everything John tried Hoover stopped him. I wish to God I could tell John that Hoover also wore a black taffeta dress! Nobody would have had more fun with that! The stories about Roy Cohn [legal counsel to Senator Joseph McCarthy]—and John had many gay friends; that wouldn't have been a problem—but J. Edgar Hoover and Roy Cohn . . . he would have just loved to know that Hoover wore that dress. Anyway, John was telling the absolute truth about why he couldn't get in the service. They wouldn't let him in. So he had to go as a war correspondent to get abroad. He went to all the dangerous spots; he didn't try to protect himself at all.

DC: Something I've been wanting to ask you about is a comment Bo Beskow [Steinbeck's friend, the Swedish artist] made to me in an interview I did with him in 1981. Bo said that he always had the impression you discouraged Steinbeck's lighthearted pieces because you wanted him to write serious novels.

ES: That is absolutely untrue. I never wanted John to write anything like that. That is the most ridiculous thing I have ever heard. Bo and John stayed the greatest friends until the Nobel Prize. Bo tried to take over everything when we got to Sweden, and they had a falling out.

DC: Didn't Bo sort of take the two of you in hand when you arrived at the airport in Stockholm?

ES: Guess who was the elbow to everybody and all the [Nobel] committee and everyone around to meet John at the plane, and who elbowed me out of the pictures? They all showed John arriving in Stockholm and with Bo Beskow instead of me. Except for one picture.

DC: He met you at the plane then?

ES: I'll say he did. When you are a laureate in chemistry, physics or literature, you are assigned an aide [upon arrival in Sweden], and John and I had the nicest aide. He eventually became the President of the Nobel Committee. Every day before you go out he tells you where you're going, what the protocol is, exactly what to do, whom you will meet, how to address certain members of the royal family and members of the committee. He's *your* aide. And this young man— we couldn't have lived without him; we just adored him. About the third day, John's aide said to John, "I'm going to have to tell you I'm having a dreadful time. I'm having to fight off Bo Beskow because he wants to take charge of everything." Bo didn't have to do that.

John and he were friends. But in every photograph with the king and the queen, you know, you had Bo right there with his arm around John. Have you ever heard the charming story about the last evening of the Nobel Prize festivities? The aide said to John and me, "Tonight you'll be going to the Royal Ball. I've watched you, and you know how to handle yourselves with anybody." One night at one banquet I had been with the prime minister and John had been with one of the princesses. Another time I was with Bertil, one of the princes, and James Watson, who was getting the award for discovering DNA, he and Crichton. Anyway, the aide said to John and me, "Now, in Sweden it's not the way it is at the White House where the guests walk around and the hosts, the president and his wife, stay still. Here, the guests form a semi-circle and the royal family go by and then they go stand in the middle of the floor and someone is chosen to accompany them in to dinner. But no literature laureate has ever been chosen for that, so you're all right. You'll probably get someone else in the royal family." We said, "Fine." Well, we were standing in a line, everybody's dressed in gown and white tie and so forth, when a man in a wig carrying a long staff and dressed in medieval clothes came and stood in front of John and me and he stamped the floor with his staff and he said, "Madam, would you advance to the middle of the floor and take the arm of the king and lead the dinner party in? Sir, would you please take the arm of the queen and lead in?" That was the first time a literature laureate had ever been chosen. Our aide was standing over there dying. John says that I said, "I sure will, Honey," but I didn't.

DC: What did you say?

ES: I said, "Thank you, yes." Then I looked at John and he was bursting with pleasure, and pride. John was selected for that because he was such a popular choice [for the Nobel Prize]. So I advanced and took the king's arm and John advanced and took the queen's arm and we led everyone. Here were all these *famous* laureates, and Steinbeck was leading them. I had never had more fun than with the king. John had never had more fun than with the queen. She was Louie Mountbatten's sister, Queen Louise. They had a marvelous time; *I* had a marvelous time. During the dinner the king said to me, "Look around the table. Anywhere you see this placemat is a member of the royal family." And I said, "Yes, sir, I noticed it." He said, "One of our forefathers was a messy eater. Now it means we're royalty." Then he said, "Where do you live?" And I said, "In the summer, in Sag Harbor." And he said, "You know I was crown prince for so long that I travelled around the world. I've even been out and seen the

Hamptons." I said, "Sir, I know all these flowers are grown in your gardens, and I know you're a great gardener." And he said, "Let me think about the climate in Sag Harbor. I'll write you down some things that will grow well there." We had the time of our lives. Bertil, the prince, was sitting on one side of me; I was sitting with the king on the other. I turned to talk to Bertil a minute, and he said, "I've been watching you have a good time for five days, and I've never known anybody to talk so much." We became close friends.

DC: Bertil is the present King's brother?

ES: Bertil was the son of the king [at that time, Gustaf VI Adolf]. He did not inherit the throne. The grandson did [Bertil's nephew, Carl XVI Gustaf]. Bertil said to me that night, "What plane are you going to use? Aren't you going to London?" And I said, "Yes." Alice Guinzburg was with John and me. Her husband, who had been John's publisher, had died just a few months before, and Alice was about to die because her husband had died—they'd been married for fifty years. John had phoned her when he won the Nobel Prize and said, "You're going to Stockholm." And Alice said, "I'll never travel again with Harold dead." And John said, "You're going to represent him, Alice. You have to come." And she went and it was wonderful. She knew so many people all over the world. She and her husband were very cosmopolitan. Anyway, Prince Bertil said to me, "Aren't you and Mrs. Guinzburg and your husband going to London?" And I said, "Yes, we're going to go there and have some parties before we go home for Christmas." He said, "You've met the woman I'm going to eventually marry." She was a commoner. "She's going to London and she's riding in steerage. Are you riding first class?" I said, "Yes, we are." And he said, "Will you invite her up for a drink?" I said, "We'd love to." So later I said to the stewardess, "Tell Mrs.—I've forgotten her name now, but they all knew who she was—I want to see her up in first class." And she came and sat in first class with us and had a ball. She said, "I've never had so much fun! Bertil and I just don't have the money to afford for me to go first-class." Now, one thing I want to say here: Whenever John is called a drunk, or an alcoholic, nothing makes me any madder. We did grow up in a time of hard drinking. We all did. I did at Texas, at the University. Zack and I did. John and I drank a lot here. I think John drank an extra lot with Gwyn because of the kind of society they lived in. But John could go anytime he wanted without a drink. And what he said to me, oh, weeks before we went to Stockholm, was, "When we go to Stockholm, will you do something with me?" And I said, "Sure, what?" He said,

"Will you go there and party those five days without taking a drop of booze?" And I said, "Why, certainly." And he said (and I love the wording), "With the possible exception of Pearl Buck, every American literature laureate who went to Stockholm has been drunk those five days." Sinclair Lewis said he was; Faulkner told in my presence that he was, and Eugene O'Neill. John said, "I'm going to represent myself, my profession, my country, and I'm not going to do it drunk." And we had not one drop. When we went to a public place I would find a waiter and say, "See that man out there? Tell the waiters to pour him nothing but water."

DC: Water looks just like aquavit anyway.

ES: Well, nobody even noticed it. The point about John is, the Austin paper had one of those gossip columns several years ago. Fran, my sister, sent one to me that said something about John's drinking, so I just sat down and wrote this story to [the columnist] and he published it. I don't think he published the letter; he just said that Elaine Steinbeck says that her husband spent five days in Stockholm going to five parties a day and never had a drop of liquor.

DC: Speaking of other American Nobel literature laureates and their wives, did you know any of them well?

ES: I got to know Mary Hemingway. We were at a big birthday party for Carl Sandburg here in New York right after Hemingway's death, and somebody at the party said to John, "Mary Hemingway is here and she's having such a hard time. Do you know her?" And John said, "I've never met her, but I would like to meet her." So John sent a note over to her table saying, "My wife and I are here. Would you care to join us for a nightcap downstairs?" We were at the Waldorf. And she did, and John was so wonderful with her. We saw her often after that. We would have a party, and if we had anybody interesting from England, or had Adlai [Stevenson], or had various people, we would always include Mary. We had a wonderful time with her.

DC: So you got to know her well?

ES: Oh, after John died, she was wonderful to me, and she and I got to be good friends. It was so funny . . . when *Steinbeck: A Life in Letters* was published [in 1975], Mary had her own book coming out. She was really not very good with an audience and got shy, I understand. Her agent called me one day and said, "I've been talking to John Steinbeck's agent, I know you're going to do a program in Connecticut that's going to be televised." I said, "Yes, I am." He said, "Would you object at all if Mary touted her book while you're touting yours?" Of course, I didn't write mine; I just edited mine. And I said, "I think it will be the greatest fun in the world." Well, we went out and Mary was scared to death. And when we got in front of the audience, I said, "Mary, tell about such and such." She started to talk. I found that during the entire show I never got to say anything about Steinbeck or my book. I was just interviewing Mary, and she was having a ball. The ladies in the audience were laughing. It was so marvelous! When it was over, Mary said, "That was fun, wasn't it?" and left. I went on to lunch with all the ladies. Mary couldn't go. And then the agent phoned the next day and said, "Mary wants to know if you'd like to do that all over the country." And I said, "Oh, Honey, I'm so sorry; I can't do that." I was so busy interviewing her and feeding her cues that I wasn't saying anything about my own book. But I would go and have dinner with her alone and would walk to her apartment, you know, filled with animal heads and all that, and the doorman would say through the button, "Mrs. Steinbeck to see Mrs. Hemingway." Once I whispered and said, "The only person who's missing is Mrs. Faulkner." And Mary said, "We don't want her. She's a party pooper."

DC: Did you ever meet Mrs. Faulkner?

ES: No. But I loved Mary. She lived over here on Sixty-Fourth Street, I think, not very far from me. She moved home when she got very sick. Anyway, she and I got along just marvelously. She did the cleverest thing, this woman, when Castro took over in Cuba. She told me this herself. She heard that Castro's government was going to take over their property. What did they call that place?

DC: The Finca?

ES: The Finca. She realized that their things left in it were everything she and Ernest valued, and so she did the following thing—Ernest was dead by then: She invited Castro to tea. She said it could be tea or coffee or whatever he chose. She said to him, "I want to present the Finca to you. I know you will give me plenty of time to get all of my possessions and all of my husband's possessions out. Don't rush me. I know you will let me do it; just give me time." What could he say? And she got all those personal things she wanted.

DC: She went back to visit the Finca right before she died, didn't she?

ES: Yes, she did.

DC: And said Castro's government had left everything exactly the way it was, right down to Hemingway's cigar butts in the ashtray.

ES: Sure they did. It was a tourist attraction. I'm sorry I never met Hemingway. John knew him when he and Gwyn were living in New York, I believe, but he never knew him well. John mourned him when he died; John really mourned him. John said, "This is the most imitated American writer of the century. All young writers want to be like him." I don't know whether John and he would have been very close friends or anything like that, but I know John loved his work. You know the first time we met Faulkner?

DC: Tell me.

ES: Jean Stein, who was Faulkner's friend in New York, phoned me and said, "Bill's coming into town and wants to meet John." And I said, "Let me talk to John." And John said, "Oh, wouldn't that be marvelous? Go on and arrange it." Jean said, "We'll come over to your house for drinks, and then we'll go out to a little bistro or somewhere." I never saw John so pleased, because he was crazy about Faulkner. Anyway, we had a library over there [house on East Seventy-Second Street] which was very informal, with a fireplace and two easy chairs on each side of it, just a very comfortable room. We were dressed very informally and so forth, and John was all excited. They came in, Jean Stein, Faulkner, and his editor, Saxe Commins, and Faulkner was blind drunk, a walking zombie. The first thing John said was, "I rarely ever give up my chair to anybody, but it would be my honor if you would sit in my chair." And Faulkner walked straight across to the other chair. Now they had asked to come, mind you, and I have never in my life seen anyone as astonished as Jean and the editor. We had the most miserable time. John never lost his composure because he knew Faulkner was drunk, and he said, "What can I make you to drink?" Faulkner said, "Whiskey and branch water." John said, "I've heard that a lot in Texas. My wife's from Texas, so I've heard that." Everybody would try to talk, and he would either not answer or would answer rudely. Somebody said, "Where should we go for dinner tonight?" And I said, "Mr. Faulkner, I've understood from Tennessee Williams and the [Elia] Kazans that they love to go to your house because you have the old Southern food." And he said,

"Don't know what they ate. I eat what's put before me." And I wanted to say, "Well, why the hell don't you . . . ." It was absolutely awful. We went to a little pub over here where we've gone a million times, and instead of ordering in English—all the waiters spoke English— Faulkner decided to order in French, in that Southern French. It was an evening . . .

DC: *Southern* French?

ES: Yes, Oxford, Mississippi, French! By the time we got home, John and I were so exhausted we were just wrecks. Trying to be civil, and, why, we were sick at our stomachs. The next morning Jean phoned me and said, "Elaine, he was so nervous about meeting John that he got drunk." About a week later John got a letter from Faulkner saying he was so sorry and asking John's forgiveness, and they became good friends. But oh, what an experience.

DC: What year was that Faulkner visit?

ES: Let's see, [it was before] we moved into this apartment in '63. I couldn't find those letters [the ones from Faulkner].

DC: So when you came back home from Stockholm, you came back to this apartment?

ES: No, when John and I heard that he had won the Nobel Prize we were in Sag Harbor and the announcement from the committee that he had won was sent to the house [on East Seventy-Second Street]. He won in the autumn of '62 and we moved here in March of '63 right after we returned from Stockholm. The prize was announced the day after we were almost blown up by the Russians—the Cuban Missile Crisis. John and I never listened to daytime television, certainly not at Sag Harbor. And neither did John have breakfast with me, ever, because he would go down to the village. But that morning—we had stayed up so late listening to the television because we felt that things were so bad—I was cooking bacon and eggs in the kitchen, and I said, "John, I think we ought to turn on the television to see if the world is still turning."

And he turned, click, and it said, "This morning John Steinbeck won the Nobel Prize for Literature." Those were the words we heard. Our kitchen and sitting room open together, and I turned around from cooking bacon and looked at John and we just started screaming. You see, the announcement, a telegram that had been sent to him, was in the mailbox at the house back here in the city. And there was nobody at the house. I put the pan with the bacon in it in the refrigerator. Three days later we came back and it was sitting there. Anyway, I said, "What do we do? What shall I do?" And he said, "First of all, I'm going to tell the boys" [Steinbeck's two sons who were away at boarding school]. So I called each school and I had such fun. I got through first to Thom's school, and I said, "Can I speak with my son, Thom?" And she said, "Now, Mrs. Steinbeck, you know he's in his first class." And I said, "Oh, never mind. Just send someone when you get a chance to tell him his father just won the Nobel Prize." And then I called Johnny's school and did the same thing. Then our phone started ringing and it rang off the wall. Viking [Press] got on the line and said, "Elaine, get him into town some way, because in spite of the Cuban Missile Crisis we'll have to have a press conference this afternoon. We've already been flooded with calls." I said to John, "Shall we fly in?" Every once in a while we fly these little planes in from Long Island because it's about 100 miles. And John said, "No, let's just drive in the car because we can talk about it and have fun and turn on the radio and listen to it being announced over the radio." He would have never said that to anybody but me, but he did say it. And it was such fun. I have wonderful pictures of us at Viking when they had the press conference—Elizabeth [Otis, Steinbeck's literary agent], and John and me. You've seen them. So that was a big thrill. But then the mail was so overwhelming from all over the world. I said to John, "We can't handle this." And he said, "Yes, let's get secretaries, but out here." So we got secretaries for Sag Harbor. All the really personal letters John would answer himself at his little house. And I just turned the big room at the house into an office and got secretaries to help. We had known Princess Grace through Tom Guinzburg [son of Steinbeck's publisher] before she became princess. John got an early telegram from her saying, "I'm so proud to be an American today." And he wrote her a letter. Then he came to me and said, "Elaine, do you know Princess Grace's address?" And I said, "Oh, I can find out." He had written, "Dear Princess Grace, Honey . . ." Later on when I saw her she said, "That's the best letter I ever got being a princess."

[Earlier that year], we were in Athens with Terrence [McNally] and the boys when Crown Prince Juan Carlos, who is now the King of Spain, married the Greek princess. And we made sure our hotel room had a balcony because we knew that during the week they were going in a procession from one church to another and we wanted to sit out there and have our breakfast and watch. And we did and it was such fun because right behind [the bride and groom] were a lot of other royalty, some of whom we knew, including Princess Grace, Honey.

I leaned out and said, "Princess Grace, Honey!" And she looked up and said, "Who in the world would call me Princess Grace, Honey, from a balcony except Steinbeck?"

DC: You were talking to me yesterday about the role that you had in the dramatic productions of two of Steinbeck's plays, *Burning Bright* and *Pipe Dream*.

ES: Yes, I thought a lot about all of this during the night. I do not believe for one minute that anybody told John what to write, ever. I think the biggest influence of anybody would have been Ed Ricketts, definitely. John always said his other passion was marine biology. Every year we went to the Caribbean John always went over to the marine station and went out with the guys and talked about what was under the water. He did that any place we went in the Caribbean and he did it at Nantucket. Ed Ricketts influenced him in many ways and I think that influence lasted all of John's life, not only while he was writing about Cannery Row. I never knew what he was going to write until he told me. I never influenced what he wrote.

DC: What about the plays he wrote after you were married? With your theatrical background, did you ever act as liaison between him and those responsible for the performances?

ES: Oh, I was always a liaison, but I didn't tell him what to write. I remember—it was very interesting—the year before we married we took a trip to Mexico. He had written *Burning Bright* and had dedicated it to me and he was turning it into a play. He would read aloud to me because he was making dialogue. And the only time that he ever accepted influence from me I would say, "Wait a minute; your scene has just ended," because, you know, a scene or an act has to end on a certain beat. Something is said and that's the curtain or the blackout. And John, as a novelist, would sometimes add two or three more lines. John's preparation for writing was thinking. That's why he rewrote so seldom. Believe me, I would know when he was beginning to think about something he was going to write because he would become very distant. And I would say, "Do you have something in mind?" And he would say, "I really do." Just before he sat down to write, nothing got through to him, nothing anybody said got through to him. He was very kind and polite, but he was just thinking what he was going to do when he sat down to write. But at that point, I never knew what he was going to write. He might say to Gadg [Elia] Kazan or Frank Loesser or some of his friends, "I think I'll write a play about such and such." But he never discussed it with me as some writers do with their wives—or their husbands. And I'm pretty sure he didn't with Gwyn. How much Carol did, I don't know. Susan Shillinglaw [editor of the *Steinbeck Newsletter*] would be able to tell you more about that. [Jackson] Benson says how helpful Carol was. She did all the typing. She worked like a *fiend*. Now whether Carol said anything to John about writing, I have no way of knowing. John never told me.

DC: But in the case of the play version of *Burning Bright* . . .

ES: When the producers would say, "Elaine, what do you think about so and so playing that part?" and when John would say, "Elaine what do you think?" I would tell them because it would have been somebody I worked with or that I had seen act a lot. I think one of the reasons John wrote *Burning Bright* was that we were coming to New York together. Remember, he had come here earlier [in 1937] with George Kaufmann and had turned *Of Mice and Men* into a play, and he had worked on various movie scripts. But the only one that I had any suggestions about was for *Burning Bright*.

DC: What about after rehearsals started? Did you have any suggestions then?

ES: Oh sure; of course, but they always had their own stage manager. I did not go on a salary and work on the play. But John would say, "How do you think such and such a scene is playing now?" And I would answer. John and I stayed together constantly, at every rehearsal and everything.

DC: What was your professional sense as a theater person of what Rodgers and Hammerstein did with *Sweet Thursday* in *Pipe Dream*?

ES: We all realized later they were the wrong ones to choose. Anybody in the world would have given a million dollars to have them, but as Billy Hammerstein said, neither one of them had ever been to a whorehouse! And then Helen Traubel had left the Metropolitan Opera and nobody had told us that she didn't have a voice any more. They never asked her to sing out in rehearsal. She was a great, great opera singer, but Rudolph Bing [then General Director of the Metropolitan Opera] had fired her and he was too much of a gentleman to say he had fired her because she had lost her voice. We got to New Haven to rehearse with the full orchestra and you couldn't hear her on the first row. And she had a run of the play contract. They should have bought her off. Everything went wrong. The second day of rehearsal, Richard Rodgers had half of his face cut away because of cancer. We knew the play was going wrong. But we kept hoping—you know when you get in those situations you keep hoping something can pull it out of the fire. But nothing ever did. It got bad reviews in Boston. But [even today] people still want to do it. Every once in a while it's done somewhere just because it's Rodgers and Hammerstein and Steinbeck. But the force of John's wonderful story, the intellectual falling in love with a whore, was lost. When it was being performed in Boston, we were all living at the Ritz, and every night after every performance, Dick and Oscar would write John notes and John would write them notes. Oscar would say, "Would you add a couple of lines in such and such a scene?" That's the way you work. Then one day, John just said to me, "I'll have to tell you what I've written Oscar: 'You've turned my whore into a visiting nurse!'" So *Pipe Dream* was Rodgers and Hammerstein's only real flop. When we were celebrating the fiftieth anniversary of *Oklahoma!* and the fiftieth anniversary of the beginning of the collaboration of Rodgers and Hammerstein, we all said, "Well, it was the only one that flopped." Linda Rodgers Emory, Dick's daughter, said to me, "Elaine, I put money myself into *Pipe Dream*. Wouldn't you know the only one you and I invested in would flop?"

DC: We were talking yesterday about a part of Steinbeck that general readers and even scholars sometimes miss, his humor.

ES: People who knew him knew his humor. And people in California knew his humor and everybody around here knew it. It's just some of the scholars now. They think he's the Great Steinbeck and that everything he wrote has to be taken seriously. I find that a lot of young people or very pompous people or people who are teaching will pick up something that John meant to be ridiculous and think that he was being profound.

DC: Let me ask you about John Steinbeck the man as opposed to Steinbeck the writer. One of my memorable experiences while I was doing research in Europe in 1981 for my book on *The Moon Is Down* was an interview in Copenhagen with Otto Lindhardt, who of course you know had been Steinbeck's Danish publisher. It was late in the afternoon, and I had been throwing questions at him for two and a half hours. He was surely weary of me, but he had remained kind and patient and responsive, if a little formal. At the end of the interview when I turned off my tape recorder and put down my pen, he asked how my research had been going, and I told him how helpful and sympathetic the Europeans I had already interviewed had been, and I said something like, "You know, the most remarkable thing I've picked up from Steinbeck's European readers whom I've interviewed so far is how profoundly John Steinbeck really touched people—all kinds of people. They speak of him almost as if they knew him personally." Then I said to Mr. Lindhardt, "You did know him personally. You had a long-standing professional relationship with him, and you were also a friend. What was he like?" I still remember his response. His face relaxed, and he told me that Steinbeck was different from most geniuses because he was so interested in other people, and so thoughtful and personal in his dealings with them, and he finished by saying, "I never met anyone like him." That last comment particularly struck me because Otto Lindhardt had had dealings over the years with many well-known authors. Obviously Steinbeck had a common touch for those who knew him personally as well as for his readers . . .

ES: But you see John was not always able to do that in person. He was only able to do that . . . that's why he liked to write. When we first started seeing each other—I didn't know it at the time but we were falling in love—he took me over to show me his house, and he said, "I started to write in that room." I said, "When was that?" And he said, "I don't remember a time I didn't write." You see, he just did not remember a time that he didn't put words on paper. His common touch came from that. I can't tell you how shy John was. Sumner Locke-Elliott, the Australian writer whom I love, once said to me, "Elaine, I had one opportunity to meet John, and he talked solemnly and I understood about every tenth word. I was too shy to say, 'I can't understand you.'" John *really* mumbled. I would say to him, "Honey, please speak up." And all of his friends would say, "Stop mumbling!" He was *genuinely* shy with new people, but not with his old friends like Otto. But his common touch was in his writing. John expressed himself well in words [when he talked]; I'm not saying that he did not. He expressed himself in the most interesting way. He was very witty and very funny. I'm a big crossword puzzler, and I used to ask him for a synonym but I would have to say, "I don't want the history of the word, John; I want the synonym." He loved words and I learned to love words from him. John was the most fun to travel with of anyone I've ever known. Somebody said to me the other day, "We're going to be in Rome a short time. Should we go out to Hadrian's Villa?" I said, "Oh my God, that is the most important and most interesting—" But then I said, "I don't know whether you should go or not. You won't be with John." When I was there with John we took a bottle of wine and some cheese and some ham and bread and went out and spent the day. The ruins are very sparse and low, and John just filled in the whole scene, right in front of my eyes. And we spent the day there, and I was *in* Hadrian's Villa. And although there was just a little of it standing, we would sit and walk in the garden and then sit and drink our wine and have a picnic. Travelling with him was simply wonderful. He always knew what to tell me to read. I always read about what I'm going to see and read about it while I'm there and then read about it more when I leave. He was a marvelous man to travel with. But—and now I'm trying to think of things about him— he was a man who wanted privacy. He didn't want to go out as much as I did. Once when we were getting ready to go abroad for several months and we were living here, he said, "Why are we going out so much?" Then he said, "We're saying good-bye to people I scarcely ever say hello to." He was very funny—and fun to live with—but also very moody. At first when he went through those terrible black moods when he was writing—I found out those were writer's block— I would think, What have I done, what have I done? He was very hard to live with in many ways. But I think most writers probably would be.

DC: You said something yesterday about his being the most compli- cated person you ever knew.

ES: Oh, his mind went in so many directions. He was very political. He knew world history very well indeed. He was very opinionated, which I liked, and he was very liberal.

DC: When you read the comments he made in the 1950s about how the Soviet empire would collapse . . . he also had amazing foresight.

ES: Where did you read that? Because he said to me, "Elaine, you have been with me this last trip"—this was just before he died—and he said, "You will live to see the downfall." And I said, "That is the most ridiculous thing I ever heard, John, that the wall in Berlin with everything I've seen—nobody is going to see it fall." And he said, "People will not stay cooped up and cut off from the rest of the world. I predict that you will see it in your lifetime." When the wall started to crumble and fall, I said to [my sister] Jean, "You remember he told us."

DC: That prediction I was talking about regarding the collapse of the

Soviet empire is in the journal he kept while he was writing *East of Eden*—the *Journal of a Novel*. Do you have a copy of it here?

ES: I think so. [Walks to bookshelves and returns with *Journal of a Novel*.]

DC: Let me see if I can find it.

ES: While you're looking, I want you to hear this marvelous story. We went to the Soviet Union during Khrushchev's last years. John wanted to meet young writers. And we did meet them, a lot of young writers, and they stayed our friends. There was a Russian man who had been in trouble, a Soviet writer who had been in prison, and who was then in hiding. The Soviets had said to John, "He's gone. You won't see him. He's not writing anymore." And John kept saying, "Maybe we'll see him someplace." Anyway, we were sitting at a long table and the press was all behind us. There were all kinds of people there; there must have been three hundred people. And suddenly the door opened and everybody went "Ah," and then a man, rather bedraggled, walked square into the room and he put his hands in front of John and said, "Nekrasov!" And John put his hands on top of his and said, "Steinbeck!" And John said, "Sit down. I want to see you. That's one of the reasons I came to Russia." And the man came and spent the night with us at the hotel. John and he sat and talked all night and then he went back into hiding.

DC: This was in 1963?

ES: Yes. And the hotel . . . of course, there were spies, and we were bugged constantly. When we first arrived there, I wouldn't talk, and then I'd say things to John such as, "What this room needs is a few more ashtrays and another chair or two." And, of course, the next day I'd have them. I would tell this at parties, and they would all laugh because they weren't used to people doing like this. John and I were just perfectly open. But there were certain things that John said we must remember: "Anything that is secret, we must be very careful about." We had the most fascinating things happen. Before we left on our trip we went by the White House to see the President.

DC: This was Kennedy?

ES: Yes, Kennedy. And I said to the President, "Can I kick up a little dust?" And he said, "I'd like you to be debriefed when John comes to be debriefed. I want to hear everything you have to tell the State Department about the women." So when I got comfortable there— we were there three months—we'd be at a party with all these men, and they'd have wonderful food—six courses—and I would say, "Just a minute. I have something I want to say." "Oh, yes, madam; yes, madam." I'd say, "Where are the wonderful women who made all this food?" And they would say, "Oh, they're off in the kitchen." And I would say, "Well, I won't have another bite or drink until I meet them." The women adored me. They'd bring them all out, and John and Ed[ward] Albee and I would toast them. And then I would get up and talk with them and go out with them. So when I came home, I had a lot to say. I had a wonderful time. John adored the fact that I did that. Let me tell you another funny story. You know the Russian toast, *za vashe zdorovie* ("to your health")? And everytime you have a forkful of food you're starting to eat, you have to put it down and say, *za vashe zdorovie!* and you have to drink. So we had been over there a long time by now, and we were sick of that. And we were down in Tbilisi, and we are at a long table again with all those men in those black suits with the vests, and some women. John's down here, and I'm here and Edward's over here. And John's very shy . He never made toasts or anything; he was strictly cordial and polite with the talk. So I was looking down and watching him, and he was getting pretty tired of trying to eat and having to toast everything, and suddenly he stood up—Edward and I were absolutely mesmerized— and he said in a loud voice, "Natchez to Mobile," and I stood up and said, "Memphis to St. Jo." And everybody stood up and drank except for Edward Albee, who fell under the table laughing. "Wherever the four winds blow." They thought it was a toast! John said to me afterwards, "Oh Honey, I knew you would pick it up for me." "Natchez to Mobile." Sounds foreign, doesn't it? They didn't know what the hell "Natchez to Mobile" meant! Now you see, if you wrote that and somebody picked it up and made something political out of it, that would be pretty silly. And one of these days, somebody will.

DC: Will see it as political commentary?

ES: Yes, somebody will say, "It's political reporting to Russia on the South." But I want to tell you, I'll never forget Edward Albee's reaction. He said, "That was the funniest thing. Imagine *Steinbeck* doing that." And I said, "He just got pissed off!"

DC: Speaking of political commentary, I can see what you mean when you say he was very opinionated. Here's what he says about General

MacArthur in *Journal of a Novel*: "April 19 . . . Today is MacArthur Day, and [he] will be filling the air with his horrid platitudes. I get such a sense of dishonesty from this man. Wonder what his wife thinks of him?"

ES: We went to the theater one night. We sat down in the center near the aisle. The curtain hadn't gone up yet when John said, "Look who just came in." It was General MacArthur with his wife. He was sitting on the aisle, and as he took off his hat and put it upside down on his lap, the hair dye was all the way around the band. John looked at me and said, "I wouldn't have missed this for the world!" John was fun like that; it was fun to be with him, because anybody else would have missed that, but not John. But you know what he did, Don? This was his whole philosophy: Whenever we were abroad and something bad was happening at home, for instance, during the McCarthy period, he always said, very seriously of course, "These are things every country has done. I discuss these things at home, but I don't discuss them away from home." And I thought it was so wonderful that he could handle that. He was always outspoken here and always wrote about such matters and discussed them, but he was not about to sit there [abroad] and slander his country in any way.

DC: Here, I've found the passage where Steinbeck predicts how the Soviet empire will unravel. It's in the entry for March 20, 1951, in *Journal of a Novel*: "This morning the Schuman Plan started its route for signature. This, I think, is the beginning of the pattern of the future—the opening of the supra-state. Our businessmen in particular and people in general are very much in fear of communism. Now mark my prophecy—The so-called communist system will break up and destroy itself in horrible civil wars because it is not a permanent workable system. It will fly apart from its own flaws. On the other hand the Schuman Plan is a workable system. The businessmen so anxious about the status quo have little to fear from communism. The Schuman Plan is the thing that will change the world. I do not believe that America can compete with this new form of sponsored and controlled cartel. We will be forced either to fight it or to join it . . . (End of prediction)." He's predicting not only the breakup of the Soviet Union and the demise of communism, but also the new European order. The Schuman Plan led to the European Common Market and to all that we're seeing unfold in Europe even as we speak—an even more united Europe with a common currency. And, of course, the [Berlin] Wall fell in 1989.

ES: When John and I stood at Checkpoint Charlie, the press said, "What do you think, Mr. Steinbeck?" And he said, "It's the most obscene sight I've ever seen." And I thought that was a great way to describe it, "obscene." And they said, "Would you like to go over and visit East Germany?" And he said, "Certainly not." That passage you read, I don't remember that at all. We ought to use that in your book somewhere. Now, please, turn that page down.

DC: Don't you want me to mark it with a slip of paper?

ES: No, just turn it down. John taught me to turn down pages. I said to him once, "Do you think it's awful to turn down pages?" He said, "Honey, mark it anyway you want, but don't put a slice of bacon between the pages. The fat would go through!" He was always saying something like that that you didn't expect him to.

DC: You know, those predictions about the collapse of communism— he was making them at the height of the cold war. And they show the same fundamental faith in democracy and human decency he proclaimed in *The Moon Is Down* during the darkest days of the Second World War.

ES: You see, John believed in *man*. That's what his Nobel Prize speech says. He said, "You believe in the perfectibility of man. Man will never be perfect, but he has to strive for it." That's the whole point. That was his whole point about life. And religion to John was very interesting. He was religious. He didn't believe in any church creeds, but he said to me when he was dying, "Don't you let a bunch of people get together and tell yarns about me. Make sure it's the Episcopal burial service." And I said to him, "Do you believe?" And he said, "I'm like Socrates before he drank the hemlock: I don't know if there are gods or not, but in case there are . . . ."

Part IV

Bibliography

Tetsumaro Hayashi: A Checklist
of Scholarly Publications[*]

Compiled by Robert DeMott

1957

"A Study of American Folklore." *Eigo Seinen* 103 (September): 455. [In Japanese.]

"Patterns of Advertising English." *Eigo Seinen* 103 (December): 659-60. [In Japanese.]

1959

"Hope for Mankind in *Adventures of Huckleberry Finn*." *Lumina* 3: vii-x.

1960

Amerika Bunka Sobyo. Tokyo: Tarumi Shobo. [In Japanese; paperback edition, 1961.]

* * *

"John Steinbeck's *The Grapes of Wrath*: The Joad Family and Women." *Lumina* 4: i-iv.

---

*This chronology does not include Professor Hayashi's "Editor's Preface" (a regular feature in each issue of *Steinbeck Quarterly* from 1976 through 1993), his many short stories in Japanese-American literary magazines, or his 2500 *senryu* poems, printed under various pen names in numerous Japanese-American publications in the United States. Wherever relevant, a triple asterisk distinguishes Hayashi's separate publications (authored and/or edited books, monographs, and pamphlets) from his contributions to that year's periodicals and other collections.

1961

"'Et tu, Brute' and Antony's Harangue." *New York Bungei* 7: 110-30. [In Japanese.]

"The Expressions and Meanings of Henry James." *Current of the World* 37 (June): 72-75. [In Japanese.]

1962

"Shakespeare Society of Japan." *Shakespeare Newsletter* 12 (April): 9.

"Was Caesar Ambitious?: An Analysis of Antony's Speech." *Lumina* 5: 39-45.

1963

"On Japan's Shakespeare Society." *Shakespeare Newsletter* 13 (November): 44.

"On the Sonnet Mystery." *Shakespeare Newsletter* 13 (November): 42.

"Vision in the Darkness: A Dramatic Dimension of *King Lear*." *Lumina* 6: 3-9.

1964

"A Bibliography of Shakespeare's *King John*." *Serif* I (October): 23-27.

1965

"*The Merchant of Venice*: The Reputation of Shylock." *New York Bungei* 9: 84-88. [In Japanese.]

1966

"Steinbeck's Women and the Principle of Continuity." *Visva-bharati Quarterly* 31 (February): 201-06.

"A Brief Survey of John Steinbeck Bibliographies." *Kyushu American Literature* 9 (December): 54-61.

1967

John Steinbeck: A Concise Bibliography (1930-1965). Introd. Warren G. French. Metuchen: Scarecrow.

* * *

"Ben Jonson and William Shakespeare: Their Mutual Criticism and Relationship." *East-West Review* 3 (Winter): 23-47.

"Henry James: A Semantic Review of His Short Stories." *Indian P.E.N.* 33 (February): 35-39.

"A Dimension of Arthur Miller's Published Works." *Serif* 4 (June): 26-32.

"Women and The Principle of Continuity in Steinbeck's *The Grapes Of Wrath.*" *Kyushu American Literature* 10 (December): 75-80.

1968

"Dr. Johnson as a Shakespeare Critic." *Lumina* 11: 17-32.

"The Function of the Joad Clan in *The Grapes of Wrath.*" *Modern Review* 33 (March): 158-62.

"John Steinbeck: A Checklist of Unpublished Ph.D. Dissertations." *Serif* 5 (December): 30-31.

"Library Research in the United States: Bibliographical Guide for the Japanese Scholar of American Literature." *Kyushu American Literature* 11 (December): 87-90.

"The Unknown Steinbeck." *New York Bungei* 10: 156-58. [In Japanese.]

1969

Arthur Miller Criticism. Metuchen: Scarecrow.

A Textual Study of A Looking Glass for London and England *by Thomas Lodge and Robert Greene.* Ball State Monograph Series, No. 17. Muncie: Ball State U.

"The Image of Steinbeck." *Eigo Seinen* 115 (May): 52. [In Japanese.]

"Thomas Lodge's Defense of Poetry." *Concept* 6 (Fall): 22-23.

"Controversy Between Gosson and Lodge." *Lumina* 12: 75-79.

"The Symbolic Function of Waymarsh in *The Ambassadors.*" *Indian P.E.N.* 35 (September): 261-63.

1970

Ed. A Looking Glass for London and England, *by Robert Greene and Thomas Lodge, an Elizabethan Text.* Metuchen: Scarecrow.

* * *

"*A Looking Glass for London and England*: Collaboration between Thomas Lodge and Robert Greene." *Calcutta Review* (New Series) 1 (January-March): 441-45.

"*A Farewell to Arms*: The Contest of Experience." *Kyushu American Literature* 12 (December): 14-19.

"John Steinbeck: A Checklist of Movie Reviews." *Serif* 7 (June): 18-22.

1971

Ed. *John Steinbeck: A Guide to the Doctoral Dissertations (1946-1969).* Steinbeck Monograph Series, No. 1. Muncie: Steinbeck Society.

Robert Greene Criticism. Introd. Louis Marder. Metuchen: Scarecrow.

Ed. with Richard Astro. *Steinbeck: The Man and His Work.* Corvallis: Oregon State UP. [Paperback edition, 1977.]

* * *

"Recent Steinbeck Studies in the USA." *Calcutta Review* (New Series) 2 (October-December): 169-72.

1972

Shakespeare's "Sonnets": A Record of 20th-Century Criticism. Metuchen: Scarecrow.

Comp. with Donald L. Siefker. *The Special Steinbeck Collection of the Ball State University Library.* Muncie: Steinbeck Society.

* * *

"The Dream Sequence in Henry James's 'The Great Good Place.'" *Lumina* 15: 2-6.

"A Brief Survey of Steinbeck Criticism in the United States." *Kyushu American Literature* 14 (December): 43-49.

1973

A New Steinbeck Bibliography (1929-1971). Metuchen: Scarecrow.

Ed. *Steinbeck's Literary Dimension: A Guide to Comparative Studies.* Metuchen: Scarecrow.

* * *

"An Explication of Robert Greene's *Orlando Furioso.*" *Lumina* 16: 6-10.

1974

Ed. *Steinbeck Criticism: A Review of Book-Length Studies (1939-1973).* Steinbeck Monograph Series, No. 4. Muncie: Steinbeck Society.

Ed. *A Study Guide to Steinbeck. A Handbook to His Major Works.* Foreword by Warren G. French. Metuchen: Scarecrow. [Trans. into Japanese as *Steinbeck Sakuhinron,* by Kiyohiko Tsuboi and others; Tokyo: Eihosha, 1978.]

A Textual Study of Robert Greene's "Orlando Furioso." Ball State University Monograph Series, No. 4. Muncie: Ball State U.

* * *

"The Agony and Ecstasy of Writing and Editing." *Contemporary Communications* 2 (February): 20-21.

"The Pearl as a Novel of Engagement." *Steinbeck Quarterly* 7 (Summer-Fall): 84-88.

"Recent Steinbeck Studies in the United States." *Contemporary Communications* 2 (September): 40-45.

"Orlando Furioso: Robert Greene's Romantic Comedy." *Studia Anglica Posnaniensia* 25 (October): 157-60.

1975

Ed. *Steinbeck and the Arthurian Theme.* Introd. Joseph Fontenrose. Steinbeck Monograph Series, No. 5. Muncie: Steinbeck Society.

* * *

"Hamlet's Satori: 'The Readiness is All' and 'Let it Be.'" *Ball State University Forum* 16 (Summer): 67-69.

With Roy S. Simmonds. "John Steinbeck's British Publications." *Steinbeck Quarterly* 8 (Summer-Fall): 79-89.

"Recent Steinbeck Studies in the United States." In *Steinbeck and the Sea.* Proc. of Conference at Marine Science Center Auditorium (Newport, Oregon). 4 May 1974. Ed. Richard Astro and Joel W. Hedgpeth. Corvallis: Oregon State University Sea Grant College Program. 11-13.

"Unknown Steinbeck." *New York Bungei* 11:137-38.

"What Values Does Shakespeare Communicate To Us?" *Ball State University Forum* 16 (Autumn): 77-80.

"Experiencing Shakespeare." *Persica* 2 (December): 77-83.

1976

An Index to Arthur Miller Criticism. Metuchen: Scarecrow.

Ed. *John Steinbeck: A Dictionary of His Fictional Characters*. Metuchen: Scarecrow.

Ed. with Kenneth D. Swan. *Steinbeck's Prophetic Vision of America*. Proc. of the Taylor University-Ball State University Bicentennial Steinbeck Seminar. 1 May 1976. Upland: Taylor University for the Steinbeck Society. [Includes Hayashi's "Steinbeck's Prophetic Vision" 10-11; and "Steinbeck's Reputation: What Values Does He Communicate to Us?" 28-34.]

Ed. *A Study Guide to Steinbeck*: The Long Valley. Introd. Reloy Garcia. Ann Arbor: Pierian. [Trans. into Japanese as *Steinbeck no Tanpen Kenkyu*, by Hiromasa Takamura and others; Kyoto: Aporon, 1992.]

* * *

"Macbeth and His Heart of Darkness: A Zen Interpretation." *Indiana Speech Journal* 10 (February): 8-11.

"*Othello*: All or Nothing—The Theme of Semantic Reduction." *Indiana Speech Journal* 10 (September): 1-5.

"Zen and the Samurai Tradition." *Indiana Social Studies Quarterly* 28 (Winter): 73-83

"Robert Greene as a Poet." *Persica* 3 (December): 111-22.

1977

Ed. *The Poetry of Robert Greene*. Ball State University Monograph Series, No. 27. Muncie: Ball State U.

* * *

"The Book of Tea: Tenshin Okakura and Zen." *Dharma World* 4 (March): 15-17.

"Steinbeck's Women in *The Grapes of Wrath*: A New Perspective." *Kyushu American Literature* 18 (October): 1-4.

"Zeami's Dramatic Time Structure in *Komachi at Sekidera*—A Shakespearean Interpretation." *Indiana Speech Journal* 12 (November): 9-16.

1978

Ed. with Yasuo Hashiguchi and Richard F. Peterson. *John Steinbeck: East and West*. Proc. of First International Steinbeck Congress (Fukuoka City, Japan). 19-20 Aug. 1976. Introd. Warren French. Steinbeck Monograph Series, No. 8. Muncie: Steinbeck Society. [Includes Hayashi's "The Theme of Revolution in *Julius Caesar* and *Viva Zapata!*" 28-39. Trans. into Japanese as *John Steinbeck: Toyo to Seiyo*, by Shigeharu Yano; Tokyo: Hokuseido, 1982.

* * *

"Macbeth: Heart of Darkness (II)." *Persica* 5 (January): 11-15.

"The Concept of Nothingness in *King Lear*: A Buddhist Interpretation." *Indiana Speech Journal* 13 (September): 27-31.

"Why is Steinbeck Widely Read?" *Persica* 6: 53-56. [In Japanese.]

1979

Ed. *Steinbeck's Women: Essays in Criticism*. Introd. Richard F. Peterson. Steinbeck Monograph Series, No. 9. Muncie: Steinbeck Society. [Trans. into Japanese as *Steinbeck no Joseizo*, by Mitsuaki Yamashita; Tokyo: Oshisha, 1984.]

Ed. *A Study Guide to Steinbeck (Part II)*. Introd. Reloy Garcia. Metuchen: Scarecrow. [Trans. into Japanese as *Steinbeck Sakuhin Ron (II)*, by Kenji Inoue; Tokyo: Eihosha, 1982.]

* * *

"Why is Steinbeck's Literature Widely Read?—What Is the Essence of His Literature?" *Kyushu American Literature* 20 (June): 42-44.

"Steinbeck's *Winter* as Shakespearean Fiction." *Steinbeck Quarterly* 12 (Summer-Fall): 107-15.

"My English Language Training." *English for the Millions* 34 (September): 17-19. [In Japanese.]

"Robert Greene as an Elizabethan Poet." *Studia Anglica Posnaniensia* 10 (October): 221-28.

1980

Ed. *Steinbeck and Hemingway: Dissertation Abstracts and Research Opportunities.* Introd. Warren G. French. Metuchen: Scarecrow.

Ed. *Steinbeck's Travel Literature.* Steinbeck Monograph Series, No. 10. Muncie: Steinbeck Society. [Trans. into Japanese as *Steinbeck Kenkyu,* by Mikio Inui; Tokyo: Kaibunsha, 1984.]

* * *

"Why Is Steinbeck's Literature Widely Read?" *Steinbeck Quarterly* 13 (Winter-Spring): 20-23.

"Robert Greene (1558-1592): A Biographical Perspective." *Persica* 7 (January): 121-25.

"Time and Timelessness in Shakespeare's Sonnets." *Indiana Speech Journal* 15 (November): 11-17.

1981

Ed. *A Handbook for Steinbeck Collectors, Librarians, and Scholars.* Steinbeck Monograph Series, No. 11. Muncie: Steinbeck Society. [Includes Hayashi's "Scholars and Collectors: How A Steinbeck Scholar Views Steinbeck Collectors," 6-7; and "A Selected Guide to Library Research in the United States for Visiting Steinbeck Scholars," 41-46.]

"Shakespeare's Sonnets: The Eternal Now." *Persica* 8 (January): 107-13.
"A Visiting Steinbeck Scholar's Advanced Studies: A Selected Guide to Library Research in the United States." *Kyushu American Literature* 21 (June): 32-62.

1982

Ed. *William Faulkner: Research Opportunities and Dissertation Abstracts.* Jefferson: McFarland.

* * *

"Robert Greene's *James IV*: Politics, Love, and Morality." *Persica* 9 (January): 1-13.

1983

Ed. *Arthur Miller and Tennessee Williams: Research Opportunities and Dissertation Abstracts.* Jefferson: McFarland.

Ed. *Eugene O'Neill. Research Opportunities and Dissertation Abstracts.* Jefferson: McFarland.

A New Steinbeck Bibliography: 1971-1981. Introd. Robert DeMott. Metuchen: Scarecrow.

* * *

"William L. Moore and His Whitman and Teilhard: A Tribute to a Great Teacher-Scholar." *Persica* 10 (March): 73-81.

"Standards for Publishable Writing: What Kind of Article Do We Accept for Publication?" *Steinbeck Quarterly* 16 (Winter-Spring): 5-8. [Rpt. in *Steinbeck Newsletter of Japan* 6 (May): 4-6.]

"Steinbeck's Political Vision in *The Moon Is Down*." *Kyushu American Literature* 24 (July): 1-10.

"Steinbeck's *The Moon Is Down*: A Shakespearean Interpretation." *Reitaku University Journal* 36 (December): 1-17.

1984

"Shakespeare's Aesthetics in *The Sonnets*." *Persica* 11 (March): 87-93.

"John Steinbeck: The Writer and His Craft." *Anglo-American Studies* 4 (April): 5-14.

"Robert Greene's *James IV*: Love, Power, and Justice." *Indiana Social Studies Quarterly* 37 (Autumn): 32-46.

"Dr. Winter's Dramatic Functions in Steinbeck's *The Moon Is Down*." *Reitaku University Journal* 38 (December): 29-40. [Rpt. in *The Short Novels of John Steinbeck: Critical Essays with a Checklist to Steinbeck Criticism*. Ed. Jackson J. Benson. Durham: Duke UP, 1990. 95-101.]

1985

Ed. *James Joyce: Research Opportunities and Dissertation Abstracts*. Jefferson: McFarland.

* * *

"Quest and Discovery in Shakespeare's *Sonnets*." *Persica* 12 (March): 1-12.

"Steinbeck's Literature Viewed from Archetypal Perspectives." *Reitaku University Journal* 39 (July): 125-33.

"A Checklist of Steinbeck's Title Changes." *Steinbeck Newsletter of Japan* 8 (May): 7-8.

1986

John Steinbeck and the Vietnam War (Part I). Introd. Reloy Garcia. Steinbeck Monograph Series, No. 12. Muncie: Steinbeck Society.

Ed. with Shigeharu Yano, Richard F. Peterson, and Yasuo Hashiguchi. *John Steinbeck: From Salinas to the World.* Proc. of Second International Steinbeck Congress (Salinas, California). Aug. 1984. Introd. Shigeharu Yano. Tokyo: Gaku Shobo Press. [Includes Hayashi's "John Steinbeck: His Concept of Writing," 34-44. Trans. into Japanese as *John Steinbeck: Salina Kara Sekai ni Mukete,* by Kyoko Ariki and others; Tokyo: Oshisha, 1992.]

Steinbeck's World War II Fiction, The Moon Is Down*: Three Explications.* Steinbeck Essay Series, No. 1. Muncie: Steinbeck Research Institute.

A Student's Guide to Steinbeck's Literature: Primary and Secondary Sources. Steinbeck Bibliography Series, No. 1. Muncie: Steinbeck Research Institute.

* * *

"Another Look at John Steinbeck's *Travels with Charley in Search of America* (1962)." *Reitaku University Journal* 41 (March): 1-13.

"Steinbeck and the Old Testament: Free Will in the Fallen World." *Anglo-American Studies* 6 (November): 149-52.

1987

Ed. *Herman Melville: Research Opportunities and Dissertation Abstracts.* Jefferson: McFarland.

* * *

"University Education in the United States." *Catena* 26: 6-15.

"John Steinbeck, Lyndon B. Johnson, and the Vietnam War." *The Torch International* 59 (Winter): 27-32.

"The Emergence of Elizabethan Feminists in Robert Greene's *James IV*." *Reitaku University Journal* 44 (July): 1-28.

1988

Ed. *John Steinbeck on Writing.* Introd. Reloy Garcia. Steinbeck Essay

Series, No. 2. Muncie: Steinbeck Research Institute. [Trans. into Japanese as *Steinbeck no Sosaku-rou*, by Toshio Asano; Tokyo: Shimbisha, 1992.]

Ed. with Thomas J. Moore. *Steinbeck's "The Red Pony": Essays in Criticism*. Introd. Warren G. French. Steinbeck Monograph Series, No. 13. Muncie: Steinbeck Research Institute.

* * *

"Natsume Soseki's *Kokoro* (*The Heart*): The Ethical Imperative." *Persica* 15 (March): 157-63.

1989

Ed. with Thomas J. Moore. *Steinbeck's Posthumous Work. Essays in Criticism*. Introd. Reloy Garcia. Steinbeck Monograph Series, No. 14. Muncie: Steinbeck Research Institute.

Comp. and Ed. with Donald L. Siefker and Thomas J. Moore. *The Steinbeck Quarterly: A Cumulative Index to Volumes XI-XX (1978-1987)*. Introd. Robert DeMott. Steinbeck Bibliography Series, No. 2. Muncie: Steinbeck Research Institute.

* * *

"Steinbeck's Literature: Its Reputation and Uniqueness—A Second Survey." *Persica* 16 (March): 141-47.

"Steinbeck's Moral Vision in *East of Eden*." *Studies in Foreign Languages and Literatures* 25 (Winter): 87-104.

"Steinbeck's Use of Old Testament Motifs in *The Grapes of Wrath*." *Kyushu American Literature* 29 (December): 1-11.

"Scholars and Collectors: How a Steinbeck Scholar Views Steinbeck Collectors." In *Essays on Collecting John Steinbeck Books*. Ed. Preston Beyer. Bradenton: Opuscula. 13-14.

"John Steinbeck: His Concept of Writing." In *John Steinbeck: A Study of the Short Fiction*. By Robert S. Hughes. Boston: Twayne. 138-49.

1990

Ed. *Steinbeck's* The Grapes of Wrath: *Essays in Criticism.* Introd. John H. Timmerman. Steinbeck Essay Series, No. 3. Muncie: Steinbeck Research Institute.

* * *

"Steinbeck's Concept of Creative Writing (Part II)." *Persica* 17 (March): 105-13.

"Steinbeck's America in *Travels with Charley.*" *Steinbeck Quarterly* 23 (Summer-Fall): 94-107.

1991

Natsume Soseki's Kokoro (The Heart): *The Ethical Imperative.* Monograph Series, No. 1. Wilmington: Museum of World Cultures.

Ed. *Steinbeck's Literary Dimension: A Guide to Comparative Studies, Series II.* Introd. Reloy Garcia. Metuchen: Scarecrow.

Ed. *Steinbeck's Short Stories in* The Long Valley: *Essays in Criticism.* Introd. Warren French. Steinbeck Monograph Series, No. 15. Muncie: Steinbeck Research Institute.

* * *

"John Steinbeck and Adlai E. Stevenson: Their Moral and Political Vision." *Steinbeck Quarterly* 24 (Summer-Fall): 94-107.

1992

"John Steinbeck: The Art and Craft of Writing." *The Torch International* 64 (Spring-Summer): 9-12.

"The Chinese Servant in *East of Eden.*" *San Jose Studies* 18 (Winter): 52-60.

"Teaching Shakespeare in the United States—Uniqueness and Universality: A Story of a Japanese Shakespeare Teacher-Scholar." *Catena* 32: 8-12.

1993

Ed. *John Steinbeck: The Years of Greatness: 1936-1939.* Proc. of the Third International Steinbeck Congress (Honolulu, Hawaii). 27-30 May 1991. Introd. John H. Timmerman. Tuscaloosa: U of Alabama P.

Ed. *A New Study Guide to Steinbeck's Major Works, with Critical Explications.* Introd. Reloy Garcia. Metuchen: Scarecrow.

* * *

"The Artful Thunder as Dramatic Technique in Shakespeare's *The Tempest.*" *Persica* 20 (January): 1-5.

"Steinbeck and Hemingway on the Craft of Writing." *Kyushu American Literature* 34 (December): 1-21.

"The A-B-C's of Steinbeck Studies: A Bibliographic Guide for English Majors." *Steinbeck Quarterly* 26 (Summer-Fall): 117-27.

CONTRIBUTORS

Debra K. S. Barker is an Assistant Professor of English at the University of Wisconsin-Eau Claire, where she teaches Native American literature. She has published articles on Native American biographies, Native American art, and archetypal forms in literature.

Donald V. Coers is Coordinator of Graduate Studies and Professor of English at Sam Houston State University. Since 1979 he has served as Associate Editor of *The Texas Review*. His book *John Steinbeck as Propagandist: The Moon Is Down Goes to War* was published by the University of Alabama Press in 1991.

Robert J. DeMott, Professor of English at Ohio University, has twice been chosen for teaching awards. A longtime editorial board member of the *Steinbeck Quarterly* and a former director of San Jose State University's Steinbeck Research Center, he has published widely in American literature and on John Steinbeck, including *Steinbeck's Reading* (1984) and an edition of Steinbeck's *Grapes of Wrath* journal, *Working Days* (1989). He is co-editor of *Novels, 1932-1937,* the inaugural Steinbeck volume in The Library of America publishing series (1994), and is author of *Steinbeck's Typewriter: Essays on Creative Dimensions of His Art* (1995).

John Ditsky, who has published over 1300 poems in journals, has several collections of poetry out, among them *The Katherine Poems, Scar Tissue,* and *Friend and Lover*. He has four critical volumes to his credit: *Essays on* East of Eden, *The Onstage Christ, John Steinbeck: Life, Works, and Criticism,* and *Critical Essays on Steinbeck's* The Grapes of Wrath. He teaches at the University of Windsor.

Warren French, a distinguished Americanist who retired from full time teaching at Indiana University-Purdue University at Indianapolis several years ago, now spends half of the year in Swansea, Wales, and the other half in intriguing places around the world. He is the author of standard books on Frank Norris, J. D. Salinger, Jack Kerouac, the San Francisco Poetry Renaissance, American Nobel Prize Winners in Literature, and the American Social Novel. His critically and popularly acclaimed study *John Steinbeck* was first published in 1961 as one of the inaugural volumes in Twayne's United States Author Series and completely revised in 1975. It recently appeared in a third revised version as *John Steinbeck's Fiction Revisited* (1994).

Mimi Reisel Gladstein has twice chaired the English and Philosophy Departments at the University of Texas at El Paso and is currently Chair of the University Graduate Council and Assembly there. She is the author of *The Indestructible Woman in Faulkner, Hemingway, and Steinbeck* and *The Ayn Rand Companion* as well as numerous articles in journals and critical anthologies.

She received the John J. and Angeline R. Pruis Award for outstanding Steinbeck Teacher (1978-1987) and the Burlington Northern Award for Teaching Excellence (1988).

Kevin Hearle, who has taught at Coe College and San Jose State University, is the author of *Each Thing We Know Is Changed Because We Know It—Poems*. His work has appeared in *American Literature, Western American Literature, Steinbeck Quarterly, Yale Review, Georgia Review, University of Windsor Review*, and elsewhere.

Cliff Lewis is Professor of American Studies and English at the University of Massachusetts at Lowell. He is the author of essays on Polish films in *Film Criticism* and *Film and History*. Co-editor of *Rediscovering Steinbeck*, he has published numerous essays on Steinbeck's fiction and political writing.

Michael Meyer is Chair of English at Hong Kong International School. An assistant editor of *Steinbeck Quarterly*, he has published chapters on Steinbeck in Jackson J. Benson's *The Short Novels of John Steinbeck*, Tetsumaro Hayashi's *A New Study Guide to Steinbeck's Major Works*, and Donald Noble's *The Steinbeck Question*. He is presently editing *Literature and the Grotesque* and is planning a book discussing Steinbeck's thematic use of brotherhood betrayed in his work.

Robert E. Morsberger is Professor of English and former department chair at the California State Polytechnic University, Pomona. He has published over 160 articles, ten short stories, and ten books, including *James Thurber* (Twayne), *Lew Wallace: Militant Romantic*, in collaboration with Katharine M. Morsberger (McGraw-Hill), *Swordplay on the Elizabethan and Jacobean Stage* (University of Salzburg Press), and two volumes on American screenwriters that he co-edited for the *Dictionary of Literary Biography*. He also edited John Steinbeck's screenplay *Viva Zapata!* for Viking/Penguin and was head of the editorial board of the *Steinbeck Quarterly*.

Brian Railsback, Director of Professional Writing at Western Carolina University, has published articles on John Steinbeck and has given papers on the author in Japan, Mexico, and the U.S. His book *Parallel Expeditions: Charles Darwin and the Art of John Steinbeck* is forthcoming from Paragon House. He is presently completing a novel, *Shadow of the Valley*.

Susan Shillinglaw is an Associate Professor of English at San Jose State University and Director of the Steinbeck Research Center. Recently she co-edited a book of Steinbeck reviews for Cambridge University Press. She has written introductions for Penguin's new *Of Mice and Men* and *Cannery Row*; and is co-editing the conference proceedings of a 1992 conference on "Steinbeck and the Environment" held in Nantucket. She is also working on a biography of Carol Henning Steinbeck.

Eiko Shiraga, author of *Lafcadio Hearn Studies: Love and Women,* is professor of English/Dean of Students at Shujitsu Women's University, Okayama, Japan. She has published articles, essays, and book reviews on Hearn and Steinbeck. She was a Visiting Fellow at the Steinbeck Research Institute, Ball State University, in the summers of 1989, 1991, and 1992. In 1994 she is publishing a book on *The Moon Is Down* in Japan.

Roy Simmonds is an independent scholar living in Billericay, England. He has published essays on Steinbeck in *Steinbeck Quarterly, The Steinbeck Newsletter, Mississippi Quarterly,* and *London Magazine* and has three books to his credit: *The Two Worlds of William March, William March: An Annotated Checklist,* and a biography of Edward J. O'Brien.

Geralyn Strecker is a doctoral student in British and American literature at Ball State University, where she was fortunate enough to participate in Dr. Tetsumaro Hayashi's final Steinbeck seminar before his retirement. Her contribution to this collection was, she writes, "originally written at his suggestion and has since been presented at the 10th Carol Ann Kendrick Memorial Steinbeck Lecture Series held at Ball State in November 1993."

THE EDITORS

Donald V. Coers, Coordinator of Graduate Studies and Professor of English at Sam Houston State University, has been Associate Editor of *The Texas Review* since 1980. He is author of *John Steinbeck as Propagandist:* The Moon Is Down *Goes to War* (1991), winner of the University of Alabama's Elizabeth Agee Prize for American Literature.

Robert J. DeMott, Professor of English at Ohio University, was a founder and longtime editorial board member of the *Steinbeck Quarterly*. Formerly a director of San Jose State University's Steinbeck Research Center, he has published widely in American literature and on John Steinbeck in particular. His books include *Steinbeck's Reading* (1984) and an edition of Steinbeck's *Grapes of Wrath* journal, *Working Days* (1989). He is coeditor of *Novels, 1932-1937*, the inaugural Steinbeck volume in The Library of America publishing series (1994), and is author of *Steinbeck's Typewriter: Essays on Creative Dimensions of His Art* (forthcoming in 1995).

Paul D. Ruffin, Editor of *The Texas Review* and Director of *Texas Review Press*, is Professor of English at Sam Houston State University. He is author of three collections of poems and a collection of short fiction, *The Man Who Would Be God* (1993); he has edited or coedited several anthologies, the latest of which was *That's What I Like (About the South)* (1993), coedited with George Garrett.

Index

Joe Elegant (*Sweet Thursday*) 183
John the Baptist 197
John Steinbeck (French) 153
John Steinbeck: A Concise Bibliography (1930-1965) (Hayashi) 157
John Steinbeck: Asian Perspectives (Nakayama, Pugh, Yano) 157
John Steinbeck's Fiction (Timmerman) 151, 177
John Steinbeck's Fiction Revisited (French) 16
"John Steinbeck: The Fitful Daemon" (Lewis) 150
John Steinbeck: Nature and Myth (Lisca) 197
"John Steinbeck: Novelist as Scientist" (Benson) 157
John Steinbeck Society 1, 13, 19
John Steinbeck: The Years of Greatness (1936-1939) (Hayashi) 4
John Steinbeck's Re-Vision of America (Owens) 103, 152-53, 176, 228
"John Steinbeck's Use of the Bible" (Timmerman) 157
Johnny (*Sweet Thursday*) 188
Johnny Bear ("Johnny Bear") 44, 53
Johnson, Lady Bird 5, 245
Johnson, Lyndon 5, 34, 242
Johnson, Nunnally 78, 88-90
Jonah 119
Jones, Lawrence William 153
Josefa (*Viva Zapata!*) 126
Joseph (*The Moon Is Down*) 85-87, 90, 95-97
Joyce, James 19
"Joyous Garde" 229
Juan Carlos, Crown Prince of Spain 262
Juana (*The Pearl*) 113-22, 126
Juanito (*To a God Unknown*) 43
Jung, Carl 114-15

-K-

Kate (*East of Eden*) 70
Kaufman, George 264
Kawata, Ikuko 154, 157
Kazan, Elia 40, 68-70, 72, 178, 260, 263
Kenderly, Molly (*The Moon Is Down*) 87
Kennedy, Jacqueline 229
Kennedy, John F. 36, 211, 229, 268
Kent State University 2, 174
Kester, Dr. Nancy 236
Kiernan, Thomas 151
Kinnaird, Clark 149
Kino (*The Pearl*) 113-22

Kirkland, Jack 54-55
Kiss of the Spider Woman (McNally) 252
Kline, Herbert 25
Knisley, Dr. Melvyn 27
Korngold, Erich Wolfgang 58-59
Krause, Stanley J. 116, 118
Kruger, Otto 88
Kruif, Paul de 23-24
Krushchev, Nikita 268
Krutch, Joseph Wood 149
"Kubla Khan" (Coleridge) 184-85
Kurtz, Efrem 64

-L-

Lacan, Jacques 154
Lady of the Lake 234
LaFollette Civil Liberties Committee 24
Lanser, Colonel (*The Moon Is Down*) 80, 82-85, 87-91, 97
Laos 242
Lancelot, Sir 210, 229, 232, 235, 252
Loft, Captain (*The Moon Is Down*) 90
Lee (*East of Eden*) 7, 42, 44, 46, 148, 156
Lee, Gypsy Rose 172
Lehr, Wilson 60
Levant, Howard 152, 176
Lewis, Cliff 4-5
Lewis, R. W. B. 150-51
Lewis, Sinclair 9, 258
Library of America 155
Library Journal 236
Lieber, Todd 197
Life 25
Light in August (Faulkner) 16
Lights Out in Europe (Kline) 25
Li'l Abner 187
Lincoln, Abraham 32, 34-36
Lindhardt, Otto 265-66
Lippmann, Walter 29
Lisa (*In Dubious Battle*) 46-47
Lisca, Peter 14, 113-14, 128, 152, 176, 197
Little Big Horn 220
Llewellyn, Richard 88
Locke-Elliott, Sumner 266
Lodge, Thomas 19
Loesser, Frank 263
Loft, Captain (*The Moon Is Down*) 90
Lomax, Alan 61, 63
Loraine (*The Wayward Bus*) 131
Lorentz, Pare 23-24, 30
Los Angeles Times 25
Los Gatos Mail-News 54
Louie (*The Wayward Bus*) 130

Walton, Sir William 58
Warfel, Harry 1-2
Washington Square (James) 67
Watson, James 256
Watt, F.W. 14
Waxman, Franz 58
Wayne, Benjy (*To a God Unknown*) 43, 45
Wayne, Burton (*To a God Unknown*) 45
Wayne, Joseph (*To a God Unknown*) 40, 43, 45-46
Wayne, Thomas (*To a God Unknown*) 45
"The Wayward Bus : Steinbeck's Misogynistic Manifesto" (Gonzales and Gladstein) 126
Webster, Harvey Curtis 149, 156, 176
Western Flyer 105, 125, 193
Westport Country Playhouse 246
White House 256
Whitey #1 (*Sweet Thursday*) 186, 190
Whitey #2 (*Sweet Thursday*) 186
Whitney, John Hay 26, 30
Who's Afraid of Virginia Woolf? (musical score by North)) 70
Wide Ida (*Sweet Thursday*) 188
Wide World of John Steinbeck, The (Lisca) 152
Wilder, Thornton 30
Wilhelmson, Carl 42
Williams, Ralph Vaughan 58
Williams, Tennessee 260
Willie (*To a God Unknown*) 45
Wilson, Edmund 150, 178
Winchell, Walter 25
Winter, Doctor (*The Moon Is Down*) 49, 81-84, 89-91, 95, 97-98
Wisconsin 221
Wolf, Naomi 131
Wolfe, Thomas 220
Wolff, Tobias 148
Woodress, James 214
World of Li'l Abner, The (Capp) 15, 173, 185-86, 188
Wright, Richard 7
Writing the American Classics (Barbour and Quirk) 153, 156
Wyatt, David 155-56, 176
Wylie, Philip 13, 235

-Y-

Yahweh 201
Yeats, W. B. 11
Yellowstone National Park 218, 222
Yergin, Daniel 25

Yokum, Zootsuit 186
Young-Hunt, Margie (*The Winter of Our Discontent*) 201, 208-10
Your Only Weapon Is Your Work 185

-Z-

Zachary Scott Theater 242
Zane, Nancy 153
Zanuck, Darryl 68
Zapata, Emiliano (*Viva Zapata*) 7, 49, 68
Zapata, Euphemio (*Viva Zapata*) 69
Zokolow, Anna 68